MICROFINANCE, LIVELIHOODS AND POVERTY REDUCTION IN GHANA

This book assesses the role of microfinance in the construction of livelihoods for poverty reduction in the Northern Savannah of Ghana, analysing the current microfinance landscape and financial services in the region.

The book analyses the current microfinance landscape and financial services in Ghana. In doing so, it demonstrates the key factors for designing microfinance products and services to ensure greater uptake and outreach enhancing the sustainability of microfinance service providers. Chapters explore the impact of access to microfinance on livelihood diversification, asset accumulation patterns and welfare outcomes. In addition to assessing the role as well as of microfinance as an anti-poverty tool, the book presents new theoretical frameworks and models, including the microfinance livelisystem framework (MFL). This unique framework, which combines and goes beyond existing frameworks, situates the microfinance industry within national and international financial and economic ecosystems and presents the interrelationships between institutions providing services for the construction of livelihoods.

Offering new theoretical frameworks and models developed for the microfinance industry with universal application, this book will be of particular use to students and scholars of Development Studies, Development Finance, Poverty and Inequality Studies, Rural Development and Sustainable Finance.

Aaron Alesane lectured with the Faculty of Business and Social Sciences at the Academic City University College, Ghana. He currently works with the Council for Scientific and Industrial Research, Institute of Industrial Research and is Head of the Business and Information Services Division.

Routledge Studies in African Development

Politics in The Gambia and Guinea-Bissau
Precolonial Influence on the Postcolonial State
Mariama Khan

Engendering Democracy in Africa
Women, Politics and Development
Niamh Gaynor

Social Protection, Pastoralism and Resilience in Ethiopia
Lessons for Sub-Saharan Africa
Edited by Zeremariam Fre, Bereket Tsegay, Araya M. Teka, John Livingstone and Nicole Kenton

Sustainable Development in Post-Pandemic Africa
Effective Strategies for Resource Mobilization
Edited by Fred Olayele and Yiagadeesen Samy

Socioeconomic Shocks and Africa's Development Agenda
Lessons and Policy Directions in a Post-COVID-19 Era
Edited by Evans Osabuohien, Gbadebo Odularu, Daniel E. Ufua and Romanus A. Osabohien

Africa's Economic Partnership with China
An Holistic Analysis
Mussie Delelegn Arega

Microfinance, Livelihoods and Poverty Reduction in Ghana
Aaron Alesane

For more information about this series, please visit: www.routledge.com/Routledge-Studies-in-African-Development/book-series/RSAD

MICROFINANCE, LIVELIHOODS AND POVERTY REDUCTION IN GHANA

Aaron Alesane

Routledge
Taylor & Francis Group
LONDON AND NEW YORK

Cover image: © Agata Lagati Photography / Getty Images

First published 2023
by Routledge
4 Park Square, Milton Park, Abingdon, Oxon OX14 4RN

and by Routledge
605 Third Avenue, New York, NY 10158

Routledge is an imprint of the Taylor & Francis Group, an informa business

British Library Cataloguing-in-Publication Data
A catalogue record for this book is available from the British Library

Library of Congress Cataloging-in-Publication Data
Names: Alesane, Aaron, author.
Title: Microfinance, livelihoods and poverty reduction in Ghana / Aaron Alesane.
Description: New York, NY : Routledge, 2023. |
Series: Routledge studies in African development | Includes bibliographical references and index. |
Identifiers: LCCN 2022037153 | ISBN 9781032332604 (hardback) | ISBN 9781032332628 (paperback) | ISBN 9781003318873 (ebook)
Subjects: LCSH: Microfinance—Ghana. | Poverty—Government policy—Ghana. | Ghana—Economic conditions—21st century.
Classification: LCC HG178.33.G4 A54 2023 | DDC 332.209667—dc23/eng/20220929
LC record available at https://lccn.loc.gov/2022037153

ISBN: 978-1-032-33260-4 (hbk)
ISBN: 978-1-032-33262-8 (pbk)
ISBN: 978-1-003-31887-3 (ebk)

DOI: 10.4324/9781003318873

Typeset in Bembo
by codeMantra

CONTENTS

ACKNOWLEDGEMENT

I am grateful, first, to the Commonwealth Scholarship Commission (CSC), UK and the Association of Commonwealth Universities (ACU), whose financial support made my PhD study a reality at the University of Reading, UK. Also, I am grateful to the Government of Ghana for my nomination via the Scholarship Secretariat. In addition, I am sincerely thankful to my supervisors, Professor Henny Osbahr and Professor Chittur Srinivasan of the University of Reading, whose constructive criticisms, attention to detail and suggestions immensely contributed to this book. Their patience, strategic interventions and directions in the course of the research work were spectacular.

To my mum, Margaret Abaane Alesane, and younger siblings Joseph, Sebastian, Roger, Nora and Dora, thank you for your prayers, moral support and most often the 'irritation' that kept me on my toes. God bless you all.

Also, I very much appreciate the management and staff of all the sampled microfinance institutions of the Upper East Region including the Naara Rural Bank; the Builsa Community Rural Bank; the Bessfa Rural Bank, Garu; Sinapi Abba, Bolgatanga Branch; the Bolgatanga Teachers Credit Union; the Garu Teachers Credit Union; Tarasum Money Lending and Leverage Services, Bolgatanga; Bencyn Susu Company, Bolgatanga; and the various Village Savings and Loans Groups across the region that took part in the study.

This acknowledgement will be incomplete without mentioning Dr Francis Boateng Agyenim, Director of the Council for Scientific and Industrial Research, Institute of Industrial Research, for all the support and all staff of the Institute. He remains a mentor par excellence.

Finally, I would also like to thank the publishing team at Routledge who have wholeheartedly supported this monograph project.

TABLES

FIGURES

ABBREVIATIONS AND ACRONYMS

AQR	Asset Quality Review
ARB	Association of Rural Banks
ARBAB	Association of Rural Banks Apex Bank
ASD	Agenda for Sustainable Development
ATMs	Automated Teller Machines
BBWA	British Bank of West Africa
BCC	Bank for Credit and Commerce Ghana Ltd
BGC	Bank of the Gold Coast
BHC	Bank for Housing and Construction
BoG	Bank of Ghana
BRAC	Bangladesh Rural Advancement Committee
CBG	Consolidated Bank Ghana Limited
CCT	Conditional Cash Transfers
CGAP	Consultative Group to Assist the Poor
COOP	Ghana Co-operative Bank
CPP	Convention Peoples Party
DFID	Department for International Development
ELA	Emergency Liquidity Assistance
ERP	Economic Recovery Programme
Findex	Global Financial Inclusion Index
FINSAC	Financial Sector Adjustment Credit
FINSAP	Financial Sector Adjustment Programme
FINSSP	Financial Sector Strategic Plan
FNGOs	Financial Non-Governmental Organizations
GAMA	Greater Accra Municipal Area
GATT	General Agreement on Trade and Tariff
GDP	Gross Domestic product

GFSDP	Ghana Financial Sector Development Project
GLSS	Ghana Living Standards Surveys
GoG	Government of Ghana
GPSDF	Ghana Private Sector Development Fund
GSE	Ghana Stock Exchange
GSS	Ghana Statistical Service
HIPC	Highly Indebted Poor Countries Initiative
ICAAP	Internal Capital Adequacy Assessment
IDS	Institute of Development Studies
IFAD	International Fund Food and Agriculture (IFAD)
IMF	International Monetary Fund
I-PRSP	Interim Poverty Reduction Strategy Paper
LEAP	Livelihood Empowerment Against Poverty
LUSPA	Land Use and Spatial Development Authority
MASLOC	Microfinance and Small Loans Centre
MDAs	Ministries, Departments and Agencies
MDGs	Millennium Development Goals
MFCs	Microfinance Companies
MFIs	Microfinance Institutions
MIVs	Microfinance Investment Vehicles
MIX	Microfinance Information Exchange
MLs	Moneylenders
MPC	Monetary Policy Committee
MSMEs	Micro, Small and Medium-scale Enterprises
MTDP	Medium-Term Development Plan
NBFIs	Non-Bank Financial Institutions
NDC	National Democratic Congress
NFIDS	National Financial Inclusion and Development Strategy
NGOs	Non-Governmental Organization
NIB	National Investment Bank
NPART	Non-Performing Assets Recovery Trust
NPLs	Non-Performing Loans
NPP	New Patriotic Party
NRC	National Redemption Council
NSCB	National Savings and Credit Bank
PAMSCAD	Programme of Action to Mitigate the Social Costs of Adjust NDC National Democratic Congress
POSB	Post Office Savings Bank
PRA	Participatory Rural Appraisals
PRSPs	Poverty Reduction Strategy Papers
PUA	Participatory Urban Appraisal
RAFiP	Rural Financial Services Project
RCBs	Rural and Community Banks
RFSP	Rural Financial Support Project

S&Ls	Savings and Loans
SAPs	Structural Adjustment Programmes
SDGs	Sustainable Development Goals
SLF	Sustainable Livelihood Framework
SPEED	Support Programme for Enterprise Empowerment and Development
SSA	Sub-Saharan Africa
SSB	Social Security Bank
UNDEA	United Nations Department of Economic Affairs
UNDP	United Nations Development Programme
USAID	United States Aid
VAT	Value Added Tax
VSLA	Village Savings and Loans Associations
WACB	West Africa Currency Board
WB	World Bank
WBUFI	World Bank Universal Financial Access
WTO	World Trade Organization
WVI	World Vision international

FOREWORD

Foreword by Professor Joshua Yindenaba Abor, *PhD, FCCA, FGA*
Professor of Finance and former Dean,
University of Ghana Business School

I first met Dr Aaron Alesane in the mid-2000s, both in the personal and academic spheres, particularly when he expressed his interest to enrol into one of the master's programmes offered by the University of Ghana. Aaron has almost a decade of experience working extensively in Development Practice in Ghana and beyond. Mostly within the international non-governmental space (e.g., Plan International, Ghana and International Cocoa Initiative, Ghana), he has managed and coordinated projects and programmes in livelihoods, including microfinance and food security, water and sanitation, health and education in deprived communities across the length and breadth of Ghana. His experiences with microfinance activities in Ghana were invaluable to both his MPhil thesis (*'A Comparative Study of the Credit with Education (CwE) and the Village Savings and Loans (VSL) Methodology of Microfinance Services on Rural Livelihoods'*) and his PhD thesis (*'Participation in Microfinance Programmes and Poverty Reduction through Clients Livelihoods: The Case of the Northern Savannah of Ghana'*), which has culminated in this book. I was personally privileged to have made some suggestions on its layout, particularly on the evolution of economic paradigms and livelihoods.

The book takes a micro, meso, macro and international outlook on livelihoods, microfinance and the poverty reduction nexus within the context of sub-Saharan Africa using Ghana as a case study. Two critical frameworks developed, the *Microfinance Livelisystem Framework* and the *Household Livelisystem Model,* theoretically and empirically contextualize this nexus. While the former situates the microfinance industry within the domestic and cross-border economic and financial eco-systems, the latter is on the interaction of household resources and activities with localized societal welfare promoting institutions for the construction of livelihoods. The third framework developed, expanded a previously developed framework for the analysis of product design from the supply side, into the demand side perspective of the microfinance industry. Using econometric techniques, the book simultaneously identified the specific macro-economic, macro-institutional, organizational, household and client-level determinants of uptake of financial services. Last, but not the least, the book examines access and livelihood diversification, asset accumulation patterns and household welfare outcomes among resource-poor population groups in a tiered microfinance landscape.

PREFACE

This book examines the nexus of the evolution of the microfinance sub-sector vis-à-vis the broader national financial sector development, households' access, livelihood diversification and poverty reduction in Ghana, focusing on the Northern Savannah. The book is largely the outcome of the PhD thesis of the author undertaken at University of Reading, UK, as a Commonwealth Scholar. The study was motivated by the following:

1 The ***personal circumstances of the author*** who had almost a decade in development practice in the INGO sector working with and through both state (MDAs) and other non-state actors across Ghana. He worked on the topic '*The Comparative Study of the Credit with Education (CwE) and the Village Savings and Loans Methodologies of Microfinance Services and Rural Livelihoods in the Awutu Senya District of the Central region of Ghana*' for his Masters of Philosophy (MPhil) study.
2 The need to ***cover gaps in the microfinance, livelihoods and poverty reduction nexus*** – both in theory and practice. For example:

   i ***in theory***: cover the gap of the absence of a single conceptual framework that holistically situates the microfinance industry within national and international economic and financial eco-systems and simultaneously shows their interrelationships with institutions providing services for livelihood construction by resource-poor populations.
   ii ***in theory***: cover the gap of the absence of a single conceptual framework that holistically presents the interactions within households and between households' resources and activities and the broader localized societal welfare promoting institutions (family, social networks, public authorities, membership organizations and markets) in the construction of livelihoods.

- iii ***empirically***: cover the gap of the absence of a single study, at least in Ghana, that simultaneously identifies the interplay of specific macroeconomic, macro-institutional, MFI (firm-level) factors, and clients and their household characteristics on the uptake of financial services, from the demand side of the industry.
- iv ***empirically***: cover the gaps between the design of microfinance products and services and the livelihood needs and wants of clients that continue to remain contested, not least because of the mixed evidence of microfinance impacts on poverty reduction and the financial self-sufficiency of microfinance institutions (MFIs).
- v ***empirically***: explore the relationship between access and livelihood diversification, asset accumulation patterns and household welfare among referenced resource-poor population groups.

3 The 2017–2020 Ghanaian financial sector crisis leading up to the revocation of the licences of some financial institutions, including 9 commercial banks, 347 microfinance institutions, 39 microcredit companies and moneylenders, 15 savings and loans companies, 8 finance houses and 2 non-bank financial institutions, for various alleged infractions of the Specialized Deposit-Taking Institutions Act, 2016 (Act 930) and the Securities Industry Act, 2016 (Act 929) did shaped the direction of this study.

The author currently works with the Council for Scientific and Industrial Research, Institute of Industrial Research (CSIR IIR) in the Business and Information Services Division.

1

MICROFINANCE AND POVERTY REDUCTION

An Introduction

1.1 Introduction

In 2010, the world had effectively attained the first Millennium Development Goal of halving the 1990 global poverty rate by 2015. It is estimated that between 1990 and 2015, the 1.85 billion people living on less than \$1.90 a day had declined to 736 million. Though the millennium development goals (MDGs) did not set targets for financial sector development, microfinance underpinned the achievement of many of its strategies. This recognition led the General Assembly of the United Nations to designate 2005 as the Year of Microcredit (Reed et al., 2015; United Nations, 2005). Also, by emphasizing access to microfinance in its recommendations, the United Nations Millennium Project also sought to focus country strategies and programmes on building inclusive and sustainable financial sectors. Besides, the Africa Commission Report (Wright, 2005) pointed to the relevance of microfinance as an anti-poverty tool.

However, according to the Findex 2017 report, almost 1.7 billion adults remain unbanked, 56% of which are female, and all coming from the poorest 40% of households with nearly half living in just seven developing countries (Bangladesh, China, India, Indonesia, Mexico, Nigeria and Pakistan). While poverty rates have declined in all regions, progress has been uneven. East Asia and the Pacific and Europe and Central Asia have all reduced extreme poverty to below 3%, effectively achieving the 2030 target. Sub-Saharan Africa is home to more than half of the world's extreme poor where 413 million are living on less than US\$1.90 a day. At this rate and trend, nine out of ten of the world's extreme poor will be living in sub-Saharan Africa by 2030 (World Bank, 2015). Significant poverty reduction did occur in a few sub-Saharan African countries.

There is an increasing need to understand how microfinance works for the livelihoods of populations in sub-Saharan Africa, not least because it is one of

DOI: 10.4324/9781003318873-1

the poorest regions, but also because it is the destination of a large proportion of development aid (Grabel, 2008). The majority of non-profit service providers are also active in the region (Gart, 2012). Historically, sub-Saharan Africa is rich in microfinance activities from the credit unions of the 1950s and 1960s (Raftopoulos and Lacoste, 2001). Group-based savings and lending (Gart, 2012) are also common. Even though there are substantial investment inflows through an array of microfinance initiatives in the region (Gart, 2012; World Bank, 2015), the microfinance industry remains undeveloped and is concentrated in relatively few countries (Gart, 2012; Campaign, 2015). There is, therefore, an opportunity for research to shape policy, especially considering new initiatives targeting capacity development (World Bank, 2015) aimed at driving effective service provision .

The united nations sustainable development goals (SDGs) and the World Bank's 2030 Agenda for Sustainable Development both seek to continue with the approaches to eradicate extreme poverty (currently measured as people living on less than $1.90 a day) globally by 2030. Furthermore, the 2020 target of the Universal Financial Access compelled major stakeholders to do more to ensure financial access for the eradication of extreme poverty. In sub-Saharan Africa (SSA), Ghana was ranked the highest recipient (about US 186 million) of development donor funding for the microfinance industry (Ivatury & Mas, 2008).

Gains in poverty reduction by successive governments based on the Ghana living standards surveys (GLSS) conducted between 1991/1992 and 2012/2013 have been impressive. The trends show that the incidence of poverty reduced by more than half over two decades. From 51.7% in 1991/1992, the incidence of poverty decreased to about 39.5% in 1998/1999, 28.5% in 2005/2006 and, recently to more than half, 24.2% in 2012/2013 (Ghana Statistical Service, 2014). Geographically, however, the fall in poverty has not been experienced equally across the country. For instance, the GLSS5 figures showed that poverty headcount rates had fallen dramatically in southern Ghana compared to northern Ghana. Urban growth, mineral extraction and, in the 2005/2006 survey period, a boom in the cocoa sub-sector in response to higher world commodity prices, domestic market reforms and production support from the government accounted for the differences. Poverty levels in the Northern Savannah have remained disturbingly high. In 2005/2006, the northern area accounted for just under 22% of the total Ghanaian population but accounted for 45% of the headcount poor and 57% of the extreme headcount poor (Ghana Statistical Service, 2007). The 2012/2013, Ghana Living Standards Survey also shows that while under a tenth of the Ghanaian population live in extreme poverty, about a quarter are generally poor, and it is a phenomenon concentrated in the Northern Rural Savannah (Ghana Statistical Service, 2014). Based on 2017 population projections, the Ghana Statistical Services reported in their '*Trends of Poverty and Inequality*' that approximately 6.8 million Ghanaians were considered poor with incomes less than GH¢1,760.80 per year (or approximately US $320.145). The UNDP in 2019 reported that for Ghana to achieve the sustainable development goals (SDGs), especially the eradication of poverty (i.e., SDG 1), substantial efforts are needed to transform the Northern Savannah.

For almost three decades, the liberalization and deregulation of Ghana's financial sector led to the establishment of several financial non-governmental organizations (FNGOs) and microfinance institutions (MFIs) in attempts to fight poverty through microfinance intermediation, and the industry has continued to receive funding and planning time from both government and development partners. However, microfinance promises to reduce poverty by building financial, physical, human, and social capital have received mixed reactions from the public, mostly due to inconclusive evidence from impact studies across time and space (Khandker, 2005; Roodman and Morduch, 2009; Imai et al., 2010; Imai and Azam, 2012; Banerjee et al., 2015). Financial NGOs and MFIs have been operating in northern Ghana for almost three decades, but the decline in poverty levels in the Northern Savannah can best be described as marginal. Thus, there is a gap in the understanding of the design of products and services, factors influencing uptake and effects of microfinance programmes on livelihood diversification, asset accumulation patterns and welfare outcomes as they relate to poverty reduction in the Northern Savannah of Ghana.

To understand the relationship between microfinance and livelihoods, it is necessary to adopt and further develop the plurality of existing concepts such as the livelisystem framework (Dorward, 2014), the household economic portfolio (Chen and Dunn, 1996) and the livelihood portfolio (Chambers and Conway, 1992) models. Two theoretical frameworks – the microfinance livelisystem framework and the household livelisystem model – are developed to better conceptually establish the functional relationship between the microfinance industry and the domestic and international financial system and the interactions between household resources and activities and their interrelationships with the broader localized societal welfare promoting institutions respectively. The book, borne out of the PhD thesis research of the author, will generate further academic understanding of the plausibility of microfinance as a development tool for poverty reduction, with Ghana as a case study. For instance, the conflicting empirical evidence of impact, according to Makina and Malobola (2004), results from definitional problems, conflicting objectives underpinning microfinance schemes and varied methodological approaches to impact assessments.

An expanded Schreiner (2002) framework for the design of microfinance products and services, irrespective of the approach to services delivery (poverty lending or the financial systems), will deepen understanding of what design features matter to clients of microfinance programmes and how these relate to the double bottom goals of increased outreach and impact on clients livelihoods and the sustainability of microfinance providers.

There is currently no single study that simultaneously identifies the interplay of specific macro-economic, macro-institutional, MFI (firm-level) factors, and clients and household characteristics that influence the uptake of microfinance from the demand side of the industry. This book explores the factors identified and their implications on uptake to improve the design of products and services, outreach and ultimately the self-sufficiency of microfinance institutions as well as macro-level policies and programmes for financial inclusion.

Moreover, the book established the role of microfinance in household livelihood diversifications, asset accumulation patterns and welfare outcomes in a three-tier industry in the Northern Savannah of Ghana. Pooled-income intrahousehold decision-making models are adapted and their interrelationships with the family, markets (including the microfinance market), public authorities, social networks, and membership institutions explored. This is particularly important in the framework of the sustainable development goals (SDGs) and more especially within the identified 'pathways' of leverage by the Microcredit Campaign (2015). As theory suggests, microfinance works differently in different regions where the population density, attitude to debt, group cohesion, enterprise development, financial literacy and financial service providers vary (Armendariz de Aghion and Morduch, 2005; Fischer and Ghatak, 2011).

The next section presents the background on which the book was written.

1.2 Background of the Book

At the macro-level, it has been theoretically and empirically established that the relationship between a well-functioning financial system and economic growth and development is positive. This relationship is a major determinant of the growth path of many countries. For instance, empirical evidence from several studies (Beck et al., 2004; Jalilian and Kirkpatrick, 2005; Jeanneney and Kpodar, 2011) concluded that financial development, particularly in developing countries, promotes growth which in turn reduces poverty. Although differing in proxies and outcome variables, others have investigated the direct relationship between financial development and poverty reduction (Honohan, 2004; Jalilian and Kirkpatrick, 2005; Beck et al., 2007; Perez-Moreno, 2011; Jeanneney and Kpodar, 2011; Sehrawat and Giri, 2015) and have come to a similar conclusion. Moreover, an imperfect financial market that excludes the poor and vulnerable segments of the population has the potential to worsen poverty and income inequality (Stiglitz, 1993). Therefore, there is an assumption within the microfinance industry that MFIs should correct the market failure that has trapped millions in poverty by providing them with access to credit, thereby creating economic and social power and helping to lift them out of poverty (Yunus, 1999).

Otero (1999), further, argues that microfinance and development essentially intersect at three key areas. These include reaching the poor through access to financial, social and human capital development; building institutions that provide broader services to the poorer sectors; and deepening the financial system via diverse regulated MFIs within the broader financial system. For many observers, microfinance is nothing short of a revolution or a paradigm shift (Acemoglu et al., 2001) away from Keynesian approaches (government-led, top-down) that have been challenged by Neoliberals theorists (market-led bottom-up) (Balassa,

1971). A 2006 Nobel Peace Prize was even awarded to microfinance pioneers Muhammad Yunus and the Grameen Bank, which signalled the extent that microfinance has become embedded in the world of international development (Armendáriz and Morduch, 2010).

However, many are still sceptical about microfinance and its links with development (Bateman and Chang, 2009; Chang, 2009; Weber, 2010). The World Bank and the IMF through the IFC continue to commit both financial resources and advisory services towards expanding and normalizing microfinance as a development tool especially where microfinance NGOs are assisted to transition towards becoming deposit-taking banks. This creates the opportunity for commercial microfinance borrowers not to rely on traditional development modalities. Microfinance borrowers are therefore co-opted into processes that have the overt objective of instilling market discipline in new locales. According to Carroll (2012), it represents the deep marketization of development continuing from the failure of the Washington Consensus Structural Adjustment Programmes and the latter Post-Washington Consensus Poverty Reduction Strategies. He called for scholars and activists to lead in the understanding of the relationship between this deep marketization and the material interests of the different factions of capital pushing for the creation of a dominant world market.

Moreover, the use of microfinance as a tool for fighting poverty has also stirred debates among practitioners, academics and policymakers about the real impact of the industry. Various studies have examined to what extent microfinance institutions have or can promote improved living standards among poor populations. While some have found positive effects on consumption and income levels (Khandker, 2005; Kondo et al., 2008; Berhane, 2009; Collins et al., 2009; Berhane and Gardebroek, 2012; Imai and Azam, 2012), housing improvements (Berhane, 2009; Berhane and Gardebroek, 2011), wages and agricultural investment at the community level (Kaboski and Townsend, 2012), savings (Kondo et al., 2008; Dupas and Robinson, 2013), health and food security (Stewart et al., 2010), others such as Chowdhury (2009) remained sceptical about its effectiveness as a tool for poverty reduction, especially amidst concerns about the commercialization of the industry. Chowdhury (2009) argues that borrowers need business skills and marketing information to leverage loans for the expansion of their businesses and the creation of jobs; otherwise, it is only a consumption smoothing tool. Buera and Kaboski (2012) built an economy-wide model of entrepreneurship of the industry, exclusive of the formal financial sector, and explored the extent of its influence on output, capital, total factor productivity, wages and interest rates. They concluded that, in some cases, MFIs not only raise output but decrease disparities between the rich and the poor. Ahlin and Jiang (2008) and Yusupov (2012) also find that MFIs promote development on a wider scale via tangible and intangible spill-overs.

As debates are beginning to shift to the demand side of the microfinance industry, researchers are questioning how innovations in products and service design can effectively mitigate the livelihood strategies of clients in existing livelisystem transitions that also ensure financial self-sufficiency of providers. Designing effective microfinance products and services remains a challenge, and according to Ledgerwood et al. (2013), the attention of the microfinance community is drawn to addressing the diverse needs of clients within the broader financial system and the transformational role of technology, such as the use of mobile phones in delivering better products and services.

Assessing the impact of microfinance on poverty reduction continues to remain difficult, not least because of the multiple dimensions of poverty, its measurement criteria, country-specific contexts and mixed evidence on the relationship between microfinance and poverty reduction (Datt and Ravallion, 1992; Pitt, 2014; Roodman and Morduch, 2014). For instance, the 2009 release of the first randomized studies in Hyderabad, India, and Manila, the Philippines, was met with mixed reactions (Banerjee et al., 2010; Karlan and Zinman, 2011). These randomized studies challenged the dominant narrative of microfinance premised on microcredit to poor micro-entrepreneurs with the ability to earn high returns from marginal capital investments while concurrently repaying and reinvesting their way out of poverty. Far from being a panacea for poverty reduction, the studies showed that these approaches could also damage livelihoods. The empirical evidence corroborated by non-randomized studies in the microfinance research literature finds only modest impacts on livelihoods from microcredit and microfinance in general. The financial needs of poor households go beyond working capital loans.

Moreover, the financial needs of individuals and households vary greatly, and the demand for different product features, payment structures and delivery structures is imperative for enabling the poor to cope with risks of irregular cash flows, smooth consumption, seize opportunities, pay for children's education, save to invest in businesses, and utilize crop and health insurance. For instance, group liability contracts promote repayment via assortative matching during screening and peer monitoring following loan disbursements. Targeting women supports the double bottom goals of greater outreach and financial self-sufficiency of providers through greater repayment rates and better welfare outcomes for households, especially children. Weekly repayments decrease credit risk for service providers of uncollateralized loans by creating immediate discipline and a pattern of repayment. Thus, if these product-centred attributes of the classic microcredit model work for service providers, do they work for borrowers?

Increasingly, empirical evidence from diverse locations and context suggests that some of these product-centred design features may be far from optimally balancing the twin goals of the industry and may rather be creating negative trade-offs against clients. Studies on variants of group liability contracts, targeting women, the timing of repayments and tools for the assessment of credit worthiness of potential clients are providing insight on the effects of alternative product design for the improvement of financial access and outcomes for segments of the population targeted.

In sub-Saharan Africa (SSA), Ghana was ranked the highest recipient (about US 186 million) of development donor funding into microfinance. The institutions responsible have been operating in northern Ghana for well over two decades. In Ghana, available studies (Afrane, 2002; Adjei et al., 2009) suggest that microfinance has had some poverty-reducing effects. In 2004, a poverty assessment and comparative study of rural microfinance institutions and government/donor credit programmes concluded among others that microfinance institutions (MFIs) had more capacity than other financial institutions to achieve better outreach when they operate in poor geographical areas; rural banks and financial non-governmental organizations (FNGOs) tended to deal more with people in the lower ends of the poverty spectrum than the rest, and nearly 80% of the recipients of loans which were less than 50 Cedis (¢50.00) were in the lowest poverty quintile. However, the decline in poverty levels can be described as marginal, as revealed by the Ghana Statistical Service (2013). This raises the question as to whether or not participation in microfinance programmes, and the products and services thereof, has had any effects on poverty reduction in the region, though reported elsewhere in the empirical literature to have the power to do so (Zeller and Sharma, 1998; Littlefield et al., 2003b). Moreover, the evaluation of products and services by customers is carried out by weighing their perceived value against the asking price, and what customers truly value can be difficult to establish because it is often embedded psychologically within functional, emotional, life-changing, and social impact categories.

The book broadly aims to assess the role of microfinance as an anti-poverty tool in the Northern Savannah of Ghana using two developed conceptual frameworks by the author and an amended existing one. First, the study theoretically filled the gap in literature created by the absence of a single conceptual framework that holistically situates the microfinance industry within national and international economic and financial eco-systems and simultaneously shows the interrelationships between institutions providing services and the livelihoods constructed by resource poor households. Second, the study theoretically established a single conceptual framework that holistically presents the interactions within households and between households and the broader localized societal welfare promoting institutions, including the family, social networks, public authorities, membership organizations and markets in the construction of livelihoods. Third, the study empirically filled in the gap created by the absence of a single study, at least in Ghana, that simultaneously identifies the interplay of specific macro-economic, macro-institutional, MFI (firm-level) factors, and clients and their household characteristics determining the uptake of financial services, from the demand side of the microfinance industry. Fourth, it explored the design of microfinance products and services and the livelihood needs and wants of clients, which has remained contested, not least because of the mixed evidence of microfinance impacts on poverty reduction and the financial self-sufficiency of microfinance institutions (MFIs) by adapting an expanded version of Schreiner's (2002) framework. Lastly, the study assessed access to financial services and patterns of household livelihood diversification, asset accumulation patterns, and welfare outcomes within the three-tiered microfinance industry of the Northern Savannah of Ghana. The case study region is the Upper East Region of Ghana. By understanding how the broader goals and objectives of financial inclusion underpin the design and roll-out of financial products and services, the factors influencing uptake and how access complements other socio-economic arrangements to support poverty reduction, the insights will inform policy and programmes, both at the local and national level, to further the case for the financial inclusion of the productive poor.

The next section presents how the rest of the book is organized.

1.3 Organization of the Book

Chapter 1 'Microfinance and Poverty Reduction: An Introduction' presents the background and motivation, the aim as well as the objectives for writing the book. The book is situated on the nexus of access to microfinance, livelihoods and the rhetoric of poverty reduction. While Section 1.1 presents the background, the problem statement is in Section 1.2. The aim of the book, objectives and the questions it sought to address are presented in Section 1.3. The organization of the book is further presented in Section 1.4.

Chapter 2 'The conceptual, theoretical and epistemological perspectives of livelihoods, microfinance, and the rhetoric of poverty reduction' discusses the conceptual, theoretical and epistemological perspectives of the study. The chapter deals with understanding the concept of poverty, livelihoods and microfinance. The evolution of economic paradigms including the Classical, Neo-Classical, Liberal, Keynesian and the Marxists views on poverty and livelihoods. The theoretical evolution of rural financial markets and rural livelihoods – including the Usurious Monopolistic Moneylender, the Perfect Information Paradigm, the Imperfect Information Paradigm and the Psychological Theory (Social Consciousness-driven Capitalism) – is also discussed. The developed Microfinance Livelisystem Framework (MFL), the Household Livelisystem Model (HLM) and the expanded Schreiner (2002) framework for designing microfinance products and services are also presented in this chapter.

Chapter 3 'The context of the global microfinance industry' presents literature on the empirical context of rural financial markets and rural livelihoods, the products and services of the industry, and the factors underpinning their design, including cost of access, worth of access, scope of access, length of access, depth of outreach, breadth of outreach, add-ons and enforcement mechanisms employed. The chapter further presents literature on clients' perceptions of the effects of macro-economic, macro-institutional, microfinance institution (MFI) level factors, as well as household and individual characteristics that influence product and service uptake. These include interest rates, the state of the rural economy, inflation, rule of law, lending models (group versus individual), household size, livelihood diversification, and client start-up requirements and uptake of financial services. The rest are the influence of other poverty interventions, level of formal education and gender. Literature on the impact of microfinance on rural livelihood diversification, asset accumulation patterns and welfare outcomes is further presented in this chapter.

Chapter 4 'The state of financial services and financial inclusion in Ghana' discusses the study country's context, including its geography, climate and population structure; an overview of its political economy and a short history of the Northern Savannah of Ghana. Also, the chapter further captures the historical evolution of Ghana's financial sector development vis-à-vis financial inclusion through microfinance programmes. Empirical literature on financial inclusion in Ghana in relation to locality, gender, credit, savings and insurance products, and payment services uptake is presented.

Chapter 5 'Designing microfinance products and services for financial inclusion in Ghana' used an expanded Schreiner (2002) framework for the design of microfinance to gauge client's perceptions of their level of incorporation in accessed products and services. These include perceptions of costs of access, both price and transaction costs; scope of available financial contracts, both between and within products; length and its demand- and supply-side complementarities; worth of access in relation to livelihood constraints and opportunities; depth of outreach, as the numbers of the poorest segment of the population reached; breadth of outreach, relating to absolute numbers of targeted unserved and underserved populations reached; contract enforcement mechanisms employed; and add-ons (i.e., microfinance plus) – the general complementary social intermediation.

Chapter 6 'Determinants of microfinance uptake in Ghana' established the macro-economic, macro-institutional, MFI level factors, as well as the household and individual client characteristics that determine the uptake of microfinance products and services. Data of 31 variables across these major themes were solicited from clients. Correlation analysis established 13 to be relevant and they are subsequently described and their signs hypothesized. A logistic regression analyses constituted the econometric method used in the determination of the factors influencing uptake of microfinance in the Northern Savannah of Ghana. Qualitative data and information provided depth behind the numbers in this chapter.

Chapter 7 'Impacts of household access to microfinance in Ghana' focuses on access and household livelihood diversification, asset accumulation patterns and welfare outcomes across a three-tier microfinance industry. The chapter provides comparative analysis of household livelihood diversification, asset accumulation patterns and welfare outcomes of those accessing services from the formal and informal MFIs and those from the semi-formal and informal MFIs. Descriptive and inferential statistics were the analytical tools, and these were complemented by qualitative data and information obtained by various methods as these outcomes relate to the pentagon of localized societal welfare promoting institutions such as family and kinship groups, social networks, markets, membership institutions and local government authorities.

The next chapter examines the conceptual, theoretical and epistemological background of livelihoods, microfinance and the rhetoric of poverty reduction.

2

THE CONCEPTUAL, THEORETICAL AND EPISTEMOLOGICAL PERSPECTIVES OF LIVELIHOODS, MICROFINANCE AND THE RHETORIC OF POVERTY REDUCTION

2.1 Introduction

This chapter presents the conceptual, theoretical and epistemological perspective of the study centred on livelihoods, microfinance and poverty reduction. The conceptualizations of poverty, livelihoods and microfinance are presented in Sections 2.2, 2.3 and 2.4, respectively. While Section 2.5 provides a critical discourse analysis of the various economic paradigms on the causes of poverty and the proffered solutions within the context of livelihood development, Section 2.6 presents the theoretical evolution of rural credit markets and rural livelihoods. Finally, Section 2.7 presents the developed conceptual and theoretical frameworks on which the content of the rest of the chapters of the book is based.

2.2 Understanding the Concept of Poverty

Over the years, the definition and measurement of poverty have witnessed considerable evolution. However, each definition represents the construction of reality through which value judgements abound and transparency remain opaque. Broadly, four approaches to defining and measuring poverty are known with each one having its own theoretical underpinnings, operational challenges and policy implications for poverty reduction. Therefore, it can be misleading when the poor are targeted based on the policy prescriptions of one type of definition and measurement criteria.

These approaches are categorized into monetary, capability, social exclusion and participatory, providing the various definitions and measurement criteria. Over all, both the classical and neo-classical economic schools underpin all four approaches. While the classical economic tradition places poverty on the failure of the individual and prescribes laissez-faire policies, the neo-classical proffers

DOI: 10.4324/9781003318873-2

diverse reasons including market failure that are beyond the control of the individual. Thus, incentives and individual productivity constitute the bedrocks within both schools from which all four approaches sprung. The monetary values are also overemphasized, the role of government is downplayed and policy prescriptions are averse to redistribution. However, neoliberals focus on macroeconomic variables and the role of government in regulation for economic stability and the provision of public goods. Here, poverty is largely recognized as involuntary due to the lack of employment opportunities. Equal weightings are given to the social and economic aspects of poverty under the social exclusion approach. Thus, the tangible and intangible precursors to situations of poverty and their long-term impact are adequately captured. Class and group discrimination, both of which have political undertones, are the primary causes of poverty according to the Marxist paradigm. Minimum wage policies and anti-discriminatory laws by the state that regulate the market can, therefore, prevent poverty and destitution. To maximize economic insights on poverty requires the synthesis of selective approaches in the design of effective policy responses. Moreover, all sources of motivation for human behaviour beyond the economic and individual need recognition in development theory and practice.

The assumption of the monetary approach is that heterogeneity across individuals, societies and environments can be accounted for with uniform monetary metrics. In each society, reference is made to a shortfall in income or consumption levels in relation to an identified minimum level of resources (the poverty line). Current market prices form the basis of valuation of the components of income or consumption; therefore, relevant markets need identification for products with intrinsic non-market values and for public goods to be imputed (Grosh and Glewwe, 2000). Here, utility maximization underpins expenditure on commodities from which the marginal utility is then derived. Expenditure or income data become the proxy for welfare defined as the total utility enjoyed. A shortfall thereof below the poverty line then implies an individual is living in poverty with reference to that society in question.

The capability approach, however, places emphasis on expanding human capabilities to live a 'valued' life as a measure of well-being (Sen, 1985; 1997; 1999). That is, "the ability to satisfy certain crucially important functioning up to certain minimally adequate levels" (Sen, 1993). The capability approach is essentially a critique of the utility considerations of the monetary approach – both as a measure of well-being and as a behavioural assumption of utility maximization. For example, if a utility is interpreted as a 'desire fulfilment' that neglects the physical condition of poor people but focuses on what seems possible economically (valuation neglect), then the outcomes analysed from the perspective of the market are misleading. This is because social context influences expectations and economic valuations (Sen, 1985). Therefore, monetary and other resource metrics are necessary but not enough for the achievement of capability. The role of externalities and social goods is highlighted, and monetary resources are instrumentally related to the achievement of well-being.

The social exclusion approach to defining and measuring poverty was coined in the Global North, where comprehensive welfare systems are common, but varied routes of marginalisation and deprivations exists. The social exclusion approach echoes the multi-dimensionality of the concept of poverty. Thus, social exclusion means wholly or partially excluding individuals or groups from the functional structures of the society in which they live (Neumark and Wascher, 2002). According to Townsend (1979), deprivation is when people "are in effect excluded from ordinary living patterns, customs, and activities".

The basic building blocks of all participatory poverty assessment are the participatory rural appraisal (PRA) tools. These are a set of tools to enable indigenes to share, analyse and take actions aimed at improving living conditions (Chambers, 1994). These approaches emerged to cover gaps in conventional poverty estimates that were increasingly being criticized as externally imposed with little or no views of locals considered. Participatory approaches are aimed at ensuring the participation of local people in decision-making around poverty and its mitigation, including the determination of its magnitude (Chambers, 1994; 1997). A variant of PRA is the participatory urban appraisal (PUA), an adaptation of the PRA tools for use in urban settings.

It is worth noting that the World Bank played a key role in scaling up participatory poverty assessments (PPAs) to complement other conventional poverty assessments (Narayan-Parker and Patel, 2000). These participatory tools were institutionalized by the World Bank and the International Monetary Fund during the imposition of both the structural adjustment policies (SAPs) in the 1990s and the poverty reduction strategy papers (PRSPs) in the early 2000s, where they were made an important conditionality. According to Cornwall (2000), participatory approaches are either for self-determination and empowerment or for the optimization of programme efficiency and mutual learning. However, participatory approaches are only adopted instrumentally for the co-option of the poor in programmes, which were some of the shortfalls during the implementation of these flagship programmes. For example, stakeholders came to the conclusion that the participatory exercises required during the preparation of the poverty reduction strategy papers (PRSPs) by countries in the Global South addressed, to a very limited extent, concerns identified during the earlier implemented structural adjustment policies (SAPs).

The contextual definition of 'the poor' varies in accordance with the perspective and objective of those defining it. Consumption and expenditure definitions of poverty are increasingly recognized as insufficient in addressing the needs of the poor, as these human and social needs are usually identified by outsiders and embedded in programmes. The self-characterization of poverty gathered from the poor themselves illustrates needs in the interactive development process. The definition of poverty by the Ghana living standards survey (GLSS) encompasses an economic index, including subsistence on a per capita income of less than two-thirds of the national average. Those with income below one-third of the national mean are classified as 'core poor'. The multidimensional nature of poverty stems from both its complexity and interwovenness, encompassing material lack and the need for assets, among others (Narayan et al., 2000). In this study, poverty permeates the personal and community life of those experiencing it. It is characterized in terms of both their occupation and their lack of access to assets and social services (Nunan and Satterthwaite, 2001). Perceptions of poverty and well-being vary across rural and urban localities and between men, women and the youth.

2.3 Understanding the Concept of Livelihoods

The conception of sustainable livelihoods began with the working paper of Robert Chambers and Gordon Conway in 1992 at the institute of development studies (IDS). Sustainable livelihoods were theoretically situated within the actor-oriented approaches in development programming, environmental studies and social sustainability frameworks, as well as the rhetoric of poverty reduction. The paper incorporated the fundamental ideas of capabilities (Sen, 1987), assets (Swift, 1989), equity and sustainability (WCED, 1987), steering away from the previous narrow conceptualizations of poverty. Since then, sustainable livelihoods encompass enhancement and diversification and are important tools for poverty reduction efforts in the Global South. Important distinctions exist between a job, work and livelihoods. While a job connotes one activity or trade that is performed in exchange for payment involving a formal agreement (a contract) between an employer and an employee, work is a broader concept that encompasses jobs and others such as creative work, unpaid care and voluntary services critical for human development.

Livelihood encompasses engagement in several activities, with or without a formal agreement, exchange of money, and it is not limited to trade. Livelihoods are self-directing and are based on income derived from 'jobs' and 'works' but also on income derived from assets and entitlements. According to Chambers and Conway (1992),

> a livelihood comprises the capabilities, assets and activities required for a means of living. It is sustainable if it can cope with and recover from stress and shocks, maintain or enhance its capabilities and assets, and provide sustainable livelihood opportunities for the next generation, contribute net benefits to other livelihoods at the local and global levels and in the short and long term.

Assets include stores, resources, claims and access. According to Scoones (2008), the concept has successfully been adapted and applied to food security, poverty reduction, disaster reduction and relief, HIV/AIDS prevention, biodiversity conservation, and development projects and research (Walpole and Wilder, 2008). 'Capabilities' was incorporated in the concept by Sen (1987). Been capable refers to "being able to perform certain basic functioning, to what a person is capable of doing and being" and is contextually dependent (Chambers and Conway, 1992). Capabilities can also be construed as the 'freedom' of individuals or households to choose pathways and participate in activities that increase their quality of life.

According to the UK's department for international development (DFID), now part of the Foreign, Commonwealth and Development Office (FCDO) "a livelihood comprises the capabilities, assets (material and social) and activities required for a means of living". It is sustainable if it copes with and recovers from stresses and shocks while maintaining or even enhancing its capabilities and assets for the present and future generations, while not undermining the natural resource base (Carney, 1998). DFID has also developed a sustainable livelihood framework (SLF) for the analysis of the concept, in which the pentagon of interchangeable livelihood assets (natural, social, physical, financial and human capitals) is key for poverty reduction in the context of vulnerabilities from shocks and stresses as well as trends and sensonalities.

Mediating access to resources at the level of government, the private sector and civil society are transformational structures but the processes are regulated by laws, policies, culture, institutions and power relations. DFID's Sustainable Livelihood Guidance Sheet outlines people-centeredness, holistic in approach, dynamism, the strengthening of local structures, micro-macro linkages and sustainability as the six core themes underpinning the application of the sustainable livelihood's framework. However, its ability to empower, respond to needs of the poor, encourage participation, build partnership, disaggregate data (i.e., into gender, household, socio-economic status, race), and be flexible in implementation is now part of the SLF (Carney, 2003).

Disaggregation of rural and urban livelihoods is increasingly difficult. Many of the rural poor live and work in urban centres for most of the year. Many of the better-off buy parcels of land or housing in urban areas so their children could be better educated (exit strategies). There is an emerging phenomenon where urban elites are increasingly expanding into the rural sphere through land purchase for agricultural purposes. In addition to multi-tasking and blurring of the rural-urban livelihood interface, rural people are increasingly developing multi-local livelihoods due to rapid urbanization and improvements in communication and transport infrastructure. The share of non-farm income in the Global South is increasing (IFAD, 2011). However, agricultural activities constitute more than 80% of all economic portfolios of rural households (Valdes et al., 2008). While farming and agricultural labour are the main sources of income for poorer households, non-farm activities remain the major source of income for better-off households. Apart from the general income gains in rural areas in the Global South, there are shifts out of agricultural wages and into self-employment.

2.4 Understanding the Concept of Microfinance

According to Robinson (2002), while the words microcredit and microfinance are often used interchangeably, they represent contrasting beliefs about the state and nature of rural financial markets and poverty. Microcredit involved the minimalist's approach of credit extension for poverty reduction and social change, initially used by MFIs such as the Grameen Bank. Microfinance was used when savings became increasingly recognized as important in the livelihoods of resource-poor households. Mostly, microfinance is associated with the integrated approach. However, the change in language occasioned the re-orientation of the industry towards the 'less poor', i.e., commercialization. This era birthed the second revolution in credit theory and practice (Woller, 2002).

The first revolution (microcredit) concentrated efforts on the dismantling of structural barriers to service (microcredit and micro-savings) provision for resource-poor population groups. These barriers are usually those arising from information asymmetries between the market participants resulting in high transaction costs and include the lack of suitable collateral demanded by creditors, high-risk environments and systematic market failures. These barriers were overcome involving methodologies such as group lending, the use of social collateral, compulsory savings, staggered lending (small initial loan size with subsequent increment upon successful repayments), using savings amounts as a determinant of loan sizes, and the deployment of frequent repayments and disbursal schedules.

From the perspective of proponents of the second revolution (microfinance), innovations tackling the structural barriers to service provision in the microcredit era were 'inward-looking' as they focused on satisfaction of donor and organizational goals rather than the real needs and wants of clients. They were 'product-centred' rather than 'client-centred', requiring customers who matched the demands of their products and services. There was, therefore, the need to replace that product-centred approach with a customer-centred one.

However, at the time, questions were being raised as to whether credit or savings (Adams and Von Pischke, 1992; Basu, 1997) provided the best pathway for the poor to work their way out of poverty. In the process, legacies of the usurious moneylender and the failure of subsidized state banks in the 1960s relationships with consumption patterns were brought to the fore. Increasingly, the widely held view of the inability of the poor to save was more of a 'mistaken' belief (Bhaduri, 1973; Bhaduri, 1977) and that the inability of the state banks to mobilize deposits was more of a capacity rather than a lack of opportunity (Adams et al., 1984). Theoretically, savings are more difficult for the poor than obtaining credit that provides large sums of money when needed quickly. The limitations of individuals to analyse complex decisions and issues of self-control in a savings culture have led to the development of innovative savings methodologies and products, including structured savings accounts. Empirically, both rich and poor households simultaneously borrow and save (Collins et al., 2009). Credit and savings are not substitutes but complementary activities that both the poor and the rich take advantage of simultaneously (Armendáriz and Morduch, 2010). A few initiatives aimed at providing micro-insurance to the poor are faced with similar challenges prevalent in credit markets, especially in rural areas that are characterized by such risk factors as floods, droughts, crop failure, pests and infectious diseases.

Free from subsidies that characterized agricultural and rural credit markets in the 1960s that discounted incentives and the role of politics in hampering poverty reduction (Adams et al., 1984), the microfinance industry represented a market-led approach to sustainable poverty reduction. It has largely remained a protected industry, and foreign investment has grown rapidly since 2008. Paradoxically, subsidies from several donors continue to drive the microfinance industry. Most of these subsidies are mostly aimed at start-ups, where it is expected that scale economies and experience will eventually drive down costs and eliminate the need for further subsidies. It is becoming imperative that MFIs mobilize capital through savings deposits and from capital markets (with proof of their profitability). Banco Compartamos, an affiliate of ACCION International, issued a large bond in 2002 and its major initial public offering (IPO) marked a shift towards commercialization of the industry. With the transformation of many non-profits into regulated institutions and established commercial banks redefining their operations to include lending to the poor, the industry has become more complex and is mainly driven by transformational structures such as the microfinance investment vehicles (MIVs). Thus, in this study, microfinance is defined as banking services provided to low-income populations mostly engaged in informal economic activities, but with little or no access to financial services. While microfinance institutions and microfinance providers are used inter-changeably in this study, microfinance providers encompass commercial banks where microfinance divisions or desks are kept in place for microfinance activities.

Access to commercial sources of funding, though, relieves MFIs' reliance on donor funding; the often-associated transfer of costs to poor borrowers through high-interest rates or the exclusion of the core poor by serving only better-off clients means 'mission drift'. According to Cull et al. (2009), the median interest rate ranges between 25% for non-governmental organizations and 13% for banks with non-bank financial institutions having 20% after adjusting for inflation. Although these transactional costs are not marginal, they are commensurate with the costs involved in handling voluminous transactions that characterize microfinance. Thus, the typical argument in line with subsidization echoes the 'infant industry' protectionist policies in international trade literature. However, the strongly anti-protectionist sentiments that have characterized trade theory for decades (Bhagwati, 1988) have led economists to justify extended protection of the industry in the development literature (Krugman, 1994; Rodrik, 1997). The microfinance movement comprised diverse institutions, varying in sizes, operational areas and focus on social change and/or financial development. For instance, while some such as ASA in Bangladesh take a minimalist approach, others such as BRAC, Catholic Relief Services, CARE and Freedom from Hunger have taken an integrated approach (Littlefield et al., 2003a) to service delivery.

Facilitating access to financial services by the poor has led to the emergence of two paradigms – the Institutionists (financial systems) and the Welfarist (poverty lending) – and debates along these two have led to what Morduch (2000) referred to as then microfinance schism. At the point of divergence are competing perceptions of their implications on the financial self-sufficiency of microfinance institutions (MFIs) and outreach, in terms of depth and breadth. Though many MFIs are adopting both approaches, finding convergence can be problematic. The double bottom line of all MFIs is meeting both the financial and social goals of the industry. Achieving both goals will require MFIs to trade off one for the other at some point or develop innovative ways (Copestake and Williams, 2011).

The recovery of operating and financing costs from programme revenues is the pre-occupation of the Institutionists approach. That is, in the long term, many parallel sets of larger profit-seeking institutions provide quality, tailor-made products and services for the productive poor sustainably. Here, institutional self-sufficiency is the cardinal guiding principle and subsidies are not encouraged. The rationale being that making a large dent on poverty requires a massive scale far beyond donor benevolence (Gonzalez-Vega, 1993). The large financial resources needed require the participation of private capital. This demands good corporate governance, efficiency and profitability. The entirely different financial sub-system that consists of privately financed and large-scale financial intermediaries will then provide sustainable financial services to the poor. Little wonder that the Institutionists position is articulated in most published literature in the field of microfinance. For example, Bank Rakyat Indonesia (BRI) and Banco Solidario (BancoSol) in Bolivia have both adapted the Institutionists approach.

However, the Welfarist paradigm focuses on the depth of outreach. That is, reaching out to segments of the poorest of the poor with financial services even if operating and financing costs are not recoverable. The poverty-lending approach purports that MFIs can be sustainable without being financially self-sufficient (Woller et al., 1999; Morduch 2000). Donations act as equity with an intrinsic social return for donors, ensuring that the alleviation of the worst forms of poverty remains the priority, even if that entails subsidies at below market rates (Robinson, 2001). Integrated service provision is encouraged and skills, literacy and numeracy, health, nutrition and family planning education are emphasized. The Grameen Bank of Bangladesh and its replications across the Global South as well as the FINCA-style village banking across Latin America, Asia and Africa have mostly adapted the Welfarist approach to service provision.

However, with the launch of Grameen II in 2002, both approaches can be witnessed simultaneously in major MFIs across much of the developing world, and individual loans and savings are now key industrial products. According to Yunus (1999), the financial systems approach represents "a non-loss, non-dividend enterprise, that is created to do good to people" to positively change the world, with long-term expectation of profits. Weber (2006) described the microfinance industry as credit distribution, credit investment, profit generation and then profits, and further lending leads to larger investments and the repetition of the cycle reduces poverty in the process. Cull et al. (2009), however, question the virtuousness of this cycle, as it requires translating high repayment rates into profits, a challenge that remains elusive to many MFIs.

These two camps differ in at least three ways: the target population to provide services, designing products and services, and the structure of organizations and financing sources (Makina and Malobola, 2004). The transition of the industry towards profit-making necessitated changes in practices and standards, management and management systems, financing and accounting, marketing, service delivery, and product design and development. The widespread adaption of these 'best practices' represents industry-wide self-sufficiency, access to capital markets and increased outreach. However, the Institutionists perception of threat emanates from the disinterest of the Welfarist approach to scale, 'best practice' and financial self-sufficiency. They argue that donor funding cannot be relied upon and subsidies undermine financial self-sufficiency and all the spin-offs possible under the financial systems approach.

Remittances from rural-urban migrants (temporary or permanent) and international (South-South and South-North) in recent decades have emerged as significant sources of household income in much of the developing world. However, migrant remittances present more gains for wealthier households in absolute terms than poorer households (Bank, 2018). And in the Northern Savannah of Ghana, remittances from migrants to urban centres in the Southern Forest and Coastal belt are vital income sources used in mitigating livelihood constraints (Pickbourn, 2011; Kwankye, 2012). Information and communication technology are playing a key role in the remittance sphere, via Financial Technology (FinTech) companies that are actively collaborating with mobile network operators across much of the developing world.

2.5 The Evolution of Economic Paradigms and Livelihoods

The evolution of the concept of livelihoods, the causal factors of poverty and the policy prescriptions along the various economic schools of thought including the classical, neo-classical, Liberal/Keynesian and Marxist paradigms are reviewed in this section.

2.5.1 The Classical Economic Paradigm and Livelihoods

Classical economic theory assumes absolute efficiency of outcomes when the invisible hand directs exchanges, with wage levels truly reflecting individuals' productivity. At the personal level, poor choices are the primary variables determining poverty. However, underlying genetic factors supporting the individual differences to decision-making in relation to choices further constitute explanatory variables. The poor choice explanation suggests little or no intervention in the social structures and/or political climate that reinforce poverty. Therefore, state intervention beyond destitution represents inefficiency, rationally generating misaligned incentives that reinforce poverty, e.g., welfare dependency. Government role should, therefore, be limited to providing a supportive environment or policies that correct perverse incentives. The focus of policy prescription should concentrate on raising the productivity potential of deprived segments of the population for full participation in the labour force. However, alternative support is to be simultaneously carved out for children, the young, the sick and the old. The broad generalizations of personal failings as the culprit of poverty in the classical tradition led to the birth of several policy approaches for tackling poverty reduction, albeit with limited success.

The behavioural/decision-based theory (Esping-Andersen, 1990) asserts that poor economic decisions as a result of individual deficiencies account for poverty. Rank et al. (2003) point out "the lack of an industrious work ethic or virtuous morality to low levels of education or competitive market skills" as some of these individual deficiencies pervasive since the mid-1970s. It was believed that these characteristics were either 'givens' or determined by the invisible hand and that the state had no business intervening.

Throughout the 19th century, the contention of the behavioural view led to the conclusion that "poverty was necessary because otherwise the labourers' would not be motivated to work" (Townsend, 1979). Laissez-faire policy frameworks were the norm often linked to the notion of 'virtue with work'. It was believed that the poor self-select into deprivation not because of market failure but because of shortcomings in capabilities and efforts (Townsend, 1979). The ethical raison d'*être for* poverty alleviation was charity-based with little or no investments in skills improvement and development. The key premise of the decision-making theory is that access or non-access to economic resources and the risks of being trapped in poverty or not are limited to failure in making the right choices at the individual level only (Blank, 2003). Subsidies are opposed as it is thought to present behavioural disincentives to escaping poverty. This brings to the fore the 'negative-decision' argument of welfare programmes, where emphasis is placed on short-term income relief instead of long-term capabilities and development needs.

Various criticisms have been levelled against the decision-making theory. For the neo-classical school, individuals' decisions can be effectively negated by market failures. Keynesians/liberals argue that inadequate aggregate demand ultimately leads to involuntary unemployment and poverty. Marxists are of the preposition that class-based oppression or discrimination is the primary causative factor underpinning poverty far beyond the individual decision-making argument.

The theory of intergenerational poverty (i.e., the 'sub-culture of poverty') claims that behavioural preferences are passed from one generation to the next via a combination of nature (genetics) and nurture (socialization). Thus, 'poverty begets poverty' as the deviant behaviour of parents is fed to children (Blank, 2003) and for Lewis 1965, quoted in Townsend (1979), "poverty in short, is a way of life, remarkably stable and persistent, passed down from generation to generation along family lines". It was thought that factors such as the lack of ability to defer gratification and accumulate private and social assets and residing in crowded quarters prone to violence underpin the theory of intergenerational poverty among certain families.

These classical theories underpinned the diversion of real solutions that addressed the root cause of poverty resulting from market failures and costly redistributive policies to training and character reformation at the individual level and low-cost social work and community psychiatry, respectively. These treat poverty as a residual personal or family issue rather than a structural social problem and are far from the allocative outcomes of a market economy. Thus, policy actions were averse to wealth and income redistribution (Townsend, 1979).

2.5.2 The Neo-Classical Economic Paradigm and Livelihoods

Building on the classical school, the neo-classical theory of poverty also posits that though market failures negatively impact poverty, the importance of the differential in individual talents, skills and capital determines levels of productivity in competitive market-based economic systems. Market failures emanating from externalities, moral hazard and adverse selection can and do impact negatively on poverty (Davis, 2007).

Creating targeted policies addressing market failures should, therefore, be the primary role of governments. For example, microfinance institutions operate on market-based principles that overcome the risk of moral hazards and limit the adverse impact of a dysfunctional financial sector, especially those targeting the poor segment of the population. The classical poor choices thesis on the cause of poverty is often rationalized as information problems under the neo-classical approach. Thus, microfinance and other pro-poor policies, e.g., food for work, are viewed as small-scale policies aimed at shifting incentives (Banerjee and Duflo, 2012).

Interpersonal comparison of utility and the related Kaldor-Hicks criterion have their limits and are not always adequate justification for proceeding with a public policy as long as it produces societal gain in excess of losses (Jung and Smith, 2007). Thus, poverty alleviation based on the neo-classical thesis places emphasis on efficiency rather than equality. This contrasts sharply with the classical notion that posited a validity in comparison of utility among individuals and a diminishing marginal utility across income groups, with the expectation that utility among the poor could be raised via redistributive policies.

Neo-classical economic thoughts on the causes and consequences of poverty, including social exclusion, are placed under the monetary and asset and financial/income risk assumptions. Under the monetary approach, the welfare of an individual is quantified as his or her total consumption, estimated in monetary terms from either the income or expenditure data. A shortfall below a certain amount stated by the specific poverty line represents people living in poverty. This is compatible with the utility-maximizing notion that welfare can be measured by consumption and income depending on the marginal productivity of labour (Laderchi et al., 2003). Monetary metric is assumed capable of capturing heterogeneous, but relevant poverty indices and units across individuals. A classic example is the minimum rights approach (Rowntree, 1901). An estimate of the monetary requirements for a nutritionally adequate diet (clothing and rent inclusive) was the established poverty line.

Expanding GDP with the expectation of increasing wages and employment outcomes to alleviate poverty is the key policy recommendation in the neo-classical thesis. Also, education completion rates are recommended instrumentally to increase the poor's productivity and income through participation in the labour force.

The asset and income paradigm posits that the lack of assets and/or income sources is the primary reason for poverty. This is because the risk of slipping into poverty with a shock to income is greater for resource-poor households. According to Ulimwengu (2008), the lack of diversified income sources from too few asset holding has implications for the rate of fluctuation into and out of poverty and the length of such episodes. It also has implications for resource-poor households' ability to accumulate both private and social assets. Yet, the transferability of assets from one generation to the next has the potential to dwarf the social mobility of household members across time.

From the neo-classical perspective, market failures in the form of information asymmetries resulting in the lack of or limited access to credit markets and other constraints such as mismatch of skills in the labour market have mutually reinforcing effects as causes and consequences of poverty. For example, many factors underpin why decisions made by resource-poor households seem to run parallel to their long-term interests. First, other desirable ends are obtained at the expense of health; lack of information may lead to obesity from deviations in optimal dieting; and there are behavioural issues with procrastination, self-control and present-consumption bias (Banerjee and Duflo, 2012). Thus, Banerjee and Duflo's (2012) proposition of integrated interventions that improve living standards for the poor while at the same time tackling the structural transformation of society via institutional reforms (Sachs, 2005) is a call in the right direction. However, gains from tackling individual-level problems are rather small in absolute rather than relative terms (Rosenzweig, 2012). Some such as Husain et al. (2014) argue that an alternative resource used in microfinance intervention could be supporting cottage industries that are labour-intensive. Moreover, standalone interventions are hardly effective. Integrated programmes that combine microfinance, health, water and sanitation, and education, among others, are highly recommended.

Pemberton et al. (2013) highlight market failure in the form of available skills mismatch in labour markets. Therefore, both the labour force and their skills sets available do matter. Thus, possessing the wrong skill or no skill at all can potentially exacerbate poverty. Asymmetric information between the labour market and the education system, in which the poor are disadvantaged due to costs and other constraints, constitutes a dysfunction of the market. Furthermore, Machin (2009) notes that children from poor households do worse in educational attainment and that declining demand for unskilled labour has implications for poverty in later life.

Moreover, Besley and Burgess (2003) concluded that public regulation of labour and product markets has the potential to reduce poverty that results from market failures. However, regulation must be prudent to have the needed impact on private entrepreneurship and the investment climate that increases economic activity and employment outcomes. Countries with higher transaction costs in starting businesses are generally those that seem excessively regulated. Therefore, regulation can potentially hurt the public interest and worsen the plight of the poor if it restricts economic growth as "gains of equality cannot outweigh the efficiency cost imposed by legislation such as the minimum wage" (Persky, 2004). Excessive regulation can also lead to the development of dual labour markets. These are the primary and secondary labour markets where job security in the former is protected by regulation while the latter is often precarious, ultimately occasioning poverty. In the Global North, Spain exhibits this characteristic.

Lack of access to credit markets by most of the world's poor has long been identified as both a cause and consequence of poverty. The combination of low levels of relevant household asset accumulation, coupled with the presence of asymmetric information, is a clear antecedence of moral hazards and adverse selections, making access to credit challenging for the majority of the world's poor (Granville and Mallick, 2012). Thus, a vicious cycle continues to evolve from the bi-directional causality between the lack of access to credit and poor accumulated household assets (both social and material). The absence of cash flows and collateral constraints hinder access. This in turn leads to the inability to present appropriate collateral to access credit, especially from formal sources, thus inducing a poverty trap (Ulimwengu, 2008).

Poor educational outcomes leading to a lack of basic financial asset management skills should not be justification for the financial exclusion of the worlds' productive poor (Besley and Burgess, 2003). The correlation between economic growth and poverty reduction can further be improved with an educated population that has easy access to financial services. In fact, resource-poor households with little or no access to flexible, low-cost credit avenues must be efficient money managers who enable shortfalls in income without a collapse in consumption. This is where the role of microfinance institutions and credit unions remains crucial.

The human capital theory (Becker, 2009) placed emphasis on the skills sets of the labour force based on the assumption of perfect competition and market equilibria, enabling a stronger correlation between wages and marginal productivity. Thus, the choice of one's education, training and mobility are key determinants explaining the differences in income among a population with little or no regard to differences in the quality of economic institutions and social norms. Poor households in many countries invest less in education, which means breaking the vicious cycle of poverty continues to remain a challenge (Machin, 2009). Policy prescriptions based on the human capital theory focusing on the redistribution of public goods such as education have the potential to moderate skill sets across a population as well as pockets of poverty and deprivation. However, health and other demographics are integral to human capital (Reinstadler and Ray, 2010). Widespread poverty among ethnic minorities is largely attributed to discrimination resulting from inequality in access and opportunity. These are structural and go beyond the individual (Western et al., 2005). However, cultural differences and attitudes to education are other explanatory variables (Farkas, 1996; Tackey et al., 2011). Several documented factors have historically been key to the vulnerability of immigrant populations in both transient and long-term poverty. These include years of residence in the host country; skills mismatch between the supplied labour of immigrants and that demanded.

2.5.3 The Liberal/Keynesian Economic Paradigm and Livelihoods

Liberal economic theory on poverty revolves around the notion that not only distortions in the market cause poverty, but also underdevelopment generally. Growth promotes economic development and, therefore, poverty reduction. Thus, Keynesians justify the use of fiscal and monetary policy interventions in the macroeconomy by governments to ensure minimal involuntary unemployment.

Underdevelopment in the liberal notion (Sachs, 2005) is characterized by a poor natural resource base; human, business and knowledge capitals; weak infrastructure and public institutions. Poverty reduction policy prescriptions under the liberal economic view involve the provision of capital goods. These include education and infrastructure to respectively improve human capital and its productive capacity with the available infrastructure to guarantee trickle-down effects within the constraints of overall economic growth and development. Therefore, the prevalence of poverty traps; the framing of economic, monetary and fiscal policies; the spatial physical differentials in geography; governance systems and failures therein; cultural barriers and geopolitical contexts must be considered when framing tailor-made policies and programmes to combat poverty. These factors underpin poverty and a 'clinical' and adaptable approach is required to avoid the one-size-fits-all design of anti-poverty interventions.

Davis (2007), however, argues that the approach should rather start with the poor (bottom up) and not with outsiders (top down) to minimize the development of black markets in the public good commodities redistribution process. Governments must devise context-specific ways of preventing the abuse of aid (Lal, 1995).

Keynes however also embraced the importance of education in the improvement of the human resource base, especially its aggregate accumulation via macro-level investment in public education. The role of government thus encompasses tackling involuntary unemployment and aggregate investment in public education to accumulate human capital and, through their multiplier effects, have the potential to concurrently stimulate economic growth and development. This contrasts sharply with both the classical and neo-classical schools' proposals of a limited or no role of government in a country's economy.

The Keynesian/liberal school holds that poverty is because of "the misfortune of certain minorities who fall out of work, cannot work or are not expected to". Labour income is the panacea to poverty. Actions of the state should entail "regulating, supplementing and exhorting, but not imposing" interventions (Townsend, 1979). Poverty is regarded more as a mirror reflection of market failures rather than individual failings, thus justifying redistributive (in cash and kind) taxation. In other words, aggregate investment that positively affects employment rates generates growth necessary for poverty reduction. Also, a low entrepreneurial investment climate is inimical to employment rates and exacerbates poverty. Government revenue from raising taxes or bonds should, therefore, be channelled into public investment such as infrastructure and education. That is, the 'socialization of investment', according to Keynes, has a high potential multiplier effect (Jung and Smith, 2007).

Though the potential for economic growth to decrease poverty is high, its effect on relative poverty is much lower. Growth reduces the variance of income distribution or increases its dispersion with no effect on the overall average level of income (Granville and Mallick, 2012). There are usually surges in relative poverty if wage dispersion rises with growth in wages from growth in GDP (Dickens and Ellwood, 2001). This holds true even with an average wage increase which also renders the absolute poverty ambiguous. The proposition gives credence to the theory that if the poor are left off the 'growth wagon' poverty rates can actually persist and even increase (Dickens and Ellwood, 2001).

Sustainable growth is necessary for poverty reduction. This implies that an aggregate supply of labour must equilibrate with the aggregate demand of capital. However, demand usually exceeds supply. This leads to unsustainable booms and a succession of recessions particularly with financial liberalization where a 5% decline in GDP potentially raises the poverty rate by as much as 10% within same year (Cline, 2002). Poorly designed financial liberalization can exacerbate poverty partly by causing unsustainable booms followed by financial crises (Arestis and Caner, 2004). However, regarding the income distribution of the bottom fifth and per capita GDP, a one-to-one relationship exists (Dollar and Kraay, 2002). Contrary to Cline (2002), they found no evidence of those in lower income brackets being disproportionately affected by economic crises.

Other macro-economic factors that can influence poverty levels are inflation and its capability of depressing workers' real income and generating poverty, especially where the prices of basic goods are affected (Agénor, 2002; Easterly and Fischer, 2000). The purchasing power reduction effects on monetary assets by inflation tax have little or no effect on lower income groups, especially those below the poverty line with little or no liquid balances (Granville and Mallick, 2012).

Sovereign debt when high serves as an impediment to economic growth and restricts the allocation of public resources to poverty alleviation programmes. This worsens during the enforcement of austerity programmes (Granville and Mallick, 2012). Also, asset market bubbles, common in industrialized economies, e.g., rising housing prices and related costs in rents, increase the risk of homelessness (Early and Olsen, 2002).

2.5.4 The Marxists Economic Paradigm and Livelihoods

The Marxists accuse the capitalist system and its class-based social and political organizations as the primary perpetrators of poverty. Adherents here argue that "the market is inherently dysfunctional" (Blank, 2003) and that to address poverty requires strict regulation of the market (e.g., in the form of minimum wages). A labour market predominantly stratified, the prevalence of discrimination and prejudices against certain groups and widespread corruption are the structural factors underpinning poverty (both absolute and relative). The enforcement of anti-discrimination laws and labour market reforms is therefore necessary to overcome these structural barriers that impede employment outcomes and poverty reduction. It is for the state to regulate the labour market to ensure working conditions and wages optimize workers' welfare (Blank, 2003). The Marxist thesis therefore proposes the implementation of a minimum wage that cumulatively sits above the poverty line to correct the inherent dysfunctional market. Jung and Smith (2007) posit that competition in low-wage job markets has the potential to further depress wages. Poor health among the subgroup further decreases the probability to escape from poverty (Pemberton et al., 2013).

Although minimum wage regulation may have a distortionary effect on efficiency, at the equilibrium wage threshold, further decline is not envisaged. Also, unionization is encouraged as it empowers the working class and serves to protect and preserve basic standards of living, especially among blue-collar and low-wage earners (Kyzyma, 2014). However, a study by Neumark and Wascher (2002) concluded that minimum wage increases only redistribute income within low income groups, but not from high to low income families. Also, the impact outcome on equal aggregate distribution is minimal.

According to the dual labour market theory, primary and secondary labour markets co-exist. Employment in the latter is unstable, with wages typically depressed with poor prospects for job satisfaction. Vulnerabilities inherent in the structurally rigid system are the root cause of poverty rather than personal traits and characteristics (Rank et al., 2003). Constraints inherent in the secondary labour market constitute the primary focus of Marxist theory and not the specific individual traits of working populations (Townsend, 1979). Thus, the social class concept constitutes the basic unit of analysis due to the unequal access of resources and opportunities. For instance, it was established by Tackey et al. (2011) that educational performance has social class as one significant influential factor.

Marxist theory diverges in spirit from the neo-classical paradigm by its emphasis on the role of employers in entrenching inequality via the dual nature of labour markets. Ayittey (2005) argues that to address the multi-layered nature of poverty, the lowest classes usually at the bottom of resource distribution should take control of production and governance structures. The element of participation is important in the Marxist interpretation of poverty (Morazes and Pintak, 2007). In investigating poverty, radical Marxist theory puts emphasis on ensuring social rights and justice for the population, contrary to classical assumption that every single person, irrespective of illness, injury and age, can work. Egalitarian principles should underpin all poverty reduction programmes according to the Marxist paradigm. Thus, policies and programmes that directly or indirectly affect the rich (Baratz and Grigsby, 1972; Levitas, 1998; Oyen, 2002) should be rolled out even in market economies because widening living standards and inequality if ignored will not make effective exclusive measures of social inclusion and poverty alleviation.

It is a combination of factors such as ethnicity, social class, gender stereotypes, age and spatial location associated with the individual and the prevailing wider social structures characterizing crime, education, health, housing and inclusiveness of occupational systems that dictates the degree of inequality among certain groups in society (Morazes and Pintak, 2007). According to Western et al. (2005), structural factors, far removed from individuals and groups, mediate access to scarce and valued social resources, resulting in social inequalities. Jung and Smith (2007) suggested that the enforcement of anti-discriminatory laws and spatially distributing economic development both constitute potent anti-poverty strategies. Thus, the principle of universal application of rights (as opposed to its selective application in the Classical thesis) strongly shapes the logic behind Marxist views (Morazes and Pintak, 2007).

However, material resource possession differential closely mirrors that of social status, which is without any precise definition among proponents of Marxist theoretical approaches to inequality. Moreover, whereas total inequality in material resource is possible, the conception of no difference in prestige, authority or status is impractical. This is because these theories rely less on quantifiable variables of analysis (occupational status and power) that are more difficult to measure (Townsend, 1979).

2.6 Theoretical Evolution of Rural Financial Markets and Rural Livelihoods

The past several decades have witnessed the persistent relevance of traditional moneylenders in rural credit markets across much of the Global South, despite interventions via institutional alternatives. Despite the prevailing competition, the cost of funds from moneylenders remains high. Moreover, financial self-sufficiency remains elusive to established institutional alternatives, due in part to heightened default risks. The use of subsidies has also not resulted in significant successes in outreach for low-income populations without appropriate collateral.

There are two strands of theoretical paradigms in microfinance. These are the economic and psychological. The economic paradigm relates the microfinance industry to the infant industry arguments needing protection. The psychological paradigm attempts to differentiate microfinance entrepreneurs from the usury modus operandi of informal credit markets.

The first theoretical literature on microfinance addresses the costs of service provision and the lack of suitable collateral by clients. The second strand concerns issues related to the gathering of reliable information on the actual and projected incomes of clients characterized by a low overall 'debt capacity' (Von Pischke, 1991). Thus, the reduction of the cost of loan screening and selection, monitoring and contract enforcement using group-lending models is central to these theoretical underpinnings. The joint liability model offers two resolution mechanisms to these three points of challenge. First, the assortative matching or screening neutralizes the outcomes of adverse selection. Second, the incorporation of peer monitoring mechanisms overcomes moral hazards (Ghatak and Guinnane, 1999). Earlier models (Banerjee et al., 1994; Stiglitz, 1990; Varian, 1990) offered limited explanation on how group liability schemes lessened issues of moral hazards and the nuanced role of peer monitoring and the problems that arise from its application. These were improved by Stiglitz and Weiss (1981), and those developed later (Ghatak, 1999; Ghatak, 2000; Aghion et al., 2000; Gangopadhyay et al., 2005) concentrated efforts on improving understanding of the role of adverse selection and other screening mechanisms in financial contract arrangements. Developing social capital within and among groups has had positive effects on repayment behaviour (Besley and Coate, 1995; Wydick, 2001). Thus, the introduction of innovative screening mechanisms that are borrower-centred such as the JLGs does overcome problems associated with adverse selection. Mechanisms within the peer monitoring system curtail both *ex ante* and *ex post* moral hazards while at the same time incentivizing repayments (Ghatak and Guinnane, 1999).

2.6.1 The Theory of the Usurious Monopolistic Moneylender and Rural Livelihoods

The theory of the usurious monopolistic moneylender anchors the reasons for the persistence of high interest rates in informal rural credit markets. The assumption is that there is no competition among these informal intermediaries (Hoff and Stiglitz, 1993). A model developed by Bell (1988) was thought to have established that monopoly power rather than the lender's risk underpins the high interest rates. It is predicted that the lending interest rate charged exceeds the marginal cost of borrowing and that these informal intermediaries earn pure profits. A study by Bottomley (1964) also concluded that the monopoly power is the key determinant of the high interest rates by moneylenders. Therefore, different policy options and conclusions can be drawn on the effects of cheap institutionalized credit on rural financial markets.

Empirically, however, the high risk of incomplete or delayed repayments as well as the high rate of return on the alternative use of funds was established by Singh (1983). He concluded that the monopoly power narrative was negligible. This is further supported by Aleem's (1990) finding in Pakistan that approximates total average costs of lending to the average interest rate charged. However, the marginal costs as a percentage of recovered loans remained low, suggesting the existence of monopolistic competition as each lender's downward sloping demand curve within his/her market share ensures that the price of loans is kept above the marginal costs. However, new entrants moderate these perceived pure profits, driving them close to zero as loan prices approach the average cost. Rural credit markets are monopolistically competitive as lender's scale of operations is usually small, spreading out the associated fixed costs over a thin clientele base.

2.6.2 Rural Credit Markets and Livelihoods within the Framework of the Perfect Information Paradigm

The perfect information paradigm of rural financial markets is associated with Stigler (1967) who argued that a market characterized by incomplete knowledge could not be imperfect, other than it being privately remunerative. Rural financial markets are inherently competitive and market clearing is too commonly observed. Thus, default risks and transaction costs underpin the high interest rates commonly observed in financial contracts of informal intermediaries. The apparent policy failure of rural credit market interventions in the 1960s vindicated non-believers of the monopoly power of moneylenders for the observed high interest rates. Thus, rural credit markets qualify under typical classical competitive markets.

For the perfect information paradigm, intervention in rural credit markets should be the least considered policy option and particularly not on the grounds of efficiency. Apart from interest rates, other puzzling observations of rural credit markets could not be explained by the usurious monopoly power or the perfect market paradigms. These include the persistent and functional co-existence of both the formal and informal service providers despite the low interest rates of the former; credit rationing that creates non-equilibrium interest rates in demand and supply functions; and the segmentation of the credit market with large variation in interest rates not explainable by default risk likelihood. For instance, contextually specific economic events including crop failures could have devastating impacts on credit availability in rural financial markets. Also, the presence of limited numbers of commercial moneylenders despite the high-interest rates, interlinkages between credit and other markets, and the specialization of formal lenders in geographical locations where land titles are available for farmers are beyond the purview of the monopoly power of moneylenders and the perfect market paradigm.

2.6.3 Rural Credit Markets and Livelihoods within the Framework of the Imperfect Information Paradigm

The imperfect information paradigm is both useful for explaining the puzzling features of rural credit markets not explainable by the usurious monopoly power or the perfect market paradigm and in the analysis of policy options for interventions. The expansion of the lending process to encompass the postponement of consumption, the introduction of insurance against default risks, innovations in screening and selection processes, improvements in incentive structures and enforcement mechanisms to ensure repayment provide grounds for the emergence of the imperfect information paradigm for explaining the workings of credit markets.

While the screening problem stems from borrower differences in the likelihoods of defaults and the costliness of obtaining information about the extent of default risk, the incentive issue relates to inducing and increasing the probability of repayment. Compelling borrower repayments is enforcement. All three constitute the fundamental problems rural financial markets must respond to, singly or in combination, during the design of financial products and services and the consideration of policy options for specific interventions.

Conceptually, two main mechanisms exist for the resolution of these three fundamental issues inherent in rural credit markets. These are the direct and indirect mechanisms. When the design of contracts expects borrowers to respond in their best interests from which the lender obtains information about their risk profiles and then provides incentives (interest rate, loan size or contracts in related markets such as rental agreements) to reduce default and increase repayment, it is called an indirect mechanism. The interest rate, for instance, serves both as the cost of credit and as an indirect screening mechanism. Therefore, the interest rate at the intersection of credit demand and supply functions need not be clear. Credit might be rationed. Changes in interest rates do have the potential to change the mix of projects of borrowers, with far-reaching implications on default rates and, therefore, the need for loan loss provisioning by MFIs. Variations in the mean gross return are associated with different risk levels such that high interest rates tilt prospective projects of clients towards riskier ones. As Adam Smith put it:

> If the legal rate … was fixed so high… the greater part of the money which was to be lent would be lent to prodigals and profectors, who alone would be willing to give this higher interest. Sober people, who will give for the use of money no more than a part of what they are likely to make by the use of it, would not venture into the competition
>
> *(Smith, 1759, p. 1, Chap. 1; Smith, 1776, Chap. 4)*

The interest rate is both a price and an instrument for regulating the risk composition of the lender's portfolio (Stiglitz and Weiss, 1981; Stigler, 1967). In a classical economic sense, an excess demand for loans should trigger lenders to increase the interest rate (price) to increase returns. However, the higher the interest rates, the higher the default risk, compelling an increase in loan loss provisioning that offsets the increase in interest income. Lenders, therefore, keep interest rates low to ensure favourable risk composition in their portfolios and available funds are rationed without changes to the interest rate, as the market will suggest. Others have argued that these processes are accountable for the thinness of many markets (including some types of credit markets) in which the quality (e.g., default risk) of the commodity exchanged depends on the price (e.g., interest rate) and where asymmetric information exists between the actors (Akerlof, 1970). The observation that interest rates in informal credit markets have not changed much, with little or no sensitivity to competition, also attests to these processes. Indirect mechanisms for screening, incentivizing and enforcing contracts are also useful both in competitive and monopoly markets.

Other indirect mechanisms are reputational effects and market interlinkages employed by lenders to incentivize desired actions by borrowers. An example of the former is the threat of cutting off future credit (Stiglitz and Weiss, 1983) that ensures defaults are not strategic. However, for reputational effects to be effective, interest rates must be moderate, and consumer surplus must exist for those with access to loans. Competition in the market with imperfect information does not drive rents to zero. The consumer surplus denied to those with no access represents rent. Second, landlords or merchants who double as lenders may interlink credit transactions with those of product or rental market contracts (Braverman and Stiglitz, 1982; Braverman and Stiglitz, 1986). For example, in a well-coordinated agricultural value chain, actors may offer reduced prices or subsidies because of the reduced probability of default. Different market interlinkages (e.g., credit and rent or labour markets) are effective as indirect mechanisms for resolving problems of information asymmetries in imperfect markets.

Direct screening mechanisms involve the lenders using their resources to screen and enforce contracts with borrowers. The cost of direct screening and monitoring of borrowers varies greatly among lenders in developing country settings with high interest rates of informal lenders reflecting these activities. Moreover, direct screening and monitoring through social ties, trade-credit linkages and usufruct loans, among others, results in a competitive market structure where the interest spread is shared. Furthermore, the usurious monopoly power of moneylenders will persist despite the entry and competition from formal credit sources until formal sources find substitutes for direct mechanisms involving transactions transcending several markets, offering greater scope for surplus.

The imperfect information paradigm, therefore, put more emphasis on the importance of costly and imperfect information, resulting in the asymmetries of information problem in the process of screening loan applicants, designing incentives and enforcement of contracts. There exists a cost advantage in favour of the informal financial intermediaries over their formal counterparts in addressing these fundamental problems because of their access to devices and mechanisms to gather necessary information about their clients. Detailed knowledge of the local community and clients is readily available. As a result, these informal intermediaries often face lower transaction costs using direct mechanisms in the resolution of the screening, incentive and enforcement problems in their service delivery. However, the enjoyment of the economy of scale and the ability to mobilize large deposits and commercial funds for credit delivery is the preserve of the formal intermediaries. The imperfect information paradigm, therefore, suggests the following policy options for the formal sector in the resolution of the problems of information asymmetry between lender and borrower. These include linkages between formal and informal financial intermediaries, the mimicking of the delivery mechanisms of the informal intermediaries by the formal sector lenders (Hoff and Stiglitz, 1993) and, in both cases, the use of small group peer monitoring systems.

Some formal financial intermediaries have opted for the linkage option. Here, it is believed that by forging links with informal financial intermediaries, more financial resources could be made available to the poor for the improvement and expansion of livelihood activities and greater employment outcomes. In the Global South, many institutions such as the Bank of Indonesia, Land Bank in the Philippines, the National Bank for Agricultural and Rural Development (NABARD) of India and BAAC in Thailand have facilitated the cooperation of banks and NGOs on the commercial terms of existing financial self-help groups (Seibel, 2001). This has led to the reduction of transaction costs and, thereby, interest rates as well as the risk to both depositors and deposit takers.

Others have used the mimicry option as a means of reaching out to the marginalized. The mimicking of some practices of the informal financial intermediaries by the formal and semi-formal sectors implies a downgrading of the latter's services with its attendant costs. Bank Dagang Bali in Indonesia and the Northern Mindanao Development Bank in the Philippines have adapted financial technologies like the daily deposit collection (Seibel, 2001). In Ghana, several formal financial intermediaries have adopted the mimicry approach (e.g., through individuals' daily *Susu* contribution) as a means of reaching out to marginalized households and enterprises within their catchment areas (Jones and Sakyi-Dawson, 2001; Sakyi-Dawson et al., 2014).

2.6.4 Rural Credit Markets and Livelihoods within the Framework of the Psychological Theory (Social Consciousness-Driven Capitalism)

The debate as to whether profits or human welfare comes first in businesses goes far back to two of Adams Smith's seemingly irreconcilable masterpieces: *The Theory of Moral Sentiments* and *...Inquiry into the Nature and Causes of the Wealth of Nations*. The *moral sentiments* theory is connected to moral psychology involving the nature of moral judgement (Raphael, 1985). According to Smith, feelings of sympathy is fundamental to moral judgement. Human selfishness certainly does preclude the innate desire to see others prosper, although there is no personal gain whatsoever. Compassion is an inborn quality exhibited in the presence of others' misfortunes or when made known. The latter, *An Inquiry into the Nature and Causes of the Wealth of Nations*, is an economic treatise aimed at establishing human selfishness as the foundation for material progress, more so in the capitalist state.

The seeming incompatibility of these two conceptions continues to remain subjects of academic debates (Tribe, 1999; Witztum; 1998). Human motivation cannot, therefore, be predicted with certainty. The selfishness of the human being, described as *homo economicus*, according to Smith, is an appropriate economic behaviour. However, this does not negate sympathy or altruism as the essential nature of human. Moral sentiments probably explain the existence and operations of charitable organizations which are as old as human history. Also referred to as 'the third sector', non-profits organize their voluntary activities centred around public tasks delegated by the state; demanded public services but for which neither the state nor commercial entities are interested; and public or commercial policies needing influence for greater positive social impact (Dobkin Hall, 1987).

While economic theories associated with the 'third sector' do not conflict with Smith's theory of moral sentiments, it does conflict with theories of economic psychology such as decision-making and the outcomes thereof regarding need satisfaction (Wärneryd, 1988). According to Gabriel Tarde, a French economic psychologist, Adams Smith failed in not reconciling his markedly different conceptions of Moral Sentiments and Wealth of Nations as social interactions should be the starting point for theorizing economic behaviour (Wärneryd, 1988). George Katona, a US psychologist, brought to prominence the relationship between economic psychology and altruism. From the neo-classical economic paradigm, altruism is non-existent since nothing is gained through charity, and when one disadvantages him/herself to favour others in the race for survival, is highly uncommon (Khalil, 2004; Walker, 2004).

The concepts of sympathy or social conscience drive poverty alleviation programmes, including that of the World Bank (World Bank, 2004a), and are embedded in the concept of social capital. According to Bebbington et al. (2004), institutions and their relationships shaped by social interactions based on the established norms are fundamental for economic growth and development.

Yunus' (1998) social consciousness-driven capitalism thesis was and is firmly grounded at the intersection of Adams Smith's *Theory of Moral Sentiments* and … *Inquiry into the Nature and Causes of the Wealth of Nations*. That is, there exists a relationship between economic psychology and altruism. It argues that a species of profit-making private ventures highly enthused about the welfare of their clientele base is possible, yet acknowledging that capitalism is premised on the self-evident notion of human selfishness. Thus, the profit maximization principle is only natural with businesses. It, however, connotes a limited interpretation of capitalism as it excludes individual and societal welfare. The maximization of a basket of profits and social goods by entrepreneurs, therefore, represents a more generalized model of capitalism.

The assumption underlying the psychological theory, according to Elahi and Danopoulos (2004), should enable a three-pronged categorization of entrepreneurs. The first category is the traditional neo-classical capitalists whose sole aim is profit maximization. The second group consists of those philanthropic organizations concerned about the maximization of social returns and includes microcredit NGOs and public credit agencies. The third and last group combines both rates of profit and social returns in their investment decisions while acknowledging that financial returns cannot be negative. These organizations include microfinance entrepreneurs with the aim of maximizing social returns and the industry, a social consciousness-driven capitalistic enterprise. Here, long-term stakeholder welfare rather than short-term shareholder profits is the goal. However, the survival of any market depends on capitalist tools, and Yunus proposes that the maximization of both financial and social returns through corporate social responsibility is preferred to the only profit maximization principle in the stricter capitalism model.

In conclusion, various theories underpin many of the empirical puzzles of rural financial markets. These are not mutually exclusive, but reinforce one another in their explanation of the workings of rural financial markets.

2.7 The Conceptual Framework(s) of the Study Grounding the Book

This section presents the three key theories, models and frameworks on which the study is grounded. These include the livelihood portfolio model, the household economic portfolio model and the meta-theoretical livelisystem framework. All these provided the basis for the development of the microfinance livelisystem framework and the household livelisystem model, so named by the author for the study.

2.7.1 Developing the Microfinance Livelisystem Framework (MLF)

The livelihood portfolio explains how individuals and households optimize welfare outcomes under the constraints of limited incomes and other resources. For resource-poor households, the risk of falling into poverty is ever-present. Households must therefore effectively plan to smoothen consumption and maintain certain welfare outcomes even during periods of shortfalls in income. However, five basic institutions are typically relied upon by households to satisfy current and future needs in any given society. Referred to as the welfare pentagon, they include the family, markets, social networks, membership institutions and public authorities. Household decision-making on their income generation, investment and consumption activities falls at specific 'production points' within the space defined by these institutions. For example, households trade effort for wages and produce products and services that can even be bartered with other household members. Moreover, current income is often traded for future income via investments, savings, insurance purchases and loans in the labour, product and capital markets. Through various mechanisms of reciprocity and solidarity, families, social networks and membership institutions help smoothen the rough edges of shocks to livelihoods.

While free entry and exit are possible with membership institutions such as unions, mutual insurance, religious groups and cooperatives, public social protection schemes directly provide pension, insurance, unemployment and child benefits. Also, the ability to enforce contracts and introduce legislation that corrects market failures such as minimum reserve requirements is indirectly made possible via public authorities. Household entitlements from the welfare pentagon of institutions to generate income, wealth, or smooth consumption can only be effectively 'fulfilled' in the presence of a certain amount of capital (acquired or endowed and neither fixed nor equalized across individuals and households).

Household members also differ in their risk exposure and preferences that define their 'needs' and, therefore, risk aversion. Thus, livelihood portfolios of individuals and households differ because of differences in initial capital endowment, risk exposures, need definitions and risk aversion that directly impact investments made in the acquisition of the necessary capital and accessing the institutions of the welfare pentagon. Within the theoretical framework of the livelihood's portfolio, households can be placed at many "points of welfare production within the 5-dimensional welfare space" based on their economic activities.

However, the household economic portfolio model (HEPM) defines the set of household resources, household activities and the circular flow of interaction between the resources and activities (Dunn and Cohen, 1996). The set of human, physical and financial resources available for use at any given period constitute the resources of the household. These include time, labour power and skills of household members; land, buildings, tools, raw materials, input stocks, inventory, equipment, livestock, personal items, and cash and other forms of liquid savings. Household resources are accessed through borrowings, social relationships or networks and may be held jointly or separately by the individual household members. Social relationships and networks such as family and kin networks, patron-client relationships, factional or political loyalties, and wider pooling or exchange networks can be drawn upon to secure human, physical or financial resources based on reciprocity or non-reciprocity. Moreover, collective goods or common resources can be accessed by households through the public sector or from common property resources.

The set of consumption, production and investment activities that the members of the household undertake at any given period is its activities (Kusterer, 1989). That is, the productive enterprises that generate marketable goods or services, strictly for household consumption and for the creation of potential additional income in future periods. While consumption activities include satisfying household members' material wants and needs such as food, clothing, medical services, liquor, ceremonies and amusements, production activities include agricultural or non-agricultural income generation, maintenance and cash earnings from wage work. Investment activities are those actions that put up household resources to build up potential additional resources. The consumption, production and investment activities of the household are meant to satisfy the current wants and needs and return resources for future periods.

Defined as

> a combination of the functions provided by assets (or resources) and activities are undertaken in and by open, structured and actively self-regulating systems in maintaining negentropy (negative entropy) and/or increasing it with informational, material and relational mechanisms for maintenance, growth or multiplication,
>
> *(Dorward, 2014, p. 7)*

the livelisystem framework draws on conceptualizations of livelihoods (Chambers and Conway, 1992), living systems (Miller, 1978) and generative replication in complex population systems (Hodgson and Knudsen, 2010). Assets (financial and non-financial) have material, informational and relational functions. While the informational and material functions match the two core elements identified in Miller's living systems theory, the information and matter-energy (Miller, 1978), conceptualization of informatics and physical (energy and material) components match those of the ecological inheritance systems (Odling-Smee, 2007; 2010). However, the relational components describe claims and obligations that systems or sub-systems have on or to other systems or sub-systems. These three functional types are structurally related to each other and are not mutually exclusive. Thus, the livelisystem framework describes how material, informational and relational functions of assets, asset services and asset pathways interact in systems with embedded and emergent properties that are constantly undergoing structural transformations (spatial, sectoral, physical, ecological, institutional, political, economic changes) and transformational processes (changes in social organization, belief systems, values, knowledge) in the decisions involving consumption, production, investment and inheritance, further shaped by the changing values and knowledge systems from the local subnational, to the national, regional, global and even external levels.

According to Dorward (2014), rural households are exposed to a broad resource base, termed 'assets, properties and attributes' (including microfinance products and services) with their material, relational and informational properties and attributes. These 'assets, properties and attributes' directly or indirectly impact the four categories of 'livelisystem transitions' which include the following: *falling down and out* (i.e., failing to maintain the status quo and falling to a livelisystem with lower attainment of sets or subsets of activities and/or assets and asset functions, possibly failing to maintain the livelisystem and survive); *hanging in* (maintaining the status quo or where assets are held and activities are engaged in to maintain livelihood levels, e.g., consumption smoothing, often in the face of adverse socio-economic circumstances); *stepping up* (where current activities are engaged in, with investments in assets to expand activities, in order to increase production and income so as to improve livelihoods, e.g., accumulation of productive dairy livestock) and *stepping out* (where existing activities are engaged in to accumulate assets which, in time, can then provide a base or 'launch pad' for moving into different activities that have initial investment requirements with higher and/or more stable returns, e.g., accumulation of livestock as savings which can then be sold to finance children's education (investing in the next generation), the purchase of buildings or vehicles (for transport or retail activities), migration or social or political contacts and advancement). Activities such as diversification, specialization, substitution, adaptation and accumulation of assets, properties and attributes determine the kind of livelisystem transitions prevalent in socio-economic contexts. Clients' households' livelihood activities are operationalized in contexts of vulnerabilities such as shocks (e.g., droughts, floods, crop/livestock pests and diseases and even death in the family); trends (e.g., migration, climate change, declining natural resource-based, inflation, currency devaluations, structural unemployment, technology change, market change and the impact of trade and globalization) and seasonality (e.g., changing rainfall patterns, price variations and production cycles).

Thus, the microfinance livelisystem framework (MLF) (Figure 2.1) developed by the author also describes how the microfinance industry and its financial and non-financial assets, with the material, informational and relational properties and attributes, contribute to poverty reduction through households' livelihood activities that are influenced directly or indirectly by localized welfare-promoting institutions including the larger family, markets, public authorities, social networks and membership institutions acting within the national and global political economy. For instance, the microfinance industry provides financial products and services that have material (e.g., loans, savings, insurance and payments), informational (e.g., health, water and sanitation, entrepreneurial and enterprise development services) and relational (e.g., clients versus MFIs, inter- and intra-household power and gender relationships and inter-MFIs collaborations and partnerships with government, bilateral and multilateral development agencies) all geared towards supporting households transitioning out of poverty among targeted populations. Moreover, the evaluation of the functions of the accessed financial resources leads to innovations in product design that better serve the livelihood needs of those with access. It is an iterative process where the evaluation of the impact of accessed products and services on client livelihoods and welfare underpins the evolution of product and service design and the direction of the industry. The evolving broader economic and financial transformational structures (top sphere in Figure 2.1) and transformational processes (bottom sphere in Figure 2.1) occurring simultaneously then influence the nature of the industry in a country. The established dynamic relationship between the domestic and international financial markets then enables the transformational structures, e.g., microfinance investment vehicles (MIVs), the role of national and international capital markets, the international financial institutions (IFIs) and transformational processes (domestic financial sector development policies, national and international legal and regulatory frameworks) to invest in

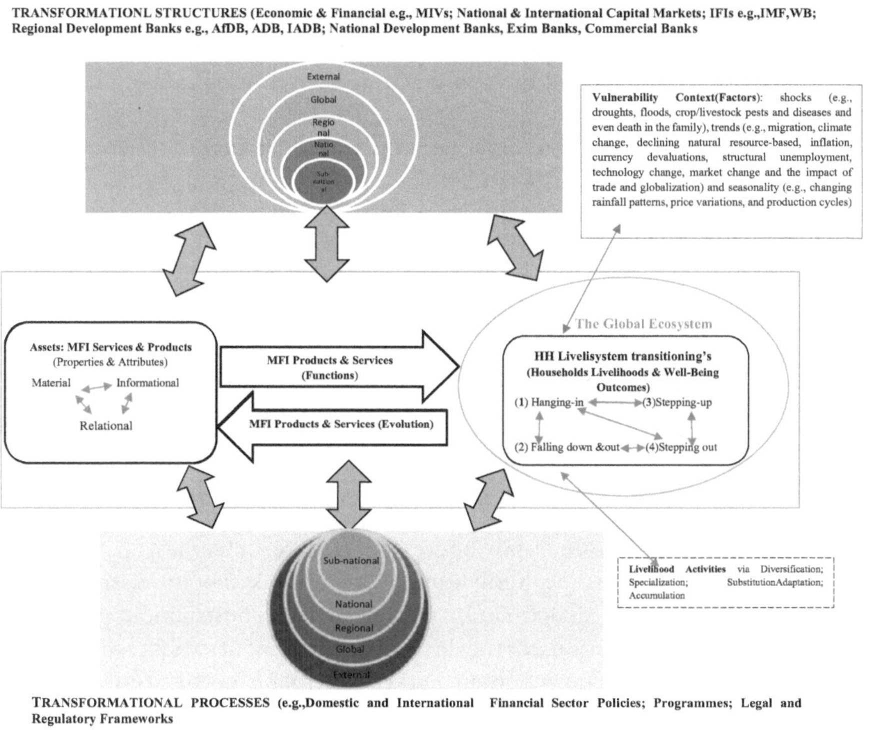

FIGURE 2.1 The Microfinance Livelisystem Framework.
Source: Author's conceptualization.

microfinance institutions for the improvement of rural livelihoods in Ghana and the Global South in general.

These iterations can affect the scope of asset portfolios and livelihood choices and worsen or improve certainty. In the background are existing transformational structures at the levels of government, the private sector, and civil society concerning funding, advocacy, information, research, capacity building, coordination, infrastructure and technical assistance, among others. The transformational processes embedded in institutions, policies, laws, rules, customs and technologies also impact the vulnerability context and are either facilitatory or not on the capabilities of households to transition out of poverty in localized livelisystems. Historically, Ghana's domestic financial sector reforms have been supported by multilateral institutions (e.g., the World Bank, the IMF) and other bilateral development partners.

In conclusion, Doward's (2014) livelisystem definition and his livelisystem framework, which draws on conceptualizations of livelihoods (Chambers and Conway, 1992), living systems (Miller, 1978) and generative replication in complex population systems (Hodgson and Knudsen, 2010), were adapted to develop the microfinance livelisystem framework (MFL) that comprehensively situates the microfinance industry within the domestic and international financial and economic eco-systems and shows how the interrelationships between these institutions provide services and the construction of livelihoods among resource-poor population groups.

Thus, the MFL by the author describes how the microfinance industry and its financial and non-financial assets (stores, resources, claims and access), together with the material, informational and relational properties and attributes, mediated by embedded and emergent economic and financial transformational structures (capital markets, IFIs, e.g., WB, IMF, AfDB) and processes (policies, legal and regulatory frameworks), when accessed by low-income population groups, contribute to poverty reduction through households' livelihood activities.

The dialectic method (Kane, 1977) was embedded to analyse and present the evolution of Ghana's financial sector vis-à-vis the microfinance sub-sector.

2.7.2 Developing the Household Livelisystem Model (HLM)

Livelihood activities that underpin household welfare outcomes occur within the household. Therefore, the study attempts to unpack the association of the accessed microfinance products and services in the construction of households' livelihoods in relation to the broader pentagon of welfare-promoting institutions – the larger family, other markets, membership institutions, social networks and public authorities. Borrowing from both the household economic portfolio and the livelihood portfolio models, the author further conceptualized the household livelisystem model (HLM) (Figure 2.2) to help unpack the interrelationships between the stock of household resources and household activities and the localized pentagon of welfare-promoting institutions for addressing risks and uncertainties in the construction of livelihoods in the Northern Savannah of Ghana. For example, households exchange effort for a (future) wage; trade effort (in producing a product or service) for a (future) profit (or in exchange of another good or service); and trade current income for future income by investing, saving, buying insurance, taking a loan in the labour, product and financial markets.

While membership institutions including unions, mutual insurance companies, religious organizations, co-operatives or neighbourhood associations offer individuals and households free entry and exit, public authorities can assist households directly through public social protection policies (the establishment of pension schemes, child benefits, unemployment, insurance and other forms of social insurance) or indirectly (by enforcing contracts through the judicial system, regulation and legislation to correct market failures such as minimum reserve requirements for banks so that the savings of households are guaranteed) and through many other public actions.

The process by which the household then re-arranges over time its mix of resources (human, physical, financial) and activities (production, consumption, investments), separately or jointly, as well as its relationship with the larger family, social networks, membership institutions, markets and public authorities to

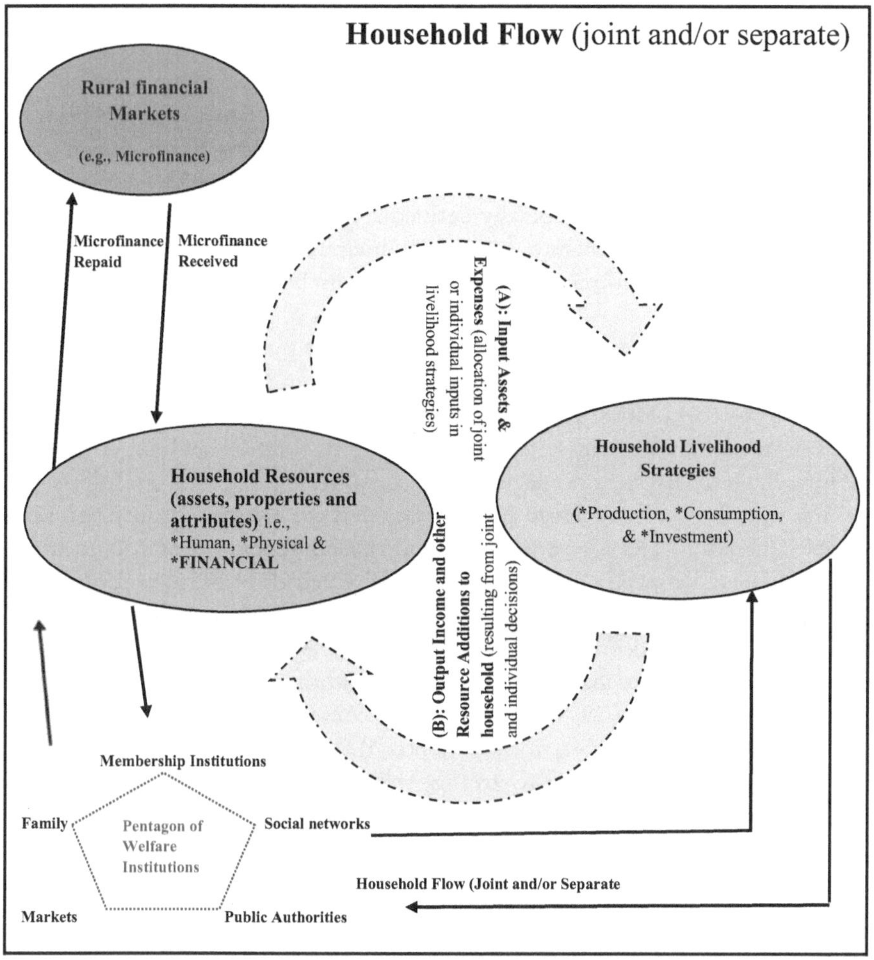

FIGURE 2.2 The Household Livelisystem Model.
Source: Author's conceptualization.

cope with its changing economic and social objectives is termed the Household Livelisystem. However, the ability of the household to transition out of poverty depends on its composition and structure, as well as the constraints facing it and the individual members. Moreover, their preferences and relationships with the five welfare-promoting institutions influence the pace of the household's transitioning out of poverty.

It is important to note that individual members of the household may have separate (if not competing) preferences, constraints and resource access and may, therefore, take the individual as well as joint decisions and activities. Also, they are involved in negotiation, bargaining and (even) conflict within the household and their relationship with the five core welfare pentagon institutions. Moreover, they may decide to cooperate in certain decisions or activities, but not in others. As a result, the household is characterized by extensive conflicts and pervasive cooperation within households (Sen, 1987). Besides, the activities of individuals within the household reflect differences in bargaining power and, therefore, access to resources (both physical and social) from the five core welfare institutions and through the socially defined roles and relationships. Thus, men and women can pursue separate, paralleled, integrated or substitutable activities that could directly or indirectly determine the household livelisystem transitioning position.

In unpacking how access to MFIs' products and services mitigate the constraints associated with livelihood construction (within the theatre of the household), and the role of localized societal welfare-promoting institutions (markets, social networks, public authorities, membership institutions and larger family), the household livelisystem model (HLM) – a pooled income intra-HH decision-making model – was conceived borrowing from the livelihood portfolio (LP) Model (Chambers, and Conway, 1992) and the household economic portfolio (HEP) model (Chen, and Dunn, 1996), both of which also have their roots in the Chayanov model (Chai͡anov, and Čajanov, 1986), the first to integrate production and consumption decisions in household analysis. Also, the 'New Home Economics' (NHE) (Ferber and Birnbaum, 1977) and the Farm Household Models (Barnum, and Squire, 1979) were reviewed to contextualize the HLM.

The Household Livelisystem Model (HLM) is defined by the author as the processes by which households re-arrange their mix of resources (assets, properties and attributes) and activities (production, consumption and investments) in relationship with the broader localized societal welfare-promoting institutions (family, markets, membership institutions, social networks and public authorities) in the construction of livelihoods to cope with their changing economic and social objectives.

2.7.3 Expanding Schreiner's (2002) Framework for Designing Microfinance Products and Services

The evaluation of the effectiveness of the role of accessed microfinance products and services spurs innovation in design to further meet the needs of the livelihood's activities of participants. Schreiner's (2002) six-factor framework (costs, worth, length, breadth, depth and scope) for designing microfinance products and services was adapted and expanded by including contract enforcement mechanisms and add-ons/microfinance plus, in assessing the demand-side perceptions of their levels of incorporation by MFIs to support livelihood construction in the Northern Savannah as well as their implications on outreach and sustainability goals of the industry. A change in the social benefits of access microfinance is underpinned by the levels of incorporation of all eight design factors and their iterative interaction. Therefore, each of these eight variables has implication(s)

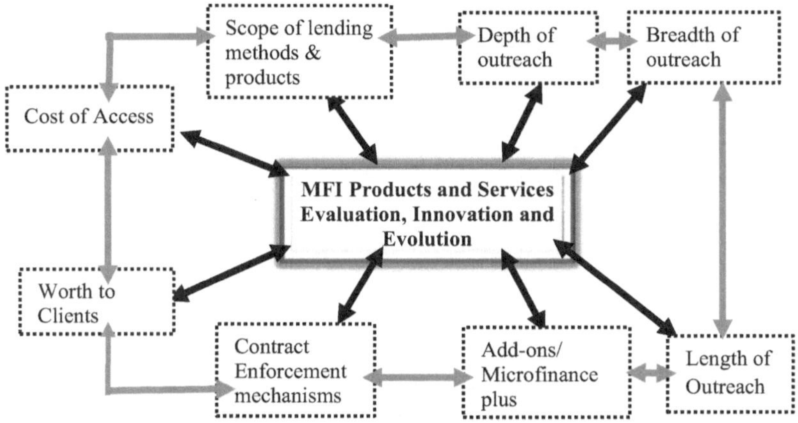

FIGURE 2.3 A Framework for Gauging the Evolutionary Innovation in Microfinance Products and Services Design (Factors Underpinning Product Design).

Source: Author's conceptualization of an expanded Schreiner (2002) microfinance product design framework.

for product uptake, outreach (both depth and breadth) and the sustainability of microfinance institution in question, regardless of whether the financial system or the poverty-lending approach is adopted and adapted (Figure 2.3). This is made use of in Chapter 6.

Understanding how to design and price products that attract more clients and serve them better is important (Karlan et al., 2010) for achieving the twin goals of financial self-sufficiency for service providers and improved living standards for those with access to financial services. Schreiner's six indices include cost, worth, scope, depth, breadth and length.

Thus, while Schreiner's (2002) framework that included his six indices was gauged from data obtained from large-scale MFIs, mostly in Latin America, this study assessed the level of perceived incorporation of these six indices, as well as contract enforcement and add-ons on designed products and services from the perspective of clients in the Northern Savannah of Ghana. These eight indices interact iteratively and concurrently in the determination of the outcome and impact of accessed financial resources on the household livelihood activities of clients. A change in the social benefits of access to microfinance is underpinned by the interaction of all eight factors and the extent of their incorporation in the design of products and services. Therefore, each variable underpinned product and service design and their implications for product uptake, outreach and the sustainability of MFIs were assessed. The eight indices are explained below.

Costs of access refers to all the economic costs incurred by a client for accessing financial product(s) from an MFI. These include price costs (interest and fees), the direct cash payments in the form of interest and fees paid by the client to the MFI to access financial products and services, non-cash opportunity costs of the time taken off by clients from other income-generating activities (IGA) to apply for and access products/services from the MFI. And the indirect cash expenses, such as cost of transportation, documentation, subsistence and taxes (where applicable), borne by clients to access financial product(s) and service(s). Client evaluation of the cost/benefits of participation is included here.

Scope refers to the number of different types of financial products and services (contracts) that are supplied by an MFI. Scope between products is the number of types of different products (e.g., number of loans, savings, payments and insurance). The scope within products is the variants of the same product (e.g., different loan types) that the MFI supplies. Thus, the scope was assessed by clients of the MFI in general, within microloans, micro-savings, micro-insurance and micropayments, the ability to employ others and the achievement of goals.

Worth describes the willingness to pay with regards to the terms of the financial contract as well as the risk profile, constraints and opportunities available to the client. Worth was assessed by clients of the MFI in general. For loans, worth increases when the terms of contracts (amount disbursed, term to maturity and instalment size) match client needs. For savings, it is the interest paid on deposits and the flexibility of withdrawals that determine whether products are tailored to a client livelihood(s) need.

Length refers to the time frame over which product(s) and service(s) are provided or capable of being provided to client groups. It is perceived in future terms and hence difficult to gauge and measure. Length was assessed as years of client access, knowledge of donor support to MFIs and client perceptions of the profitability of their MFIs.

Breadth of outreach for an MFI is absolute the number of clients that it serves with financial products and services. Budgetary constraints and the varied needs and wants of the poor make breadth an imperative for analysis. Breadth was assessed along client perceptions of the targeting orientation, interest rates, donor partnership with the MFI as well as group individual products and services offered.

Depth of outreach refers to the value society places on the net gain of a given client for participating in microfinance programmes. The level of poverty of targeted clients is a good proxy for gauging depth of outreach as society would prefer that net gains of programmes are associated with the vulnerable. Depth was assessed by the preference of MFIs for women, rural populations, those with less or no formal education, and ethnic minorities. The housing conditions and loan sizes of clients were also explored.

Contract enforcement refers to the mechanisms MFIs use to ensure clients honour their side of the contract agreements in the case of default. Client perceptions of the effectiveness of the MFIs' employed enforcement mechanisms were assessed.

Add-ons (microfinance plus) are additional products or services provided by the MFI or based on the MFI's main product(s) and/or service(s) that enhances uptake of the main product(s) and service(s). Add-ons are assessed along with client perceptions of MFI staff and management relationships with clients; add-ons on microloans, on micro-savings, on micro-insurance, and on micro-payment services (see Appendices V and VI).

3

THE CONTEXT OF THE GLOBAL MICROFINANCE INDUSTRY

3.1 Introduction

This chapter presents the relevant empirical perspective on microfinance, livelihoods and poverty reduction efforts. While Section 3.2 presents the nature of rural financial markets in the context of rural livelihood construction, Section 3.3 broadly presents an exploratory assessment of the prevailing products and services of the global microfinance industry. Section 3.4 captures the factors underpinning the design of the products and services of the industry aimed at balancing the double-bottom goals of outreach for poverty reduction and sustainability of microfinance institutions. Section 3.5 then presents the determinants of microfinance product and service uptake.

3.2 The Nature of Rural Financial Markets and Rural Livelihoods: A Global Perspective

Agriculture is the predominant economic activity in rural areas of developing countries the world over. In these environments, seasonal variation of agricultural production and income results in the need for short-run financial intermediation as a liquidity management device over seasonal production cycles (Conning and Udry, 2005). Therefore, the demand for financial intermediation as an effective device for risk-pooling and risk-sharing is potentially immense. Stiglitz (1989) described the financial market as an important set of institutions whose operations are characterized by imperfect and incomplete information that is most often costly to obtain. Appropriate governance mechanisms are therefore needed to deal with the agency problems that can result in moral hazards and adverse selection. Stiglitz's hypothesis of the imperfect information paradigm shares commonalities with the institutional economists' analysis of the need for appropriate

DOI: 10.4324/9781003318873-3

governance mechanisms (Williamson, 1985; North, 1990; Coase, 1992). Both criticized the conventional neo-classical model for its failure to include the role of transaction costs in exchanges and the role of institutions in the formation and operation of markets. Institutions can potentially alter transaction costs and uncertainty levels. Thus, both focus on how costly and incomplete information aligns with enforcement, which agents in the real world must contend with when navigating financial markets.

The rural financial system in most developing countries comprises the activities of formal and informal financial markets, together with their respective institutions (Nwanna, 1989). Hoff and Stiglitz (1990) and Conning and Udry (2005) also segmented the rural financial system into formal and informal markets based on the structural differences in cost and risk features. Regulation involving official and direct monetary controls is carried out in the formal financial market, while informal financial markets are not subject to regulatory controls by monetary authorities (Nwanna, 1989). Meanwhile, the formal financial sector in most West African countries has at its apex the central bank, commercial banks, finance houses, building societies, development finance institutions, savings institutions and the insurance industry added to its structure (Nwanna, 1996). The informal financial market actors include moneylenders, traders, estate owners, grain millers, friends, relatives, neighbours, businesses and employers.

Systemic and idiosyncratic risks are the two types of risks involved in the lending process. While systemic risks originate from exogenous factors leading to unpredictable variation in income, idiosyncratic risks stem from the asymmetric distribution of information between lender and borrower. This asymmetric information can be costly to re-align with the result that moral hazards and adverse selection can be pervasive. Segmentation of the rural financial market, as the new institutional economist points out, can lead to market specialization, with each serving a niche by exploiting its comparative advantage in the assessment of borrowers' specific idiosyncrasies within that market niche.

The high systemic risk originates from unpredictable variations in income because of exogenous factors. The high idiosyncratic risk stems from the costly acquisition and asymmetric distribution of information, which can lead to the pervasive problems of moral hazards and adverse selection. Asymmetric information makes it difficult for a would-be creditor or insurer to be sure whether the expected probability distribution over state-contingent payoffs associated with a contract promise is the one being represented by the seller or not, as in the case of adverse selection or moral hazard.

The new institutional economics thus points to a possibility of segmentation of the rural financial system leading to market specialization. Each specialized market segment would then serve specific market niches by exploiting its comparative advantages in the assessment of borrower-specific idiosyncratic risks in the inherent environment of imperfect information. Typically, institutions are burdened with agency problems resulting from the costly and imperfect information inherent in the markets they operate (Aryeetey and Nissanke, 1998).

This agency problem leads to adverse selection, moral hazard and contract enforcement difficulties (Hoff and Stiglitz, 1990). Karlan and Zinman (2004) found that about 40% of defaulters in a South African credit market were attributed to asymmetric information leading to moral hazards and adverse selection. The resolution of the screening, incentive and enforcement problems associated with imperfect information by lenders leads to the demand for collaterals, which can be seized in the case of default (Binswanger and Rosenzweig, 1986).

Costly screening and monitoring implies the restriction of loan amounts, loan size rationing or not lending to some potential borrowers at all (Gonzalez-Vega, 1977). Missing institutional infrastructure can also lead to high costs in contract enforcement that further limit access to formal loans (Fleisig and de la Peña, 1996). The formal financial sector often views most rural sector activities as non-bankable for several reasons, including the high risk of default, high transaction costs associated with small operations, inappropriate collaterals, and none or limited experience with formal banking among rural households (Binks, 1979). High uncertainty in production cycles is associated with infrastructural problems caused by government policies.

In place of legal frameworks for contract enforcement, social mechanisms are often used. Thus, informal financial intermediaries with a comparative advantage in devices and mechanisms appropriate to rural firms and households dominate (Besley and Coate, 1995). These, however, lack the breadth, depth and term transformation to provide the full range of necessary financial services (Nwanna, 1996).

Informal loans are usually timely, reliable, and have low transaction costs. While the informal financial infrastructure complements the formal system, most charge usurious interest rates but lower defaults and delinquencies (Udry, 1994). In Ghana, between 70% and 80% of informal lenders surveyed reported that they had no delinquent borrowers in 1990 and 1991 (Udry, 1994). Some form of co-insurance also existed in the informal financial system, with the level and timing of debt repayment in Nigeria dependent on whether either party to a contract suffered shocks to income or not (Udry, 1995).

3.3 Microfinance Products and Services: A Global Perspective within the Microfinance Livelisystem Framework

3.3.1 Introduction

This section presents the literature on microfinance products and services for poverty reduction among resource-poor households. Poor households are extremely vulnerable to risk and external shocks and have traditionally managed risk and coped with external shocks through a combination of informal social support networks, savings and borrowing from informal sources. Participation in microfinance programmes offers another set of risk management and coping strategies for poor households. Participation in formal micro-insurance schemes offers yet another option. Payment services for remittances, albeit small, from migrated family members (temporary or permanent) can sometimes offer vital lifelines.

Microfinance products and services (savings, loans, insurance and payment services) are like the formal sector financial services, but the methods of delivery and scale differ. Enterprise lending (loans for enterprise formation and development) has remained the dominant product offered by MFIs (Nourse, 2001; Woller, 2002). But this has gradually changed with the addition of various products, including savings, consumption/emergency loans, insurance and business education. Nourse (2001) reviewed MFI products and services and recommended the need for flexible savings and insurance services for the poor in addition to credit products. Eyiah (2001) went on to develop a model of small construction management contractors and MFIs in developing countries that provides tailored lending structures for microenterprise contractors. Similarly, Dunn (2002) further argued that MFIs should be more client-focused, offering a mix of products tailored to the needs of target clients.

3.3.2 Microloans in the Microfinance Livelisystem Framework

Within the lending function of microfinance institutions, loans can be classified into enterprise loans and consumption/emergency loans. However, enterprise loans dominate the industry landscape. Nonetheless, there exists a large gap between the demand for consumption/emergency loans and its current level of provisioning (Woller, 2002). Microloans are either provided to individuals or groups. Group loans enlist the joint liability concept to minimize adverse selection and moral hazards. With the joint liability, the potential loss of access to future loans upon default(s) incentivizes group members to monitor one another's projects (Zeller and Sharma, 1998). According to Stiglitz (1990), the success of the classic Grameen Bank model and other group-lending methodologies is largely based on the peer monitoring strategy.

According to Anane et al. (2013), access to enterprise credit by SMEs has led to increased productivity and incomes in Ghana. In rural areas where agricultural activities dominate, enterprise loans enable farmers to increase their production, accumulate assets and reinvest in new income-generating activities that further reduce business risks and vulnerabilities (Grameen Foundation, 2010). In evaluating the impact of the classic Grameen-style enterprise-lending model in Hyderabad, India, Banerjee et al. (2010) found that more durable consumer goods were bought by households that pre-owned businesses. Households that purchased non-durable consumer goods were those not starting new businesses. For those households starting new businesses, there were limitations in the consumption of temptation goods such as tobacco, alcohol, tea, betel leaves, gambling and food consumed outside the home. Thus, access to microloans can potentially alter the households' decision-making based on what matters, as loans are invested in making the most of new opportunities. Access to consumer credit by poorer segments of the population can have positive effects on borrower well-being. Emerging innovations in credit design stem from researchers questioning the group liability model, gender and returns to capital, the role of timing in scheduling repayments and the effect of different incentives for clients' repayments (Karlan and Zinman, 2011).

The concept of group lending is claimed to have provided mechanisms for overcoming problems associated with imperfect credit markets, particularly information asymmetries (Armendáriz de Aghion and Morduch, 2005; Armendáriz and Morduch, 2010) and therefore adverse selections and moral hazards. The concept of joint liability also assumes that groups, when allowed to self-form, ensure trust and reliability (assortative matching). However, the empirical evidence suggests that there can be unintended negative consequences, including the possibility that a borrower's social and community support system unravels if they default on repayment.

Giné et al. (2011) carried out a study in collaboration with the Green Bank in the rural Philippines beginning in 2004 that examined the consequences on default rates when existing group clients were switched to individual liability models, compared to new borrowers who started under individual liability loans. The results showed negligible negative impacts on loan repayment rates for either set of clients. The unintended consequence was rather an increased outreach, as the individual liability models were attractive to more new clients. This confirmed the long-held view that fewer poorer people may be taking formal credit because the joint liability of group loans repels risk-averse individuals, unwilling to co-sign for their peers (Giné et al., 2011).

Gender targeting in microfinance programmes has added commercial as well as social value for microfinance. First, serving women is associated with higher repayment rates. Second, the extant literature also suggests that access to microfinance by women has direct relationships with positive household welfare than men (Pitt and Khandker, 1998; Steele et al., 2001; McKernan, 2002). Littlefield et al. (2003a) state that accesses to MFIs have proven capable of empowering women to become more confident, assertive and likely to take part in family and community decisions and in confronting gender inequities. Thus, MFIs serving more women is good for both business and the social mission of the industry. By making available credit, cash or business inputs to women is theoretically placing resources at their disposal that enable them to take advantage of income-generating activities and overcome socio-cultural and economic barriers to their well-being. In practice, however, increasing women's access to credit does not always lead to increased income. Three microcredit impact studies conducted in India, the Philippines and Morocco support this view (Banerjee et al., 2010; Karlan and Zinman, 2011; Crépon et al., 2011). In testing the hypothesis that credit to women does not necessarily produce increased income in even environments with higher female participation in the workforce, Fafchamps et al.'s (2014) study of women in Ghana produced no return on the capital of women micro-entrepreneurs. However, the use of in-kind gifts of inventory and equipment led to a significant average return for women, especially those with functionally established businesses. With cash, women split some for other household necessities, reducing investment capital in the process. This suggests opportunities exist to adjust client groups of MFIs and the structuring of products and services and targeting for optimal livelihood outcomes for those with access.

The role of timing in the loan repayment schedule can be critical to project success and repayment rates. Most product designs in microcredit programmes are inflexible, requiring weekly or monthly instalments following loan disbursements (Feigenberg et al., 2013). Less time than necessary is, therefore, available for investment to make meaningful returns. All of the microloans may not be invested and entrepreneurs may avoid investments characterized by long gestation periods. Field et al. (2011) find that in the United States, build-in grace periods of a few months with enterprise loans yielded higher default risks between 13% and 15% than the typical 2%–5% of microcredit programmes in developing countries without grace periods. Testing the grace period concept in the developing country context, the authors found that overall, 9% of the individuals in the grace period group ultimately defaulted on their loans, compared to a 2% default rate among those in the standard weekly repayment regime in rural India. Moreover, Feigenberg et al. (2013) compared the effects of weekly and monthly meetings and observed that monthly meetings had no adverse effects on repayment rates, and they suggested that MFIs could make substantial savings on operational costs with monthly meeting regimes rather than weekly ones.

Innovations in direct screening mechanisms require that the lenders screen loan applicants, monitor project implementation and enforce contracts, where necessary. Costs of direct screening and monitoring vary with the structure of the MFI and the adapted lending approach. Direct screening increases the operating costs of MFIs. On client screening as a product design tool (a direct mechanism), Banerjee et al. (2010) attempted to establish shared characteristics of clients most likely to start businesses with microloans. Iyer et al. (2015) focused on the creation of a selection tool for lenders to screen potential entrepreneurs, especially those of the 'missing middle' using automated psychographic evaluation tools already in use in other contexts, difficult to play tricks, and correlated highly with entrepreneurial success.

Tools within the credit market including credit pricing, staggered loan sizes and the ability to interlink credit to related markets such as rent, labour (Braverman and Stiglitz, 1982; Stiglitz and Weiss, 1983; Braverman and Stiglitz, 1986) as well as output markets that use warehouse receipt systems and other functional commodity exchanges (Goodland et al., 1999; Coulter and Onumah, 2002; Onumah, 2003; Onumah et al., 2007; Onumah, 2010) constitute indirect mechanisms available to lenders. Here, borrowers are expected to respond based on their own considered best interest. Information about client riskiness is then assessed to reduce the probabilities of defaults. The interest rate, for instance, serves a dual function. It is the price paid for the loan and an indirect screening mechanism when clients accept to pay based on their considered best interest. Therefore, credit rationing is observed because the equilibrium interest rate need not be clear, and loan loss provisions by MFIs are necessary, as interest rate changes have the potential to change the project mix of borrowers. Thus, competition in imperfect markets does not drive rents to zero. Interlinkages across different markets (e.g., credit, rent, labour) are also effectively used as an indirect mechanism for the resolution of information asymmetries and enforcement problems inherent in imperfect credit markets.

The empirical evidence of indirect screening mechanisms is the focus of a study by Giné et al. (2011), which focuses on the impact of withholding credit from previous bad borrowers and expanding the same for those with good credit histories. The study sought to improve the MFI's ability to identify borrowers using bio-metric identifiers and found significant changes in behaviour. Clients least likely to repay took smaller loans, allocated more land for crop production and applied more inputs. The authors hypothesize that saving the good credit histories of clients could have future implications for credit access from other financial institutions.

3.3.3 Micro-Savings in the Microfinance Livelisystem Framework

Savings as a tool in the microfinance arsenal against poverty are key to maintaining the financial stability of the household. It is key to consumption smoothing, especially during emergencies, external shocks and life-cycle events that can be tasking financially. Savings have the potential to help households build up assets, smoothen fluctuating seasonal consumption needs, self-insure against major shocks and self-finance investments (Grosh and Somolekae, 1996; Cull and Morduch, 2007; Diop et al., 2007). Savings services offered by MFIs are frequently seen as a way of securing savings and encouraging the poorest to save more and more systematically (Beverly and Sherraden, 1999; Diop et al., 2007; Dupas and Robinson, 2013). MFIs also encourage SMEs savings (Anane et al., 2013).

Savings services offered by MFIs are either mandatory or voluntary. The former requires clients to save a minimum amount each week (or some other time intervals). Clients learn financial discipline and can use savings as collateral for the loans, while the frequency of deposits enables the provider to obtain vital information that narrows the information asymmetry between lenders and borrowers (Armendáriz de Aghion and Morduch, 2005). Voluntary savings, however, are flexible forms of savings (Nourse, 2001; Montgomery and Weiss, 2005). Savings as an entry to service provision can be critical sometimes. Christen (2001), for example, reports that over a few years, retail banks in Latin America opened millions of small deposit accounts in countries where fewer than 200,000 credit lines were given out over the same period.

Moreover, MFIs that offer both enterprise loans and voluntary savings found that savers typically exceeded borrowers by large proportions. Rutherford (1998) showed that poor people are active money managers. They can 'save up' by storing a usefully large sum somewhere or 'save down' by taking a loan and repaying later out of future savings. The pertinent question to ask is what motivates clients to save and what institutional features attract savers in the Northern Savannah of Ghana?

Theories underpinning savings attitude are rooted in psychology. First is the theory postulating differences in attitude towards the present and the future. Some people value the present more than the future without any consideration of the potential benefits that can be derived from postponing consumption. Second, savings culture is tied to issues of self-control that have implications on whether an individual spends in the present or the future. Self-control varies across individuals. Third, people differ in the way they plan *ex post* needs in *ex ante* situations. This does have implications on people's attitudes towards savings. Lastly, pressure from family, friends and relations on the windfalls of 'wealthy' individuals can be a daily occurrence. This puts a toll on people's ability to save. Innovations in savings product design are therefore geared towards overcoming one or more of these challenges. Few of these innovations include commitment savings accounts, reminders to save and labelled accounts.

With commitment savings accounts, a saver is required to continue depositing money into his/her savings account until a certain set date, or a certain amount is realized before he/she can make withdrawals. There are certain obvious advantages associated with a commitment savings account. Savings can finance investment expenditure as well as protect against arbitrary expenses, especially the demands of family members, friends and neighbours. Brune et al. (2011) evaluate commitment savings accounts with cash crop farmers in Malawi and show that treated groups had significantly higher absolute amounts deposited and withdrawals made before the commencement of the planting season for the purchase of inputs as well as other positive unintended outcomes.

Reminders to save, however, are innovations that regularly bring to the attention of low-income savers the need to save towards their own set goals, albeit long term. This is based on the theory that daily struggles of low-income people, which are characterized by risks and vulnerabilities, distract them from long-term goals. Therefore, they need reminding to save. Reminders to save makes the future look more real and relevant to their livelihoods' improvement needs. Sending regular SMS text messages to savers in Bolivia and the Philippines and letters to savers in Peru, Karlan et al. (2016) found that reminders to save led to an overall increase in average savings balances by 6%, and substantially by 16% for the Peruvian savers when the message reminding them to save referred to the particular purchase goal that the savers set themselves.

Account 'labelling' is an innovation that aligns well with both reminders to save and commitment savings accounts. Karlan et al. (2016) built on the concept of account labelling in Eastern Ghana, where people have long used it in the allocation of funds for different purposes, e.g., rent, education of children, among others. Cash was stashed away at places until a time when needed or a certain amount is realized. They find that savers who were eligible to open parallel accounts and were tagged specifically for a purchase goal with the MFI saved on average 31% more than those in the comparison group with just one savings account that is not labelled. The greatest effect was however observed with the education label (Karlan et al., 2016). These innovations in savings product design do show that design changes have great potential to help low-income people save more. This has the potential to increase and improve the living standards of poor savers as they finance investment expenditures, educate children and finance other welfare expenses.

3.3.4 Micro-Insurance in the Microfinance Livelisystem Framework

Generally, micro-insurance for low-income people is still at their infancy stages world-wide, especially in the Global South. However, several initiatives are being carried out to design replicable products and services to formalize the sub-sector within the microfinance industry. For example, FINCA Uganda offers clients' health and other micro-insurance products through an AIG subsidiary, based in South Africa. However, progress has been slow and two key reasons account for this. First, the divergence of insurance markets from credit markets needs specialized skills and expertise. Second, few MFIs possess the requisite human resource base with these necessary skills and expertise to set up and run insurance programmes.

The problem of information asymmetry is common in imperfect markets such as insurance and credit markets. This makes designing good insurance products impractical. For instance, people who will not possibly be affected by risk will portray behaviours differently from those fully exposed that same risk (moral hazard). Moreover, high-risk individuals are more likely to buy an insurance product (adverse selection). Therefore, the fundamental problem for the insurance seller is identifying and isolating higher-risk individuals to charge higher premiums and low-risk individuals so they can be charged low premiums. This impracticability causes designing insurance products to respond by averagely increasing the premium for all clients.

Karlan et al.'s (2014) study with farmers in Ghana on rainfall insurance products designed to lower risks of smallholder farmers overall and counter their risk aversion revealed that when coupled with a subsidy component, the impact was greater on the variables than those exposed to the insurance only or the subsidy only or none (the control group). For example, farmers exposed to both insurance and subsidies increased (farm input expenditure increased by 47%; land area under cultivation increased by 22%); and household members missed fewer meals than the comparison groups. The implication of these results for micro-insurance programmes targeting low-income population groups was that risk reduction through insurance products could be beneficial by themselves alone. However, the much greater impact could be achieved when poorer households' financial needs, risks and vulnerabilities are comprehensively understood and incorporated in the design of micro-insurance products. The question then is, 'what micro-insurance products are offered to clients in the Northern Savannah of Ghana, and what are their mitigating roles in household's livelisystem transitioning?'

3.3.5 Payment Services in the Microfinance Livelisystem Framework

Remittances from rural-urban migrants (temporary and permanent) and international migration (South-North and South-South) have become a significant source of household income in much of the Global South (Adams and Page, 2005; Gupta et al., 2009) and payment service providers are the primary drivers. For example, M-Pesa processes more transactions domestically in Kenya than Western Union does globally (Mas and Radcliffe, 2010). In 2015, the World Bank estimated that $439 billion was channelled back home by migrants from developing countries (World Bank, 2016). Earlier studies on the effects of migration and remittances on poverty and inequality in sub-Saharan Africa included those by Gustafsson and Makonnen (1993) on Lesotho and Litchfield et al. (2002) on Ghana. Remittances from migrant workers have been found to increase household incomes, support consumption smoothening, the education of children, household investments and increased standard of living. There is an additional positive spill-over impact on the wider community as well. Organized migration programmes are increasingly recognized as an effective development policy (Adams and Page, 2005; McKenzie and Gibson, 2010; Gibson et al., 2014). Wealthier households generally benefit more, but for the poorer households, remittances are an important source of income for risk mitigation and coping (Gupta et al., 2009). Remittances have a far-reaching positive impact on recipient households than most other development interventions, on the migrant workers themselves and the GDP of the world (Yang, 2008; McKenzie and Gibson, 2010; Gibson et al., 2014).

In September 2008, the World Bank established the first international database of remittance prices which covers over 200 countries. Remittances to sub-Saharan Africa through banks are restrictive due to legal and related issues. Large money transfer companies such as Western Union or MoneyGram readily fill in the gap, but the cost can be as high as 12% of the transferred amount. At the G20 2011 Summit in Cannes, Bill Gate stated that "...if the transaction costs on remittances worldwide were cut from where they are today at around 10% to an average of 5%...it would unlock $15bn a year in poor countries". Apart from traditional payment service providers such as Western Union and MoneyGram, new players armed with modern technologies are beginning to disrupt the remittance payment market, including pricing models of the established money transfer operators (MTO). These new players including Xoom, World Remit and Willstream, among others, are using the fast-pace mobile phone penetration rates in sub-Saharan Africa to provide services at competitive prices. In Ghana, three mobile network operators are active in the money transfer services and are disrupting traditional money transfer services across the country. These are MTN, Vodafone and Tigo.

3.4 Factors Underpinning Microfinance Product and Service Design: A Global Perspective within the Microfinance Livelisystem Framework

3.4.1 Introduction

The diversity of microfinance service providers and the products and services they provide have a direct correlation with the needs and wants of clients. As a result, Bennett and Goldberg (1993) argue that there is little understanding of the differential needs, goals, risk profiles, investment opportunities and barriers to financial inclusion of the productive poor working themselves out of poverty. This is of concern because Otero (1999) posits that microfinance as an industry facilitates financial, social and human capital development of the productive poor and builds institutions that provide broader development services. This is important because financial self-sufficiency remains the over-riding goal of those MFIs oriented towards the financial systems approach. Moreover, scale remains limited for those MFIs oriented towards the poverty-lending approach, even though subsidies from both public and private sources are intended for increased outreach (Woller et al., 1999). Furthermore, theoretical underpinnings of rural financial markets are focused on reducing the costs of services provision via product design that counters prevailing barriers to financial inclusion such as the lack of suitable collaterals and the pervasive information asymmetries between lenders and resource-poor borrowers, characterized by low 'debt capacity' (Von Pischke, 1991; Ghatak and Guinnane, 1999; Armendáriz de Aghion and Morduch, 2005; Hill and Sarangi, 2012). Thus, theories of rural financial markets (Stigler, 1967; Stiglitz and Weiss, 1981; Hoff and Stiglitz, 1993; Yunus, 2007) are drawn upon to contextualize the gaps in product and service design. For instance, experience with interventions in rural credit markets of developing countries suggests that the introduction of regulated formal financial institutions has failed to drive out usurious moneylenders, despite their competitive interest rates (Bottomley, 1964; Singh, 1983; Bell, 1988) and economies of scale. What then are the reasons for the continued patronage of the services of such informal providers? Bhatt and Tang (2001) conclude that the future success of microfinance would depend on MFI's ability to design products and services tailored to the specific needs and preferences of clients. Bhatt and Tang's assertion highlights the importance of research to develop sound practices of MFI product and service design and management.

3.4.2 The Eight Factors Underpinning Microfinance Product and Service Design

The point of divergence between the financial systems and the poverty-lending approaches is the difference in their implications on the design of products and services to concurrently improve sustainability and large outreach (Morduch, 2000), and, therefore, poverty reduction. Achieving both goals requires a careful balancing of both the sustainability and outreach goals or innovation to achieve both goals. Schreiner (2002) developed a framework for the design of products and services regardless of the approach an MFI adopts for achieving these broad goals of the industry. He identified six factors including cost, worth, depth, breadth, length and scope. While the cost of supply includes interest and fees charged to borrowers, the cost of access includes the interest and fees and the transactional costs (i.e., the opportunity costs of time and the indirect cash expenses incurred for access). While worth is simply those factors that affect the willingness of clients to pay the price of access, depth considers levels of access by the poorer segments of targeted populations. Breadth, however, describes the absolute numbers of the population with access. Also, while the length is more related to the sustainability of microfinance intermediation, scope describes the varieties of products and services provided by the industry including the lending methodologies.

Schreiner used data reported to MIX Market by a group of MFIs for the estimation of the extent of their incorporation and their implications on clients' livelihoods. While this study diverges from Schreiner's by focusing on the demand side of the industry, it expanded the framework by the inclusion of contract enforcement mechanisms and add-ons. This chapter focused on the assessment of all eight design factors across the three institutional types of the Northern Savannah of Ghana using data obtained primarily from clients but supplemented with secondary and qualitative data obtained from the microfinance providers. The extent to which each feature underpinned product and service design and their implications for product uptake and the ability of clients to honour contractual obligations were assessed. A change in the social benefits of microfinance to clients is underpinned by the interaction of all eight design features.

Regardless of approach and the plurality of institutional types, what remains important is the incentive structure of contracts that optimizes supplier efficiency and the livelihood outcomes of clients. It is worth noting that length offers the greatest effect on the social benefits of microfinance (Schreiner, 2002). Thus, the profitability of the MFI or donations or both determines how long an MFI will remain in operation to serve clients. All other things constant, increasing profits for the MFIs requires that products and services be priced higher, which increases costs and limits net gain for clients. However, a profitable MFI can drive innovations that reduce costs of supply and, therefore, costs of access in the long run. Increased net gain results in an increased willingness to pay by clients (Woller et al., 1999; Woller, 2002). The high worth of products and services is priced high and does not compromise net gain for clients. Moreover, profitable MFIs have the potential to increase the number of clients (outreach both breadth and depth) accessing products and services in the long run such that the short-term decreases in net gain, because of the initial high prices, are off-set in the long run (Schreiner, 2002).

The poverty-lending approach with an affinity for subsidies does not provide strong incentives for innovations. Here, innovations are hardly rewarded, nor lack of growth punished. However, because clients' welfare directly depends on how well products and services meet their livelihood needs, the reward of innovations can be envisaged in the long run. Also, donations for subsidies negate the need to price products and services highly. This increases the net gain for clients. Thus, for MFIs that are pro-poverty lending, increasing net gain is paramount, even if subsidies stifle innovations and profits (Schreiner, 2002). By contrast, the financial systems approach assumes that the overall benefits derived from prolonged length (sustainable programmes) made possible by profits do compensate for the short-term decreases in net gain from the high pricing of products and services. The comparative nature of the study, which also segments clients into formal, semi-formal and informal, is expected to provide evidence to support policy for access to microfinance and the productive inclusion of the poor in rural economies.

The point of divergence between the financial systems and the poverty-lending approaches is the differences of their implications on the design of products and services that concurrently improve sustainability and increase outreach (Morduch, 2000), and therefore poverty reduction. Achieving both goals requires a careful balancing of the two or finding innovative ways to achieve both. Schreiner (2002) developed a framework for the design of products and services regardless of the approach an MFI adopts for the contextualization of the social benefits of microfinance. The six factors Schreiner identified were cost, worth, depth, breadth, length and scope. Schreiner used data reported to MIX Market by a group of MFIs to estimate the extent of their incorporation and their implications on clients' livelihoods. Contract enforcement and add-ons (microfinance plus) affect the incentive structure of contracts both for the MFI and for clients and are thus included in this study. The chapter focused on the assessment of all eight design factors across the three institutional types of the Northern Savannah of Ghana using data obtained from clients. The extent to which each feature underpins product and service design and their implications for product uptake and the ability of clients to honour contractual obligations are assessed. A change in the social benefits of microfinance to clients is underpinned by the interaction of all eight design features (see Appendices IV and V).

3.5 The Determinants of Product and Service Uptake: A Global Perspective within the Microfinance Livelisystem Framework

3.5.1 Introduction

Client and industry specificities traditionally segment financial sectors (Richter, 2004). However, institutions (Acemoglu et al., 2002), infrastructure and governance (Beck et al., 2007), and income levels (Edison et al., 2002) play a significant role in financial sector development. Huang and Temple (2005) identified three groups of factors including policy, geography and institutions that underpin financial sector development. The literature is also awash with studies on country-specific factors that were needed to create well-functioning microfinance markets. Vanroose (2008) further groups these factors into four different categories for the microfinance sub-sector owing to the dual goals of the industry – financial self-sufficiency and increased outreach (Meyer, 2002; Hartarska and Nadolnyak, 2007). Vanroose (2008) shows that the most feasible way to measure the development of the microfinance sector is by the number of clients served.

Concerning policy, four factors defined as 'macro-economic policy' are found in the extant literature. These are income levels, geographic variables, institutional variables and the legacies of colonialism and regulatory frameworks. Westley (2005) found that regions with higher levels of income have less developed microfinance sectors and provided two contrasting reasons. First, high-income micro-entrepreneurs usually self-finance through savings. Second, these high-income micro-entrepreneurs have easy access to credit from informal family and friends, as well as from the commercial banks. Similarly, Schreiner and Colombet (2001) further argue that Argentina's microfinance sector remained relatively undeveloped due to the general prevalence of higher wages. Thus, the microfinance industry focuses on the excluded poor and marginalized, poor regions should have high microfinance activities.

Transaction and information cost most often related to geography also influence financial sector development. These can sometimes underpin market failures (Stiglitz and Weiss, 1981). Easy interconnectivity across regions, power availability, communication and sanitation networks, and high population density lower transaction and information costs. Sriram and Kumar (2005) offered two contradictory arguments on transaction and information costs. First, they argued that formal financial institutions – the commercial banks – are likely to be in regions with high connectivity and population densities. This can hinder the development of the microfinance sub-sector. However, a complementary formal banking sector should stimulate the development of the microfinance sector. Rhyne (2001) found that Latin American MFIs are more urban than rural. Generally, poor infrastructure and lower population densities hinder the development of microfinance activities (Yaron et al., 1997; Schreiner and Colombet, 2001; Hulme and Moore, 2006).

The role of institutions in the development of countries is well documented. Education directly affects the human capital base needed for the development of the financial sector. Colonial legacies and regulatory frameworks are also important variables in the development of the financial and microfinance sub-sectors in the extant literature. For example, Paulson (2002) finds that regions with higher levels of education in Thailand have much developed financial markets, while Guiso et al. (2004) also found better outcomes in social capital formation in the same region. Thus, higher education and literacy rates associated with human capital development enhance the outreach of MFIs.

Factors influencing client participation in microfinance programmes from the individual and household as well as the MFI level and the role of macro-economic and macro-institutional variables are also well documented in the extant microfinance best practice literature. Factors such as interest rates, targeting, lending models, economic growth, sex/gender, availability and access to other poverty interventions, opportunities for livelihood diversification, microfinance commercialization, MFI customer relations, the rule of law, client enterprise start-up requirements, household size, inflation, and MFI governance structures and management systems do influence participation and uptake. However, Dunford (2000) argued that best practices vary and constantly change due to the nature of the MFI clientele and the disparate environments in which MFIs operate. Best practices must be adaptable to specific contexts in order to thrive.

3.5.2 Interest Rates and Participation in Microfinance

On regulatory and macro-economic policy impacts on MFIs, Franks (2000) discusses macro-economic stabilization and its impact on microenterprises. He concludes that macro-economic stabilization can ultimately be very beneficial to the microfinance sector, although it may be costly in the short run. While consultative group to assist the poor (CGAP) estimates that only about 5% of MFIs worldwide are financially sustainable, the International Monetary Fund (IMF, 2005) puts that figure at only 1%. The achievement of financial self-sufficiency, according to Havers (1996), requires an MFI to cover the cost of funds, the operating costs, loan write-offs and the eroding effects of inflation from revenues generated from fees and interest charged. According to the IMF (2005), self-sustainable MFIs tend to be larger and target the less poor to improve efficiency through larger loan sizes. However, those focusing on the poorest tend to remain dependent on donor funds. MFIs face apparent contradictions regarding interest rates with dual goals of financial self-sufficiency and poverty reduction with invariably poorer client bases. High interest rates can potentially constrain borrowers' capacity to work themselves out of poverty and credit ration those at the bottom of the pyramid. Involuntary defaults undermine sustainability goals and, in the case of group-lending models, weaken safety nets offered in solidarity groups.

Moreover, MFI loans are typically small in principal amounts, offering little economies of scale in the lending process that sufficiently cover fixed costs. Achieving financial self-sufficiency, therefore, requires charging relatively high interest rates that usually reflect factors such as operational location, access to infrastructure, the macro-economic environment, the level of technology, the prevailing credit and savings culture of the society, and the efficiency of the MFI in question, among others. According to De Aghion and Morduch (2004), "achieving profitability and strong social performance is the ultimate promise of microfinance. It is not impossible, but neither is it easy". Thus, the challenge of the microfinance industry is threefold. It concerns not only financial sustainability, but the breadth (larger numbers of the poor reached) and depth (larger numbers of the poorest of the poor reached) of outreach.

Conning (1999) constructs a theoretical model of the contract design problem facing MFIs seeking to maximize impact by targeting poorer borrowers and financial self-sufficiency. Their analysis of data from 72 MFIs revealed that those who were sustainable targeted poorer borrowers charged higher interest rates, had higher staff costs and were less leveraged. In contrast to this finding, the mid-19th-century Irish loan funds were able to lend to the poor at competitive interest rates without subsidies (Hollis and Sweetman, 1998), efficiently handling information and enforcement problems, while operating at a surplus in markets that formal commercial banks could not. There is a shred of indirect evidence that the poor can and do pay high interest rates. The evidence of the capability of the poor to pay higher interest rates was that of Perry (2002) who found that in Senegal, some moneylenders borrow from MFIs and successfully on-lend at higher interest rates. Robinson (1996) also argued that interest rates charged to microfinance borrowers should cover all costs and that the working poor can afford those rates relatively lower than other available alternatives. Finally, Fafchamps (1997) used a simulation methodology to show that interest rate subsidizations have little impact on whether the poor in India invest in profitable projects.

Apart from interest rates, Yaron (2004) lists 'eight pillars' of pro-urban policies that have often worked against the development of rural communities and rural financial markets. These include: (1) overvalued exchange rates; (2) low, controlled and seasonally invariant prices of agricultural products; (3) high effective rates of protection for domestic industry, the output of which is used for agricultural inputs; (4) disproportionately high budgetary allocations for urban over rural infrastructure (roads, electricity and water supply); (5) disproportionately high investment in human resources in urban over rural areas (health and education); (6) usury laws that rule out the loans typical in rural areas – small, risky and high-cost loans; (7) underdeveloped legal and regulatory provisions regarding land titling and collateral for typical rural assets (land, crops, and farm implements) relative to urban assets (cars, durables and homes); and (8) excessive taxes on agricultural exports. These pillars characterize many developing countries and have resulted in the uneven distribution of infrastructure, an essential ingredient for mass poverty reduction.

3.5.3 Lending Models (Group versus Individual Models) and Participation in Microfinance

Microcredit is most often extended without traditional collateral. Instead, social collateral, via group lending, is commonly used. Group lending encompasses a variety of methodologies, but all are based on the principle of joint liability. Joint liability implies that if a member does not repay a loan, then the other members of the joint liability group will have to repay on that member's behalf (Ahlin and Townsend, 2007) or the entire group lose access to future credit facilities. The group takes over the underwriting, monitoring and enforcement of loan contracts from the lending institution (Wenner, 1995). Reputational effects on group members, especially the maintenance of their social standing in the community (Woolcock, 2001), further enhance the effectiveness of the use of social collateral in rural credit markets. Joint liability transfers the risk from the MFI to borrowers and helps mitigate problems of adverse selection, moral hazards, the lack of insurance and enforcement difficulties (Simtowe and Zeller, 2006). Goldmark (2003) suggests methods that may help build social collateral, thereby making loans even more secure. Van Tassel (1999) constructs a model in the determination of optimal group-lending contracts under asymmetric information and concludes that agents will always form groups with agents of the same characteristics (assortative matching) and that agents' types can be distinguished according to the rate at which they are willing to trade increased joint liability commitments for lower interest rates. Also, Ghatak (1999) concludes that group lending increases repayment rates and welfare not only via social collateral, but also due to peer selection by members of the lending group.

Moreover, Islam (1996) concludes that lenders using peer-monitoring systems can charge lower rates relative to conventional lenders and that, at same interest rates the expected rate of repayment is higher when peer monitoring mechanisms are deployed. Marr (2002), however, states that it is important not to assume group-lending dynamics as existing in a vacuum but to perceive the process as embedded in social, economic and cultural spheres, as group behaviour is conditioned by power structures, evolving risks, constraints and opportunities. Simtowe and Zeller (2006) used a model to explain the strategy of group lending in microfinance.

In that model, each stage is associated with an inherent problem that group lending, through social collateral, is expected to help address. Allowing self-selection at the group stage ensures that potential borrowers utilize local information and devices in the understanding of one another's projects or attributes and, therefore, the selection of the best partners (Ghatak, 1999; Ghatak, 2000; Armendáriz de Aghion and Morduch, 2005; Hadi and Kamaluddin, 2015). It also reduces the incidence of adverse selection (Ghatak, 1999). Johnson and Rogaly (1997) propose that members' control of groups devoid of manipulation by MFI officials is key to the success of group-lending schemes.

The incentive for service users to monitor the use of loans among themselves stems from the joint liability and the potential loss of access to future loans (Zeller et al., 1997; Zeller and Sharma, 1998). According to Stiglitz (1990), the success of the Grameen Bank and other similar group-lending models is largely the result of the peer monitoring strategy. Aghion et al. (2000) argue that peer monitoring in group lending prevents strategic defaults by the ability of members to verify project returns (*ex post* moral hazard) just as peer selection mitigates *ex ante* moral hazards (Stiglitz, 1990, Ghatak, 1999).

Stiglitz (1990) shows that group lending can increase the choice of safer projects when service users select peers willing to engage in safer projects (assortative matching). However, project officials can play an important role in monitoring to improve repayments (Fuglesang et al., 1993). Enforcement using peer pressure

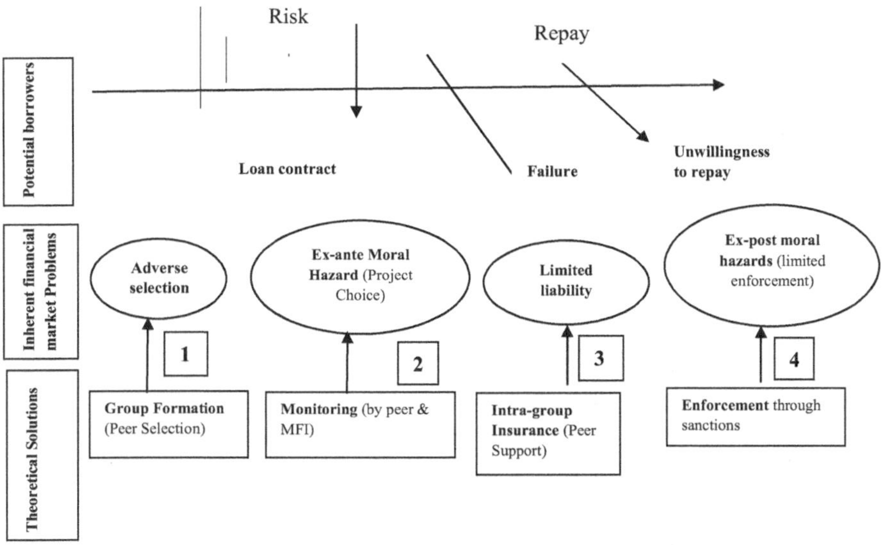

FIGURE 3.1 The Dynamics of Group Lending.
Source: Adapted from Simtowe and Zeller (2006).

and sanctions to induce repayments by service users mitigates the problem of *ex post* moral hazards (Figure 3.1).

Others have argued that stage four should precede stage three because the burden of repayment falls on the entire group (joint liability). Marr (2002) argues for the addition of an audit stage at the point of enforcement where group members can determine whether a default is wilful or due to investment failure. The last stage is the peer support/joint liability which occurs when peer pressure and sanctions, among others, have been applied but fail to secure repayments. Simtowe and Zeller (2006) call this the limited liability problem. Though presented as a stage in the group-lending scheme, joint liability underlies the entire process of the group-lending model (Ghatak and Guinnane, 1999). And it is the idea that compels peers to monitor and apply pressure and sanctions to ensure repayments.

MFIs often rely on social collateral within loan groups to secure their loans (Woolcock, 2001). Addressing the issue of group-lending design, Woolcock (1999) analysed five cases of MFI failures in Ireland, Bangladesh and India and concluded that group performance depends on lending policies, cost structures, the nature and extent of social relations among group members, and the staff of an MFI. Bhatt and Tang (2001) offer recommendations for setting up and managing an MFI based on their discussion of group lending under the frameworks of incomplete information theory and transaction cost theory. Gomez and Santor (2001) also provide empirical evidence of the importance of social collateral.

In an empirical study of 612 group borrowers and 52 individual borrowers in Canada, they report that group lending and the presence of neighbours have a positive correlation with self-employment earnings.

Although group loans form most microloans within the microfinance industry globally, individual lending is equally significant in some areas and is growing in popularity. Aghion et al. (2000) consider microfinance beyond group lending in Eastern Europe, Russia and China and describe the mechanisms that allow MFIs to successfully penetrate rural credit markets to include direct monitoring, regular repayment schedules and threats of non-refinancing.

3.5.4 Household Size and Participation in Microfinance

Household size describes the number of people who live together and share food cooked from a common pot. It could be wife, husband and their children, but it is not uncommon to find other relations. The size of the household can have an impact on the economic and social capital accumulation capacity of the household, including participation in microfinance programmes. The size of the household and the dependency ratio do impact production, consumption and investment decisions. Larger households with a high dependency ratio may aim more at consumption smoothening rather than investment capital. However, if the dependants are productive, then it can be expected that such labour is employed in productive investments, thereby increasing the need for credit. Smaller households are more likely to be self-sufficient than larger households.

3.5.5 Livelihood Diversification and Participation in Microfinance

Studies by Remenyi and Quinones (2000) indicated that the household income of families with access to credit was significantly higher than comparable households without access to credit. According to Markowski (2002), while the social mission of microfinance is to provide financial services to large numbers of low-income populations to improve livelihoods, the commercial mission is providing those financial services in a financially viable manner.

Diversification in rural environments represents a dynamic adaptation process in response to threats and opportunities. Through diversification, farmers can manage risk as well as gain extra income and resources, securing their livelihoods and improving their standard of living (Ellis, 2000; Csáki and Lerman, 2000; Ellis and Allison, 2004). Rural households traditionally rely on diversified income portfolios (Reardon, 1997; Reardon et al., 2007). Non-farm earnings in developing countries constitute around 35%–50% of rural-household incomes (Reardon et al., 2006; Haggblade et al., 2009). These percentages tends to be even higher in sub-Saharan African countries (Ellis, 1999), where livelihood diversification is very commonly observed (Ellis, 1999; Barrett et al., 2001; Davis et al., 2010).

Mosley and Rock (2004), in a study of six African MFIs, concluded that MFI services provided to the non-poor could reduce poverty by sucking up the poor into labour markets as employees of microfinance participants. They also stated that microfinance services often enhance human capital through increased spending on education and health that may extend to poor households through intra-household and inter-generational effects. Also, Zohir and Matin (2004) found that MFI loans are mostly used for agricultural production, trading, processing and transport. Increased outputs of agricultural production from increased input use then translate to higher income for farmers. The enhanced employment opportunities in these sectors for the wider community increase supply and, therefore, price reductions. The authors further observed that trading activities financed by MFIs could help to establish new market links that increase the income of traders. The tide of migration can be beaten down when poor people are employed to earn incomes. From a social perspective, reduced migration increases family cohesion and can significantly contribute to improving child-upbringing.

The motivations for livelihood diversification strategies in the extant literature suggest that both push and pull factors determine the levels and types of diversification. Farmers' asset endowments and the availability of off-farm opportunities as well as other exogenous factors underpin rural livelihood diversification. Mostly the push factors include managing risk (market and price risks) and income variability, adapting to heterogeneous agro-ecological production and changing weather conditions (Lipper et al., 2010; Cavatassi et al., 2012). Diversification may, thus, be considered as a deliberate household strategy to smoothen incomes or to manage risks, or it may be an involuntary response to the crisis of coping with shocks (Bryceson, 1996; Bryceson, 1999; Delgado and Siamwalla, 1999; Toulmin and Quan, 2000; Barrett et al., 2001).

While a safety net for the rural poor, diversification serves as an asset accumulation strategy for the rural rich (Ellis, 1998). In regions where rainfall variability is high, *ex ante* decisions for diversification are common for managing risks of possible shocks. Such climatic shocks can exert *ex post* diversification (e.g., harvest shortfalls). Climate variability, associated with farm-income variability, is a key driver of diversification in many developing countries (Newsham and Thomas, 2009). Diversification, as a risk-management and shock-coping strategy, may yield lower average welfare outcomes, but should lead to more income security when an extreme event does occur (Barrett et al., 2001; Bandyopadhyay and Koufias, 2012; Skoufias et al., 2017). Diversification is also an essential strategy in the transition from subsistence to market-based agriculture, and from poverty to higher levels of well-being (Pingali and Rosegrant, 1995).

Wydick (1999) finds that upward class structure mobility increases significantly with access to credit. Using the same Guatemala data set in a subsequent study, Wydick (2002) further finds that rapid gains in job creation following initial credit access were subsequently followed by prolonged periods of stagnant job creation. Dunn and Arbuckle Jr (2001) find that programme clients' enterprises performed better than non-client enterprises in terms of profits, fixed assets and employment. Anderson et al. (2002) analyse 147 MFIs and find that microfinance participation increased environmental awareness and common resource stewardship. Owusu Ansah's (2001) study on Ghana attests to the fact that microfinance can indeed be used as a strategy for reducing poverty. Using impact analysis studies on the clientele of microfinance institutions operating in Ghana, i.e., Sinapi Aba trust (SAT) and BRI-UD, it was revealed that by providing microcredit to SAT's clientele, household incomes increased on average by 157% for the period August 1994 to July 1997. Thus, the study expects clients' livelihood diversifications in the Northern Savannah of Ghana to be associated with increased product uptake in the increasingly fragile weather and variable climatic conditions of the region.

3.5.6 Targeting and Participation in Microfinance

Targeting is central to poverty reduction policies and programmes in developing countries (Wodon, 1997). One of the key roles microfinance has to play in development is in bringing access to financial services to the poor, "essentially invisible, in government plans and budgets, in economists' models, in bankers' portfolios, and national policies" (Acemoglu et al., 2001). Client targeting in microfinance involves gender and poverty targeting. Gender targeting refers to lending to women versus lending to men while lending to the very poor versus the marginally poor is poverty targeting. Targeting the poor aims to improve income and access to social services (Zeller and Meyer, 2002).

Competition can increase outreach (Rhyne and Christen, 1999; Olivares-Polanco, 2005) or improve targeting of the poor by MFIs (Nagarajan, 2003). Simanowitz (2001) highlights several factors leading to the marginalization of the poorest such as self-exclusion, exclusion by other members, exclusion by MFI staff, and exclusion by product and service design, weakening the impact of microfinance as a poverty reduction tool. Markowski (2002) and Rogaly (1996) argue that MFIs in their project designs are failing to meet the needs of the very poor and destitute, who do have a demand for microfinance services, especially for savings (Dichter, 1999; Littlefield et al., 2003a).

However, women are among the poorest, yet are most apt to use household income to better the nutrition and educational opportunities of their children (Grasmuck and Espinal, 2000). Pitt and Khandker (1998) showed that the impact of the Grameen Bank's lending activities included the increased household income, assets held by women and moderately positive impact on the education of sons. This was interpreted as an indication of a lack of fungibility of capital and income within the households when women exercise control. But since loans to males are larger on average, the difference can also be explained by the standard theory of declining marginal returns to capital.

Exploring a related question, Kevane and Wydick (2001) found no significant differences between men and women borrowers in generating business sales, but a slight advantage of employment opportunities by men. The triple roles of women, including productive, reproductive and community managing, explained the differences observed. Amin and Becker (1998) used qualitative and quantitative evidence in Bangladesh to also show that membership in microfinance programmes, among other factors, was positively related to women's empowerment. However, Johnson (2004) states that having women as key participants in microfinance projects do not automatically lead to empowerment. Sometimes negative impacts such as increased workloads, increased domestic violence and abuse can be witnessed.

Earlier published studies outside Bangladesh have assessed the impact of microfinance programmes in Bolivia (Mosley, 2001), China (Park and Ren, 2001), Ecuador (Woller and Parsons, 2002), Ghana and South Africa (Afrane, 2002), Guatemala (Kevane and Wydick, 2001), Honduras and Ecuador (Smith, 2002), Indonesia (Bolnick and Nelson, 1990), Peru (Dunn and Arbuckle Jr, 2001), Thailand (Coleman, 1999, Coleman, 2006), Uganda (Barnes et al., 1999), Zambia (Copestake, 2002), and in multiple countries (Mosley and Hulme, 1998; Anderson et al., 2002). The findings of these studies vary considerably, suggesting that the impacts of microfinance programmes are highly context specific.

Targeting the very poor versus the marginally poor relates to one of the most significant and controversial debates in microfinance. That is, whether and to what extent there exists a trade-off between financial self-sufficiency of MFIs and the very poor reached with financial services (depth of outreach). Integral to this debate has been whether MFIs aiming at financial self-sufficiency should target the marginally poor to take advantage of economies of scale and cover costs. Addressing this issue, Navajas et al. (2000) analysed the outreach of five Bolivian MFIs and found that most clients were near the poverty line (i.e., the marginally poor), group lending had more depth than individual lending, the urban poorest were more likely to borrow, but overall, the most poorest borrowers were found in rural localities.

In addressing who participates and who does not in microfinance programmes and whether micro-entrepreneurs are subject to credit rationing, Evans et al. (1999) conduct an empirical examination of microfinance clients in Bangladesh and report that only 25% of eligible households participate and that poorer households had higher rates of participation. Multivariate analysis indicated low female education levels, small household size and landlessness constituted the bottlenecks for nonparticipation by households. McIntosh and Wydick (2005) show that non-profit MFIs cross-subsidize within their pool of borrowers. Thus, when competition eliminates rents on profitable borrowers, it is likely to yield a new equilibrium in which poor borrowers are worse off. The research envisaged that targeting should be positively associated with increased uptake.

3.5.7 Growing Rural Economy and Participation in Microfinance

Keynes, in his thesis 'General Theory of Employment, Interest, and Money', hypothesized that national income depends on the level of employment. Full employment is achieved when economic resources are fully utilized in an economy and can be described as optimal. This is a desirable state for all economies.

However, according to the neo-classical school of thought, it is impractical to achieve full employment in an economy (Samuelson and Modigliani, 1966), although both paradigms agree that full employment is desirable.

At the macro-level, it has been established theoretically and empirically that the relationship between a well-functioning financial system and economic growth and development is positive and is a major determinant of the growth path of many countries and poverty reduction (Jalilian and Kirkpatrick, 2002; Jalilian and Kirkpatrick, 2005; Beck et al., 2008; Jeanneney and Kpodar, 2011). Differing in proxies and outcome variables, others have investigated the direct relationship between financial development and poverty reduction (Honohan, 2004; Jalilian and Kirkpatrick, 2005; Beck et al., 2007; Perez-Moreno, 2011; Jeanneney and Kpodar, 2011; Sehrawat and Giri, 2015) and came to similar conclusions.

Increased access to financial services by the rural population empowers the human resources for productive economic activities and vice versa. An imperfect financial market that excludes the poor and vulnerable segments of the population has the potential to worsen poverty and inequality (Stiglitz, 1993). Thus, microfinance should correct market failure that has trapped millions in poverty by providing them with access to credit, creating economic power and translating that into social power to lift many out of poverty (Yunus, 1999). Also, Otero (1999) further argues that microfinance and development essentially involve reaching the poor through access to financial, social and human capital development, building institutions that provide broader services and financial system's deepening via diverse regulated institutions within the broader financial sector ecosystem. Thus, the study anticipates a positive relationship between rural economic boom and microfinance product and service uptake.

3.5.8 Inflation and Participation in Microfinance

A large body of empirical literature supports the proposition that inflation affects financial sector development negatively. Thus, price stability must be an essential precondition for successful financial development (Boyd and Smith, 1996; Khan and Ssnhadji, 2001; Boyd and De Nicolo, 2005; BenNaceur and Ghazouani, 2005; Keho, 2009; Huang and Temple, 2005; Huang and Wang, 2014; Bittencourt, 2012).

However, variations exist among monetary authorities on the definition of what levels of inflation constitute price stability and what means to achieve it. In Ghana, price stability between 11% and 16% points (i.e., year-on-year consumer price index (CPI) inflation rates) is found to support financial sector development in overall size, liquidity of assets and efficiency in resource allocation.

High rates of inflation affect financial sector development negatively by exacerbating the information asymmetry problems in imperfect markets, including credit markets and the subsequent inefficient allocation of resources (Huybens and Smith, 1998; Huybens and Smith, 1999; Boyd and Smith, 1998). The definition and the framework for achieving price stability in Ghana have been murky following a sharp downward trend (70.82% in 1995 to 10.82% in 2006) and the marginal financial sector development, resulting in the 2018 financial sector crisis.

The impact of inflation varies across population segments. In general, the rich with greater asset holdings and higher incomes are less affected than the poor, especially in environments with little or no safety nets. Wage workers are more affected by inflation than enterprise owners. Boyd and Smith (1996) also predicted that high rates of inflation induce endogenous volatility (instabilities) of important economic variables, including equity returns and low real returns to savings.

Overall, available theoretical literature posits a negative relationship between inflation and financial sector development (English, 1999; BenNaceur and Ghazouani, 2005; Kim and Lee, 2010). Inflation has a direct effect on the costs of capital and lending rates in Ghana (Osei-Assibey, 2010). The interest rate also serves both as a price and as an instrument for regulating the risk composition of the lender's portfolio (Stiglitz and Weiss, 1981) and can be difficult to manage during high inflation (Stugler, 1987). Financial development supports growth under low or moderate inflation rates (Huybens and Smith, 1998; Huybens and Smith, 1999; Rousseau and Wachtel, 2002; Lee and Wong, 2005). It is therefore expected that inflation will have a negative relationship with microfinance product and service uptake in the Northern Savannah of Ghana.

3.5.9 Rule of Law and Participation in Microfinance

The rule of law encompasses a country's overall legal system as well as the implementation of laws (Kaufmann et al., 2009) and government policies and regulations that impact MFI operations (Mersland and Strøm, 2009). Earlier studies suggest that governments do have an interest in the microfinance industry because credit and deposit services support poverty reduction among resource-poor populations (Claessens, 2006; Hossain, 2013), when organized sustainably by MFIs.

MFIs must, therefore, be protected (Hartarska and Nadolnyak, 2007) with the right mix of policies and regulations. The operations of MFIs fall under all that universe of legal provisions and administrative regulations that directly or indirectly affect their operations. These include, but not limited to, non-profit organizational-related rules, rules governing formal financial intermediaries and financing activities, and the rules applicable to small businesses in Ghana.

The rule of law affects both the social and commercial logic of MFI operations (Im and Sun, 2015). The state of the rule of law should have an association with the uptake of microfinance products and services by clients, but its direction cannot be established *a priori*.

3.5.10 MFI Corporate Governance and Participation in Microfinance

Governance refers to the systems and processes defining and upholding an organizational mission and goals. It guides strategic decisions that ensure accountability and manages risks. Governance incentivizes management to pursue objectives for the achievement of organizational goals. Good governance structures of MFIs should ensure effective monitoring, feedback, and prudent decisions and resource use.

The ownership and governance of financial institutions largely depend on the legal, regulatory, supervisory and shareholder frameworks upon which they are established. Governance of microfinance institutions is complex because of the double (or triple) bottom line implicit in financial inclusion. Over the years, the governance structures of MFIs have evolved to adapt to industry growth, including product and service diversification and private sector investments (Mersland and Strøm, 2009) and further complicating the operational processes and reinforcing the need for strong and relevant governance structures and practices (Barry and Tacneng, 2014). Governance issues feature prominently among the reasons for the revocation of the licences of 192 insolvent microfinance institutions and another 155 insolvent microfinance companies that had already ceased operations in May 2019. Furthermore, 15 savings and loans companies and eight finance houses also had their licences revoked in August 2019 (Bank of Ghana, 2019). Thus, the influence of MFI governance could not be determined *a priori*.

MFI governance structures and management systems must look out for strategic risks, including adverse business decisions or improper implementation. Poor leadership or ineffective governance can result in reputational risk (Strøm et al., 2014) and can lead to the loss of value from negative public opinion (Ekkaand EDA Rural Systems, 2011). In addition to managing strategic and reputational risk, there is the need to balance both the financial and social performances of microfinance institutions. The level of effectiveness of these governance issues has implications for product and service uptake. Good governance structures and systems should, therefore, be associated with increased product and service uptake and vice versa.

3.5.11 Client Start-up Requirements and Participation in Microfinance

The Government of Ghana recognized the need to support micro-, small and medium-sized enterprises (MSMEs) as early as the early 1990s and thus established the national board for small-scale industries (NBSSI) and merged it with the Ghana enterprises development commission (GEDC) for the delivery of credit to small-scale entrepreneurs except in agriculture, real estate and trading. However, repayments were unsatisfactory. Several research studies confirm that the demand for external financing among MSMEs in developing countries is not overly high, except when planning growth, with young firms more strongly preferring bank loans compared to mature firms.

Buera and Kaboski (2012) built an economy-wide model of entrepreneurship of the industry outside the formal financial sector and explored the extent to which it influenced output, capital, total factor productivity, wages and interest rates and came to the conclusion that, in some cases, MFIs not only raise output but decrease disparities between the rich and the poor. Ahlin and Jiang (2008) and Yusupov (2012) also find that the industry promotes development on a wider scale via tangible and intangible spill-over effects.

Debates are beginning to shift marginally to the demand side of the industry, and according to Ledgerwood et al. (2013), the focus is now on how to address the diverse needs of clients and the transformational role of technology in delivering better products and services to clients. Gubert and Roubaud (2005) found that the impact of microcredit on employment was positive and significant in Madagascar. Data from Zimbabwe also showed that microcredit had no impact on employment levels in businesses (Barnes et al., 2001). Buckley (1997) discusses field summary data from Kenya, Malawi and Ghana and concluded that fundamental structural changes in socio-economic conditions and a deeper understanding of the psychology of informal sector entrepreneurs are needed for microfinance to prove effective. Schreiner and Woller (2003) compare evidence about the effectiveness of microenterprise programmes in developing countries and the United States. They conclude that microenterprise development is much more difficult in the United States than in developing countries. It is expected that the requirements for enterprise start-ups will spur increased demand for microfinance products and services.

3.5.12 Other Poverty Interventions and Participation in Microfinance

Adams and Von Pischke (1992) attempt to establish the viability of the microfinance industry as a poverty reduction tool relative to other poverty alleviation policies. By directly comparing the operational frameworks of the failed rural credit programmes of the 1960s and 1970s with the modern MFIs, the authors conclude that the latter were bound to fail just like the former. In contrast, Woller et al. (1999) also concluded that the current microfinance movement differs from the earlier rural credit programmes, and a direct comparison was inappropriate. They list several reasons why the prospects for success of the modern microfinance industry look positive.

In Bangladesh, for instance, McKernan (2002) reported that programme participation could exert a large positive impact on self-employment profits. Woller and Woodworth (2001) argued that, to date, top-down macro-level poverty alleviation programmes also have significant failure rates. Consequently, they argue that microfinance constitutes a potentially viable bottom-up policy option capable of complementing macro-level policies for effective poverty reduction.

Moreover, Snow and Buss (2001) studied the industry in sub-Saharan Africa and concluded that better goal-oriented assessment is needed to determine if microfinance is an effective policy for poverty alleviation. This study, therefore, sought to establish to what extent clients perceive other poverty interventions to have on the uptake of microfinance products and services in the Northern Savannah of Ghana. Participation in other poverty interventions should have a positive association with microfinance uptake.

3.5.13 Formal Education and Participation in Microfinance

Village banks, initiated by Freedom from Hunger, have found substantial benefits in bundling financial services with client education (MkNelly and Dunford, 1996, MkNelly and Dunford, 1998). Analysing credit rationing in Ecuador by MFIs, Baydas et al. (1994) constructed and estimated a supply and demand model that analysed factors MFIs use to ration credit and found that micro-entrepreneurs with less profitable enterprises and less education have a smaller demand for microcredit.

In Northern Ghana, socio-economic, cultural and environmental factors limit female education and their educational attainment. Females are, therefore, targeted by MFIs with financial and social intermediation such as vocational skills for self-employment, information on support services for improving business outcomes and for capital accumulation (Akudugu, 2009). Formal education is expected to have a positive association with microfinance uptake in the Northern Savannah.

3.5.14 Gender and Participation in Microfinance

Microfinance institutions (MFIs) have been recognized as organizations that can advance social causes in developing economies by improving the economic prospects and living conditions of people at the base of the pyramid (Hudon and Seibel, 2007; Khavul et al., 2009; Hermes et al., 2011; Boehe and Cruz, 2013). Of importance in the financial self-sufficiency debate, women's involvement has been a key driver to MFI performance. Women are considered to exhibit better debt repayment performance (Akula, 2008; Yunus, 1999). However, the empirical evidence is rather mixed: whereas some studies suggest that female MFI membership positively affects debt repayment (Hossain, 1988; Zeller et al., 1997; Mersland and Strøm, 2010; Strøm et al., 2014; Afrane and Adusei, 2016), others do not (Wydick, 1999; Bhatt and Tang, 2002; Godquin, 2004) without consideration of the context.

In the extant literature, institutions matter (North, 1990; Kostova and Zaheer, 1999; Scott, 2001; Peng et al., 2008) because a society's institutional framework creates incentives that influence the socio-economic opportunities available as well as the capabilities of economic actors contextually (North, 1990).

In Northern Ghana, economic and socio-cultural factors limit female formal education attainment. MFIs, therefore, target women with financial and non-financial services such as vocational skills for self-employment, information on support services for improving their businesses and the ability to earn an income for capital accumulation (Akudugu et al., 2009). Localized socio-cultural and economic factors associated with gender (kinship and marriage systems, norms regarding female behaviour, and the nature of local labour, product and credit markets) do influence participation and product uptake of men and women differently. Women are mostly targeted by MFIs in the Northern Savannah of

Ghana (Akudugu, 2012), with the widespread notion that women's repayment rates are much higher than men's and that access by women guarantees household welfare. Most government credit programmes target women (Microfinance and Small Loans Centre, 2014). They are mostly found in the dominant informal trade sector of the study region.

3.6 The Impact of Microfinance on Rural Livelihood Diversification, Asset Accumulation and Welfare Outcomes: A Global Perspective within the Microfinance Livelisystem Framework

The impact of microfinance on the livelihoods of rural households has been well documented. These range from diversification, asset accumulation and household welfare. As discussed in Section 3.3 on the impact of access to major products and services of the microfinance industry, reports of the multi-dimensional impacts of microfinance on households' livelihood activities by development practitioners, academics and policymakers have so far been mixed. Some have found positive effects on consumption and income levels (Khandker, 2005; Kondo et al., 2008; Berhane, 2009; Collins et al., 2009; Imai and Azam, 2012; Berhane and Gardebroek, 2012), housing improvements (Berhane, 2009; Berhane and Gardebroek, 2011), wages and agricultural investment (Kaboski and Townsend, 2012), improvements in savings (Kondo et al., 2008; Dupas and Robinson, 2013), health and food security (Stewart et al., 2010). Others such as Chowdhury (2009) remained sceptical about its effectiveness as a tool for poverty reduction especially amidst concerns of commercialization of the industry. Chowdhury (2009) further argues that borrowers need business skills and marketing information to leverage loans for the expansion of their businesses and the creation of jobs; otherwise, it is only a consumption smoothing tool. Ahlin and Jiang (2008) and Yusupov (2012) also find that MFIs promote development on a wider scale via tangible and intangible spill-over effects.

Earlier studies by Remenyi and Quinones (2000) indicated that the household income of families with access to credit was significantly higher than that of comparable households without access to credit. The results of the study in Indonesia found that there was a 12.9% annual average rise in income from borrowers, while only a 3% rise was reported from non-borrowers (the control group). They noted that, in Bangladesh, a 29.3% annual average rise in income was recorded for borrowers and a 22% annual average rise in income for non-borrowers. In Sri Lanka there was a 15.6% rise in income from borrowers and only 9% rise from non-borrowers. In the case of India, 46% annual average rise in income was reported among borrowers with a 24% increase reported by non-borrowers. The effects were higher for those just below the poverty line while income improvement was lowest among the very poor. Chowdhury et al. (1991) asserted that women (and men) participating in BRAC-sponsored activities have more income, own more assets and are more often gainfully employed than non-participants. Mustafa et al. (1996) confirmed this and noted that members have better-coping capacities in lean seasons and that these increased with length of membership and amount of credit received.

Zeller and Sharma (1998), in their assessment of the impact of microcredit on household income, found that access to credit positively affected household income in four out of five countries assessed. Households with improved access to credit were also better able to adopt technologies, spend more on food and, in some cases, have higher calorie intake. Owusu Ansah's (2001) study in Ghana attests to the fact that microfinance can indeed be used as a strategy for reducing poverty. Using impact analysis studies on the clientele of microfinance institutions operating in Ghana, i.e., Sinapi Aba trust (SAT) and BRI-UD, it was revealed that by providing microcredit to SAT's clientele, household incomes increased on average by 157% for the period August 1994–July 1997. Mosley (2001) and (Copestake et al., 2001) assessed the impact of microloans in Bolivia and Zambia, respectively. Both found a positive impact of loans on the clients' economic situation. Mosley also found evidence for poorer clients benefiting less because they prefer low-risk and low-return investments.

Moreover, concerns with gender in microfinance programmes are motivated by the observation that women tend to be more reliable borrowers than men, with much lower probabilities of delinquency, and that women may allocate resources differently from their spouses (Wood and Sharif, 1997). Studies show that when women are given greater autonomy over their lives and the lives of their children, living conditions invariably improve. This is mostly because women are most apt to use household income to better the nutrition and educational opportunities of their children (Grasmuck and Espinal, 2000).

Pitt and Khandker (1998) interpreted the finding that loans to women have higher marginal impacts than loans to men as an indication of a lack of fungibility of capital and income. But since loans to males are larger on average, the difference can also be explained by the standard theory of declining marginal returns to capital. Although the average loan sizes in Pitt and Khandker (1998) showed females with much higher average borrowings (e.g., women borrowed 956 takas from Grameen versus 374 takas borrowed by men), the average is for the entire sample with zeroes included for non-borrowers. Hulme and Mosley (1996) stated that microfinance projects could reduce the isolation of women as when they come together in groups, they have an opportunity to share information, discuss ideas and develop bonds. From studies of the Grameen Bank and BRAC, the authors showed that clients of these programmes suffered from significantly fewer beatings from their husbands than they did before they joined the MFI. However, in a separate study of a BRAC project, Chowdhury and Bhuiya (2004) found that violence against women increased when women joined the programme, as not all men were ready to accept the change in power relations, and so resorted to violence to express their anger. However, this violence decreased over time. The study found that when the violence did rise, the increased awareness made victims report back to the group on their marital life and they got support in diverse ways.

Additionally, Sachs (2005), on a visit to a BRAC project, was amazed to find that women he spoke to had only one or two children when he was expecting them to have five or six as he had become accustomed to for Bangladeshi women. When he asked those with no or one child how many children they would like to have, the majority replied two. He called this a 'demonstration of a change of outlook' and a new spirit of women's rights, independence and empowerment. On women clients and groups, Osmani (1998) analysed the impact of credit on the well-being of Grameen Bank women clients. The project was found to have increased their autonomy in that they were able to spend family income more freely than non-clients. They had greater control over family planning. However, the project was not shown to have had an impact on clients' control over other decision-making even though they were found to have greater access to household resources than non-clients. However, Johnson (2004) states that having women as key participants in microfinance projects does not automatically lead to empowerment. Sometimes negative impacts such as increased workloads, increased domestic violence and abuse can be witnessed.

On enterprise profits, McKernan (2002) and Madajewicz (1999) analysed the impact of participation in microfinance programmes and found significant impacts, with profits increasing by roughly 175% for participants. Madajewicz focused on the distinction of group loans versus individual loans on enterprise profits and found that when compared to individual loans, group loans from the Grameen Bank increase profits by 8% for households with no land and less for wealthier households. That is, wealthier households benefit more from individual loans than from group loans. Coleman (2006) analysed a microfinance programme in Northeast Thailand and after correcting for selection bias, he found that the impact of microfinance institutions on household wealth was either not significant or negative. He attributed the negative impact to the small size of the loans. Being too small for investment, the loans were used for consumption, and households turned to moneylenders to finance the repayments, leading to a vicious cycle of poverty. Distinguishing between wealthy and poor clients, it was observed that only the wealthy clients benefited from the loans. The results by Coleman (2006) and Madajewicz (1999) showed the influence of wealth. The authors found negative or insignificant effects but considering averages, there were significant positive effects for groups with high wealth (Coleman, 2001) and those groups with individual loans or low wealth (Madajewicz, 1999).

The next chapter examine the state of financial services and financial inclusion in the case study country, Ghana.

4

THE STATE OF FINANCIAL SERVICES AND FINANCIAL INCLUSION IN GHANA

4.1 Introduction

This chapter focuses on the assessment of the evolution of the microfinance landscape in the Northern Savannah of Ghana in the context of the broader financial sector developments. The assessment covers the period before, during and after Ghana's independence from Great Britain. Descriptive statistics are mostly used for the analysis and presented in tables. The chapter explores how the broader development of the financial system of Ghana is conditioned by the evolution of the social, political, economic and institutional frameworks, precipitating its current state, with a special focus on the Northern Savannah of Ghana. The dialectic method embedded within the Microfinance Livelisystem Framework aided the presentation of the evolution of financial services in general and the contextualization of microfinance landscape in particular in the Northern Savannah of Ghana.

The assessment draws on archival records and surveys of government ministries, departments and agencies such as the National Development Planning Authority, the Ministry of Finance and Economic Planning, the Bank of Ghana and the Ghana Statistical Services, among others. Reports of programmes and projects carried out by bilateral and multilateral development agencies such as the world bank (WB), the international monetary fund (IMF) and international fund for food and agriculture (IFAD), private sector actors, scholarly journals and articles based on the financial system of Ghana were reviewed and data and information obtained and used. While Section 4.2 presents the study country context in terms of geography, climate and population and a short history of the Northern Savannah of Ghana, Section 4.3 explores the evolution of Ghana's financial sector and financial inclusion from its pre-independence stage to its present post-independence state. The dialectic method was particularly employed in this section. Also, while Section 4.4 focuses on the contemporary state of

DOI: 10.4324/9781003318873-4

financial services and financial inclusion in Ghana, Section 4.5 summarizes and concludes the chapter.

4.2 The Study Country Context

This section provides the Ghanaian context under which the study was carried out (Map 4.1). While Section 4.2.1 presents the geography, climatic conditions and population structure, Section 4.2.2 explores the political economy of the Northern Savannah of Ghana briefly. However, Section 4.2.3 focuses on the historical context of the Northern Savannah of Ghana.

4.2.1 Geography, Climate and Population of Ghana

As shown in Map 4.1, Ghana is situated on the West Coast of Africa, with a total land area of 238,540 km^2. Politically and administratively divided into ten regions, Ghana shares borders with Côte d'Ivoire to the west, Burkina Faso to the north and Togo to the east. To the south are the Gulf of Guinea and the Atlantic

MAP 4.1 Map of Ghana within Sub-Saharan Africa.

MAP 4.1 continued

Ocean. Ghana's 2020 population is estimated at 31,072,940, equivalent to 0.4% of the total world population (UNFPA, 2020). The population density in Ghana is 137 per km^2 (354 people per mi^2).

The five distinct geographical regions include the low plains, the Ashanti uplands, the Akwapim-Togo range, the Volta Basin, and the Northern and North-Western high plains. The five geographical regions are further classified into six agro-ecological zones based on climate, soil types and vegetation cover. From the northern part of the country to the southern part, these agro-ecological zones include the Sudan savannah, the Guinea savannah, the transition zone, the semi-deciduous forest, the rain forest and the coastal Savannah. The climate is tropical, and temperature varies with the seasons and elevation above sea level. The forest, transitional and coastal zones experience bimodal rainfall patterns. However, across the Sudan and Guinea savannah, rainfall is unimodal and unreliable. Complete crop failures are commonly experienced once in every five or three years. Annual rainfall ranges from about 1,100 mm (about 43 in) in the north to about 2,100 mm (about 83 in) in the southeast. The country's population is approximate 28 million (2015), with a density of 116.3 people per km^2 as of April 2016 (UN, 2016). The total dependency ratio is 66.7%, made up of 60.8% and 5.9% for children and the aged, respectively (UN Statistics Division, 2016), while total life expectancy (both sexes) at birth stands at 61 years which is below the global average of 71 years. The literacy rate is above the region's average at 76.67% of the adult population (aged 15 years and above).

4.2.2 Overview of the Political Economy of Ghana

According to the World Bank, Ghana's annual economic growth continued on a strong path at 6.3% in 2018, although at a slower pace than the 8.1% in 2017. This trend was led largely by strong growth in mining, petroleum, agriculture, and sustained expansion in forestry and logging. Non-oil GDP reached a strong 6.5% growth in 2018. The fourth edition of the Ghana Economic Update of the World Bank that focused on financial sector development and financial inclusion notes that universal financial access is an achievable target in Ghana if innovative technology and approaches are deployed. The government must, therefore, continue to lead the implementation of its financial inclusion strategy over the medium term, and stepping up effective domestic resource mobilization will ensure that gains on fiscal consolidation remain robust.

Ghana's economic growth was projected to close the year 2019 at 7.6%, driven by both the oil and non-oil sectors. Policy interventions in agriculture and industry are expected to revitalize the other productive sectors, leading to accelerated growth in the non-oil sector (Bank, 2018). There is also the need to invest Ghana's current natural resource wealth in non-natural resource sectors for sustainable growth in the medium to long term.

The government sustained its fiscal consolidation efforts in 2018 despite shortfalls in revenue that likely impacted the slower fiscal consolidation in 2019. However, the overall outlook will likely remain intact over the medium term (World Bank, 2019). Weaknesses in the financial sector over the past decades have resulted in the government closing nine domestically owned universal banks between 2017 and 2018. Providing substantial financial support to cover the gap between the liabilities and the assets of these collapsed banks has further closed the fiscal space for the government. Specific recommendations from the World Bank to enhance financial inclusion in Ghana include the digitization of government payments and utilities, the linking of the informal financial service delivery channels to those of the formal providers, the promotion of agent banking and other low-cost models that increases the footprint of financial services countrywide, and improvements in financial capability via financial literacy programmes to equip consumers with the information needed to identify the benefits and risks associated with the uptake of financial products and services. These are all but very limited in the Northern Savannah of Ghana.

4.2.3 A Short History of the Northern Savannah of Ghana

The section presents the historical and colonial legacies that have shaped and continue to shape the current state of development of the Northern Savannah of Ghana. First, the Anglo-French Treaty of June 1898 ended the hostile competition in the area and delimited their respective spheres of influence. The Gold Coast Order-in-Council passed on 26 September 1901 annexed the Northern Territories as a British Protectorate, and its legal status was defined and established during the Northern Territories Order-in-Council in the same year of 1901.

The British colonial development policy towards the northern territories and the nature of the financial sector in pre-independent Ghana continue to shape the microfinance landscape in north-eastern Ghana. The migration of people from northern to southern Ghana was a common phenomenon before the arrival of the colonialist (Hart, 1971; Cleveland, 1991). However, the colonial administration's active labour policies including the use of forced and indentured labour initially promoted the outward migration of labour from the Northern Territories to the southern part of the country (Thomas, 1973). The general neglect of infrastructural development for promoting education, health and transport sectors continues to 'push labour' out of the area and the current phenomenon of Kayayei, where young adolescent girls migrate to the commercial centres in the southern parts of Ghana, has its roots in these colonial policies. According to the land use and spatial development authority (LUSPA) 2015 report, life-time out migrants from the Upper West Region represented 37% of its population in 2010. That of the Upper East was close to a third (32%) and under a fifth (17%) for the Northern Region. These factors, coupled with low levels of in-migration, meant the figures represented a net out-migration from the area, mostly to southern Ghana.

Four factors during colonial rule exacerbated the under-development of the Northern Territory. First, primary commodities from the Ashantis were redirected to the coast for export. This annihilated profitable trade routes with western Sudan and, therefore, the 'middleman' of the Northern Territory. Second, the colonial government deliberately scrapped tolls on cattle caravans and kola nuts in 1908, two important sources of revenue for the area. Third, there were conscious policy directives by the British administration in luring young men to the South to work in the mines (Dickson, 1968). In 1914, it was estimated that 3,800 Northern Territory migrants were working in these gold mines (Lentz, 2006). Those who worked on the cocoa farms were even more extensive. Finally, the British imperialist cost-saving policy that dictated that the inhabitants of the Northern Territories be given limited and marginalized formal education just enough to support the 'native administration' was a major contributory factor. One chief commissioner of the colonial state put it well when he declared that only "a few crumbs from this feast of instruction", that is, from the educational activities of the colonial government and the various missions in the South, "might well be spared for the children of this Dependency" (Bening,

1971; Bening, 1990; Songsore and Denkabe, 1995). These colonial policies culminated in what Plange (1979, p. 659) pointed out that "relatively self-sufficient peasants and traders were rapidly transformed into unskilled wage labourers in the mines, in public works, and in various expatriate enterprises in the eastern, central, and southern regions of the country".

This section concludes that these historical narratives, among others, continued to undermine the development of the Northern Savannah of Ghana and helped to situate its current development context within the contemporary political economy of Ghana. This hypothesis is supported by the high levels of poverty still pervasive in the Northern Savannah today. Thus, notwithstanding the significant gains in poverty reduction in recent decades, the persistently high levels of poverty in the region compared to the national averages and other parts of the country have historical and colonial antecedences. The next section focuses on the evolution of the microfinance industry and financial inclusion in the Northern Savannah of Ghana.

4.3 Ghana's Financial Sector Evolution and Financial Inclusion: The Pre- and Post-independence Eras

This section presents the evolution of the microfinance sub-sector within the financial eco-system of Ghana, with emphasis on the Northern Savannah using the dialectic method (Kane, 1977). The dialectic model is embedded in the Microfinance Livelisystem Framework conceptualized by the author and presented in Chapter 2 (Figure 2.1). It assessed the past development policies and programmes of the government that underpin the current state of the microfinance landscape in the Northern Savannah of Ghana. With the dialectic model, the microfinance industry at any point in time is presented as an outcome of the transformation of a pre-existing, less functional industry – the thesis – into an improved and more functional system – the anti-thesis. The clash of the thesis and anti-thesis then produces synthesis and the microfinance industry experiences progress in deepening financial inclusion within the constraining goals of financial sustainability and greater outreach. It is worth noting that this process is continued with the resulting synthesis becoming the next thesis, which in turn results in the anti-thesis when untenable features develop, which necessitates further change, and the process thus repeats itself.

The section proposes that the microfinance landscape of the Northern Savannah of Ghana mirrors developments in the broader financial sector eco-system in Ghana. These developments are often reactionary, spanning several epochs, each mutating into the next through the interaction of embedded and opposing emergent factors. This section, therefore, concludes that the microfinance industry of the Northern Savannah of Ghana has not been markedly different from Ghana's economic growth and financial development trajectories. Table 4.1 presents the major reform eras of the financial system of Ghana, aimed at deepening the financial sector as well as increasing financial inclusion.

TABLE 4.1 Major Reform Eras and Key Microfinance Initiatives (Policies and Programmes) in Ghana

Reform Era (the Thesis)	*Characteristics (Untenable Features – the Anti-thesis)*	*Major Financial Sector Initiatives (Policies and Programmes) (the New Thesis)*	*Goals/Objective(s)*	*Major Microcredit/Microfinance Initiatives (Programmes/Policies)*
Colonial Era (up to 1957)	Limited banking services; banks controlled from Metropolitan London; exclusion of indigenes; agitation for an inclusive financial sector	Establishment of a national bank (BoG) to operate on a commercial basis; maintain government accounts and float bonds	Increase financial inclusion	Post office savings bank (POSB) established in 1905 to provide deposit services for small savers Cooperative Bank also established in 1935 engaged in thrift and credit activities, mostly with cocoa farmers and their cooperatives
Centrally Planned Economic Era (1957–1983)	State-sponsored development of the financial sector; inefficient banks; financial repression; overconcentration sectorally and spatially	State controlled; new banks established; development banking commences; interest rate ceilings; and sectoral credit ceilings in place	Develop the financial sector to drive industrialization for economic growth and development	Agricultural Credit and Cooperative Bank, established in pursuance of the Agricultural Credit and Cooperative Act 1965 (Act 286); the Bank of the Gold Coast was renamed Ghana Commercial Bank to undertake commercial banking activities; the Social Security Bank (Nussbaum) – established in 1977 to improve access to financial services for workers; The Post Office Savings Bank, reorganized and renamed the national savings and credit bank (NSCB) in 1975; Ghana Cooperative Bank founded in 1975 had the explicit objective of expanding cooperative banking services; the introduction of rural banking in 1976 led to the setting up of rural and community banks (RCBs) to provide basic banking services in rural and hard-to-reach areas upper region agricultural development project (URADEP) (1976/77–1980/81)

The Era of Structural Adjustment Programmes, Economic and Financial Sector Liberalization and Banking Reforms (1983–2001)	Bank-dominated economy; absence of money and capital markets; weak non-bank financial sub-sector; dysfunctionally distressed banking system; prevalence of illiquidity and insolvencies in the banking sector; credit rationing; interest rate control	Introduction of the economic recovery programme (ERP); financial sector adjustment programme (FINSAP) which included the financial sector adjustment credit (FINSAC 1 and FINSAC 2 from 1988 to 1997); the non-bank financial institutions (NBFI) Project	Restructure financially distressed banks; improve the regulatory and supervisory framework; develop liberalized money and capital markets; improve savings; and promote non-bank financial institutions	The Social Investment Fund Project (SIF) (1998–to date); IFAD Land Conservation and Smallholder Farmer Project (LACOSREP) (1990–1996); IFAD Upper West Agricultural Development Project (UWADEP) (1995–2005)
Post ERP, Liberalization Reforms (2003–2019)	Macro-economic and financial sector eco-system divergence, high inflation and interest rates; uncertainty and market volatility; the lack of credit information system; and lack of long-term debt markets; poor corporate governance; poor risk management practices; shady related party transactions; poor regulatory regime; non-compliance with prudential guidelines; poor supervisory regimes; undercapitalization	Financial sector strategic plan (FINSSP 1 and FINSSP 2) National financial inclusion and development strategy (NFIDS) (2017-2023) have	promote a balanced financial eco-system that fully integrates the bank and non-bank sub-sectors; ensure financial stability; improve access, quality and usage; improve financial infrastructure; consumer protection and capability	The microfinance and small loan centre (MASLOC) (2006-to date); Northern Region Poverty Reduction Programme (2001–2009); Livelihood Empowerment against Poverty (2008–to date); A Tiered Regulatory Environment (2011–to date); Rural Enterprises Programme (Crépon et al., 2011) (2011–2019); The rural financial services project (RAFiP) (2010–2016); rural finance support project (RFSP)(2002–2008); Northern Rural Growth Programme (2007–2015); IFAD Ghana agriculture sector investment programme (GASIP) (2014–2020); IFAD adaptation for smallholder agriculture programme (ASAP) (2012–to date); financing Ghanaian agriculture project (USAID-FinGAP); The support programme for enterprise empowerment and development (SPEED I and SPEED II) (October 2006–June, 2010); Ghana private sector development facility (GPSDF) Phase I:-2004–2007 Phase II: 2007–2008); A Tiered Regulatory Environment (2011–to date)

Source: https://datatopics.worldbank.org/financialinclusion/country/ghana.

1 The dialectic was first espoused by the German Philosopher Hegel in Science of Logic first published in German (1812–16). Originally used as a method of reasoning, the dialectics has been applied in the study of how societies and institutions evolve as in Karl Marx's dialectical materialism. Kane (1977) was the first to seminally apply the dialectics in analysing financial sector development.

Table 4.1 presents the various reform eras of Ghana's financial sector; the characteristics necessitating the reforms; the policies, programmes and institutional reforms undertaken; the goals and objectives of each reform era; and the major microcredit and/or microfinance initiatives aimed at increasing the financial inclusion of the country's productive poor. Other development initiatives that had microcredit programmes mainstreamed to promote rural financial market development and economic activities are also presented. Like many African countries, Ghana's financial sector has gone through several epochs of transformations (Ackah and Asiamah, 2016). Several processes, policies and measures continue to be put in place to improve the regulatory framework and the strengthening of supervision for the efficiency and profitability of the banks in the country (Wampah, 2015; Obeng and Sakyi, 2017).

In the late 19th century, the colonial era financial system was characterized by limited financial services that largely excluded indigenous populations. This resulted in agitation for greater financial inclusion and the first-ever financial sector reforms including the establishment of the Bank of the Gold Coast under the Bank of Ghana (BoG) ordinance in 1952. After independence in 1957, the government focused on expanding a development-oriented financial system aimed at driving industrialization, economic growth and development.

However, the domestic political climate, coupled with internal and external economic forces, resulted in a government dominated by an inefficient and dysfunctional financial system that was characterized by low profitability, high non-performing assets, inadequate liquidity and capital reserves, obsolete technology and the absence of competition (Brownbridge and Gockel, 1996; Antwi-Asare and Addison, 2000). Innovation stagnated as a result of poor governance structures (Thompson, 2015; Ackah and Asiamah, 2016). Credit decisions were not based on commercial interest and the repressed, inefficient and over-concentrated financial system became the anti-thesis that heralded reforms that saw distressed banks being restructured, the regulatory and supervisory frameworks improved, the liberalization of the money and capital markets, increases in the mobilization of domestic deposits and the promotion of the role of non-bank financial institutions (Brownbridge and Gockel, 1996). These reforms aligned the Ghanaian economy with emerging global financial developments and broader macroeconomic policies of the country. However, the establishment of the post office savings bank (POSB) in 1905 initially provided deposit services for small savers. Moreover, the Cooperative Bank established in 1935 also engaged in thrift and credit activities, mostly with cocoa farmers and cooperative societies that borrowed on a short-term seasonal basis to finance members' production, storage and processing. Sales of these seasonal commodities repaid contracted loans. Medium- or long-term loans were not easily made available, while the women-dominated agro-processing and trade sectors were most disadvantaged in access to formal credit.

The first post-independence Ghana's financial sector reforms were necessitated by the Economic Recovery Programmes introduced in the 1980s. This was the financial sector adjustment programme (FINSAP) implemented between 1988 and 1997. FINSAP led to a restructured financial sector with regulatory frameworks that rescued distressed banks and other financial institutions from collapse by ensuring improvement in deposit mobilization, the efficient allocation of credit, the development of the money and capital markets and the removal of distortionary market policies (World Bank, 1997). These reforms deepened financial intermediation as well as the development of non-bank financial institutions under the non-bank financial institution (NBFI) Assistance Project (1996–2002) that targeted the resolution of the challenges of the Bank of Ghana, the Ghana stock exchange (GSE), the Ghana Reinsurance industry, the then securities and regulatory commission (SRC), the state insurance company (SIC) and the social security and national insurance trust (SNITT) and further facilitated their integration and relevance to the broader financial sector eco-system. During this era, several development programmes with credit facilities were introduced to the Northern Savannah, including the social investment fund project (SIF), the IFAD land conservation and smallholder rehabilitation (LACOSREP) and the IFAD upper west agricultural development project (UWADEP) (see Appendix I).

Recognizing that the development and improvement of the rural sector's productivity and competitiveness was central to growth and poverty reduction, the 2001 Ghana Poverty Reduction Strategy Papers, which were based mostly on the accelerated long-term growth and poverty reduction of the Vision 2020 Plan, included rural financial intermediation as central to deepening outreach and expanding services in the rural economy. Thus, the entry of Ghana into the highly indebted poor countries initiative (HIPC), the passage of the new Bank of Ghana Act, 2002 (Act, 612), the amendments of the Securities Industry Law, the restructuring of Ghana's domestic debt and the establishment of the National Bond Market Committee all necessitated an overall review of the financial sector in consonance with these developments. While it was acknowledged that the narrow focus of both the financial sector adjustment programme (FINSAP) and the non-bank financial institution (NBFI) project created many other imbalances in the financial system, the financial sector strategic plan (FINSSP) launched in 2003 promoted a balanced financial system that integrated the activities of the bank and non-bank financial sub-sectors. FINSSP was thought of as comprehensive and futuristic in its consideration of possible linkages and synergies in the overall financial eco-system. Reforms brought in by FINSSP further deepened financial intermediation and integrated the domestic economy with global financial markets that have since spurred economic growth and development. The policies and programmes on microfinance and financial inclusion that were rolled out during this era, some with development partners, included the following: the microfinance and small loan centre (MASLOC), the Northern Region Poverty Reduction Programme, the livelihood empowerment against poverty (LEAP), the rural financial services project (RAFiP), the rural finance support project (RFSP), the Northern Rural Growth Programme and the Rural Enterprises

Programme (Crépon et al.). The rest were the IFAD Ghana agriculture sector investment programme (GASIP), IFAD adaptation for smallholder agriculture programme (ASAP), financing Ghanaian agriculture project (USAID-FinGAP), support programme for enterprise empowerment and development (SPEED I and SPEED II), Ghana private sector development facility (GPSDF I and II) and a tiered regulatory framework for the microfinance sub-sector (see Appendix I).

However, the fundamental factors restraining broader financial inclusion remain prevalent with substantial inefficiencies in savings mobilization and allocation of resources to the real sectors by the financial system (Senbet and Otchere, 2006; Nampewo et al., 2013). Also, commercial banks generally had no proven methodologies for financing the poor due to high transaction costs and risks (Aryeetey and Nissanke, 1998; Opare, 2001). Thus far, Ghana's financial system, like many other sub-Saharan African countries, remains liberalized with institutional and market reforms positively supporting economic growth (Moyo et al., 2014). Reforms have also enabled the integration of global financial markets with substantial flows (Senbet and Otchere, 2006). The numbers of financial services institutions have also increased substantially, and increased competition and improved efficiency have increased accordingly (PWC, 2016). Moreover, the government's draft national financial inclusion and development strategy (NFIDS) (2017–2023) has outlined a series of necessary further reforms that are structured around five key mutually reinforcing priorities including financial stability; access, quality and usage of financial services; financial infrastructure; financial consumer protection and financial capability aimed at sustainable financial inclusion and development.

Moreover, a comprehensive asset quality review (AQR) by the Bank of Ghana in 2015 and updated in 2016 revealed that over the years several legacy problems had plagued the banking sector including macro-economic factors, poor corporate governance and risk management practices, shady related party transactions, regulatory non-compliance, and poor supervision (including questionable licencing processes and enforcement shortfalls). This has led to a significant build-up of vulnerabilities within the financial system itself and the economy at large. These vulnerabilities include deteriorated asset quality, substantial loan loss provisioning shortfalls, declined credit to the private sector and higher lending rates and spreads (BoG, 2018). Thus, using the newly promulgated Banks and Specialize Deposit-Taking Institutions Act, 2016 (Act 930), the BoG under the current NPP administration increased the capital adequacy requirements to ¢400 million for commercial banks. The reasons given by the BoG for the increase in the minimum capital requirements were to ensure a stable financial sector, reduce costs to banks and clients through an economy of scale, a diversified investment portfolio, more resilient banking sector capable of absorbing shocks in a growing economy, easing the burden of supervision requirements by the BoG and the consolidation of the banking industry, through sustainable mergers and acquisitions, stronger corporate governance structures, and risk management systems and practices (BoG, 2017). So far, 16 banks have successfully met the minimum paid-up capital requirement and nine had their licences revoked due to insolvency and were forced into mergers and acquisitions with the creation of the Consolidated Bank Ghana Limited. There are now 23 banks, down from 32 after the new minimum capital adequacy directive and the financial sector clean-up. Government indebtedness to some of the failed banks was cited as a major cause of the collapse of the banks. Some of the accusations included political interference in the work of the BoG, which emanated from the lack of due diligence in the licencing and supervision of the banking sector.

The securities and exchange commission (SEC) also revoked the licences of 53 fund management companies in pursuant of Section 122 (2) (b) of the Securities Industry Act, 2016 (Act 929). The SEC accused the fund management companies of failing to return client funds that remained locked up and, in some cases, had even folded up operations. According to the SEC, its action was to protect investors and the integrity of the capital market as the companies failed to perform their functions efficiently, honestly and fairly and in some cases are continuing to breach relevant securities laws, rules or conditions, despite space provided them to resolve all regulatory breaches.

The problems witnessed in the broader financial sector (Chapter 3, Section 3.4) were also reflected in the microfinance sub-sector, comprising seven groupings of organizational types broadly classified into three: formal, semi-formal and informal. Over the same period, most MFIs also witnessed highly impaired capital adequacy ratios, low asset quality and liquidity challenges (BoG, 2018).

After the promulgation of the Non-Bank Financial Institution Act, 2008 (Act 774) and the rapid growth of the microfinance industry into the late 2000s, the Bank of Ghana deemed it necessary to introduce a licencing regime for the industry. Existing microfinance institutions hitherto without licences from the BoG were roped into the new licencing regime introduced in 2011. Following the repeal of the Banking Act of 2004 (Act 673), these microfinance institutions were re-licenced, and many others issued licences. By the end of 2015, approximately 484 microfinance institutions had been licenced by the Bank of Ghana (BoG). However, off-site reviews and on-site examinations of these 484 microfinance institutions as early as 2014 revealed signs of distress resulting from severe undercapitalization, high cost of operations, inordinate losses from poor lending and investment practices, diversion of customer deposits into unprofitable and speculative ventures, poor corporate governance, non-compliance with prudential guidelines, weak internal controls and fraud, among others. Efforts by the Bank of Ghana to have these affected institutions and their shareholders and directors to diffuse the identified deficiencies and vulnerabilities yielded no positive result. This placed a substantial number of depositors' funds at risk. Many had their financial position deteriorated to the point of insolvency. Many others ceased operations. Yet others closed their outlets with depositors' funds locked up, while some had their offices open but could not pay depositors. By 2015, more than hundred microfinance companies folded up due to mismanagement of funds and other irregularities (Appiah-Konadu et al., 2016).

According to the Bank of Ghana, of a total of 566 licenced microfinance institutions as at the end of the second quarter of 2018, 211 were active but distressed, while others folded up altogether (BoG, 2018). Besides, there were 37 rural and community banks from a total of 141 that were distressed, while some folded up altogether. It was further estimated that of an overall total of 707 institutions that made up the sub-sector, 272 (38.5%) were at risk with a combined monetary value of about GH¢740.5 million. In percentage terms, total industry deposits under distress consisted of 8.81% contribution from RCBs and 52.49% from all other MFIs (BoG, 2018). Thirty other microfinance companies were dragged to court by the Bank of Ghana (BoG) and investigated by the economic and organized crimes office (EOCO) for alleged embezzlement and fraud (*ibid*).

The Bank of Ghana, in a bid to address the liquidity crises of the microfinance sub-sector and indeed the broader financial eco-system, directed all financial institutions to recapitalize to a higher minimum capital requirement towards the end of 2018. For the Tier 1 MFIs comprising Savings and Loans (S&L) companies and rural and community banks (RCBs), the new minimum capital requirement was set at GH¢15 million and GH¢1 million, respectively. It was GH¢2 million for the Tier 2 MFIs (deposit-taking microfinance companies). For the Tier 3 MFIs (non-deposit–taking money lending companies and financial non-governmental organizations (FNGOs)), it was set at GH¢2 million and GH¢300,000, respectively. There were no minimum capital requirements for the Tier 4 MFIs (individual moneylenders and Susu collectors). These could self-regulate exclusively via their apex bodies that are, in turn, supervised by the Bank of Ghana (BoG).

In the directive, the Board of Directors were responsible for the banks meeting the new capital requirements as per the Banks and Specialized Deposit-Taking Institutions Act, 2016 (Act 930). Three options were made available for these financial institutions to recapitalize, which included the issuance of ordinary shares, the use of income surplus or retained earnings as statutory reserves (i.e., the amount of money that a bank must hold to remain solvent and attain partial protection against a substantial investment loss). The capacity of the regulator (the BoG) to adequately regulate, supervise and monitor the many and diverse financial institutions operating within the financial eco-system remains questionable. As the principal regulator, the Bank of Ghana's (BoG) initial position was that the activities of MFIs were relatively insignificant and posed no potential systemic risk (Belnye, 2011).

There was, therefore, the need to sanitize the microfinance sub-sector by the orderly resolution of the failed institutions under Sections 123–137 of Act 930. It is in the light of the above that the approval of a US$30 million International Development Association (Hollis and Sweetman, 1998) facility by the World Bank to the Government of Ghana on 20 September 2018 in support of the Ghana financial sector development project (GFSDP) is important. As a key component of the World Bank Group's comprehensive portfolio supporting financial stability, financial inclusion and private sector competitiveness, the goals of the project include improving financial sector regulatory oversight and market transparency and discipline, increasing the outreach of RCBs and MFIs and linking VSLAs to the formal financial sector, bolstering financial capability and consumer protection, and enhancing the capacity for the implementation and monitoring of financial sector policies.

Regulatory bodies are expected to be strengthened to help build confidence in the financial sector, and the microfinance sub-sector to benefit from savings mobilization and financing of investments. Educational campaigns would enable consumers to understand their rights and be equipped with the requisite skills and knowledge to make informed choices on the financial services landscape. Rural and community banks will be supported to expand financial services in rural areas and the underserved segments of the Ghanaian population.

On 31 May 2019, the Bank of Ghana (BoG) revoked the licences of 192 insolvent microfinance institutions and another 155 insolvent microfinance companies that had already ceased operations. The action of the BoG was taken in pursuance of Section 123 of the Banks and Specialized Deposit-Taking Institutions Act, 2016 (Act 930). The Act requires the BoG to revoke the licence of any bank or specialized deposit-taking institution (SDI) if it establishes insolvency or likely insolvency on the part of the institution within the next 60 days. In line with Section 123(2) of Act 930, a receiver was appointed to transition the institutions that had their licences revoked. In so doing, the BoG hopes to minimize, if not eliminate, the threat to the stability of the financial system and protect depositors by insolvent and dormant institutions with no reasonable prospects of rehabilitation. Funds were made available by the Government of Ghana that enabled the Receiver to pay depositors, following the validation of claims. It is worth noting that the hierarchy of creditor claims set out under Act 930 stipulated that the Receiver settles other creditors of these failed institutions that had their licences revoked upon the validation of their claims and to the extent to which the Receiver realizes value from the remaining assets of the institutions.

Moreover, on 16 August 2019, the comprehensive assessment of the savings and loans and finance house sub-sectors by the BoG led to the revocation of the licences of 15 savings and loans companies and eight finance houses and a road map was announced for their orderly resolution per Sections 123–137 of Act 930. Reasons for the revocation of the licences included highly impaired capital adequacy ratios that violated the minimum regulatory capital required by Act 930, posing risks to depositors and other direct and indirect counterparties; excessive risk-taken without the required risk management function to manage them; the use of depositors' funds to finance non-commercial personal or related-party projects or businesses, compounding their liquidity challenges; weak corporate governance leading to poor accountability and overrides of internal controls; creative accounting practices and under-provisioning for impaired assets; persistent regulatory breaches, involving non-compliance with prudential rules; and failure to implement on-site examination recommendations by the Bank of

Ghana (BoG). The regulator further stated that its efforts to get the shareholders and directors of the affected institutions to put in remedial actions, especially the significant capital deficiencies, yielded no positive results.

Overall, the BoG had revoked the licences of nine universal banks, 347 microfinance companies (of which 155 had already ceased operations), 39 micro-credit companies/moneylenders (ten of which had already ceased operations), 15 savings and loans companies, eight finance house companies and two non-bank financial institutions that had already ceased operations. To ensure that the remaining institutions remain resilient, the Bank of Ghana committed to proactive vigilance, intensification of on-site examinations and enforced compliance with statutory, prudential and other requirements. The regulator also said it would move in to quickly resolve identified early warning signs of distress and work in collaboration with the ARB Apex Bank to reposition the rural and community banking sector to better support rural economic development. The launch of the Ghana Deposit Protection Scheme in September 2019 will serve as a conduit to further strengthen the protection of depositors in Ghana. Currently, a total of 137 microfinance companies are active and the BoG has put in place measures to ensure they remain safe and sound by complying with relevant prudential regulations and norms. These include a comprehensive review of licencing and supervisory policies and directives; reviewing the minimum capital requirements for microfinance companies and encouraging possible consolidation through voluntary mergers and acquisitions; the introduction of proportional corporate governance, fit and proper, and risk management directives; strict supervision of licenced institutions and enforcement of relevant regulatory requirements; and an increase in the resources available for effective supervision of all licenced microfinance institutions.

Table 4.2 presents a summary report of Ghana's Financial Inclusion Index by the World Bank Global Financial Index compared to other lower middle-income countries and that of sub-Saharan Africa. It showed that account ownership for all adults aged 15+ years stands at approximately 58% in 2017 (up from 40.7% in 2014 and 29% in 2011) and that was on par with the lower middle-income countries and 18 percentage points higher than the average for sub-Saharan Africa. Financial institutional account ownership is also trending upwards at 42.3% in 2017, up from 34.6% in 2014. Though higher than the sub-Saharan average of 33%, it was lower than the 56% average for lower middle-income countries. Mobile money usage also saw an increase to 39% in 2017 from a low of 13% in 2014. Approximately half of the adult population of women, those in the bottom poorest 40%, those out of the labour force and those living in the rural areas, own an account and 49.5% carried out digital payments in 2017 from a low of 25% in 2014.

However, savings in financial institutions dropped to 16.2 from a high of 18.6 in 2014. This was still higher than the sub-Saharan African average of 14.9%, down from 15.8%, but compared favourably with an upwardly trending average of 15.9% of the lower middle-income countries. The financial sector clean-up

TABLE 4.2 Financial Inclusion Indicators of Ghana 2014 versus 2017 (Findex Report, 2017)

Sub-Saharan Africa			*Lower Middle Income*
Population, Age 15+ (Millions)	*17.3*	*GNI per Capita ($)*	*1,380*
	Ghana Country Data	*Sub-Saharan Africa Average*	*Lower Middle Income*
Account (% age 15+)			
All adults, 2017	57.7	42.6	57.8
All adults, 2014	40.5	34.2	41.9
All adults, 2011	29.4	23.2	28.9
Financial institution account (% age 15+)			
All adults, 2017	42.3	32.8	56.1
All adults, 2014	34.6	28.8	40.6
All adults, 2011	29.4	23.2	28.9
Mobile money account (% age 15+)			
All adults, 2017	38.9	20.9	5.3
All adults, 2014	13.0	11.6	3.2
Account, by individual characteristics (% age 15+) 2017			
Women	53.7	36.9	53.0
Adults belonging to the poorest 40%	48.3	31.9	50.7
Adults out of the labour force	48.4	31.4	50.8
Adults living in rural areas	52.5	39.5	57.6
Digital payments in the past year (% age 15+)			
Made or received digital payments, 2017	49.5	34.4	29.2
Made or received digital payments, 2014	25.1	26.9	19.7
Used an account to pay utility bills	8.6	7.7	7.5
Used an account to receive private sector wages	9.0	5.7	5.5
Used an account to receive government payments	10.8	7.3	8.3
Used the internet to pay bills or to buy something online	7.8	7.6	6.8
Used a mobile phone or the internet to access an account	35.5	20.8	8.3
Used a debit or credit card to make a purchase	6.3	7.5	10.0
Inactive account in the past year (% age 15+) 2017			
No deposit and no withdrawal from an account	6.7	5.5	21.6

(Continued)

TABLE 4.2 Continued

Sub-Saharan Africa			*Lower Middle Income*
Population, Age 15+ (Millions)	*17.3*	*GNI per Capita ($)*	*1,380*
	Ghana Country Data	*Sub-Saharan Africa Average*	*Lower Middle Income*
Domestic remittances in the past year (% age 15+) 2017			
Sent or received domestic remittances through an account	32.2	22.7	10.1
Sent or received domestic remittances through an OTC service	17.8	11.7	4.7
Sent or received domestic remittances through cash only	5.6	9.4	8.8
Saving in the past year (% age 15+)			
Saved at a financial institution, 2017	16.2	14.9	15.9
Saved at a financial institution, 2014	18.6	15.8	14.4
Saved using a savings club or person outside the family	19.0	25.3	13.0
Saved any money	50.2	54.4	39.7
Saved for old age	15.1	10.3	13.2
Credit in the past year (% age 15+)			
Borrowed from a financial institution or used a credit card, 2017	11.6	8.4	9.8
Borrowed from a financial institution or used a credit card, 2014	8.3	7.5	10.0
Borrowed from family or friends	22.8	31.0	30.4
Borrowed any money	40.3	45.7	42.9
Outstanding housing loan	7.5	4.7	5.0

by the regulator, the Bank of Ghana, closing more than nine banks, and the current crisis in the microfinance sub-sector, where deposits are not easily made available, probably eroded public and consumer confidence in the financial institutions, leading to this downward trend.

However, borrowings from financial institutions or the use of credit cards continued an upward trajectory from 8.3% in 2014 to 11.6% in 2017. Informal credit from mostly family and friends continues to remain an important source of credit for adult populations in Ghana, at almost 23% of the adult population.

4.4 Rural Financial Markets and Financial Inclusion of Households in Ghana

4.4.1 Introduction

This section reflects on the state of financial services and financial inclusion in Ghana, but with a focus on the Northern Savannah. Generally, rural financial markets' development and inclusion in the Northern Savannah remain limited. While Section 4.4.2 explores the available types of financial institutions in the different localities, accounts held by households and in gender terms, Section 4.4.3 presents the uptake of credit products in rural financial markets and livelihood investments. It explores households' access to credit, the sources of credit, the collateral mechanisms employed and barriers to access by locality and gender. However, Section 4.4.4 presents the uptake of savings products, reasons for households' savings and non-saving by locality as well as gender. Section 4.4.5 also presents household uptake of insurance products (both long- and short-term insurance products) by locality as well as those of non-insurance. Section 4.4.6 presents the uptake of payment services, with a special focus on mobile money. Lastly, Section 4.5 presents the summary and conclusion of the chapter.

This section draws from national survey data and reports of the Ghana Living Standards Surveys, the united nations children's fund (UNICEF) and the Ghana Poverty and Inequality Analysis, among others. While it takes a national outlook to the analysis of the uptake of financial services, it highlights these same variables as they pertain in the context of the Northern Savannah, comprising the Northern, the Savannah, the North-East, the Upper East and the Upper West regions where poverty remains relatively high. The Upper West (70.7%), the Northern, the Savannah and the North-East regions (50.4%) retain a very high incidence of poverty. However, that of the Upper East Region is marginally lower (44.4%). Compared to Greater Accra (5.6%) and Ashanti (14.8%) (Ghana Statistical Service, 2014), poverty incidence in the Northern Savannah are unimaginably high. It is worth noting that the microfinance industry in Ghana comprises seven groupings of financial institutions broadly classified into formal (rural and community banks and the savings and loans companies), semi-formal (credit unions, financial NGOs and microfinance companies) and informal (Susu companies/individuals and moneylenders) microfinance institutions. However, the drive to increase deposit mobilization has led many commercial banks operating in the area to engage in microfinance activities via special units or desks, created to carry out microfinance activities mostly with informal economic actors predominantly in the urban centres.

4.4.2 Rural Financial Markets, Gender and Livelihoods in Ghana

This section presents a snapshot of the financial institutions operating in the rural financial markets of Ghana and the disparities in service uptake by locality and gender. The types of financial institutions operating in the rural financial market include commercial banks, investment/mortgage providers, community/rural banks, savings and loans schemes, cooperative/credit unions, Susu schemes (individuals and companies) and other providers, as presented in Table 4.3. Among all the institutional types, urban households holding accounts were disproportionally higher than those from rural localities. Over 90% of urban households accounted for all investment/mortgage accounts. For households with accounts in the commercial banks, urban households held over 80%, while rural households held about 19%. Ironically, the community/rural banks, savings and loans schemes, cooperative credit unions and Susu schemes that are pro-rural in orientation had more than 50% of their account holders living in the urban centres.

These results show that even interventions such as the rural and community bank's concept aimed at increasing access to financial services in rural areas are not having the desired impact. Moreover, while Rural Coastal performed poorly in terms of households' accounts ownership across all institutional types, it was second only to the Rural Savannah. Household account ownership in the Rural Savannah was lower compared to the Rural Forests and all the urban centres. These results for the Rural Savannah potentially also masked disparities across social groups such as gender, employment type and even ethnic origins.

For example, Table 4.4 indicates that male household members held proportionally higher institutional accounts than females, both in the urban and rural localities. While men accounted for 67.8% of all checking accounts, women held only 32.2%. This pattern is repeated in almost all urban and rural localities, except the Rural Savannah, where females held higher account numbers for fixed deposits (84.9%) and E-zwich accounts (72.0%) than their male counterparts at only 15.1% for E-zwich and 28.0% for fixed deposits. This result is indicative of the dominance of women in commerce especially in the informal economy in the Rural Savannah.

However, the patriarchal nature of the social structure in much of the Rural Savannah can sometimes leave women vulnerable to exploitation by their male

TABLE 4.3 Financial Institutions and Household Account Ownership by Locality in Ghana

Financial Institutions							
Locality	*Commercial Banks*	*Investments/ Mortgages*	*Community/ Rural Banks*	*Savings and Loans Scheme*	*Cooperative/ Credit Unions*	*Susu Schemes*	*Other*
Urban	80.76	90.89	60.36	65.96	66.89	54.91	68.14
Accra	36.4	53.8	4.2	22.5	6.9	9.1	51.5
Other Urban	44.4	37.1	56.2	43.5	60.0	45.8	16.6
Rural	19.2	9.1	39.6	34.0	33.1	45.1	31.9
Rural Coastal	2.9	1.9	4.2	2.4	1.2	4.2	12.8
Rural Forest	11.4	5.3	26.4	28.2	20.6	30.9	13.2
Rural Savannah	5.0	2.0	9.0	3.5	11.3	10.0	5.9
All	100.0	100.0	100.0	100.0	100.0	100.0	100.0

Source: GLSS Main Report, 2014.

TABLE 4.4 Financial Product Uptake by Locality and Gender in Ghana

Account Type	*Urban*				*Rural*								
	Accra		*Other Urban*		*Rural Coastal*		*Rural Forest*		*Rural Savannah*		*Country-Wide*		
	Male	*Female*	*Male*	*Female*	*Male*	*Female*	*Male*	*Female*	*Male*	*Female*	*Male*	*Female*	*No.*
Current	68.2	31.8	64.3	35.7	68.1	31.9	78.0	22.0	70	30	67.8	32.2	2,243
Investment	69.2	30.8	59.8	40.2	100.0	0.0	59.8	40.2	53	47	64.6	35.4	7,138
Savings	56.3	43.7	54.6	45.4	70.6	29.4	67.0	33.0	74	26	58.6	41.4	203
Fixed deposit	62.9	37.1	51.2	48.8	46.3	53.7	61.6	38.4	15.1	84.9	53.3	46.7	58
E-zwich	55.9	44.1	50.2	49.8	0.0	0.0	61.5	38.5	28	72	50.4	49.6	37
Other	55.1	44.9	68.6	31.4	33.6	66.4	55.3	44.7	45.3	54.7	54.1	45.9	58
Total	55.4	44.6	52.3	47.7	63.1	36.9	58.5	41.5	62.1	37.9	55.1	44.9	9,737

Source: GLSS (IV) Main Report.

counterparts, hence the high percentages of female fixed deposits (85%) and E-zwich accounts (72%) in the region. Also, it is posited here that potential theft or armed robberies linked with the convenience of E-zwich usage could be the primary drivers for the higher percentages among the women in the Northern Savannah.

4.4.3 Uptake of Credit Products within Rural Financial Markets and Livelihoods in Ghana

This section presents the percentages of households accessing loan facilities by locality and explores the sources of such credit, also along with locality and gender. The broader purposes for accessing credit facilities, the modes of collateralization and the inherent barriers to accessing credit by locality and gender are further explored. Those of the Northern Savannah are emphasized.

From Table 4.5, access to credit presented a dull scene for households in the Northern Savannah of Ghana. Only about 9.9% of households in this part of the country had accessed credit in 2012/2013, according to the GLSS VI survey report (Ghana Statistical Service, 2014). This leaves almost 90% of all households in the Rural Savannah without access to any form of institutional credit. However, while an average of only 11% of all urban households across the country had accessed institutional credit during the same period, the other urban centres fared better at 13% than the GAMA at only 5%.

In general, rural households stood at only 12%, but much higher in the Rural Forest (14%) than in the Rural Savannah (10%). The poor state of loan product uptake from commercial financial institutions by households in both the urban and rural localities is indicative of a large informal economy and low levels of financial inclusion among the productive poor in Ghana.

Also, Table 4.6 presents the sources of credit for households by locality and gender in Ghana. While savings and loans companies and the private banks supplied 34% and 25% of all loans in Accra, respectively, more than one-fifth of households in the other urban centres obtained loans from savings and loans schemes (i.e., 23%) and the private banks (i.e., 22%). While private banks (24%) and Susu

TABLE 4.5 Percentage of Households Applying for Loans by Locality in Ghana

Loan Application			
Locality	*Yes (%)*	*No (%)*	*Number*
Urban	**10.9**	**89.1**	**7,44**
Accra	5.9	93.5	1,697
Other Urban	13.2	86.8	5,748
Rural	**12.0**	**88.0**	**9,327**
Rural Coastal	8.0	92.0	1,156
Rural Forest	14.1	85.9	3,863
Rural Savannah	9.9	90.1	4,308
All	**11.4**	**88.6**	**16,772**

Source: GLSS (IV) Main Report.

TABLE 4.6 Source of Loans to Households by Locality and Gender in Ghana.

Locality									
	Urban		*Rural*			*Ghana*			
Source of Loan	*Accra*	*Other Urban*	*Rural Coastal*	*Rural Forest*	*Rural Savannah*	*Male*	*Female*	*All*	*Number*
State bank	16.3	17.6	9.9	5.7	7.1	14.4	9.9	12.2	220
Private bank	24.7	21.6	24.9	15.3	9.2	20.9	16.3	18.6	318
Cooperative	6.1	7.4	0.7	5.5	4.6	5.9	6.2	6.1	117
Gov't Agency	0.9	1.5	2.3	0.5	0.4	1.4	0.7	1.0	18
NGOs	1.1	0.9	0.7	1.9	8.4	1.9	2.2	2.1	50
Business firm	2.1	0.8	1.2	1.1	1.0	1.1	1.0	1.0	20
Employer	5.0	1.6	0.0	0.4	0.3	1.4	1.2	1.3	23
Moneylender	0.7	2.4	2.8	6.6	3.3	3.5	3.9	3.7	73
Savings and loans scheme	34.3	23.4	9.4	16.3	7.1	13.2	26.0	19.6	336
Susu scheme	3.8	3.7	23.4	10.4	14.7	4.5	11.3	7.9	239
Trader	0.0	2.0	0.0	2.0	1.8	2.6	0.8	1.7	35
Farmer	0.0	0.4	0.3	2.8	1.6	2.2	0.4	1.3	33
Relatives/friends/neighbours	4.0	14.9	20.2	30.8	39.3	25.8	18.3	22.0	476
Other	0.9	1.8	4.1	0.8	1.1	1.2	1.6	1.4	30
All	**100.0**	**100.0**	**100.0**	**100.0**	**100.0**	**100.0**	**100.0**	**100.0**	**1988**

Source: GLSS (VI) Main Report.

schemes (23%) were the preferred sources of loans for households in the Rural Coastal areas, most of loans for the Rural Savannah were from relatives/friends/neighbours at 39%. '*Susu*' schemes and private banks supplied 15% and 9% of loans, respectively, in the Northern Savannah. NGOs were serving 8.4% of households. These results suggest that the majority of loan sources in the Rural Savannah are from informal providers and revealed a shallow penetration of formal financial institutions and services in the region. Barriers to accessing institutional credit in the Rural Savannah are still structurally embedded, hence the low rate of uptake.

Table 4.6 presents the sources of household credit among Ghanaian households. Irrespective of sex, most Ghanaians access loans from four main sources. These included relatives/friends/neighbours (22%), savings and loans schemes (19.5%), private banks (19%) and state banks (12%). Many Ghanaian females preferred savings and loans schemes (26%), relatives/friends/neighbours (18%) and private banks (16%) as loan sources. The high rates of credit sourced from relatives/friends/neighbours (i.e., informal lenders) are underpinned by the dominance of the informal economy and the ability of the informal lenders to provide products and services that better meet the needs and wants of the actors in the informal economy.

The modes of collateralization of credit facilities in the Ghanaian financial market are presented in Table 4.7. While 92% of households in urban areas use the documentation of vehicles as collateral, vehicle documentation only involved 8% of rural households. For the use of houses and buildings for collaterals, it was 83% for urban households and only 17% for rural households. The presence of high-valued housing in urban centres as a result of high incomes from businesses and wages explains the high percentage of their use for collateral.

The use of employers as collateral stood at 78% and salary payment services via banks at 72% in the urban centres. Livestock (cattle) as collateral only occurred in the Rural Savannah. The use of land as collateral was dominant among rural households (63%). Land as collateral was only used by 37% of urban households. More than half (54%) of the loans accessed by all rural households and approximately half (46%) of the loans accessed by all urban households in Ghana were unsecured. The high levels of uncollateralized loans from both the urban and rural areas confirm the dominance of the informal economy, limited formal financial services and the inherent ability of informal suppliers to meet the needs of certain population segments better.

In terms of barriers to accessing credit in the Ghanaian rural financial markets, especially from formal lenders, presented in Table 4.8, over 60% of rural and 40% of urban households claimed over-indebtedness as a key barrier to accessing credit. Also, while more than half (58.5%) of all loan applicants from rural households do not possess the appropriate collateral, 41.5% of urban households held similar reasons as a barrier to access. Besides, interest rates being too high accounted for 57% of non-access by urban households and 43% of rural households across Ghana.

While about 89% of urban households indicated that an inability to provide the required collateral constituted a major barrier to access, this was a barrier for only about 11% of households in the Greater Accra Metropolitan Area.

TABLE 4.7 Collateralization of Credit Facilities by Locality in Ghana

Locality	*Urban*			*Rural*				
The Purpose of Contracting Loans	*Accra*	*Other Urban*	*Total*	*Rural Coastal*	*Rural Forest*	*Rural Savannah*	*Total*	*Number*
None (unsecured)	4.4	41.4	45.8	3.2	37.2	13.9	54.2	**1,173**
Land	3.7	32.9	36.7	1.0	59.6	2.7	63.3	**27**
Cattle	0.0	0.0	0.0	0.0	0.0	100.0	100.0	**4**
House/building	33.0	50.3	83.4	2.2	12.0	2.4	16.6	**24**
Employer	16.3	62.1	78.4	6.4	3.3	12.0	21.6	**52**
Relatives	31.0	37.7	68.7	3.5	18.4	9.4	31.3	**82**
Non-relatives	1.9	67.3	69.2	6.0	21.9	2.8	30.8	**72**
Land title (with or without a house)	0.0	60.2	60.2	0.0	39.8	0.0	39.8	**8**
Salary via a lending institution	17.1	54.6	71.8	2.3	19.7	6.2	28.2	**130**
Vehicle documents	40.3	51.3	91.6	0.0	8.4	0.0	8.4	**11**
Cash or bank account or loan	8.9	42.7	51.6	8.8	31.4	8.2	48.4	**270**
Third-party security	15.8	32.6	48.4	7.0	27.5	17.2	51.6	**79**
Other	19.0	35.0	54.0	5.7	31.0	9.3	46.0	**56**
All	**8.7**	**43.5**	**52.2**	**4.3**	**32.1**	**11.4**	**47.8**	**1,988**

Source: GLSS (VI) Main Report.

TABLE 4.8 Barriers to Accessing Financial Services by Locality in Ghana

Locality								
	Urban			*Rural*				
Reason	*Accra*	*Other Urban*	*Total*	*Rural Coastal*	*Rural Forest*	*Rural Savannah*	*Total*	*Number*
No need	27.8	72.2	50.9	11.3	52.6	36.0	49.1	44,617
Interest rate too high	40.8	59.2	57.5	14.8	65.7	19.5	42.5	6,264
Demand for collateral	43.3	56.7	45.4	15.8	41.3	42.9	54.6	3,516
Already has too much debt	30.2	69.8	39.8	16.7	44.1	39.2	60.2	491
Cannot obtain the amount needed	10.6	89.4	41.5	4.1	50.7	45.2	58.5	2,584
Other	58.9	41.1	43.6	5.6	40.8	53.6	56.4	1,476
All	**30.4**	**69.6**	**50.8**	**11.5**	**52.8**	**35.7**	**49.2**	**58,948**

Source: GLSS (VI) Main Report.

However, an estimated 66% of households of the Rural Forest and only 20% of the Rural Savannah could also not provide the appropriate collateral constituting as a barrier to access. Other reasons for non-access to institutional credit in the Rural Savannah made up almost three-fifths (58.5%) of all the barriers to access. However, the perception of the amount requested not granted (45%), demand for collateral (42.9%), households already in debt (39%), no need for institutional credit (36%) and interest rates too high (19.5%) constituted critical barriers to household access to credit in the Northern Savannah. The implication of these results is not far-fetched.

Economic and market activities in the Northern Savannah have historically been sub-optimal. A combination of under-investment in socio-economic and other infrastructural facilities, as well as the unfavourable prevailing climatic conditions of the area, continues to exacerbate under-development of the Northern Savannah. Poverty levels remain high and the fact that the least barrier to accessing institutional credit in the Rural Savannah was interest rates confirms earlier findings that the poor can pay high interest rates and that when credit is needed, interest rates matter little for the productive poor.

Interest rates as a barrier to access also accounted for about 15% in the Rural Coastal but 66% for the Rural Forest. In the Rural Forests, most cash crops such as cocoa, coffee and citrus are capital intensive and have longer gestation periods. The larger loan amounts and longer durations required for repayments meant that most MFI loans, usually rigid, are ill-suited for such economic activities; hence the relatively high-interest rate premiums reflect longer repayment durations and the associated risks to lenders.

On household usage of accessed credit from rural financial markets presented in Table 4.9, while over 81% of all loans to rural households went into the purchase of agricultural inputs, only 19% of urban households used theirs for agricultural inputs.

About two-thirds of rural households (70.2%) also used acquired credit for purchasing agricultural equipment compared to only 30% of urban households. Moreover, about 55% and 48% of rural household loans were used for other consumer goods and educational purposes, respectively.

For urban households, 82% of all loans went into the acquisition of land. Housing (72.6%) and vehicle purchase (64.5%) followed a distant second and third, respectively, for the urban households. And commitments such as weddings, travels and bride price payments collectively made up 56% of all the reasons for loan product uptake by urban households across Ghana.

The Rural Savannah saw about 34% of all loans used in the purchase of agricultural equipment and slightly over 30% for farm inputs. The acquisition of consumer goods and weddings, travel and bride price payments collectively made up 17% of loan product uptake in the Rural Savannah. Taking loans to service household debts (13%), housing (10%), education/training (8%), vehicle purchase (6%), business start-up (6.9%) and other undefined reasons (12.4%) were some of the reasons for loan product uptake in the Rural Savannah of Ghana, as presented in Table 4.9. These all point to low levels of financial services and financial inclusion in the zone. The above evidence shows that there are low levels of financial

TABLE 4.9 Use of Contracted Loans by Locality in Ghana

Locality								
	Urban			*Rural*				
The Purpose of Contracting Loans	*Accra*	*Other Urban*	*Total*	*Rural Coastal*	*Rural Forest*	*Rural Savannah*	*Total*	*No. of Persons with Accounts*
Land	26.3	55.6	81.9	2.4	11.6	4.1	18.1	26
Agricultural equipment	0.0	29.8	29.8	3.6	31.8	34.8	70.2	37
Agricultural inputs	0.0	19.3	19.3	8.2	42.1	30.4	80.7	246
Business	9.7	52.3	62.0	3.5	28.6	5.9	38.0	733
Housing	7.7	64.9	72.6	3.5	13.8	10.0	27.4	155
Education/training	6.3	45.5	51.8	4.1	35.8	8.3	48.2	278
Wedding, travel, B. price	2.3	54.1	56.4	0.0	25.9	17.7	43.6	21
Vehicle	24.3	40.2	64.5	10.8	18.8	6.0	35.5	42
Debt payment	21.1	36.4	57.5	2.1	27.1	13.3	42.5	52
Other consumer goods	8.2	37.2	45.4	3.7	33.7	17.2	54.6	188
Other	1.5	30.7	32.2	4.3	51.1	12.4	67.8	210
Total	**7.8**	**44.4**	**52.2**	**4.3**	**32.1**	**11.4**	**47.8**	**1,988**

Source: GLSS (VI) Main Report.

services and financial inclusion in the Northern Savannah. When looked at in the context of historical colonial and policy neglect, as well as the unfavourable climatic conditions of the area, described earlier in Section 4.4.2, they have contributed to the low levels of financial services and inclusion.

4.4.4 Uptake of Savings Products within Rural Financial Markets and Livelihoods in Ghana

This section explores the dynamics of household deposit account ownership and contributions to deposit schemes by locality and gender. It further assesses the reasons for the non-ownership of deposit accounts and non-contributions to savings schemes by households along with gender and locality in Ghana, with special emphasis on the Northern Rural Savannah.

From Table 4.10, while about 35% of all households (both rural and urban) in Ghana had savings accounts or are contributing to a savings scheme, about 67% neither had savings accounts nor contributed to any savings scheme. For those households with deposits, the proportion of males was more than half (58.6%), compared to less than half (41.3%) of females. This reflects the pervasive gender inequalities in access and control of resources between men and women in Ghana. Overall, deposit account ownership among urban households is about half (46.4%) and almost a fifth (21.5%) among rural households. The Northern Rural Savannah was much worse, at only 18% among households. This suggests that over 80% of households in the Northern Rural Savannah do not have a deposit account and do not contribute to any savings scheme. Of the 18% of those households with deposit accounts, males made up over three-quarters (74%) of the real owners. This is indicative of the general under-development and poor financial services availability and accessibility by populations of the Northern Savannah, especially among females.

TABLE 4.10 Households Deposit Account(s) or Contribution to Savings Schemes by Locality in Ghana.

	Households with			*Households with Individuals Having Savings Accounts*		
Locality	*Savings*	*No Savings*	*Total*	*Male*	*Female*	*All*
Urban	**46.4**	**53.6**	**100.0**	**55.2**	**44.8**	**75.6**
Accra	54.1	45.9	100.0	56.3	43.7	28.2
Other Urban	42.9	57.1	100.0	54.5	45.4	52.7
Rural	**21.5**	**78.5**	**100.0**	**69.2**	**30.8**	**24.4**
Rural Coastal	22.6	77.4	100.0	70.2	29.8	3.4
Rural Forest	23.3	76.7	100.0	67.1	32.9	15.1
Rural Savannah	**17.6**	**82.4**	**100.0**	**74.0**	**26.1**	**5.8**
All	**35.4**	**64.6**	**100.0**	**58.6**	**41.4**	**100.0**

Source: GLSS (VI) Main Report.

Reasons for households not prioritizing savings are presented in Table 4.11. While about 44% of households identified inadequate income as key reasons for not having savings accounts or contributing to savings schemes, about 29% considered a lack of regular income a key reason for not saving or contributing to savings schemes.

However, about 20% of both urban and rural households said they saw no need to save. Only about 2% of all households attributed their lack of savings or non-contribution to savings schemes to unawareness of the need to save and 1% attributed it to the distance to the financial institution.

Regarding the Northern Rural Savannah, while approximately 47% said they don't have enough money or income to save, 26% said it was because they had no regular income. About 19% said they saw no need to save and an estimated 4% attributed their lack of savings or contribution to a savings scheme to the long distance to the financial institution. In terms of gender, higher proportions of both males (42.3%) and females (45.1%) attributed their non-ownership of savings accounts or non-contribution to savings schemes to inadequate financial resources or income. Irregular income came in second for males (29.1%) and slightly higher for females (29.6%).

However, about 21% of males and 19% of females said that having a savings account was either not necessary or they had no interest in having a savings account. About 1% each of males and females also attributed their non-ownership of savings accounts to the cumbersome process involved at the institutions.

For the entirety of urban households in Ghana, about 42% also attributed not saving or contributing to a savings scheme to the inadequacy of cash at home or income flows. However, not having regular income and the perception of savings not been necessary accounted for about 30% and 22% for the urban households, respectively.

Also, for all rural households across Ghana, not having enough money or income accounted for about 45%, while 29% attributed their non-savings to the lack of regular income. About 18% found owning deposit accounts not necessary. This pattern was repeated in the Northern Rural Savannah, with about 47% citing a lack of adequate money or income as the reason for not having deposit accounts. Furthermore, only about 26% of the Northern Rural Savannah households attributed their non-ownership of deposit accounts to irregular income flows, while a much lower (19%) did not find it necessary to have institutional deposit accounts. Not aware of the need to save, the financial institution being too far and processes involved in institutional savings being too cumbersome accounted for about 2%, 1% and 0.8%, respectively, for the non-ownership or non-contribution to savings schemes in the Northern Rural Savannah households. These results showed that poverty and poor human development are pervasive in the Northern Rural Savannah.

4.4.5 Uptake of Insurance Products within Rural Financial Markets in Ghana

The section explores the status of insurance penetration among Ghanaian households with a focus on the Northern Rural Savannah. Short-term and long-term

TABLE 4.11 Reasons for Non-ownership of Deposit Accounts and/or Non-contribution to Savings Schemes by Locality and Sex in Ghana

Reason								
Gender/Locality	*Not Necessary/Interested*	*Not Aware of One*	*Process Cumbersome*	*Financial Institution Too Far Away*	*Don't Have Enough Money or Income*	*Don't Have Regular Income*	*Other*	*Total*
Male	21.1	2.6	0.9	1.4	42.3	29.1	2.6	100.0
Female	18.9	2.3	0.7	1.2	45.1	29.6	2.3	100.0
Urban	**21.7**	**2.3**	**0.7**	**0.4**	**41.9**	**29.6**	**3.5**	**100.0**
Accra	27.7	2.1	1.0	0.7	39.4	21.0	7.9	100.0
Other Urban	19.5	2.3	0.6	0.3	42.7	32.7	1.8	100.0
Rural	**18.4**	**2.6**	**0.8**	**2.0**	**45.4**	**29.2**	**1.6**	**100.0**
Rural Coastal	22.5	1.8	2.0	1.3	47.4	21.8	3.2	100.0
Rural Forest	17.2	2.1	0.7	1.0	44.1	33.3	1.5	100.0
Rural Savannah	**18.8**	**3.4**	**0.7**	**3.5**	**46.6**	**25.9**	**1.2**	**100.0**
All	**19.9**	**2.4**	**0.8**	**1.3**	**43.8**	**29.4**	**2.4**	**100.0**

Source: GLSS (VI) Main Report.

insurance products are assessed along with urban and rural localities as well as the reasons underlining the state of insurance product uptake among households.

Table 4.12 shows that the average coverage of household insurance uptake across Ghana was only 34% as of 2013. However, uptake by urban households (41.5%) was almost twice that of rural households (24.9%). Moreover, uptake from the other urban localities (45%) was about ten percentage points higher than the GAMA (35%), suggesting a huge informal sector in Greater Accra. In general, non-uptake of insurance products among rural households' country-wide was as high as 75%. Households in the Northern Rural Savannah had the lowest average penetration of insurance product uptake at only 22%. There is, therefore, a huge niche for micro-insurance products in the region, where the majority live in rural settings and subsist on farming – both crop and animal.

About 52% of households of the Rural Coastal, 57% of the Rural Forest and 34% of the Northern Savannah cited unaffordability as the main reason for non-insurance. Reasons for not holding insurance policies for Ghanaian households, in general, were more related to a lack of affordability (48.5%). While the lack of affordability of insurance products constituted 49% for urban households, it was 48% for rural households. No knowledge of the availability of insurance products and how they work accounted for about 33% of non-insurance of rural households and only 15% for urban households.

Over 50% of the Rural Savannah households did not know insurance products in the financial markets and 1.4% accused insurance companies and their product offerings of deception. The relatively underdeveloped insurance market explains the low penetration. Meanwhile, less than 4% of households in the Rural Savannah cited other reasons for not having any insurance policies.

In terms of short-term insurance policies held by households across urban and rural localities, more than six out of ten households that held some form of insurance reside in the urban centres. While about nine out of ten urban households held commercial or business insurance policies, approximately eight out of ten held property and vehicle/motor insurances.

TABLE 4.12 Proportion of Households Holding Insurance Policy by Locality in Ghana

Locality	*Yes*	*No*	*Total Number*
Urban	**41.5**	**58.5**	**7,445**
Accra	34.9	65.1	1,697
Other Urban	44.6	55.4	5,748
Rural	**24.9**	**75.1**	**9,327**
Rural Coastal	25.3	74.7	1,156
Rural Forest	26.3	73.7	3,863
Rural Savannah	**22.1**	**77.9**	**4,308**
All	**34.1**	**65.9**	**16,772**

Source: GLSS (VI) Main Report.

However, four out of ten rural households in Ghana held medical insurance products. Also, in rural Ghana, about three out of ten held funeral plans and two out of ten had vehicle/motor insurance. Together, these two constituted the main short-term insurance policies among rural households across Ghana.

For the Northern Rural Savannah, insurance penetration for medical was only 12% among households. For funerals, it was only 5% and for property only 0.7%. Also, households in the Northern Rural Savannah held 1.5% of commercial/business policies, 10.3% travel and 9.3% for vehicle/motor insurance policies. Although these results were slightly higher than those of the Rural Coastal, they were much lower than those of the Rural Forest, as shown in Table 4.13. Overall, these figures point to limited short-term insurance penetration among households of rural localities in general and the Northern Savannah ecological zone.

For the long-term insurance policies such as life, education and retirement annuities, Table 4.14 showed similar trends as those of the short-term policies, including vehicle, funeral, property and travel. Urban households generally held approximately 71% of all life insurance policies paid up by individuals or the household and 74% by employers.

Urban households also accounted for 79% of all retirement annuities and 63% of endowment/investment savings plans. Overall, 60% of urban households did not have any formal insurance policy and over 86% did not hold any informal insurance, whatsoever. This has implications for urban poverty and the rate of growth of urban population because rural-urban migration is further compounding issues of poverty, housing and sanitation. Also, the proportion of households with life insurance policies paid for by individuals or households in other urban areas apart from the GAMA was 52.9%.

In the Greater Accra Metropolitan Area (Fuglesang et al.), households with life insurance only accounted for 17.9% and 19% for education. The penetration of these two policies in the GAMA was much lower compared to the other urban centres combined at 52.9% and 51.6%, respectively.

In the rural areas, the uptake of life insurance policies paid for by individuals or households was about 29%. Approximately 26% of these life insurances held by households were paid for by employers. Also, while 21.4% of rural households held retirement annuities, 29.4% had education policies, and those with endowment/investment savings plans made up 37.4%. Overall, about 40% of all rural households had any form of a formal insurance policy. Other forms of insurance policies constituted about 14% held by rural households. These results effectively leave the endowment or savings plan as the dominant insurance policy in the rural localities at 37.4% of households.

In the Northern Rural Savannah, the dominant long-term insurance policy was also the endowment/investment savings plan held by about 14% of households. Those households that had education insurance policies made up only about 9%. About 10% of the Northern Rural Savannah households held life insurance policies paid for by the individual or household, 7% were paid for by the employer and 9% held retirement annuity/plans.

TABLE 4.13 Reasons and Percentages for Not Having an Insurance Policy/Cover by Locality in Ghana

Reason								
Locality	*Do Not See It Necessary*	*Cannot Afford It*	*Insurance Companies Are Deceptive*	*Inadequate Compensation*	*Don't Know How Insurance Works*	*Procedure for Claims Takes Too Long*	*Other*	*Number*
Urban	**26.7**	**49.1**	**4.3**	**1.0**	**14.7**	**1.5**	**2.8**	**16,171**
Accra	33.8	46.0	7.9	0.4	5.3	2.0	4.7	3,761
Other Urban	22.9	50.8	2.4	1.3	19.6	1.2	1.8	12,410
Rural	**15.1**	**48.0**	**1.2**	**0.2**	**32.5**	**1.1**	**1.9**	**31,171**
Rural Coastal	23.7	52.3	2.4	0.2	18.2	2.1	1.1	3,118
Rural Forest	16.7	56.9	0.7	0.3	23.4	0.9	1.0	10,698
Rural Savannah	**10.1**	**33.7**	**1.4**	**0.1**	**50.2**	**0.9**	**3.4**	**17,355**
All	**20.5**	**48.5**	**2.6**	**0.6**	**24.2**	**1.3**	**2.3**	**47,342**

Source: GLSS (VI) Main Report.

TABLE 4.14 Type of Short-Term Insurance Policies Held by Households and Locality in Ghana

Policy									
Locality	*Vehicle/Motor*	*Medical*	*Funeral*	*Property*	*Commercial/Business*	*Travel*	*None*	*Other*	*Number*
Urban	**77.4**	**61.9**	**74.3**	**83.3**	**89.4**	**87.1**	**77.7**	**84.4**	**23,600**
Accra	32.1	9.4	29.6	31.6	42.4	33.0	36.2	40.9	4,913
Other Urban	45.4	52.5	44.7	51.7	47.1	54.0	41.5	43.5	18,687
Rural	**22.6**	**38.1**	**25.7**	**16.7**	**10.6**	**12.9**	**22.3**	**15.6**	**37,544**
Rural Coastal	3.0	3.6	4.9	3.9	–	1.2	2.1	5.4	3,824
Rural Forest	10.3	22.6	15.8	12.1	6.1	1.3	13.8	7.1	13,713
Rural Savannah	**9.3**	**12.0**	**5.0**	**0.7**	**4.5**	**10.4**	**6.4**	**3.1**	**20,007**
Total	**100.0**	**100.0**	**100.0**	**100.0**	**100.0**	**100.0**	**100.0**	**100.0**	**61,144**

Source: GLSS (VI) Main Report.

TABLE 4.15 Types and Percentages of Long-Term Insurance Policy Held by Households and Locality in Ghana

Type of Policy								
Locality	*Life Insurance Paid by Holder*	*Life Insurance Paid by Employer*	*Retirement Annuity/Plan*	*Education*	*Other Endowment/ Investment Saving Plan*	*None*	*Other*	*Number*
Urban	**70.8**	**74.4**	**78.6**	**70.6**	**62.6**	**60.5**	**86.3**	**23,600**
Accra	17.9	37.7	36.4	19.0	23.6	9.7	9.6	4,913
Other Urban	52.9	36.7	42.2	51.6	39.0	50.8	76.7	18,687
Rural	**29.2**	**25.6**	**21.4**	**29.4**	**37.4**	**39.5**	**13.7**	**37,544**
Rural Coastal	6.4	5.3	3.0	2.5	4.7	3.0	2.0	3,824
Rural Forest	12.9	13.1	13.0	17.7	18.4	23.6	8.7	13,713
Rural Savannah	**9.8**	**7.3**	**5.3**	**9.2**	**14.4**	**12.8**	**3.1**	**20,007**
All	**100.0**	**100.0**	**100.0**	**100.0**	**100.0**	**100.0**	**100.0**	**61,144**

Source: GLSS (VI) Main Report.

Though on average, these results were higher than the Rural Coastal, they suggest that the penetration of formal insurance in the Northern Rural Savannah is relatively undeveloped. The market for micro-insurance products is potentially large for the microfinance industry.

There is therefore the need for the microfinance industry to collaborate in the development and testing of pro-poor micro-insurance products in the zone. This is because it is the insurance industry that underwrites policies. Understanding the livelihoods of the people of the Northern Rural Savannah is critical to the success of the development and roll-out of micro-insurance products in Ghana.

4.4.6 Uptake of Payment Services within Rural Financial Markets in Ghana

This section presents the status of payment services in Ghana vis-à-vis those of the rest of sub-Saharan Africa and the cohort of other middle-income countries from the Global Findex data for 2014. The section further explores the penetration of all account types for payments, digital payment platforms and the domestic remittances landscape.

Improvements in mobile handset functionality, advances in network technology and the upgrades of point-of-sale infrastructure have made mobile money operators efficient as they open longer than banks and MFIs in Ghana. The recent launch of mobile money interoperability services, allowing transfers across mobile networks, other e-payment platforms and banks, is increasing transaction values and volumes. Mobile money is generally used for peer-to-peer payments, utilities and salaries via mobile wallets. However, as mobile network operators are not permitted to hold deposits, it offers opportunities for microfinance institutions and banks alike to increase customer numbers and deposit mobilization. Mobile network operators such as MTN, Vodafone and Airtel are leading the mobile money revolution in Ghana. The ubiquitous penetration of mobile phones is creating low-price offerings and innovative distribution models for banking and microfinance sub-sectors.

Mobile account ownership in Ghana for all adults (% age 15+) recorded 13% in 2014 compared to averages of 11.5% for sub-Saharan Africa and 2.5% for the cohort of lower middle-income countries. Mobile money services are significant players in the financial inclusion agenda in Ghana and many other African countries. Table 4.15 presents the results of data from the Global Findex survey for 2014. It shows that domestic remittances via mobile phones (i.e., % senders) reached 38.9% in 2014 for Ghana compared to averages of about 31% for SSA and 8% for the cohort of other lower middle-income countries. However, debit and credit cards used for payments (4.4%) remained below the averages of sub-Saharan Africa (8.7%) and the cohort of other lower middle-income countries (9.6%). The use of internet payments (2.7%) in Ghana was, however, marginally higher than the averages of SSA and the other lower-income countries.

TABLE 4.16 Payment Services in Ghana (Findex Report, 2014)

Sub-Saharan Africa			
Ghana			
Population, Age 15+ (Millions)	*15.9*	*GNI Per Capita ($)*	*1,770*
	Ghana	*Sub-Saharan Africa*	*Lower Middle Income*
Mobile account (% age 15+) All adults	13.0	11.5	2.5
Use of account in the past year			
Use an account to receive wages	5.8	7.3	5.6
Use an account to receive government transfers	2.0	3.8	3.3
Use a financial institution account to pay utility bills or making purchases	0.7	2.8	3.1
Other digital payments in past year (% age 15+)			
Used a debit card to make payments	4.4	8.7	9.6
Used a credit card to make payments	0.6	1.9	2.8
Used the internet to pay bills/purchases	2.7	2.4	2.6
Domestic remittances in the past year (% age 15+)			
Sent remittances	26.5	28.7	14.2
Sent remittances via a fin. institution (% Sender)	16.8	31.0	30.9
Sent remittances via a mobile phone (% Senders)	38.9	30.8	7.7
Sent remittances via a money transfer operator (% senders)	17.2	21.021	18.3
Received remittances	36.9	37.2	17.8
Received remittances via a financial institution (% senders)	16.2	26.6	26.0
Received remittances via a mobile phone (% senders)	34.6	27.6	5.7
Received remittances via a money transfer operator (% senders)	13.0	22.1	16.6

Source: http://datatopics.worldbank.org/financialinclusion/country/ghana.

As a conduit for domestic remittances in Ghana, mobile money led in sending (38.9%) and receiving (34.6%) remittances via mobile phones in Ghana. These were higher than the averages of 30.8% and 27.6% for SSA and 7.7% and 5.7% for the cohort of lower middle-income countries. Mobile money services via domestic remittances are also creating jobs for people, with 17.2% and 13% of users sending and receiving remittances, respectively, via mobile money operators in Ghana. The averages of those sending and receiving money via mobile money operators were much higher for SSA (21% and 22%, respectively) and lower middle-income countries (30.9% and 16.6%, respectively). Mobile money operators offer conveniences and are fast eroding traditional remittance payments via financial institutions.

Remittances by migrants to mostly the urban middle and coastal urban centres and increasingly the rural middle belt of Ghana play significant roles in improving household livelihoods and welfare in the Northern Rural Savannah of Ghana (Adaawen and Owusu, 2013). Mobile phone penetration and improvement in their functionality have created opportunities for the expansion of financial services and increased the role of non-financial institutions such as e-money issuers.

Recent data from the BoG showed that mobile money accounts stood at about 12.7 million in the first quarter of 2019 compared to 345,000 in 2012. However, more policies are needed to facilitate the growth of financial technologies to support new products and services in the market and deepen cybersecurity through standardization. Changes in regulations, interest payments, consumer protection, agent management, deposit protection, partnership and interoperability services have given a boost to the expanded mobile money services. The three mobile network operators – MTN, Airtel-Tigo and Vodafone, in collaboration with the banks – continue to champion mobile money in Ghana (Table 4.16).

4.5 Summary and Conclusion

The meta-theoretical livelisystem framework (Dorward, 2014) was adapted for the study to contextualize the microfinance landscape of the Northern Savannah. The chapter concludes that although the Ghanaian financial eco-system has undergone drastic changes in recent years (Díaz Serrano and Sackey, 2015; Ackah and Asiamah, 2016; Diaz-Serrano and Sackey, 2016), it is the collective successes and failures of these historical policies and reforms that underpinned its current state.

Also, based on reports from the Ghana living standards surveys (GLSSs), there has been remarkable progress in poverty reduction in Ghana since 1991 and in microfinance. As of 2013, about one-quarter of the Ghanaian population lived below the poverty line and about 10% of those in extreme poverty (down from 52.7% and 37.6% below the poverty line and extreme poverty in 1991, respectively). A broadly shared and sustained economic growth is at the bottom of this success story. Moreover, a major contributory factor to structural transformation is an increasing share of services and industry. The rural economy has also witnessed increased agricultural productivity and higher incomes. A broader education and skills acquisition over the years has led to better wages. However, persistent spatial inequality (including access to financial services) has led to intra-regional disparities. The three northern regions continue to exhibit the highest poverty headcount ratios, exceeding the national averages by large margins (Ghana Statistical Service, 2015).

In the late 19th century, the colonial financial system was characterized by limited financial services that largely excluded indigenous populations. This resulted in agitation for greater financial inclusion and the first-ever financial sector reforms including the establishment of the Bank of the Gold Coast under the Bank of Ghana (BoG) ordinance in 1952. After independence in 1957, the government focused on expanding a development-oriented financial system aimed at driving industrialization, growth and development. These policies had limited long-term impact on access and financial inclusion. Necessitated by the Economic Recovery Programmes introduced in the 1980s, the first post-independence Ghana's financial sector reforms were introduced aimed at restructuring the financial system (World Bank, 1997). These reforms deepened financial intermediation as well as the development of non-bank financial institutions and facilitated its integration and relevance to the broader financial sector eco-system. These policies and programmes were described as narrowly focused as they created many other imbalances. Later, further reforms led to the deepening of financial intermediation and integrated the domestic economy with global financial markets to spur economic growth and development.

However, the fundamental factors restraining broader financial inclusion remain prevalent with substantial inefficiencies in savings mobilization and allocation of resources to the real sectors of the economy (Senbet and Otchere, 2006; Munyambonera, 2013) and commercial banks generally had no proven methodologies for financing the poor due to high transaction costs and risks (Aryeetey et al., 1994; Opare, 2001). So far, Ghana's financial system, like many other sub-Saharan African countries, remains liberalized with institutional and market reforms positively supporting economic growth (Moyo et al., 2014). Further reforms such as the national financial inclusion and development strategy (NFIDS) have outlined five key mutually reinforcing priorities, including financial stability; access, quality and usage of financial services; financial infrastructure; financial consumer protection; and financial capability, all geared towards sustainable financial inclusion and development.

The financial sector witnessed low liquidity, especially that of the banking sector, largely due to low capitalization, as was identified in the asset quality report (AQR) in 2016. This led to the revocation of nine commercial banks as part of a financial sector clean-up that began in August 2017 by the Bank of Ghana. Also, 347 microfinance companies (of which 155 had already ceased operations), 39 microcredit companies/moneylenders (ten of which had already ceased operations), 15 savings and loans companies, eight finance house companies and two non-bank financial institutions that had already ceased operations had their licences revoked. The Securities and Exchanges Commission also revoked the licences of 55 fund management companies as of 11 November 2019.

Though the financial sector clean-up will address structural and systemic weaknesses, the challenges in short to medium term are enormous. The exercise is having negative impacts on access to financial services by SMEs and, therefore, the level of economic activities generated in the economy. For example, in November 2019, the BoG reduced the primary reserve rate of the remaining commercial banks from 10% to 8% and directed that the 2% be made available to SMEs. The ability of the government and the closed financial institutions to reimburse depositors and investors is being called into question. It is estimated that a combined investment of $1.6 billion could be affected by the closures. The launch of the Ghana Deposit Protection Scheme in September 2019 will serve as a conduit to further strengthen the protection of depositors in Ghana. Through the national financial inclusion development strategy and the payment systems strategy, mobile money will continue to play a critical role in the formalization of the Ghanaian economy. The Ghana Financial Sector Development Project since June 2018 has been expected to improve financial stability, inclusion and private sector competitiveness that will further build the public confidence, thus helping the population to make informed choices especially in the rural settings.

In terms of financial services, household institutional account ownership in the Rural Savannah, in general, has remained abysmally low. Data available revealed that only 5% of households in the Rural Savannah have accounts with commercial banks, 2% with investment/mortgage houses, 9% with rural and community banks and 3.5% with savings and loans schemes. The rest include 11.3% with cooperative/credit unions, 10% with 'Susu' schemes and 5.9% from other informal microfinance sources such as family and friends and the VSLAs. In terms of gender, men owned 62.1% of all account types in all financial institutions, as against 37.9% for females in the Rural Savannah. Only 9.9% of households accessed loans in the Rural Savannah.

Moreover, the loans were mainly secured through third-party security employers and relatives. The demand for collateral and households' lack of same, as well as previous debt burdens, were the key barriers to access by households in the Rural Savannah. Furthermore, the advanced loans were mostly used for agricultural equipment, agricultural inputs and social consumer goods.

Also, according to the Ghana Living Standards Survey (VI), only 17.6% of households in the Rural Savannah had deposit accounts with financial institutions. Over 74% of households had no form of deposits or contributions to a savings scheme. Major reasons for the high levels of non-savings of households were not having enough money or income, no regular income and not having a need to save. Not aware of the need to save, the distance to financial institutions and cumbersome processes also constituted barriers to savings. Insurance penetration also fared no better in the Rural Savannah. Only 22.1% of households had one form of an insurance policy or the other. No knowledge of how insurance products work, a lack of affordability, not necessary and perception of insurance companies being deceptive made up key barriers to access in the Rural Savannah.

The next chapter assesses the factors underpinning the design of microfinance products and services for greater outreach and sustainability in Ghana, based on an expanded Schreiner (2002) framework discussed in Chapter 3 and presented in Figure 3.1.

5

DESIGNING MICROFINANCE PRODUCTS AND SERVICES FOR FINANCIAL INCLUSION IN GHANA

5.1 Introduction

The chapter presents results of an exploration of factors underpinning microfinance product and service design within the context of rural livelihood activities. It focuses on assessing perceived gaps between the design of microfinance products and services (microcredit, micro-savings, and micro-insurance and payment services) and the needs and wants of those with access. The Upper East Region of the Northern Savannah served as the case study area. Understanding how to design and price microfinance products and services that broaden outreach and serve them better is important (Karlan and Zinman, 2010) for the achievement of the goals of the industry.

Microfinance product and service design are underpinned by the normative approach adopted by the microfinance institution as first postulated by Schreiner (2002) (see Chapter 2, Section 2.7.3). While the financial systems approach advocates recovery of programme costs, and profit-making by service providers based on market principles, a poverty-lending approach focuses on poverty alleviation, even if subsidies are required. In both cases, the double bottom goals of financial sustainability and outreach remain imperative. However, according to Schreiner (2002), the adoption of either of these two approaches must address six fundamental issues in the design of products and services to achieve the dual goals of financial sustainability and increased outreach. These six indices are scope, length, worth, cost, breadth and depth. Section 5.2 will assess the perceptions of clients for each of these indicators to reveal the extent of their incorporation in product and service design in the Northern Savannah of Ghana. How the incorporation of these indicators differentially affects clients' livelihood strategies, as well as their ability to honour financial contracts in the segmented industry, is then explored.

Moreover, perceptions of clients about the effects of add-ons as a product design feature and how they navigate contract enforcement mechanisms employed

DOI: 10.4324/9781003318873-5

by MFIs are also explored, as these two factors influence the incentive structure for both the MFI and the client.

Data collected via household in-depth interviews, focus group discussions and key informant interviews between July and November 2017 across the eastern (Garu), central (Bolgatanga and Navrongo) and western (Sandema) corridors of the Upper East Region (see Table 5.1) were used. At the institutional level, the researcher carried out desk review and content analysis of products and services available, MFI-specific product and service design features, the needs (and wants) of clients targeted by the various products and services, the terms and conditions attached, contract enforcement approaches used and add-ons as product design features, among others. Table 5.1 presents the microfinance institutional and client sampling.

The key informant interviews involved identifying and interviewing one or more persons knowledgeable in a subject area while taking notes (Diccicco-Bloom and Crabtree, 2006). These were carried out with managers and project heads of all participating microfinance institutions. Selected clients (one male and one female) from the formal, semi-formal and informal categories of MFIs were interviewed as key informants at the household level. Furthermore, focus group discussions were held with selected clients from each of the three MFI groups to provide depth behind the numbers. Moreover, the case study methodology was used to study two clients (male and female) each from these three institutional types to validate other findings. Gender, the number of years of client participation, and the products and services accessed were key considerations in the selection of case study participants. Audio recordings (with permission) were taken and transcribed for the qualitative analysis. Field diaries and observations were made to support the qualitative analysis. Key informant interviews have been widely adopted and adapted in studies across different social phenomena and disciplines (Chaskin, 2001; Cowles et al., 2002; Barker et al., 2005; Nyamukapa and Gregson, 2005; Burns et al., 2007). The key informants with their particular knowledge and understanding provided insights on the nature of the social interactions between clients in the communities, between clients and the MFIs, and the general subject matter under study. The themes covered in the key informant interview guided the achievement of the research objective (see Appendices IV and V).

Each of the six indices, as well as add-ons and contract enforcement mechanisms, is explained in Section 5.2. The summary and conclusion of the chapter are also presented in Section 5.3.

5.2 Product Design and Financial Inclusion within the Microfinance Livelisystem Framework in Ghana

5.2.1 Introduction

The diversity of microfinance service providers and the products and services they offer correlate with the varied needs and wants of clients. As a result, Bennett and

TABLE 5.1 Sampling: Microfinance Institutions, Locations and Client Types

Region	*Districts*	*Formal MFIs*	*No.*	*Semi-formal MFIs*	*No.*	*Informal MFIs*	*No.*	*Non-Participants*	*No.*	*Sub-Total (Clients)*
Upper East Region	**Bolgatanga/ Navrongo Municipal.**	1RCB (Naara RB) = 9 + S & Ls (Sinapi Abba) = 9	18	CUA (Bolga TCU) = 9 + MFC (Innovative MFC) = 9	18	ML (Taarasum) =5 + Susu (Bencyn) =9	14	Via Snowball	17	71
	Builsa North and Builsa South	RCB (Bucobank) = 16	16	CUA (NTCUA=8 & AG CUA=8) **NB:** from Navrongo Municipal	16	VSL groups (various)	20	Via Snowball	17	65
	Garu/ Tempane	RCB (BESSFA) = 16	16	CUA (GTCUA) = 16	16	VSL groups (various) = 16	16	Via Snowball	16	64
Total institutional sampling		**50**		**50**		**50**		**50**		**200**

Legend: RCB = Rural and Community Banks are NRB = Naara Rural Bank; BuCoBank = Builss Community Bank; BESSFA = Garu Rural Bank; S&L = Savings and Loans Companies are Sinapi Abba S&L; CUA = Credit Union Association; FNGO = Financial Non-Governmental Organization; MFC = Microfinance Company; ML = Moneylender; Susu (ind/co) = Susu individual/company.

Goldberg (1993) argued that there is little understanding of the differential needs, goals, risk profiles, investment opportunities and barriers to financial inclusion of the productive poor working themselves out of poverty. This is of concern because Otero (1999) posits that microfinance as an industry facilitates financial, social and human capital development of the productive poor, and builds institutions that provide broader development services. There is, therefore, the need for the assessment of the gaps between the design of microfinance products and services to explore how they differentially meet the needs of different clients and add value to the dual goals of the industry (Morduch, 2000). This is important because financial self-sufficiency remains the over-riding goal of those MFIs oriented towards the financial systems approach. Moreover, scale remains limited for those MFIs oriented towards the poverty-lending approach, even though subsidies from both public and private sources (Woller et al., 1999) are intended for increased outreach. Furthermore, theoretical underpinnings of rural financial markets are focused on the reduction of the cost of service provision via product design that counters prevailing barriers to financial inclusion. For example, the lack of suitable collaterals and the pervasive information asymmetries between lenders and resource-poor populations, characterized by low 'debt capacity' (Von Pischke, 1991; Ghatak and Guinnane, 1999; Armendáriz and Morduch, 2010; Hill and Sarangi, 2012). Thus, theories of rural financial markets (Stigler, 1967; Stiglitz and Weiss, 1981; Hoff and Stiglitz, 1993; Yunus, 2007) are drawn upon to contextualize the gaps in product and service design. For instance, experience with interventions in rural credit markets of developing countries suggests that the introduction of regulated formal financial institutions has failed to drive out usurious moneylenders, despite their competitive interest rates (Bottomley, 1964; Singh, 1983; Bell, 1988) and economies of scale. What then are the reasons for the continued patronage of the services of such informal providers?

The point of divergence between the financial systems and the poverty-lending approaches is the difference in their implications on the design of products and services to concurrently improve sustainability and large outreach (Morduch, 2000), and therefore poverty reduction. Achieving both goals requires careful balancing of both the sustainability and outreach goals or generally finding innovative ways to achieve both. Schreiner's (2002) framework for the design of products and services regardless of the approach an MFI adopts for the contextualization of the social benefits of microfinance included cost, worth, depth, breadth, length and scope. While Schreiner (2002) used data reported to MIX Market by a group of MFIs to estimate the extent of their incorporation and their implications on clients' livelihoods, this study diverges by using data primarily from clients to gauge the incorporation of these design features in the microfinance industry of the Northern Savannah of Ghana. Contract enforcement and add-ons (microfinance plus) affect the incentive structure of contracts for both the MFIs and clients and are therefore included in this study. The chapter focused on the assessment of all eight design factors across the three institutional types operating in the Northern Savannah of Ghana using data predominantly from the demand side of the industry. The social benefits of microfinance to clients overall is underpinned by the extent of incorporation of all eight design features and their interactions as perceived by clients. Thus, the chapter assessed the perception of clients on each factor of design and their implications on the livelihood's activities of clients and their ability to uptake products and repay (see Table 5.2 and Appendices IV and V).

Concerned with an assessment of the evolution of the microfinance landscape of the Northern Savannah of Ghana in the context of the broader financial sector developments, conceived based on the meta-theoretical livelisystem framework (Dorward, 2014), the microfinance livelisystem framework (MLF), complemented by the dialectic approach, formed the boundaries within which the evolution of the microfinance sub-sector within the broader financial sector eco-system was assessed. Descriptive statistics in the form of tables provided the basis of the analysis which drew on archival records and data from surveys of government ministries, departments and agencies such as the National Development Planning Authority, the Ministry of Finance and Economic Planning, the Bank of Ghana, the Ghana Statistical Services and reports of multilateral and bilateral programmes as well as scholarly journals and articles on the financial sector of Ghana were examined.

On the cost of access, while interest and fees are low among the formal MFIs, they are perceived as unaffordable compared with clients of the semi-formal and informal suppliers. There seemed to be a general recognition of the negative implications of the non-cash opportunity costs that clients of the formal and semi-formal MFIs incurred accessing microfinance products and services. In responding to this challenge, most of these MFIs in the Upper East Region of Ghana have deployed mobile staff, armed with vehicles and predominantly motorbikes, to take banking to the doorsteps of clients. In so doing, the burden of indirect cash expenses, principally on transportation and subsistence, was also substantially removed (see Table 5.2).

In terms of product scope, the formal MFIs were the most integrated with different loan products ranging between 1 and 10, and 1 and 5 for savings products. For insurance, it was 1–3, and that included weather-indexed crop insurance apart from the Ghana Agricultural Insurance Pool programme. There were 1–5 different payment services, where Western Union and MoneyGram featured prominently. The semi-formal MFIs had lower loan and savings product scope and provided only mobile money transfer services. The only insurance product was the credit risk management instrument on deposits (a kind of quasi-insurance product) for small savers. The informal MFIs were minimalist and either provided loans and/or savings services, but not insurance products and payment services (see Table 5.2).

Worth relates to the willingness of clients to pay for services. Worth was more driven by commercial and sustainability motives by the formal MFIs where loan amounts disbursed were based on the creditworthiness of the client rather than any other considerations. The duration of repayment and the regular repayment

TABLE 5.2 Perceptions of Levels of MFIs' Incorporation of Factors of Product and Service Design Based on an Expanded Schreiner (2002) Framework

Design Factor	*Sub-design Factors*	*Formal MFIs*	*Semi-formal MFIs*	*Informal MFIs*
Cost of access	**Interest and fees affordability**	Low (but perceived more unaffordable)	Medium (but perceived affordable)	High (but perceived highly affordable)
	Non-cash opportunity costs	Low (because of mobile staffs)	Moderate (because of mobile staffs)	Low (live near MFIs)
	Indirect cash expenses	Low (because of mobile staffs)	Medium (because of mobile staffs)	Low (live near MFIs)
	Client cost-benefits evaluation	High-value activities	Medium-value activities	Low-value activities
Scope	**MFI delivery approach**	Highly integrated approach	Lowly integrated into the approach	Mostly minimalist in approach
	Loans	Highly varied (between 1 and 10 products)	Moderately varied (between 1 and 5 products)	Lowly varied (1 and 2 products)
	Savings	Moderately varied (between 1 and 5 products)	Lowly varied (between 1 and 3 products)	Single products
	Insurance	Moderately varied 1–3 (including weather-indexed insurance)	Only credit risk management	None (except VSLA welfare funds)
	Payments	Moderately varied (1–5 products including Western Union and MoneyGram)	Only mobile money transfer services	None
Worth	**Worth at MFI level**	More related to commercial banking	More of quasi-commercial banking	Very informal
	Loan amounts disbursed	Loan amounts based on creditworthiness	Loan amounts tied to savings	Based on credit worthiness and KYC
	Duration of repayment (term to maturity)	Less flexible, with options for clients to choose from	More flexible, with options and open to negotiation	Highly flexible
	Regular repayment amounts (size of instalment)	Less flexible, but with options for client to choose from the start	More flexible with options and open to negotiation	Highly flexible

	Interest paid on deposits	Mostly fixed, but negotiable on fixed deposit instruments	Fixed on savings, but no fixed deposit instruments offered	None
	The flexibility of deposit withdrawals	Highly flexible	Moderately flexible	Highly inflexible
	Access and ability to diversify income sources	High-valued activities; used for enterprise loans	Medium-valued; used for consumption loans	Low-valued activities; mostly for low value IGAs
	Access and ability to employ others	More numbers of others employed	Moderate numbers of others	Few household members
	Access and ability to meet personal goals	High-value goals achieved	Medium-value goals achieved	Low-value goals achieved
Length	**Years of access**	High number (between 1 and 17 years)	Medium number (1–12 years)	High number (between 1 and 17 years)
	Awareness of donor support for sustainability	NGO present (USAID)	NGOs absent (formed by professional associations, religious groups)	NGOs present (World Vision International for VSLAs)
	Awareness of MFI profitability	High (AGMs)	High (AGMs)	Low
Depth	**Preference for women**	Very low (women not particularly targeted)	Very low (women not particularly targeted)	None (women not targeted except VSLAs)
	Preference for rural	Very low (rural clients not particularly targeted)	Very low (more on client membership)	Very low (except for the VSLAs)
	Preference for less/not educated	Very low (the educated not particularly targeted)	Very low (more on client membership)	Very low (except for the VSLAs)
	Preference for ethnic minorities	Very low (minorities not particularly targeted)	Very low (more on client membership)	Very low (except for the VSLAs)

(Continued)

TABLE 5.2 Continued

Design Factor	*Sub-design Factors*	*Formal MFIs*	*Semi-formal MFIs*	*Informal MFIs*
	Client primary housing material	High use of cement blocks as primary housing materials	High use cement blocks as primary housing materials	High use cement blocks as primary housing materials
	Client Loan Sizes	Larger loan sizes	Medium-sized loan sizes	Smaller loan sizes
Breadth	**Numbers of clients**	High numbers of clients	Moderate numbers of clients	Few numbers of clients
Enforcement	**Enforcement methods**	A mixture of legal and traditional informal methods	A mixture of legal, but mostly informal traditional methods	Very informal
Add-ons	**MFI-client relationship**	Cordial relations between staff and clients held very importantly	Cordial relations between staff and clients very important	Cordial relations between clients and lender
	Microloans add-ons	Moderate credit risk management	High credit risk management	No credit risk management (co-insurance existed)
	Micro-saving add-ons	Moderately varied	Low varied	No variation
	Micro-insurance add-ons payment services add	Highly varied (including weather index)	Less varied (only credit risk management instrument)	Non-existent

amounts involved were also less flexible once a client opted for a plan. Interest payments on the client's deposits were mostly fixed but could be negotiated in the case of fixed deposit instruments according to officials of the Rural and Community Banks. The flexibility of withdrawals for clients, in terms of both amounts and frequency, was also highly flexible with the formal MFIs. Moreover, formal clients had highly diversified income sources, employed more people from their communities and said they accomplished more personal goals (see Table 5.2).

About length (sustainable participation), many formal and informal clients had stayed with their MFIs for much longer. This ranged between 1 and 17 years for formal and informal clients. Those of the semi-formal MFIs (Credit Unions and Financial NGOs) had worked with their MFIs between 1 and 12 years. This suggests that the semi-formal MFIs were relatively new service providers on the microfinance landscape in the study region. Most of these clients were also not aware of the existence of any donor partnerships with their MFIs and could have implications for sustainability, worth and scope of product offerings. However, the formal clients had the greatest perception of the profitability of their service providers (i.e., the MFIs) (see Table 5.2).

Depth relates to MFIs' outreach to poorer clients (bottom of the pyramid). This design feature saw no special preferences for women, people living in rural localities, those with little or no formal education and ethnic minorities across all three institutional types. The only exception was a leaning towards more women among the informal VSLA groups. Ironically, most clients across all institutional types had concrete blocks as primary construction materials for their houses and homes. However, the use of mud bricks was more pronounced with the informal clients' houses and homes than with the formal and semi-formal clients. For the formal MFIs, loan amounts disbursed were more based on set criteria of creditworthiness. For the semi-formal MFIs, it was more on membership and the amount of savings. In an increasing breadth of outreach, MFIs assess clients based on their capacity to use, benefit and repay, not just on need. This suggests that MFIs prioritize sustainability goals more than poverty alleviation goals across all three categories of institutional types (see Table 5.2).

Interest rates were relatively lower in the Upper East Region than the national averages of 36%, 45% and 65% per annum for formal, semi-formal and informal MFIs, respectively (Osei-Assibey, 2013). In the Upper East Region of Ghana, the study found that interest rates per annum for the formal, semi-formal and informal MFIs averaged 32%, 35% and 40%, respectively. These have implications for the depth and breadth of outreach (i.e., poorer clients and absolute numbers served, respectively). However, the VSLAs were an exception in that group members set their interest rates and accumulated interest and fees were paid to members as dividends in proportion to shares bought by the end of the cycle. Donor partnerships with MFIs were targeted at pre-determined enterprises and income-generating activities (IGAs). While USAID partnership with Rural and Community Banks targeted SMEs including rural cottage industries, World Vision was typically involved in the formation and linkage of VSLA groups to the Rural and Community Banks. These partnerships had implications on the levels of breadth of outreach.

Moreover, group products that have the potential of increasing access to poorer clients without suitable collaterals were more common with the formal MFIs than with the semi-formal and informal clients. Furthermore, depending on the MFI in question, enforcement mechanisms consisted of both legal actions in the law courts and informal devices. For example, informally summoning defaulting clients to the local chief palace most often induces repayments.

And the mere threat of legal action also triggers repayments. Product add-ons were more pronounced for loans of the formal MFIs and most often have access to commercial funding sources. The semi-formal MFIs relied on deposits more often than not for lending, and compulsory savings were used by many as an instrument for the mobilization of deposits. In summary, the incorporation of all eight features of product design was more pronounced among the formal MFIs (rural and community banks and the savings and loans companies) than the semi-formal (credit union associations and financial NGOs) and informal MFIs (moneylenders and 'Susu'). While interest and fees were low among the formal MFIs, these were perceived as unaffordable compared to similar perceptions by the semi-formal and informal clients. Increased non-cash opportunity costs negatively affected access and uptake by clients of the formal and semi-formal MFIs. This challenge has been resolved through the deployment of mobile staff, armed with vehicles for transportation, to take banking to the doorsteps of clients.

This also effectively reduced the indirect cash expenses incurred by clients through transportation and subsistence. The formal MFIs also offered a much more varied scope, reached out to poorer clients (depth) and had larger client numbers participating (breadth). The formal MFIs also had more ongoing partnerships, both with government and the private sector aimed at increasing outreach. However, the incorporation of factors that increase the willingness to pay, such as ensuring good customer relationships and flexible duration of repayments, was much higher with the semi-formal clients than with the formal ones. This shows that ownership, voice and accountability can make differences in clients' willingness to repay and the degree of flexibility in the duration of repayments. However, worth in terms of loan amounts accessed, the flexibility of deposit withdrawals and the ability to diversify income sources, employ others, and achieve personal goals were more widespread among the formal MFI clients than was the case with semi-formal and informal MFI clients. The formal MFIs also had varied contract enforcement mechanisms and add-ons (microfinance plus) on group products. Forging linkages and collaborations between these three institutional types is key to the achievement of the broader goals of financial sustainability, increased outreach and financial inclusion with likely greater impacts on livelihoods and poverty reduction. Interest rates across the formal, semi-formal and informal providers were relatively lower in the Upper East Region than the national averages.

These averaged 32%, 35% and 40% for the region, compared to the national averages of 36%, 45% and 65% per annum for formal, semi-formal and informal MFIs. These have implications for depth and breadth of outreach (i.e., poorer clients and absolute numbers served, respectively).

The next sections take a detailed look at each of these design features and their implications on product and service design on client's livelihoods.

5.2.2 Clients' Perceptions of Costs of Microfinance Intermediation and Livelihoods in the Northern Savannah of Ghana

From the microfinance supply side of rural financial markets, interest rates are both the price and an instrument for regulating the risk composition of the lender's portfolio (Stiglitz and Weiss, 1981; Stiglitz, 1987). In other words, the interest rate serves a dual function of being the price of the loan and an indirect screening mechanism. Reputational effects (Stiglitz and Weiss, 1983) (e.g., the threat of cutting off future credit) and market interlinkages (Braverman and Stiglitz, 1982, 1986), where credit transactions are interlinked with product or rental market contracts to steer borrowers away from moral hazards and increase the probability of repayment, constitute other indirect mechanisms used by MFIs. However, for reputational effects to be effective, interest rates must be moderate and consumer surplus must exist for those with access.

On the demand side, the cost to clients comprises both price costs and transaction costs. While price costs are the direct cash payments in the form of interest and fees, transaction costs are the sum of both the non-cash opportunity costs (e.g., the time to apply for a loan) and indirect cash expenses (e.g., transport, documents, food, taxes, among others) incurred for the use of a financial service (Schreiner, 2002). Whereas price costs are revenue for the MFI in question, transaction costs borne by clients are not. Also, while the internal rate of return of price costs would make the present value of the cash flow of a financial contract zero for the client, transaction costs can be estimated from survey data by miles, minutes and money required to use a financial service. However, a distinction exists between costs to clients, costs of supply and costs to society. While the cost to clients includes price cost, transaction cost, non-cash opportunity cost (time lost from income-generating activities) and indirect expenses incurred for access, cost of supply is the opportunity cost of the resources (public and/or private) used for financial and non-financial intermediation via existing MFIs within the microfinance livelisystem framework. Cost to society includes the cost of supply (the opportunity costs of resources used in microfinance) and any other costs borne by non-clients (e.g., displacement costs borne by non-clients when out-competed from markets by those with access).

Clients' perceptions of the various elements of the costs of access associated with the design of MFIs' products and services are explored. The section focuses on (a) interest and fees charged by MFIs on products and services, (b) the opportunity costs (i.e., time-off from other income-generating activities to obtain products and services from their MFIs) and (c) the indirect cash expenses from transportation, documentation and subsistence, among others, during attempts to have access. The overall assessment of the benefits and costs of participation in microfinance by clients in the Northern Savannah of Ghana concludes the costs of access.

Table 5.3 presents the percentages of clients' perceptions of the affordability of interest and fees (price costs), non-cash opportunity costs, other indirect cash expenses and the overall cost-benefits verdict of accessing financial products and services from the various MFIs in the Northern Savannah of Ghana. Overall, 72% of all clients regarded interest and fees as affordable (Table 6.2, column A). It was 99% for non-cash opportunity costs, 93% for indirect cash expenses and 93% for cost-benefits analysis of participation in the microfinance livelisystem

TABLE 5.3 Perceptions of the Appropriateness of Price Costs, Non-cash Opportunity Costs, Indirect Cash Expenses and Overall Cost-Benefits Analysis by Microfinance Clients

(A) Total Sample (N = 150)			*(B) Formal Clients (N = 50)*			*(C) Semi-formal Clients (N = 50)*			*(D) Informal Clients (N = 50)*		
Freq.		*%*	*Freq.*		*%*	*Freq.*		*%*	*Freq.*		*%*
Price cost (interest and fees) to clients appropriate											
Yes	108	72	**Yes**	20	40	**Yes**	40	80	**Yes**	49	98
No	42	28	**No**	30	60	**No**	10	20	**No**	1	2
Non-cash opportunity (time-off other income-generating activities) costs to clients as a product design feature											
Yes	148	99	**Yes**	49	98	**Yes**	49	98	**Yes**	50	100
No	2	1	**No**	1	2	**No**	1	2	**No**	0	0
Indirect costs (indirect cash expenses/transport, food and documentations) appropriate											
Yes	140	93	Yes	45	90	Yes	45	90	Yes	50	100
No	10	7	No	5	10	No	5	10	No	0	0
Client overall costs/benefits Analysis (positive) of access appropriate											
Yes	140	93	Yes	45	90	Yes	45	90	Yes	50	100
No	10	7	No	5	10	No	5	10	No	0	0

of the Northern Savannah of Ghana (all in Table 6.2 column A). And 93% said that overall, benefits exceeded the costs of access (column A). These generalized results on costs of access suggest that microfinance may not necessarily be transformational, but the goals of the industry are being achieved in the Northern Savannah of Ghana.

Disaggregating the respondents into formal (Tier 1), semi-formal (Tier 2) and informal (Tier 3), it was observed that as high as 98% of the informal clients considered interest and fees charged affordable (column D). For the semi-formal clients, it was 80% (column C) and only 40% for the formal clients (column B).

Therefore, the informal clients were the least likely to have interest rates and fees charged on loans or paid on deposits as an obstacle to access. Smaller loan sizes make interest and fees seem negligible. There existed some form of co-insurance, where the amount charged or paid as interest depended on whether the debtor or creditor suffered losses. The reverse was true for formal MFIs where loan sizes were relatively larger and contracts less flexible.

When cash flows become irregular and sometimes unpredictable, servicing loans from the formal MFIs can be distressing. This confirms the findings of earlier studies that concluded that high-interest rates do not deter the need to access financial services by the poor (Robinson, 1996; Fafchamps and Pender, 1997; Perry, 2002). The flexibility in contract design features common with the informal intermediaries could be more valuable for resource-poor people with irregular cash flows, than the interest and fees charged (Magill and Meyer, 2005; Tejerina et al., 2006). That is, just as loan contracts offered by informal lenders (e.g., rapid loan approval, flexible terms, repayment periods measured in days or weeks and lump sum payments at exorbitant interest rates) are generally ill-suited for enterprise financing, those from formal MFIs are characterized by slow turnaround, inflexible repayment periods measured in months or years, and regular small repayments at relatively low-interest rates are generally ill-suited for emergency/consumption purposes (Perry, 2002). Moreover, the high approval rating of the affordability of interest and fees by the semi-formal and informal clients could also signal the lack of alternative sources of access (Hoff and Stiglitz, 1993) in clients' localities rather than affordability.

Also, the disaggregation of the non-cash opportunity costs – a form of transaction costs – incurred by clients showed that 98% each of the formal and semi-formal clients and all the informal clients discounted it as limiting participation. The trend wasn't different in the case of indirect cash expenses. Plausible reasons proffered include limited time spent on farms because of the unimodal rainfall pattern of the region, which is made worse by weather variability and climate change. Nevertheless, these costs were high, leading to the adaption and adoption of the mobile staff concept by mostly the formal but also some of the semi-formal MFIs. This involved taking banking to the doorsteps of clients by staff using vehicles. Transactions take place at the field (client's homes or enterprise locations) and staff enters transactions into the computer systems upon return to the MFI's offices. For the informal clients, participants were found to belong to close social networks and most often lived in the same community.

The disaggregated evaluation of perceived cost/benefits of participation across the three institutional types revealed that 90% of the formal and semi-formal clients claimed that benefits exceeded costs. All the informal clients said that benefits exceeded costs, suggesting that although microfinance may not be transformational, the broader goals of the industry have been met.

In addition, the study carried out focus group discussions to provide depth behind the numbers for the claims of affordability of interest and fees, the transaction costs of non-cash opportunity costs and indirect cash expenses, and overall client evaluation of cost-benefits of participation. Table 5.4 provides quotes on how clients from each microfinance finance institutional category perceive the cost elements including price costs, non-cash opportunity costs, indirect cash expenses and overall client evaluation of the cost-benefits of participation.

Moreover, the first two and/or three ranked reasons for the affordability of these cost elements, as presented in Appendix V, are discussed and their implications to the conceptual framework and the extant literature are further explored. For instance, the key reasons given for the affordability of interest and fees by the formal clients were that many clients repeat loan contracts, and that is if the terms and conditions, including interest and fees, were favourable, hence the repetition. Another reason was that the sustainable provision of services meant

TABLE 5.4 Perceptions of the Various Cost Elements of Microfinance Intermediation, Including Cost-Benefits Evaluation

Institutional Category	*Price Cost (interest and fees)*	*Non-cash Opportunity Cost*	*Indirect Cash Expenses*	*Overall Benefits*
Formal MFIs	Low but perceived high	Low	Low	High
Quotes	"*You are made aware of the interest before taking the loan, so it must be affordable once you sign, take the loan, repay and take another loan and keep repeating*" FC_RCB_ M_Navrongo	"*We have the bank agents coming to us at our workplaces or even homes to conduct business. This has made us not spend any monies on traveling to the bank. It's a good thing the banks are doing to help us and help themselves because if we don't spend on some of these things, we can repay our loans and save more*" *FC_M_ S&L_Bolga*	"*The same bank agents coming to us has reduced the money I have to spend buying petrol for my motorbike to travel there. Even the risks of maybe an accident on the road is reduced*" *FC_RCB_ Sandema*	"*Most of our individual clients use loans to expand existing enterprises. However, most of the group loans went to women groups that are either into a group or individual income-generating activities*" *Credit Officer Naara Rural Bank Bolgatanga Branch*
Semi-formal MFIs	Medium	Low	Low	High
Quotes	"*As for our Credit Union, interest rates way, way lower than these commercial banks in town and even the Rural Banks. That is why I have left all of those and have been working with Vavrongo Teachers Credit Union for more than 10 years now*" *SFC_ CUA_M_Nav*	"*The union agents do come around and no much time is wasted, but for me getting the loan at the end of the day is the most important thing. Because, no money, no business, no profits*" *SF*	"*The agents come around, so we don't usually go to the office especially for the savings and most of us live not too far away*" *SFC_F_ Navrongo*	"*Because a client must buy shares (save) and be able to take a loan twice that amount, the savings culture is gradually improving among our clients and most useful for businesses like rice farming and tomato farming at the Tono Irrigation project site. It's really helping our people*" *Manager, Assemblies of God Credit Union Navrongo*

Informal MFIs	High but perceived low	Low	Low	High
Quotes	*"As for the VSLA groups, we all set our interest rate according to what is comfortable for many of us. We don't have problems with interest rate on loans because the interest money we pay along with the amount borrowed eventually comes back to us and each member get his/her share according to the amount you contributed at first"* *IC_F_VSLA_ Sandema*	*"Most of us live near our sources of money and we don't waste time because there is trust after working with him for years now, but the important thing is getting the money and using it for the purpose you are looking for it to do"* IC_M_Tarasum_ Bolga	*"We just walk to our meeting place at the primary school there late afternoon when the sun is hot, and we don't usually waste time because we have to go home and start cooking for our children and husbands. But using the money to do business or solve your problems is more important"* *IC_VSLA_ Sandema*	*"Most of my group members use not to have anywhere to borrow. The sad part was when you go to friends or family members to borrow money and after you finish telling them all your problems they refuse and tell you why you didn't come yesterday or a week earlier and that they have used all their monies. Now most of us can pay school fees for our children, buy fertilizer and do business. Others to don't spend carelessly again. They save the money and get interested on it"* *IC_F_VSLA Chair Sandema*

the interest and fees are needed for the MFIs to stay in business. This implied that clients must be benefiting from repeating contracts and understood the need for sustainability of service provision profitability. These insights may also suggest that more of the formal clients in the Northern Savannah of Ghana were better educated and not necessarily found at the bottom of the microfinance pyramid. These sentiments were captured in the following quote:

> You are made aware of the interest before taking the loan, so it must be affordable once you sign or thumbprint and obtain the loan and repeat another loan when you finish paying.
>
> *FC_RCB_M_Garu*

It is also worth noting that clients are not homogenous, and livelihood strategies are affected by both individual household circumstances and the broader socio-economic environment.

The semi-formal clients perceived that interest and fees were lower in comparison to commercial banks, and the formal and informal intermediaries. This perception was generally not true, but this was accounted for by the flexibility of the financial contracts with this group of MFIs that probably matched the irregular and unpredictable cash flows of clients. Clients here also contended that service provisioning was less time-consuming, which pointed to better MFI-client relationships where voice and accountability mattered in product design and roll-out. It also suggests an orientation towards the poverty-lending approach by this group of MFIs, mostly the credit unions and financial NGOs. The following quote sums up the views on the affordability of interest and fees by the semi-formal clients.

> As for our Credit Union, interest rates and fees charged are very much lower and affordable than the commercial banks and even some other microfinance institutions. Here you can negotiate and pay later with very small charges for late repayments. That is why I have left all the others and have been working with them for over 10 years now.
>
> *SFC_CUA_M_Nav*

However, it was financial contract flexibility that ranked first for the informal clients. Most perceived interest and fees as moderate, suggesting smaller loan sizes have a dampening effect on the perceptions of interest and fees paid for the use of financial contracts, mostly loans. This confirmed Robinson's (1996) finding that the working poor can pay relatively higher interest rates, which they consider relatively lower than their alternatives.

Fafchamps (1997) also showed that interest rate subsidizations have little impact on client product uptake and livelihood activities, more especially on profitable investments. For the village savings and loans (VSL) groups – a form of Accumulating Savings and Loans Association (Dupas and Robinson, 2013) – interest and fees were self-determined and groups self-managed. Generated revenues from interest and fees charged become dividends paid in proportion to what each member contributes to the pool at the end of the cycle. The promotion of the VSLA concept by international NGOs is partly in response to the need for affordable financial services in rural localities and the widespread commercialization of mainstream microfinance. The following quote sums this view.

> As for we the VSLA groups, we all sit down to set our interest rate according to what most of us are comfortable with. We don't have problems with interest rates on loans because the interest money we pay on loans eventually becomes ours. This is paid to each member according to the number of shares bought by the member.
>
> *IC_F_VSLA_Sandema*

On designing products that ensure non-cash opportunity costs of clients are kept to the barest minimum, most of the formal and semi-formal MFIs in the Northern Savannah of Ghana have largely deployed mobile staff who reach out to clients. Using motor-bikes and sometimes pick-ups for transportation, they take banking to the doorsteps of clients. This phenomenon represented a recognition of the need to minimize non-cash opportunity costs of participating clients that have implications for the outreach and sustainability goals of the industry. However, for the formal clients, having access at the end of the day, even if the non-cash opportunity cost is high, was ranked first. To them, access was all that was important. The next highest-ranked reason was that MFIs were reaching out via mobile staff. This, clients contend, has made non-cash opportunity costs negligible. For the semi-formal clients, the deployment of mobile staff by the MFIs has made non-cash opportunity cost negligible. Thus, the call that commercial banks and microfinance institutions should form links or that commercial banks mimic (Hoff and Stiglitz, 1993) the activities of informal intermediaries to enable clients to take advantage of both is critical. The rest of the perceptions of clients on product design to minimize non-cash opportunity costs for clients are presented in Appendix VI.

Moreover, on product design to minimize indirect cash expenses clients incur for financial inclusion, the use of mobile staff drastically cuts down on such expenses by the formal and semi-formal MFIs where such expenses feature prominently. The following quote confirms this assertion:

> We have the bank agents coming to us at our workplaces or even homes to conduct business. This has made us not spend any monies on traveling to the bank. It's a good thing the banks are doing to help us and help themselves because if we don't spend on some of these things, we can repay our loans and save more.
>
> *FC_M_S &L_Bolga*

Clients are not homogenous. For the formal and semi-formal clients, there was the recognition that the use of mobile staff yields broader dividends for both MFIs and clients. It had a positive impact on outreach and the sustainability goals of the industry and, therefore, financial inclusion in the Northern Savannah of Ghana. The second reason was that loans are needed for investments. Working capital is the lifeblood of any enterprise, so discounting any indirect cash expenses can only be compelling when cash is needed to replenish stocks. The following quote captured this view.

> I use the MFI products and services to buy stocks for my shop and once I make a profit and I able to repay the Credit Union, does it matter whatever indirect expenses I might have made while chasing the loan? Not at all.
>
> *SFC_F_CUA_Bolgatanga*

However, for the informal clients, less time consumed in accessing financial products and services from the MFIs was ranked first and this was because most live near the MFIs. There was the additional advantage of providers having access to sufficient information about their potential clients and devices such as reputational effects (Woolcock, 2001) and interlinked markets (Braverman and Stiglitz, 1982, 1986) were easily used to overcome adverse selection and moral hazards in these informal rural credit markets. The following quote puts these assertions into perspective.

> Most of us live around where we get our loans. We just walk there. No transportation costs, no need to buy food because we will easily get back home and eat even our left-over foods because we don't travel to Sandema town.
>
> *IC_F_VSLA_Sandema (Fumbishi)*

On the overall evaluation of benefits against the cost of participation, over 93% of microfinance clients (Table 5.3, column A) in the Northern Savannah of Ghana claimed that the benefits of access far exceeded all cost considerations. On usage, while the majority of the formal clients expanded existing businesses with loan products, many also used savings instruments and invested some in mostly consumption smoothening needs. These were succinctly revealed in the following quote:

> I was able to expand my business through working with the MFI products, particularly the loans. There are other things I benefit from the bank that somebody who is not a member cannot get. I was able to buy stocks for my shop and I am doing rice farming too from the profits I make from my shop.
>
> *FC_M_RCB_Bolga*

For the semi-formal clients, the majority claimed that the savings culture developed because of compulsory savings instruments required before loans can be disbursed to as much as twice the deposit amount has been helpful. Savings, they claimed, have been a critical component of their households' livelihood strategies while loans were instrumental in enabling them to expand their non-farm enterprises, as captured in the following quote:

> I was able to expand my Coal Tar business by taking a loan from the Navrongo Teachers Credit Union and buying in large quantities during the rainy season when the prices are relatively very low. I then sell it immediately the Dry Season is starting, and people need it to repair their homes, especially in the rural areas. I am then able to pay back the loan balance on time. So, what I do is, I keep part of the loan amount in my account to take care of the monthly installment required for at least 3 months before

> the dry season when I can sell the coal tar and pay off the balance with my profits at a go.
>
> *SFC_F_CUA_Navro*

This statement aligns with the recognition that the role of timing in loan repayment schedules can be critical to a client's success or failure with implications on repayments. Inflexible repayment schedules, involving weekly or monthly repayments, usually begin the first week or month following loan disbursal, take away some of the investment's capital and stifle outcomes. Some investments require longer periods to yield appreciable returns. Moreover, it confirms Perry's (2002) finding that just as contract terms of informal service providers that include rapid loan approval, flexible repayment periods and lump sum repayments at exorbitant interest rates made them generally ill-suited for enterprise financing, those of the formal providers with slow turnaround time, inflexible and regular repayments at relatively low interest rates also made them ill-suited for emergency/consumption purposes. It also confirmed the findings of Banerjee et al. (2010) in India that people with access to microcredit were likely to start businesses, especially so if the credit was sourced from formal MFIs.

However, informal MFIs such as the VSLA groups were emphatic that their profits were mostly saved for emergencies and that the majority of loans and savings went into providing the educational needs of their children. Consumption smoothening was the dominant use of most financial products among informal clients as narrated in the following quote:

> The benefits are more because I used not to have anywhere to turn to in times of need. These groups are a saviour for most women in this community. It has helped us to bring together our small, small monies into one 'big' money and we can borrow and repay in an orderly way. The good thing is that we ourselves set the interest and at the end of the cycle everyone gets some of the interest according to how much your total contribution is. No cheating of one another.
>
> *IC_F_VSLA_Sandema*

In summary, the results showed that designing products and services that simultaneously reduce the cost of access, including interest and fees paid to MFIs, the non-cash opportunity cost and indirect cash expenses incurred by clients, and at the same time match livelihood needs, ultimately adds weight to microfinance as an anti-poverty tool. However, the cost of access varies across the three tiers of MFIs operating in the Northern Savannah of Ghana. Those accessing products and services from the formal MFIs perceived interest and fees paid to be the lowest in the market, but two-thirds said it was unaffordable. The larger absolute loan amounts involved largely accounted for the perception of unaffordability by clients of the formal MFIs. The semi-formal clients also perceive interest and fees paid lower than those charged by commercial banks and both the formal and informal MFIs. However, it was the flexibility of contract designs by most semi-formal MFIs that largely accounted for the perception of sub-market interest rates. The notion of contract flexibility accounting for the perception of lower interest and fees paid was much more pronounced among clients of the informal MFIs than with those of the semi-formal MFIs. Among such informal organizations as the Village Savings and Loans, groups self-manage and set their interest and fees charged to members.

Limiting the non-cash opportunity costs and indirect cash expenses incurred by clients was the critical determinant of increased outreach, product uptake and MFI sustainability. The use of mobile staff by most MFIs in the region confirmed the recognition of this fact. However, MFIs need to effectively estimate these additional transactional costs and efficiently transmit the same through the design of contracts, without upsetting the demand and supply dynamics of the financial market. While the deployment of mobile staff constrained non-cash opportunity costs and indirect cash expenses by clients of the formal and semi-formal MFIs, it was the proximity of clients to the informal MFIs that limited such transactional costs for both clients and their service providers. Furthermore, a disaggregated evaluation of client perceived cost/benefits analysis of access to microfinance in this study revealed that while over 90% of clients accessing products and services from the formal and semi-formal MFIs claimed benefits exceeded all cost considerations, no informal client claimed otherwise. These results suggest that despite challenges limiting the transformational role of microfinance as an anti-poverty tool, microfinance is working for those with access (see Appendices V and VI and also II, III and IV).

5.2.3 Clients' Perceptions of Scope of Microfinance Intermediation and Livelihoods in the Northern Savannah of Ghana

In basic terms, the scope is the number of different types of financial products and services (contracts) that an MFI is supplying to its clients within the microfinance livelisystem framework. However, while scope between products describes the number of different product types (e.g., number of loans and savings), the scope within products describes the number of different types of the same product that the MFI offers (e.g., the different loan products). MFIs that are poverty-lending oriented tend to limit the scope to loans, while those inclined to the financial systems approach do little on savings services (Schreiner, 2002). Within the lending function of MFIs, loans are for either enterprise development or consumption smoothening purposes, or emergency needs. Also, MFI loans are provided either individually or in groups where joint liability is enlisted to curtail adverse selection and moral hazards. The exploration of scope in this study relates to clients' perceptions of whether the different products – loans, savings, insurance and payment services – provided by the MFIs of the Northern Savannah of Ghana are meeting clients' diverse financial needs and the satisfaction with the scope of products and services generally. The reasons for product

TABLE 5.5 Perceptions of Scope of MFI Product and Service Offering

	MFI Level	*Loans*	*Savings*	*Insurance*	*Payments*
Formal MFIs	High	High	High	High	High
Semi-formal MFIs	Medium	Medium	Medium	Low	Low
Informal MFIs	Low	Low	Low	None	None

scope meeting clients' livelihood needs and the satisfaction thereof were further assessed. Table 5.5 provides an overview of scope across the formal, semi-formal and informal microfinance institutions of the Northern Savannah of Ghana. While product scopes for the formal MFIs were highly varied and integrated, those of the semi-formal was moderate to low in variation and less integrated into their delivery approach. Those of the informal MFIs were less varied, providing basic credit and secure savings services. They can best be described as minimalists in their delivery approach.

Table 5.6 presents the dominant product scope of the sampled MFIs of the Northern Savannah of Ghana that reflects the diverse client livelihood needs of the study region. The dominant products were loans and savings that targeted clients at different levels of the microfinance pyramid. The presence of individual and group products, especially for loans, was indicative of clients belonging to different levels of the microfinance pyramid. Thus, while some MFIs were pre-financial systems and others pro-poverty-lending, others were hybrids, in that they designed products that served different layers of clients in the Northern Savannah of Ghana. For the formal MFIs, loans, savings, insurance and payment services mirrored those of the banking sector. While within loan scope ranged between five and ten different products, this was averaged four and five for savings per each formal MFI. Also, there existed the presence of a credit risk management instrument designed to protect both the MFIs and clients from income loss resulting from unintended defaults. Other insurance products included credit life, bancassurance and weather-indexed crop insurances. However, none but the BESSFA Rural Bank had successfully rolled out the weather-indexed crop insurance with small-holder farmers. Payment services for the formal clients included salaries of mostly public and civil servants, E-zwich, Western Union Money Transfer, National Lotteries, MTN Mobile Money and ARB Apex Link transfers.

For the semi-formal clients, loan scope ranged between three and seven products, while those of savings were between two and three products per institution. Moreover, all the semi-formal clients had an insurance product designed with support from their apex bodies to protect income loss from unintended loan defaults. The informal VSLA groups also had their own insurances, albeit informal co-insurances where interest rates paid are conditional upon whether the client or provider suffered a loss to income. These were either financial or non-financial and more pronounced among the VSLA groups.

TABLE 5.6 Product and Service Scope of Sampled MFIs in the Northern Savannah of Ghana

	Name of MFI	*Loans Products*	*Savings Products*	*Products*	*Payment Services*
Formal MFIs	Naaara Rural Bank	1. Naara Micro Credit (NMC); 2. Credit with Education; 3. Susu Loan; 4. Construction Business Loan; 5. Overdrafts/ business; 6. Salary	1. Susu Savings; 2. Ordinary Savings; 3. Child Trust Account; 4. Fixed deposit	1. Insurance on all loans (various) (underwritten by an insurance company, Star Life)	1. Western Union; 2. MoneyGram; 3. ARB Apex Transfer Link; 4. E-zwich; 5. MTN Mobile Money
	Builsa Community Bank	1. Commercial Loans; 2. Agricultural Loans; 3. Microfinance Group Loans; 4. E-Susu Loans; 5. Quick/ smart Loans; 6. Salary Loans/Construction Loans	1. Buco Savings Account; 2. Buco Child (Kiddo) Account; 3. Buco Susu Savings Account; 4. Buco Microfinance Savings Account; 5. Fixed Deposit; 6. Savings deposit; 7. Current deposit; 8. Fixed deposit; 9. Susu deposit; 10. Trust account deposit	1. Susu loans; 2. Savings-linked insurance	1. Western Union; 2. MoneyGram; 3. ARB Apex Transfer Link; 4. E-zwich; 5. MTN Mobile Money
	BESSFA Rural Bank	1. Individual non-salaried loan; 2. Individual salaried loan; 3. Farming loan; 4. Credit with education loan; 5. Overdraft facilities	1. Savings deposit; 2. Current deposit; 3. Fixed deposit; 4. Susu deposit; 5. Trust account deposit	1. Credit Life; 2. Bancassurance; 3. Weather-Indexed Crop Insurance (Underwritten by Star Life Insurance Company)	1. Western Union; 2. MoneyGram; 3. ARB Apex Transfer Link; 4. E-zwich; 5. National Lotteries; 6. MTN Mobile Money

	Sinapi Abba	1. Group Loans (Trust Bank and Cluster Group Loans); 2. Micro-Enterprise Loans; 3. Sinapi Festive Loan; 4. Sinapi Agro-Loans (Project); 5. Micro-School Loans; 6. Tractor Loans; 7. Susu Loans; 8. Educational Loans; 9. Asset Loans; 10. Home Improvement Loans	1. Mandatory Savings; 2. Susu Savings; 3. Flexi Savings; 4. Kiddy Savings	1. Insurance; 2. Welfare Schemes (various)	1. Western Union; 2. MoneyGram; 3. E-zwich; 4. MTN Mobile Money
Semi-formal MFIs	Navrongo Teachers CUA	1. Long-Term Loans; 2. Loans within Savings; 3. Soft Loans	1. Member saving (MS); 2. Special savings (SS); 3. Youth Savings	1. Credit and income risk management insurance on loans; 2. Savings	1. Mobile Money
	Navrongo Assemblies of God CUA	1. Provident Loans; 2. Agricultural Loans; 3. Business Loans	1. Ordinary Savings; 2. Group Savings; 3. Youth Savings	1. Credit and income risk management insurance on loans; 2. Savings	1. Mobile Money
	Bolgatanga Teachers CUA	1. Education Loan; 2. Business Capital Loan; 3. Housing Loan; 4. Medical (Healthcare Loan)	1. Ordinary Savings; 2. Youth Savings (No Charges on Savings)	1. Credit and income risk management insurance on loans; 2. Savings	1. Mobile Money

(Continued)

TABLE 5.6 Continued

	Name of MFI	*Loans Products*	*Savings Products*	*Products*	*Payment Services*
	Garu Teachers CUA	1. Individual loans; 2. Group loans; 3. Soft loans; 4. Business loan; 5. Personal loan; 6. Agri-business loan; 7. Individual loans	1. Ordinary normal Savings; 2. Group Savings; 3. Youth Savings	1. Credit and income risk management insurance on loans; 2. savings	1. Mobile Money
	Innovative Microfinance Company	1. Group Loan; 2. Community Group Loan; 3. Individual Loan; 4. Susu Loan; 5. Hire Purchase	1. Edumapa Saving; 2. Inno Saving; 3. Inno Kids Saving	-	1. Mobile Money
Informal MFIS	Bencyn Susu Company	-	1. Susu Original; 2. Susu Myway; 3. Susu Education; 4. Susu Savings; 5. Susu Old Age	-	-
	Tarasum Lending	1. Tarasum Microloans	-	-	-
	VSLA	1. Microloans; 2. Micro-savings	1.Share purchase (equity)	1. Informal (cash and non-cash) insurances	-

TABLE 5.7 Percentages of Products and Services Accessed by Microfinance Clients

Products	*Loans (N = 150)*		*Savings (N = 150)*		*Insurance (N = 150)*		*Payments (N = 150)*		*Fin. Advice (N = 150)*		*Fin. Literacy (N = 150)*	
	Freq.	*%*	*Freq.*	*%*	*Freq.*	*%*	*Freq.*	*%*	*Freq.*	*%*	*Freq.*	*%*
Yes	115	76.67	119	79.33	29	19.33	13	8.67	51	34	30	20
No	35	23.33	31	20.67	121	80.67	137	91.33	99	66	120	80

Table 5.7 presents the percentages of product and service uptake by clients of the microfinance industry of the Northern Savannah of Ghana. Over 76% of all sampled client's take-up loans. This was three percentage points higher for savings, at 79%. This confirms the findings of Diop et al. (2003) that an expanded microfinance industry that included savings services was key to securing deposits and enabling the poor to save more and more systematically. Insurance uptake was low at only 19% while that of payments represented only 13%. This mirrors the findings in the GLSS IV report that insurance penetration was low in the Northern Savannah, with almost 78% of households without any form of insurance. The low penetration of payment service uptake via MFIs in the Northern Savannah of Ghana was attributed to a well-developed and growing mobile money transfer service that was making traditional money transfers unattractive. Financial advice and financial literacy training for clients by the MFIs were also not impressive at 34% and 20%, respectively, common with the formal and semi-formal clients. The diverse product and service availability lend credence to microfinance as a development tool, where both financial and non-financial intermediation are used as poverty reduction instruments. Thus, services are integrated to ensure favourable livelihood outcomes for participants.

Table 5.8 presents quantified perceptions of the convergence of microfinance products and services to the diverse needs of participants and the general satisfaction thereof across the three institutional types. While over 83% of all participants said loan products from their MFIs were meeting the diverse needs of their livelihood's strategies, a similar percentage of 83% expressed satisfaction. Drivers of loan product satisfaction among the formal clients included low interest and fees compared to the commercial banks. The perception of low interest rates also drove loan satisfaction for the semi-formal and informal clients except for the VSLA groups, where interest and fees become revenue for the group. It is worth noting that the drivers of satisfaction with products and services were perceived at the institutional and product-specific levels as captured in the following quote:

> Our bank has many different loans and savings products. Some are for single people who have guarantors or collateral. Some are also for we the poor ones don't have guarantors or collateral and are made to form groups so that loans can be given to us. The good thing is that, once you are in

TABLE 5.8 Frequency of MFI Product and Service Mix (Scope)

(A) MFI loan(s) products meeting needs?			*Overall satisfied with loan product(s) offering?*		
	Freq.	*%*		*Freq.*	*%*
Yes	125	83.33	Yes	124	82.67
No	25	16.67	No	26	17.33
(B) MFI saving(s) products meeting needs?			*Overall satisfied with saving product(s) offering?*		
	Freq.	*%*		*Freq.*	*%*
Yes	116	77.33	Yes	130	86.67
No	34	22.67	No	20	13.33
(C) MFI Insurance (if any) meeting needs?			*Overall satisfied with the Insurance product(s) offering?*		
	Freq.	*%*		*Freq.*	*%*
Yes	66	44	Yes	16	10.74
No	84	56	No	133	89.26
(D) MFI Payment Services (if any) meeting needs?			*Overall satisfied with MFI Payment Services (if any)*		
	Freq.	*%*		*Freq.*	*%*
Yes	13	8.67	Yes	13	8.67
No	137	91.33	No	137	91.33
(E) Generally, products and services meeting the need of the clients?			*Generally, satisfied with the products and services offered?*		
	Freq.	*%*		*Freq.*	*%*
Yes	91	61.49	Yes	132	88
No	57	38.51	No	18	12

> the group and the rules of the group are made known to you, you wouldn't want to break them. So, our bank is doing well because the well-off people get loans and the poor ones also get loans to help ourselves.
>
> *FC_F_RCB_Bolga*

This suggests that factors determining optimal product uptake and satisfaction must be considered in the organizational cultural setting that relates to structures and systems of management and the specific product features that clients value and can afford.

On savings, while slightly over 77% of clients said microfinance deposit products met their needs, over 87% claimed satisfaction with the same in the Northern Savannah of Ghana. This confirms the findings of Christen (2001), in Latin America, that the estimated market for savings among low-income populations far outweighed that for enterprise loans. These savings products were either mandatory or voluntary. While the mandatory savings teaches financial discipline and provides suppliers with additional information that narrows the information asymmetry between lenders and borrowers, voluntary savings products allow clients to save up (i.e., in anticipation of hard times), save down (i.e., take out a loan and repay in instalment) and save through (i.e., insurance and group-based savings VSLAs) (Rutherford, 2011). Moreover, key informant interviews with credit officers revealed that mandatory savings, especially with the credit union associations, served as loanable funds and a quasi-collateral for loans (Armendariz and Morduch, 2005; Morduch, 2007), but withdrawals were typically restrictive with this group of institutions. The build-up of savings within the microfinance industry constitutes a promising contribution to reducing the vulnerability of resource-poor, low-income groups in the Northern Savannah of Ghana. Besides, while the formal clients (RCBs and S & L) considered good customer relations and encouragement as key to increased deposits, the deployment of mobile staff who regularly visit clients contributed to increased savings by the semi-formal clients (CUAs and FNGOs). However, accepting even the smallest amounts from clients for purposes of saving it was critical to increased frequency of savings for the informal clients.

In general, more than 61% of microfinance clients in the Northern Savannah of Ghana agreed that all products and services accessed from their MFIs were meeting their needs. On satisfaction, over 88% of microfinance clients of the Northern Savannah of Ghana were satisfied with all products and services accessed. This is fundamental to the assertion that microfinance is working. The rest of the drivers of savings product uptake and their rankings are presented in Appendix VI under product scope.

Although micro-insurance was in its early stages of development, efforts had been made to formalize and design the process in the Northern Savannah of Ghana, but with limited success. A consortium of 14 rural and community banks located in the Northern Savannah, a private insurance company and some NGOs partnered in the development of weather-indexed insurance products from which the BESSFA Rural Bank in Garu continue to run this day. Over 44% of respondents with insurance products, including those tailored to credit risk management, said the products were serving their intended purpose—however, less than 11% of those expressed satisfaction. The low penetration of insurance product uptake in the microfinance industry of the Northern Savannah of Ghana was reflected in the low uptake of insurance products by households of the Northern Savannah, at only 22.1% (GLSS VI, 2014). The differences between insurance markets and credit markets are reflected in the financial sector regulatory framework of the country. MFIs are legally not allowed to underwrite insurance products. There was also limited capacity on the part of existing MFIs in partnering, designing and rolling out insurance products with the insurance companies. Setting up and/or running insurance programs requires specialized knowledge completely at variance with credit markets. Information asymmetry continues to hamper the growth of existing insurance programmes in the sector. For instance, people insulated from risk may behave differently from those fully exposed to it (moral hazard). Also, high-risk individuals are more likely to buy insurance products (adverse selection) than low-risk individuals. The inability of the insurer to isolate and charge high-risk individuals higher premiums compels the design of products to charge high premiums, contributing to low uptake averagely. Most often, it is a lack of knowledge of the existence of insurance and the need to ensure it that hinders penetration. It remains important that insurance products that improve upon traditional risk-sharing arrangements and informal insurance networks are co-opted in micro-insurance product designs to support resource-poor households deal with shocks emanating from the vagaries of the weather and irregular income flows. A well-designed inclusive insurance scheme should target and effectively offer safety nets for poor families, for whom the impact of crop failure, livestock death, bad weather, and pests and diseases can have devasting consequences for household livelihoods and welfare.

No perfect design solution has been found to deal with the problems of asymmetric information, but some types of risk should be easier to insure than others. Rainfall insurance stands out among these (Karlan and Morduch 2009; Duflo and Banerjee 2011), and though a piloted weather index insurance scheme involving 14 rural and community banks in the northern Savannah had limited success, the BESSFA Rural Bank in Garu has been successful in rolling it out with smallholder farmers in partnership with Star Insurance Company. Rainfall insurance pays a set amount when rainfall, as measured by a local weather station, is lower or higher than established thresholds. Because rainfall is not under the control of clients, the outcome of a sold insurance product is not influenced by their behaviour (i.e., the elements of moral hazards are absent). Also, because rainfall is a public event, insured households do not need to file claims and insurance companies do not need to spend time and resources verifying the validity of those claims. In short, weather-indexed insurance is simpler and cheaper to administer than many other types of insurance. However, key informant interviews revealed that there were disagreements over the gaps between rainfall amounts and the actual losses suffered by farmers even during the pilot stage, leading to disaffection not only by clients but also by the collaborating rural and community banks as it affected their immediate and future portfolios and the relationship with the underwriting insurance company. Rainfall micro-insurance has the potential of supporting rural households to reduce their exposure to risks. It also modifies smallholders' incentives to invest in riskier, but profitable crops and crop varieties (Giné et al., 2011). But take-up rates remain puzzlingly low in the Northern Savannah of Ghana due to some confounding problems (Karlan and Zinman, 2009; Karlan et al., 2014). The Ghana Agricultural Insurance Pool was actively collaborating with many financial institutions including the BESSFA Rural Bank to roll out weather-indexed insurance products in the Northern Savannah.

The key driver of micro-insurance product uptake for the formal and semi-formal microfinance institutions in the Northern Savannah of Ghana was the low premiums. This aligns with the findings of Cole et al. (2004) in India that the price of an insurance policy was the most important determinant of client uptake increasing by about 10.4% on average when premiums are pegged downwards by 10%. The second reason was the evidence of other clients benefiting from being insured when the risk does occur among both client groups. The following confirmed these reasons during a focus group discussion:

> For me, the deductions (premiums) are almost negligible especially those of the loan insurance and I have seen relatives' of some customers benefiting when the customers himself died from motorbike accidents. So, I always ask the bank to be sure they are deducting on my behalf and I encourage friends to do the same because death comes at the time no one expects it.
>
> *FC_RCB_M_Garu*

It was further noted that in piloting the weather-indexed insurance programme with the rural and community banks in the Northern Savannah, the limited understanding of how the rainfall regime was measured against set thresholds and issues of mistrust between the collaborating partners aggravated by the high illiteracy rates among the farmers contributed to its limited success (Cole et al. 2004). The farmers were of the view that regular updates on insurance policy statuses and providing continuous education will be helpful. All of these suggest that effective collaboration remains compelling to better design, price and market micro-insurance products that meet the real needs of resource-poor households cost-effectively in the Northern Savannah of Ghana.

Payment services for remittances have become useful for rural-urban migrants (temporary and permanent) and international migrants (South-North and South-South). Remittances continue to remain significant for households' income sources in much of the developing world, although wealthier households generally gain more in absolute terms than poorer households. Remittances via payment services remain an important source of household income, a risk mitigation tool and a coping strategy. The importance of payment services as a conduit for remittances was captured by Bill Gates at the G20 2011 Summit in Cannes when he stated, "If the transaction costs on remittances worldwide were cut from where they are today at around 10% to an average of 5%...it would unlock $15bn a year in poor countries". In Ghana, remittance payments are not restricted to banks alone where exclusive arrangements are entered into with large money transfer companies such as Western Union or Money Gram. This has created a niche for microfinance institutions. However, mobile technology is fast disrupting the hitherto traditional models in Ghana, and different rate structures are facilitating patronage in the domestic and international spheres. The three mobile network operators (MNOs) active in the money transfer services in Ghana include MTN, Vodafone and Airtel-Tigo.

Microfinance institutions are active in the payment services in the Northern Savannah of Ghana despite the disruptions. These payment services by the MFIs were in partnership with Western Union, MoneyGram, ARB Apex Link, E-Zwich and National Lotteries. These services were, however, common with the formal and semi-formal MFIs and most had joined in the disruptive money transfer services in partnership with the mobile network operators (MNOs) such as MTN, Airtel-Tigo and Vodafone. New financial technologies compatible with smartphones (e.g., World Remit, Global Reach, Currencies Direct and TransferWise) enable same-day international transfers redeemable at some of these MFIs. The informal MFIs offered no such services. Described as affordable and convenient services characterized by good customer relationships from dedicated staff, payment services were said to be transparent and less time-consuming. Overall, six out of ten clients said that accessed payment services met their expectations and livelihood needs and that nine out of ten expressed satisfaction with payment services offered by MFIs in the Northern Savannah of Ghana. Though cyber-fraud is on the ascendancy in Ghana, these payment services remain a niche, which, if well harnessed, could provide significant conduits for migrant labour to southern Ghana. This will thus securely send back necessary cash to mitigate risks and build sustainable enterprises in the Northern Savannah of Ghana.

In conclusion, scope represents the diversity of products and services. Microfinance products and services in the Northern Savannah of Ghana included loans, savings, insurance, payment services, financial advisory and business development services. The extant literature that established that poverty-lending oriented MFIs often limit the scope to loans and those oriented towards the financial systems approach do little savings services did not entirely reflect the reality of the microfinance landscape in the Northern Savannah of Ghana. While product scopes for the formal MFIs were said to be highly varied and integrated, those of the semi-formal MFIs were moderate to low in variation and less integrated into the delivery approach. Basic credit and savings services dominate the scope of informal MFIs and are described as minimalist in approach. Processes and procedures for the provision of services by the formal MFIs generally mirrored those of commercial banks. Loans and savings products dominated the product baskets of all three tiers of microfinance institutions in the Northern Savannah of Ghana. This was indicative of the primacy of loans and savings in the arsenal of microfinance as an anti-poverty tool. While the formal MFIs offered a broader range of insurance products including weather-indexed crop insurances, credit risk mitigation measures and life assurances, most of the semi-formal MFIs offered credit risk insurances. Compulsory savings were also widely reported among clients of the semi-formal and informal MFIs. This was less pronounced among clients of the formal MFIs, suggesting credit as an entry point. Traditional payment services hitherto offered by the formal and semi-formal MFIs were fast being disrupted by cheaper and more convenient mobile money transfer services by the mobile network operators such as MTN, Airtel-Tigo and Vodafone.

Moreover, product use patterns showed consumption smoothening was high among informal clients and low for the semi-formal and formal clients. The reverse was true for the usage of products for enterprise development, high among formal clients and low among informal clients. In addition, while microfinance products from formal MFIs targeted specific enterprises, it was more relaxed for the semi-formal and informal clients. While 61% of all microfinance clients said accessed products and services met their needs, 88% expressed satisfaction in participation. Overall, 83% said accessed credit met their needs and an approximate percentage expressed satisfaction with loan uptake. For savings, 77% said accessed savings met their needs while 87% expressed satisfaction in participating in savings. These results further confirm the case of the primacy of loans and savings in microfinance.

For the accessed micro-insurance products, while 44% of clients said it met their needs, only 11% expressed satisfaction in participation. Credit risk management schemes were instituted by the formal and semi-formal MFIs that protected both the MFI in question and clients against income loss in the case of involuntary defaults. These credit risk micro-insurance instruments were limited to the 'Susu' savings product of the formal MFIs and the compulsory savings product of the semi-formal MFIs. The insurance claim is triggered once an unintended default is established from either death or permanent disability. This confirms the findings of the GLSS (VI) report that only 22.1% of households in the Northern Savannah are covered by any insurance product. Only 11% of clients accessing micro-insurance products were satisfied. It is worth noting that the financial sector regulatory framework of Ghana does not allow MFIs to design and roll out micro-insurance products. This directive has stifled capacity and innovation in the design of effective insurance products in the microfinance landscape of the Northern Savannah of Ghana.

Only the formal and semi-formal MFIs offered payment services and only 9% of clients expressed satisfaction and needs being met. Traditional payment services provided by the microfinance institutions in the Northern Savannah of Ghana, such as Western Union, MoneyGram and ARB Apex Transfer, were increasingly being disrupted by mobile money offered by mobile network operators. Domestic and international transfers via financial technology apps are now common. These also come with lower costs and increased convenience. But uptake of all payment services, including mobile money via MFIs in the Northern Savannah of Ghana, remains relatively low at 13%, from which only 9% expressed satisfaction. Generally, 60% of clients accessing financial and non-financial services from their MFIs claimed their needs were met and 90% said they were satisfied.

The drivers of satisfaction came from the governance structures and systems of the MFI as well as the product-specific characteristics. Though there were commonalities, these drivers vary from one institutional group to the other.

Good customer relationships and the frequency of visits by mobile staff increased savings and loans product uptake. For insurance products, it was low premiums that were driving uptake. The other drivers of satisfaction and dissatisfaction of scope as product design factor are provided in Appendix VI under '*Scope*' (see also Appendices II, III and IV).

Several collaborations between the government, private sector and international development agencies exist in the microfinance space of the Northern Savannah of Ghana and are helping expand the scope. An example was the Ghana Agricultural Insurance programme that was collaborating with rural and community banks to roll out weather-indexed crop insurance.

5.2.4 Client's Perceptions of Length of Microfinance Intermediation and Livelihoods in the Northern Savannah of Ghana

Length is the time frame for the provision of microfinance products and services to targeted populations. Length concerns the sustainability of MFIs, and it is important for ensuring the prospects of greater welfare for the poor both in the present and in the future. The concept of length is perceived in future terms and therefore, it is difficult to gauge, quantify and measure. Financial self-sufficiency of MFIs emanates from profitability and/or donor funding for the subsidization of costs of services. These two constitute the key determinants of length. On the supply side, the profitability of the MFI is a proxy for length in the absence of guaranteed donations. Profitability further serves as a proxy to gauge and measure the ability of the MFI to access commercial funding either on the domestic or on the international capital markets (e.g., via Microfinance Investment Vehicles). In principle, profitability is necessary, but not sufficient for length (MFI sustainability) in service provision to targeted poorer populations. Financial products and services must meet the needs and wants of clients and positively impact their livelihoods to provoke a reverse reaction of increased demand and product uptake. Moreover, donations have never been given in perpetuity, and therefore profitability matters.

On the demand side, the length will be explored along with clients' perceptions of MFI profitability and knowledge of donor support. Also, the length is explored along clients' livelihoods' preferences and outcomes as they work with their MFIs across the years (see Table 5.9).

The formal MFIs are regulated by the Bank of Ghana and, therefore, subject to the broader financial system regulatory framework. These MFIs are continuing to partner with bilateral and multilateral development agencies to extend credit to critical poverty-reducing real rural sectors. In the Northern Savannah of Ghana, while USAID had ongoing collaborations with some RCBs, World Vision International was partnering with communities in the formation and training of VSLA groups. Most of these VSLA groups were then linked to the RCBs, where they are exposed to a broader scope of products and services and for financial inclusion purposes.

TABLE 5.9 Perceptions of Factors Promoting Sustainable Services Provision (Length)

MFI Category	*Donor Support*	*Profitability*
Formal MFIs	Yes (USAID partnership with RCBs)	High
Semi-formal MFIs	Yes (professional bodies, e.g., GNAT and religious groups (churches) received technical support from Apex bodies	Medium
Informal MFIs	Yes (World Vision, e.g., VSLA formation)	Medium

TABLE 5.10 Percentages of Sustainability (Length) Factors of MFIs in the Northern Savannah of Ghana

Do you think your MFI is making profits?		
	Freq.	*%*
Yes	123	82
No	27	18
Is your MFI donor or government-supported?		
	Freq.	*%*
Yes	19	12.67
No	131	87.33
Range of years clients worked with MFIs		
	Lowest	*Highest*
Formal	1	17
Semi-formal	2	12
Informal	1	17

Table 5.10 presents the findings, in percentage terms, of client's perceptions on length (i.e., the sustainability of service provision). On average, eight out of ten clients of MFIs in the Northern Savannah of Ghana perceived them to be profitable. For the formal and semi-formal clients, the fact that interest and fees were charged on all loans advanced and, to large customer bases, implied that the large transactions enable profitability.

The following quotes, from two of the three study sub-areas, captured the perceptions of MFIs being profitable succinctly:

> For me, I know my bank is making lots of profits because all the loans they give to customers attract interest. When I take the interest, I pay on my loan and look at all the people that go to take loans and paying back, the bank should be making lots of profits.
>
> *FC_F_RCB_Sandema*

> This bank has a very large number of customers. Even they have branches in Bawku and Tempane and almost all the customers take loans all the time. If they are not making profits will they open these branches? Even the "Adaka" groups (VSLA Groups) are now joining the bank and increasing the number of customers. I can't think of anything that can prevent this bank from making profits.
>
> *FC_M_RCB_Garu*

These quotes suggest that clients are not passive stakeholders but are active participants with expectations that the accessed financial products leverage livelihoods and enable MFIs to make profits in order to provide services sustainably. The other reasons clients gave for the profitability of MFIs in the Northern Savannah of Ghana and their rankings are presented under '*Length*' in Appendix VI (see also Appendices II, III and IV).

However, on knowledge of donor support, nine out of ten clients in the Northern Savannah of Ghana had no idea of any donor support or partnership engagements with their MFIs. While USAID had programmes with some of the RCBs, World Vision International was involved in the informal rural credit market by partnering with communities in the formation of VSLA groups. This attests to the international recognition of the need for available, accessible and affordable financial services for poverty alleviation in the Global South. It also suggests the pervasive orientation of MFIs towards the financial systems approach in an increasingly commercialized landscape with considerable barriers for the poor and marginalized in the Northern Savannah of Ghana and the country as a whole. Moreover, the involvement of non-governmental organizations in microfinance attests to the role of financial services in the anti-poverty arsenal in the Global South.

The formal and informal MFIs had the highest number of years of exposure to products and services. This ranged between 1 and 17 years. Thus, outreach in terms of both breadth and depth was much broader and deeper with the formal clients in the Northern Savannah of Ghana. The semi-formal MFIs were relatively new players in the microfinance landscape with client exposure of between 1 and 12 years of clients with access. The widespread compulsory savings among these institutions, more or less as client equity as a conduit to the entrance, may explain their limited outreach. The formal and majority of informal MFIs usually start with loans (debt) for clients.

Analysing the consistency of MFIs in the Northern Savannah of Ghana in rolling out their products and services over the years, agro loans from Sinapi Aba (a formal MFI) was the newest product in its third year, and the oldest was Salary Loans from the Naara Rural Bank in its 36th year. For deposits, Kiddy Savings Accounts also provided by Sinapi Aba and Ordinary Savings Accounts by Naara Rural Bank also had 3 and 36 years, respectively. It is important to note that the oldest rolled-out product usually mirrored the year of the MFI establishment of the MFI in the locality. All other things being constant, the longer the years of exposure, the better the livelihood outcomes of participants. Furthermore, most of the oldest products were either loans or savings, further reaffirming the primacy of these two in the basket of microfinance products and services in the Northern Savannah of Ghana.

In conclusion, length refers to the time frame in the provision of microfinance services to targeted populations. It concerns the sustainability of MFIs that ensure greater prospects of client welfare. Length, perceived in future terms, remains difficult to gauge, quantify and measure. Profitability and/or donor funding determine the length. MFIs' profitability and donor partnerships have implications for length. While over 87% of clients believed their MFIs were profitable, less than 13% had any knowledge of donor support or partnership(s). This has implications for customer loyalty, including repayment behaviour and moral hazards. Open communication between MFIs and clients is therefore key. While clients of all MFIs in the Northern Savannah of Ghana had only one-year minimum exposure to participation, the maximum was 17 years for the formal and informal MFIs. It was 12 years maximum for the semi-formal MFIs. This suggests that the semi-formal MFIs are late entrants to the financial market of the region. Analysing the consistency of products and services roll-out revealed consistency with the year of establishment of the MFI in the localities. All other things being constant, the longer the years of exposure to participation, the better the livelihood outcomes of participants. Loans and savings constituted the oldest product offerings further reaffirming the primacy of these two in the basket of microfinance in the Northern Savannah of Ghana (see also Appendix VI under '*Length*' and II, III and IV).

5.2.5 Client's Perceptions of Worth of Microfinance Intermediation and Livelihoods in the Northern Savannah of Ghana

Worth describes client's willingness to pay the price of a financial contract in relation to the client risk profile, as well as their livelihood constraints and opportunities. For loans, worth increases when the terms of contracts in relation to loan amounts disbursed, duration of repayments (term to maturity) and regular repayment amounts (size of instalment) match client livelihood needs. For savings, interest is paid on deposits and the flexibility of savings contracts, including lower minimum balances, unrestricted access and convenient withdrawals, matches the livelihood needs of clients. The total worth of microfinance, therefore, includes worth to clients and worth to society. New hires and forward and backward linkages, improved entrepreneurial capabilities and business environment increase worth to society. Access to financial services can and do improve welfare without necessarily increasing profits or diversifying household income sources (Morduch, 1998; Mosley and Hulme, 1998).

This section first explores worth-promoting factors along with the governance structures and management systems of MFIs in the Northern Savannah of Ghana. Second, it explores the nuances of product and service design features promoting participants' willingness to pay. The specific nuanced design features promoting worth for credit included loan amounts disbursed, duration of repayments (terms to maturity of loans), the regular repayment amounts (size of instalment), the interest paid on client deposits, and withdrawal flexibility (in amounts and frequency) and convenience. The contribution of access to livelihood diversification of income sources, employment of others (new hires) and forward and backward linkages to the achievement of client personal and household goals were included in this study as worth-promoting factors for MFI credit products.

Two key outcomes, related to governance and management systems, that promoted worth for the formal and semi-formal clients were experiences of friendly customer relations and easy access to loan facilities (screening, selection and disbursal). Unsurprisingly, poor customer relationships were the single most worth-depressing factor. Moreover, smaller staff-client ratios and poor internet connectivity also affected the client's willingness to participate and product up-take (Table 5.11).

Conscious efforts by management and staff to create and maintain mutual respect and understanding between staff and clients can have positive impacts on outreach and sustainability goals. More broadly, understanding the socio-cultural environments of target populations is important to the willingness of clients to participate. For the semi-formal MFI clients, the lack of weekend banking opportunities and the low interest rates on deposits both decreased worth. Easy access to secure savings facilities and group member support promoted the willingness to pay for the VSLA groups. Cash boxes being stolen and the placement of ceilings on the number of shares an individual can purchase in VSLA groups tended

TABLE 5.11 Perception of Factors Promoting Worth of Microfinance at the MFIs Level

MFI Category	*Key Worth Promotional Factors*	*Key Worth Drawback Factors*
Formal MFIs	Friendly staff-client relationship	Bad staff-client relationships
	Easy access to loans	Fewer staff at MFI
	Easy access to savings services	Unreliable internet connectivity
	Target clients within a limited geography	Low interest in client savings
Semi-formal MFIs	Friendly staff-clients relationship	No weekend banking/no ATMs
	Easy access to loans	Low interest on savings
	Flexible savings contracts	
Informal MFIs	Social support from VSLA group members	Theft of VSLA boxes
	Affordable interest on loans	A ceiling on the number of shares a member can buy (VSLA)
	Flexible loan contracts	Restrictions on withdrawals till maturity (Bencyn 'Susu')

to decrease worth. Institutional governance and management systems factors that increased and/or decreased worth for clients of the microfinance industry of the Northern Savannah of Ghana are ranked and presented in Appendix V.

In addition, product-specific factors influencing worth for clients across the three institutional types are also presented in Table 5.12. Client loan sizes could be described as large, medium and small for the formal, semi-formal and informal clients, respectively. Terms to maturity (duration of repayments) showed a continuum from less flexibility for the formal clients to high flexibility for the informal clients. This flexibility trend was repeated for the size of the instalment (regular repayment amounts). Interest paid on deposits was said to be low for the formal clients, moderate for the semi-formal clients and high for the informal clients. The presence of high numbers of the VSLA group members in the informal client sample may have contributed to the perception of high deposit interest earnings (dividends). The reasons for this were not far-fetched, as formal MFIs were pro-financial systems in approach where the profit and sustainability motive supersedes outreach and social intermediation concerns. But partnerships with other organizations are enabling the targeting of marginalized women's groups in the hinterlands. Moreover, these institutions operate under the financial sector's regulatory regime and are, therefore, prone to the use of standard banking practices. However, on the flexibility of deposit withdrawals, the formal clients had the most flexible withdrawal regime in terms of amounts, frequency and convenience. Those of the informal clients had the least flexible withdrawal arrangements.

Compulsory savings products were not very common with formal MFIs and clients. It was the norm for the semi-formal MFIs and clients. The diversification of income sources was high for all three client groups. However, while the formal clients established new enterprises predominantly, the semi-formal clients invested in long-term household human resource development via education and training. Given the fact that most of the semi-formal clients were professionally educated salaried workers, the premium placed on education and training of family members was relatively much higher. For the informal clients, it was more of consumption smoothening, while investment into income-generating activities came in second.

For formal clients, goals achieved were based mostly on non-farm and/or off-farm activities. This outcome was much lower for the semi-formal clients while the majority of the informal clients were mostly farm-based.

Table 5.14 presents the specific product design features that increased worth for microfinance clients of the Northern Savannah of Ghana and the revelation of the same in the segmented landscape. While 69% of clients generally obtained loan amounts as applied for, the disaggregated data revealed that this was 66%, 80% and 62% for the formal, semi-formal and informal clients, respectively. The Welfarist orientation of the semi-formal credit union associations and financial NGOs, whose clients start on equity instead of debt and where clients are made to understand from the onset that loans could only be as much as twice a client

TABLE 5.12 Perception of Factors Negatively Affecting Worth of Microfinance Provisioning

Design Factor	*Formal MFIs*	*Semi-formal MFIs*	*Informal MFIs*
Loan amounts disbursed	Larger sizes (loan amounts usually based on client ability to repay)	Medium sizes (loan amounts usually tied to client savings amount)	Smaller sizes (loan amounts highly personalized)
	High awareness that smaller amounts easily gets disbursed	High awareness loan amounts twice as savings amounts	VSLA loans are thrice client savings
Term to maturity of loans (duration of repayment)	Less flexible (client chooses the term to maturity of loans from limited options)	Medium flexibility (client chooses the term to maturity of loans from broader options)	Highly flexible (personalized terms to maturity)
	Medium match to client needs	Medium match to client needs	High match to client needs
Size of instalment (regular repayment amounts)	Less flexible (clients chooses the size of instalment from limited options)	Medium flexibility (client determines the size of the instalment)	Highly flexible (no limitations on amounts)
	Medium satisfaction (size of instalment matches client needs)	Medium satisfaction (size of instalment matches client needs)	Very high satisfaction (any amounts are accepted)
Interest paid on deposits	Low (fixed deposits attract quarterly interest)	Medium (interest on savings lower than expected)	Two extremes (negative interest/no interest for susu to high dividends for the VSLAs)
The flexibility of deposit withdrawals	High flexibility (good for emergencies and business opportunities)	Medium flexibility (allowed only when there are no outstanding loans)	Low flexibility (only at the end of the cycle for VSLA and end of 30 days for Susu)
	Low levels of compulsory savings	High levels of compulsory savings	Medium levels of compulsory savings
Diversified income sources	High new enterprises formation	High household welfare expenditure	High consumption smoothing expenditure
Achieved personal goals	High off-farm income sources	Medium off-farm income sources	Mostly on-farm activities and low off-farm income sources
	Limited consumption smoothing activities	Medium consumption smoothing activities	Limited scope limiting benefits

deposit amount, may have accounted for the high percentage of the semi-formal clients. With economic activities mainly agricultural in the Northern Savannah of Ghana, enterprise loans were key to farmers' ability to increase production, accumulate assets and re-invest in other non-farm income-generating activities to reduce risks and vulnerabilities (Anane et al., 2013) during the prolonged dry season.

Worth associated with duration for the repayments of loans (term to maturity) saw 64% of microfinance clients in the Northern Savannah of Ghana claim it matched their livelihood needs and expectations. Different durations for repayments are usually presented to clients who then choose the best fit for their peculiar livelihood circumstances to ensure cash flows for the repayment of the loan. Based on the historical repayment performances of clients, terms to maturity can further alter client-specific needs. Key informant interviews with credit officers of the formal and informal MFIs revealed that presenting clients with choices on the term to maturity of loans was associated with lower default rates as captured in the following quote:

> You know the economic activities around here are very low. For example, those women who process paddy rice to sell couldn't make weekly repayments because they must buy the rice and process it and that can take 3 to 4 days before they then look for buyers. So, we decided that instead of weekly repayments, we made it bi-weekly for such women groups.
>
> *Deputy Manager, BESSFA Rural Bank, Garu*

Disaggregating the best fit for the term to maturity across the three institutional types showed that satisfaction was highest for the semi-formal clients, with eight out of ten claiming satisfaction (Table 5.13). This was six and five out of ten for the formal and informal clients, respectively. This suggests the institutional structures and governance systems of the semi-formal MFIs probably allowed more voice and accountability in these pro-poverty lending institutions. The low percentage of five out of ten for the informal MFIs also suggests that the pressure for moneylenders to make margins, avoid delayed repayments and abscond with borrowers can place considerable limitations on the terms to maturity of advanced loans.

In addition, worth related to regular repayment amounts (size of instalment) saw over 75% of clients (Table 5.13) asserting that it met their livelihood needs and expectations in the Northern Savannah of Ghana.

But the disaggregated data (Table 5.14) also revealed that this was highest among the semi-formal MFI clients, with nine out of every ten clients claiming regular repayment amounts met their livelihood needs and expectations. This was eight and six out of every ten of the formal and informal MFIs clients, respectively. Again, this points to the poverty-lending orientation of and better 'know-your-customer' indices for the semi-formal MFIs. The low score of the informal clients could reflect the generally irregular and unpredictable cash

TABLE 5.13 Frequency of Worth Features by Sampled Clients

Worth factor (N = 150)	*Response*	*Frequency*	*Percent*
Loan amounts always same as requested?	Yes	104	69.3
	No	46	30.7
Duration of repayment (term to maturity of loans) appropriate?	Yes	96	64
	No	54	36
Regular repayment amounts (size of instalment) appropriate?	Yes	113	75.3
	No	37	24.7
Interest paid on your deposits appropriate?	Yes	94	62.7
	No	55	37.3
Allowed withdrawal of any amount and time (flexibility)?	Yes	94	62.67
	No	55	37.33
Diversified income sources?	Yes	96	64
	No	54	36
Employed other people in the diversified strategies?	Yes	48	32
	No	102	68
Achieved personal goals?	Yes	138	92
	No	12	8

flows from a culmination of low-valued and low-turnover livelihood activities associated with this group of clients. It could also conceal higher levels of harsh collection modus operandi by the informal lenders than the formal and semi-formal MFIs.

Furthermore, with an average of 63% (Table 5.14) of MFI clients in the Northern Savannah of Ghana claiming satisfaction with the interest paid on their deposits, the disaggregated data revealed that eight out of every ten informal clients expressed satisfaction with the interest spread (the difference between interest paid by the MFI on client deposits and that which the client pays on loans from the MFI). This points to the VSLA groups, where dividends payments can be quite high as interest on loans from the pooled pot are retained and distributed in proportion to the number of shares held by each member. It was seven and five out of every ten of the semi-formal and formal clients, respectively, that claimed satisfaction with interest on deposits. Thus, the formal clients were the least satisfied when it came to interest paid on deposits by MFIs in the Northern Savannah of Ghana.

This could have serious implications on the formal MFI ability to mobilize savings (a cheaper source of loanable funds). It also suggests an alignment of the formal MFIs towards the financial systems approach, with profitability as the overarching goal. Paying lower interest on deposits could be explained by cost saving that boosted profitability. It could also be that the formal MFIs had access to cheaper loanable commercial funding that did not necessitate deposit mobilization derived for on-lending purposes.

TABLE 5.14 Disaggregated Frequencies of Worth Sub-features by Clients

Worth Factor	*Response*	***Formal Clients***		***Semi-formal Clients***		***Informal Clients***	
		Freq.	*%*	*Freq.*	*%*	*Freq.*	*%*
Loan amounts	Yes	33	66	40	80	31	62
	No	17	34	10	20	19	38
Duration for repayments (terms to maturity)	Yes	30	60	40	80	26	52
	No	20	40	10	20	24	48
Regular repayment amounts (size of instalment)	Yes	38	76	46	92	29	58
	No	12	24	4	8	21	42
Interest on savings	Yes	23	46	33	66	39	78
	No	27	54	17	44	11	22
Flexible withdrawals	Yes	40	80	35	70	19	38
	No	10	20	15	30	31	62
Diversified income sources	Yes	37	74	34	68	25	50
	No	13	26	16	32	25	50
Employed others	Yes	13	26	21	42	16	32
	No	37	74	29	58	34	68
Achieved set goal(s)	Yes	48	96	43	86	47	94
	No	2	4	7	14	3	6

Moreover, in Table 5.14, almost 63% of clients of microfinance institutions in the Northern Savannah of Ghana generally claimed that the flexibility of allowing withdrawals of deposits met their needs and expectations. However, it was the formal MFI clients that had access to ATMs that commanded the greatest outcome on flexibility and convenience of withdrawals (Table 5.14) at eight clients out of every ten. The most restricted withdrawal regimes were associated with the informal clients, where only four out of ten claimed satisfaction with the flexibility of withdrawals. The savings product being the *Susu* from the informal intermediaries' withdrawals is only allowed at the end of every 30 days. Thus, the low flexibility score for withdrawal was therefore understandable.

Additionally, almost 64% of clients in the Northern Savannah of Ghana were generally able to diversify their income sources as a result of access to microfinance products and services (Table 5.14). This implies that the goals of microfinance are being achieved, even if they are not transformational. However, at 74%, the greatest outcomes of access and the diversification of household income were observed with the formal MFI clients (Table 5.14). This outcome was 68% and 50% for the semi-formal and informal clients, respectively. Generally poor and marginalized, with little or no access to formal MFIs, the informal clients relied on sources where interest rates are usurious and generally yielding limited benefits of access.

Approximately three out of ten microfinance participants generated employment opportunities for others in their livelihood activities in the Northern Savannah of Ghana (Table 5.14). This constituted worth. These employees were either family members and/or non-family members whose labour was engaged in on-farm and non-farm or off-farm activities. The disaggregated data showed that the semi-formal MFIs had the highest employment outcomes with four out of ten clients having employed others within the last 12 months. With marginal spill-overs in employment outcomes, microfinance can be said to be working.

Last, but not least was the achievement of set goals from the access to microfinance. On average, nine out of ten clients in the Northern Savannah of Ghana claimed access was instrumental in their achievement of set personal and household goals (Table 5.14). The disaggregated data, however, revealed that the formal MFI clients had the greatest outcome on this indicator. The least overall achievement on this was observed with the informal MFI clients.

In conclusion, worth refers to the willingness to pay the price of financial contracts taking into consideration clients' risk profiles, livelihood constraints and available opportunities. Worth was also assessed at the governance and management level of MFIs as well as the degree to which specific product features match clients' needs, preferences and satisfaction. While friendly customer relationships, stress-free access to flexible loans and savings contracts were key drivers of worth for clients of the formal and semi-formal MFIs, it was disrespectful MFI staff, lower staff to client ratios, the lack of weekend banking including automated teller machines (ATMs), lower interest paid on deposits and unreliable internet connectivity that lowered it for clients of these two tiers of MFIs. The social support from group members as well as the flexible nature of informal contracts promoted worth for clients accessing products and services from informal MFIs. Theft and the fear of theft of cash boxes of VSLA groups or even armed robbery lowered worth of clients working with informal MFIs such as the *'Susu'* collectors. Restricted withdrawals of savings and limited product scope depress worth further for clients of the informal MFIs. These findings suggest that the incorporation of relevant local socio-cultural values and norms in the management and the design and delivery of products and services by MFIs in targeted markets can have implications on participation and the willingness of product and service uptake. There is, therefore, a need for management and boards of MFIs in the Northern Savannah to prioritize the creation of organizational cultures that encompass governance management structures and systems for microfinance intermediation (see also Appendix VI under '*Worth*' and II, III and IV).

For specific product and service design that promotes worth for clients, approximately 70% of microfinance clients of the Northern Savannah said loan amounts requested are approved without changes. Increasing this percentage higher means MFIs need to work on factors that improve customer loyalty to warrant tailored loan amounts with implications for the success or failure of projects and, therefore, repayments. An interconnected credit market that collaborates in providing credit services is best placed to meet the diverse needs of its constituents. Having one-size-fits-all MFIs that provide one-size-fits-all products and services is at odds with reality. The formation of interlinkages and mimicry of product and service design has the potential to increase the worth of credit products to targeted populations.

Slightly over 64% of clients said the duration of repayments (term to maturity) met their needs. The peculiar circumstances of clients' livelihood need to require contracts to be tailored to increase the willingness to pay for financial contracts that limit defaults and increase repayment rates. The prevailing regime of presenting clients with different durations of repayments for the same loan products and having clients then opt for that which optimally matches their needs does have implications on repayment behaviour. Taking this further will require client-centric loan products that place the client at the centre for the determination of the term to maturity of loan products.

Approximately 80% of microfinance clients of the Northern Savannah of Ghana said the regular repayment amounts (size of instalment) of loan repayments matched their livelihood needs and expectations. However, the irregularity and unpredictability of cash flows associated with the livelihoods of the informal MFI clients impacted negatively on how the size of instalments matched their needs. This revealed the marginalized socio-economic status of those accessing microfinance from informal sources. Thus, the need to complement microfinance services with broader rural development policies and programmes continues to remain critical for sustainable microfinance intermediation in the Northern Savannah of Ghana, not least because of the high incidence of poverty in the region.

The interest spread (differences in what clients pay for loans and that which the MFI pays on clients' deposits) continues to remain a challenge, especially for clients of the formal MFIs in the Northern Savannah of Ghana. Only 50% of all clients of the formal MFIs expressed satisfaction with interest paid on deposits. This was 70% and 80% for semi-formal and informal clients, respectively. This meant clients of informal MFIs valued deposits and the interest obtained more. With only 50% of clients of the formal MFIs expressing satisfaction with interest on deposits, more need to be done to improve interest on deposits to spur deposit mobilization by these MFIs. Deposits are cheaper alternative sources of loanable funds. However, MFIs need to balance the interest spread that can have profound implications for loan pricing and ultimately repayment rates. The high satisfaction with interest on deposits by informal depositors was as a result of the security of savings services and, for the VSLA groups, the dividends earned by members. Restricted access to deposits, especially by the informal MFIs, had negative implications for client welfare during emergencies. Making withdrawals convenient through the use of ATMs in high-population areas and for weekend banking activities was noted to increase the worth of savings (see Appendix V under '*Worth*').

Access to microfinance and the ability to diversify livelihoods increase worth. Overall, 64% of clients said access to financial services from MFIs supported the diversification of livelihoods and therefore their willingness to pay and participate. The clients of formal MFIs had the greatest outcome on livelihood diversification. This was attributed to higher average education levels, wage employment, larger loan sizes as well as the choice of investments. Marginal spillover effects included the employment of others in the diversified livelihoods of clients. Only 30% of microfinance clients had employed a non-household member in the past 12 months. Approximately 90% of all clients said their set personal as well as household goals had been achieved. Microfinance is certainly working in the Northern Savannah of Ghana with households transitioning in different directions as postulated by Dorward (2014) (see Chapter 2, Section 2.7.1). For the minority, it has been transformational where livelihoods are *stepped up* or *stepped out and* production meant for the market. Few *fell down and out* and missed out on the promise of leveraging livelihoods with the accessed financial products and services to better their lot. This calls for broad-based rural development policies and programmes. Yet the majority are transitioning from *hanging in* to *stepping up* for both markets and improvement in household welfare.

5.2.6 Clients' Perceptions of Depth of Microfinance Intermediation and Livelihoods in the Northern Savannah of Ghana

The depth of outreach in the microfinance livelisystem framework is the value that society places on the net gain of clients for participation in microfinance programmes. The poverty levels of targeted clients are a good proxy for the depth of outreach. All other things being constant, society would prefer positive net gains for poorer clients than for richer clients. Direct measurement of depth (poverty levels) through income or wealth is difficult, but certainly not impossible. Enlisted indirect proxies for the measurement of depth of outreach included sex (preference for women), location (preference for rural dwellers), education (preference for those with little or no formal education), ethnicity (preference for marginalized minorities), housing (preference for those living in poorer housing structures and neighbourhoods) and public services (preference for those with little or no access to public social services). However, the most important indicator for gauging the depth of outreach is the loan sizes. And when complemented with an estimation of the duration of repayment, regular instalment amounts and time in-between instalments gives added value (Schreiner, 2002). Along each aspect of loan size, smaller amounts or shorter durations of repayment signal greater depth, as poorer clients must obtain smaller loans to ensure a reduction of the lender's exposure to credit risks, and repeat contracts allow for the monitoring of clients' projects (Schreiner, 2002). Differentiating between first loans and repeat loans estimated in means or medians is further useful for depth analysis. However, it is the median loan size that best gauges loan size and hence the poverty status of clients (depth).

It is important to discuss depth because greater depth increases social benefits, but also the social costs per unit of provided services by MFIs. The smaller and more frequent the transactions (Schreiner, 2002), the higher the cost for the microfinance institution and the client. Therefore, either more donations or higher prices (interest) or both are needed to cover the higher costs of supplying microfinance products and services to resource-poor households. Moreover, group or joint-liability contracts increase the depth of outreach at lower costs than individual collateralized contracts that target the better-of. Furthermore, while the self-sustainability or financial systems approach trades off the poorest in favour of the less-poor, the poverty-lending approach places a premium on the poorest. However, the non-homogeneous nature borrowers make it difficult for MFIs to adequately assess risks and creditworthiness (Conning 1999) of clients. Thus, depth is assessed along MFIs' preferences for women, rural dwellers, those with no or little education, and ethnic minorities. Loan sizes and the quality of housing of clients were also assessed.

In Table 5.15, the preference for the educated, women, rural dwellers and ethnic minorities was low across all three MFI client groups. In other words, there was little or no discrimination in favour of the better educated, women, rural dwellers and ethnic minorities regarding the provision of microfinance services. However, loans were much larger among the formal clients and much smaller with the informal clients. The use of concrete blocks for walling and corrugated aluminium or iron sheets for roofing of housing was almost at par for all three client groups.

Owning or living in a house constructed with cement and roofed with corrugated aluminium or iron sheets was a status symbol and extended family members usually jointly pool resources to undertake such housing projects, especially at the extended family compound mostly found in the rural localities (see Table 5.15 and Appendix VI under '*Depth of Outreach*', II, III and IV).

In Table 5.15, the preference for women by MFIs in the Northern Savannah of Ghana showed that over 78% of clients claimed no discrimination in favour of females. Factors accounting for this outcome were not far-fetched.

Both men and women were active economic agents, even in the predominantly patriarchal societies of the Northern Savannah of Ghana. From cultivating crops to rearing small ruminants and processing and marketing foodstuffs, women were active participants, even if not the dominant gender. Generally, meeting contract terms and requirements were the key considerations for those who have access regardless of sex and gender. However, the informal VSLA groups acknowledged the prevalence of all-female groups being promoted by some NGOs.

On the locality of residence (Table 5.15), more than 92% of clients perceived MFIs as preferring neither rural nor urban clients. The inter-connectedness of the urban and rural economies of the Northern Savannah of Ghana made it prudent for MFIs not to discriminate based on either rural or urban settlements of clients. People live in urban settlements but have economic interests such as farms (crop and animal) in rural areas. For the formal clients, meeting the set terms and requirements for the product was the key determinant of access. With the

TABLE 5.15 Perceptions of Factors Affecting Depth Outreach of Microfinance Outreach

	MFI Category		
Depth factor	*Formal*	*Semi-formal*	*Informal*
Preference for educated clients	Low (no discrimination based on educational status; more based on who can make use of products and repay)	Low (no discrimination based on education; the formally educated just understand issues better)	Low (no discrimination based on education; mostly women groups in communities (VSLA))
Preference for women clients	Low (no discrimination between men and women; more based on client meeting requirements for product access)	Low (no discrimination and women); more based on client meeting product access requirements	Low (no discrimination based on gender/ sex; however, most VSLA groups were only women)
Preference for rural clients	Low (more based on client meeting product access requirements; based on who can repay)	Low (deal more with urban clients where turnovers are high; once a client, there is no discrimination)	Medium (provider live in community with clients)
Preference for ethnic minorities	Low (no discrimination based on ethnicity; based on meeting product terms)	Low (no discrimination based on ethnicity; more on being a member)	Low (no discrimination based on ethnicity; more on one ability to repay)
Primary hosing construction material	High (concrete walls and corrugated iron sheets)	High (concrete walls and corrugated iron sheets)	High (concrete walls and corrugated iron sheets)
Loan sizes	Larger sizes	Medium sizes	Small sizes

turnovers higher in urban centres, it was observed that the semi-formal clients were more inclined to be market traders apart from the majority of professional salaried worker shareholders.

On educational levels (Table 5.15), more than 90% of clients said there was no preference for the formally educated over those with little or no education in the context of the Northern Savannah of Ghana. Entrepreneurship is a skill. Being productive, with the ability to make profitable use of financial products and services, may have little correlation with formal education. MFI assessment of the client's ability to repay or honour contractual obligations constituted the key determinant of access. However, being formally employed with evidence of monthly wages increased access via informal moneylenders in the Northern Savannah of Ghana.

On targeting (Table 5.15), over 82% of clients of microfinance institutions in the Northern Savannah of Ghana had no special preferences for ethnic minorities. The provision of microfinance services was ethnicity blind with the implication that ethnicity constituted no barrier to access. Economic opportunities had fewer barriers to entry in the Northern Savannah of Ghana more broadly. Even the Fulani, made up of nomadic tribesmen, who traverse national boundaries herding cattle in the sub-region, was said to have access to microfinance services. However, a few had made permanent settlements around villages and towns in recent years.

Approximately 7% of clients across the three microfinance institutional types in the Northern Savannah of Ghana either owned or lived in homes constructed with concrete blocks and roofed with corrugated iron or aluminium sheets. It is worth noting here that, in the Northern Savannah of Ghana, having the extended family home constructed with concrete blocks and roofed with corrugated aluminium or iron sheets was regarded as a status symbol and usually involved family members pooling resources together for such projects. The implication here is that poverty is reducing in the Northern Savannah of Ghana and microfinance might be playing significant roles in the poverty reduction trends observed as captured in the following quote:

> Farmers make up most of the people in this area and we target them and make sure we design the products to meet their needs. And we don't just allow them to be at the same poor economic positions year after year. We make sure there is real improvement in their lives. For example, I was traveling with my boss to Accra when we decided to pass through the Gambaga instead of through Bolgatanga and when we got to Nakpanduri we saw that people, almost all the children were walking to school and for several miles, I saw just one child riding a bicycle. So, I asked my boss what is happening here? why is it that they are walking long distances to the schools? My boss told me why do I ask? And I said I don't see that in our bank operational areas. In our operational area parents buy their children bicycles or drop them off and go for them during the closing on motorbikes. He said it's the living conditions that make all the differences and that if I look at the houses that we are passing by, I will realize that the people are poor. It's not their fault. They need people to help them. They need people to come with 'light' so that they can follow because they are in darkness. Our operational area wasn't different a few decades ago.
>
> *Deputy Manager, BEESFA Rural Bank, Garu*

In addition, loan sizes were larger among the formal clients but much smaller among the informal clients with the implication that the informal clients were generally poorer and more marginalized than those of the formal and semi-formal clients. Over 86% of clients of microfinance organizations said MFIs targeted those clients capable of making use of financial services and not just poorer clients with no debt capacity. This orientation suggested limited donor support for MFIs in the Northern Savannah of Ghana and the need to cover costs, make margins and stay in business was even more compelling. Most MFIs seemed to align with the financial systems approach where profit-making was the overarching goal.

Table 5.16 provides quantitative data and information on whether or not MFIs preferred women, the educated, ethnic minorities, primary construction

TABLE 5.16 Percentages of Depth of Design Features of Sampled Clients

Depth Factor	*Response*	*Frequency*	*Percent*
Do your MFI prefer women as clients to men? (N = 150)			
	Yes	32	21.33
	No	118	78.67
Do your MFI prefer rural clients to urban clients? (N = 150)			
	Yes	11	7.33
	No	139	92.67
Do your MFI prefer the less or not educated clients to the more educated ones? (N = 150)			
	Yes	14	9.33
	No	136	90.67
Do your MFI prefer ethnic minorities as clients? (N = 150)			
	Yes	26	17.33
	No	124	82.67
What are the primary construction materials of your home? (N = 142)			
	Cement blocks	104	73.2
	Mud blocks (unburnt)	19	13.4
	Mud blocks (burnt)	4	2.8
	Mud and sticks	13	9.2
	Others	2	1.4
Loan sizes (N = 106)			
	50–150	15	14.15
	151–300	16	15.09
	301–450	7	6.60
	451–600	14	13.21
	601–750	4	3.77
	751–900	5	4.72
	901–1,050	10	9.43
	>1,050	35	33.02
Client targeting orientation (N = 150)			
	Those can repay	130	86.6
	Very poor people	20	5.4

materials, loan sizes, targeting orientation and certain residential locations of their clients.

In conclusion, designing products and services for the poorest segment of the population directly relates to the depth (those at the bottom of the pyramid) that they have access among targeted populations. Using income or wealth measurements remains difficult and therefore proxies assessed for depth included gender (designed to increase female uptake), location (designed to increase uptake by rural people), education (designed to increase uptake by people without or with little formal education), ethnicity (designed to increase uptake by marginalized ethnic minorities), housing (designed to increase uptake by those living in poorer neighbourhoods) and public services (designed to increase uptake by those without or with little access to public social services). Though loan sizes best predict depth of outreach, smaller and frequent transactions increase the overall costs of microfinance intermediation that must be covered by donor subsidies or increased pricing.

Loan sizes were a continuum from the generally larger loans of clients of the formal MFIs to the generally smaller loan sizes of clients of the informal MFIs. This result mirrored the social and economic status of the clients. Over 90% of all client groups claimed to have their homes constructed with cement blocks and roofed with either corrugated iron or aluminium sheets. This suggests access to microfinance services may not necessarily be the driver of cement-constructed homes in the study region. Overall, 70% of microfinance clients claimed MFIs had no special preferences for women, the formally educated, rural populations and the livelihoods of ethnic minorities in the Northern Savannah of Ghana. These results suggest that MFIs were probably compromising on depth of outreach with the implication that women, rural dwellers, ethnic minorities and the poorer communities were the most excluded and that microfinance may be worsening inequalities rather than redistribution in the Northern Savannah of Ghana (see also Appendix VI under '*Depth of Outreach*' and II, III and IV).

5.2.7 Client's Perceptions of Breadth of Microfinance Intermediation and Livelihoods in the Northern Savannah of Ghana

The breadth of outreach for an MFI is the absolute number of clients that it serves with financial products and services. Budgetary constraints and the non-homogeneous nature of resource-poor households make the analysis of breadth imperative. All other things being constant, an MFI that is poverty lending in approach may need donations to subsidize below-market interest and fees, among others. Also, an MFI that adopts a financial systems approach with wider breadth may reach as many of the productive poor as a poverty-lending one with narrower breadth. Murdoch (1999) argues that the poverty-lending approach produces better outcomes on the social welfare function for clients than the financial systems approach. It is estimated that for two MFIs, one adopting the poverty-lending and the other, the financial systems approach to yield equal net gain for clients, the latter must have between 15 and 125 times the breadth of the former to produce similar effects on the social welfare function. Profound depth (the targeting of poorer clients) compensates for narrower breadth (fewer, less poor clients). Perception of clients on the effects of the orientation of MFI targeting, donor partnership, current average interest, fees charged, and group product and service availability have implications on the absolute numbers of clients an MFI serves and are therefore explored in this section.

In Table 5.17, perceptions of clients on the targeting orientation of MFIs in the Northern Savannah of Ghana showed that over 86% believed that MFIs target those capable of repaying. A disaggregation of the data further revealed that this was as high as 96% of the formal, 90% of the semi-formal and 74% of the informal clients. This has the implication of the formal MFIs tending to serve

TABLE 5.17 Perception of Factors Affecting Breadth of Microfinance Outreach

Your MFI target clients are mostly? (N = 150)		
	Category	%
Client targeting orientation	Those can repay	87
	Very poor people	13
Identified partners (N = 150)		
Formal MFIs	Semi-formal MFIs	Informal MFIs
USAID partnership via the Development Credit Authority	Religious groups (churches); professional bodies (Ghana National Association of Teachers – GNAT)	World Vision International – WVI, VSLA
Average annual interest rates per annum loans (N = 150)		
Formal MFIs	Semi-formal MFIs	Informal MFIs
27%–32%	20%–30%	Can be as high as 45% (Tarasum leverage)
Average annual interest rates per annum savings (N = 150)		
Formal MFIs	Semi-formal MFIs	Informal MFIs
8–19% depending on deposit type	7–8%	–39.6 for Susu savings (individual) to as high as 60% for the VSLAs
Group products		
Formal MFIs	Semi-formal MFIs	Informal MFIs
High group products offering (enable poor people with no collaterals to form groups and have access)	Low group products offering (enable poor people also to form groups and have access)	Low (except the VSLAs)

better-off clients and the informal MFIs serving much poorer clients, probably in hard-to-reach, marginalized communities and groups such as the VSLA groups.

The involvement of international non-governmental organizations, such as World Vision International, in the formation and linkage of the VSLA groups to rural and community banks in the Northern Savannah of Ghana attests to the limited financial services available to the majority of the population in the study region and the need for financial inclusion as a tool to drive down poverty levels. The United States agency for international development (USAID) was also involved in some partnerships with some of the rural and community banks through its development credit authority (DCA)P for the extension of credit facilities via ecobank to microfinance institutions to on-lend medium to long-term loans to specific rural sectors. The semi-formal MFIs were mostly professional associations and/or religious bodies, initiated (e.g., the Ghana national association of teachers (GNAT) and some churches) with the primary goal of ensuring the welfare of members, and therefore lending rates were found to be below market rates.

The interest rate is both a price and an instrument for regulating the risk composition of the lenders' portfolio (Stiglitz and Weiss, 1981) and especially the institutional providers (Stigler, 1967). In other words, the interest rate serves a dual function of being the price of the loan and an indirect screening mechanism and therefore has implications for breadth. Lower interest rates incentivize increased loan uptake. Also, higher deposit rates incentivize savings, potentially providing a cheaper source of loanable funds for the MFIs. The transaction costs (non-cash opportunity costs and indirect cash expenses) that potential clients incur need to be taken into consideration as well. The use of mobile staff was in response to the need to curtail such costs of clients with dividends for both the institutions and the clients.

Group products have the potential to reach out to poorer clients by enlisting the principle of joint liability to reduce the costs of policing moral hazards. Groups, if allowed to self-form, have the added benefit of assortative matching that reduces the risk for both the groups and MFI. Group product offering, especially loans, was high among the formal MFIs. There were conscious efforts to segment clients and offer tailor-made products that match livelihood needs and debt capacity. For the semi-formal MFIs, group products were offered sparingly. The informal MFIs only offered individual savings and loans, except for the VSLA groups commonly found at the hard-to-reach, marginalized communities. The VSLAs have a potential of increased outreach, especially when linkages are established with the formal MFIs, such as the rural and community banks, to mop up excess liquidity of groups that attract deposit interests and expose groups and individuals to a greater scope of product offerings.

In North-Eastern Ghana, MFI interest rates on loans from the formal MFIs ranged between 27% and 32% per annum and varied across different loan products. Though relatively lower than the national average lending rates of between 2% and 8% per month and 45% per annum (Osei-Assibey, 2011), these rates were considered unaffordable by clients, given the high endemic poverty prevalence of the region. For the semi-formal MFI loans, interest rates on loans ranged between 20% and 30% and up to 45% maximum on informal MFI loans. Interest paid by formal MFIs on deposits varied between 8% and 19% per annum, depending on the type of savings instrument. Fixed deposits attracted higher interest than other savings instruments. For example, amounts between GHS 1,000.00 and GHS 2,000.00 attract 8% interest rates per annum. Those more than GHS 2,000.00 up to GHS 20,000.00 attract a maximum of 19% per annum. However, interest rates for amounts above GHS 20,000.00 were usually negotiated between the client and the MFI management in the case of the rural and community banks. For the semi-formal MFIs, savings rates averaged between 7% and 8% per annum and most clients held no fixed deposits as this product was absent in the MFI product scope. Most informal MFIs do not offer interest on deposits, and the individuals or companies offering *Susu* savings deduct a day's savings out of every 30 days' daily savings of the client as charges. This was estimated to be as high as negative 39.6% per annum for the *Susu* savers. However, depending on the volumes of transactions, VSLA groups could earn substantial dividends up to 60% of invested equity at the end of the group cycle, usually six months or year period. Group loans from the formal MFIs were mostly targeted at poor and marginalized populations in hard-to-reach areas, where suitable collaterals are difficult to find. VSLAs hold off potential increased outreach and financial inclusion in marginalized rural and peri-urban communities of the Northern Savannah of Ghana. This was captured by the following quote:

> Those in the towns have many places to go for loans. For those of us in the villages, the Adaka (VSLA) is what most of us have now. It has helped me a lot. I use not to have anywhere to go and get a loan for even the smallest of need. Now we are better-off.
>
> *IFC_F_VSLA_Sandema*

In conclusion, the breadth of outreach describes the absolute numbers of the population participating in microfinance intermediation. The opportunity costs of committed resources for microfinance activities and the fact that clients and their households are not homogenous make breadth analysis an imperative. The perception of the targeting orientation of MFIs, knowledge of MFI donor partnership, the prevailing interest rates been paid by clients and group product offerings all have implications for the breadth of outreach. Approximately 87% of microfinance clients in the Northern Savannah of Ghana perceived MFIs to target people with the capability of making use of the financial services and not just those in need. Donor partnerships were found to be common among the formal and informal MFIs, but most clients did not know about such partnerships. In order to maintain transparency and buy-in purposes, the goals and objectives of such a partnership should be communicated to clients. While the formal MFIs operate under the financial and banking regulatory regime, the semi-formal MFIs do not and have their services downgraded and tailored to the needs of members. Compulsory savings are encouraged through a share purchase. Bridging the interest spread gap has the potential to increase savings mobilization. Effective deposit mobilization was thought to have knock-on effects on interest rates of the semi-formal MFIs. Interest rates of the formal and semi-formal MFIs in the study region were found to be below the national averages. However, the variation of deposit rates was prominent among the informal MFIs that had negative rates up to –39.6% per annum for the '*susu*' savers and could earn a VSLA group member as much as 60% or more per annum. Group products, particularly loans, were observed to be critical for financial intermediation with poorer clients (women and rural localities) in the Northern Savannah of Ghana (see Appendix VI under '*Breadth of Outreach*' and also II, III and IV).

5.2.8 Client Perception of Contract Enforcement in Microfinance Intermediation and Livelihoods in the Northern Savannah of Ghana

A contract refers to a legally binding exchange of promises or agreement between two or more parties with which the law expects compliance. Contract enforcement is, therefore, the process of persuading a non-compliant party or parties to take remedial actions to comply with the terms of the contract. Laws that relate to financial transactions do influence borrower behaviours. Exchange and production transaction costs are usually constrained when property rights are not well defined and contract laws lack clarity. Minimizing transaction costs frees up resources that can be used to increase overall welfare (USAID 1995). The civil courts in Ghana handle financial contract enforcement. However, in the microfinance industry, imprisonment or fines are not common. Threats of jail or co-opting a police officer's visit are usually effective deterrents to defaulting loan clients. Thus, MFIs are employing various legal sanctions available, including traditional methods such as summoning a defaulting client to the much-respected local chief's palace, as well as the law courts as a last resort to enforce financial contracts.

In terms of processes and procedures for enforcing contracts by the formal MFIs in the Northern Savannah of Ghana, defaulting clients are issued demand notices up to the third time. Upon failure to comply after the third notice of demand, reports are submitted to the loans recovery committees that then kick-start series of actions aimed at recovering the loans. Again, when all these fail, the next steps are for the MFIs' Legal Department to initiate legal action(s) to recover the loan. However, it was reported that the mere threat of legal action usually triggers repayment by defaulting clients. Also, the mere threat or actual announcement of the names of defaulting clients at the local radio station ensures repayments from defaulting clients. Sometimes, formal MFIs also outsource the recovery of loans to third parties. This was said to be effective in increasing loan recoveries. Furthermore, the design of contracts requiring third parties (guarantors) to co-sign, which makes them liable for the loan repayment in case there is a default, was said to have a positive influence on the client's project choices and repayment behaviour. Moreover, some MFIs make use of localized traditional structures and systems in their efforts to recover loans from arraigning defaulting clients at the local chief's palace to invoking deities to ensure repayments were common.

The enforcement methods and procedures of the semi-formal MFIs were not markedly different from the formal ones. For the informal clients, personalized relationships between providers and clients that limit information asymmetries ensure defaults are not wilful. Moreover, the limited scope of product offering means clients can be targeted with tailor-made contract terms that enhance the client's livelihood experiences and ensure repayments.

Across all institutional types, there was a consensus that amicably resolving default problems with the right enforcement mechanisms positively influences the client's behaviour in relation to project choices, product uptake and repayment rates. It was also acknowledged that it was in the interest of both clients and the financial institutions for management to amicably resolve default issues. This perception was highest among the formal MFI clients, with 72% agreeing to this assertion in Table 5.18. Clients also contend that built-in flexibility of contract designs has the potential to decrease default rates.

Table 5.19 thematically presents the enforcement methods and how clients perceive the same in the context of the microfinance landscape of the Northern Savannah of Ghana. These contract enforcement design themes include threats of legal action and/or legal actions; threats to the air and/or the airing of loan defaulters' names on the local radio; the outsourcing of loan recovery to third parties; allowing of guarantors (third parties) to co-sign contracts; the use of traditional social structures and systems; and the lending to close networks by mostly the informal providers, where information asymmetry is limited and repayments can be assured.

In conclusion, contracts are legally binding exchanges of promises or agreements between two or more parties to which the law expects compliance. Thus, the process of persuading a non-compliant party or parties to take remedial actions is referred to as enforcement. The application of laws in enforcing financial

TABLE 5.18 Perceptions of Enforcement Methods on Microfinance Uptake

Do enforcement mechanisms affect client behaviour regarding repayment and product uptake?

	Formal MFIs		*Semi-formal MFIs*		*Informal MFIs*	
	Freq.	*%*	*Freq.*	*%*	*Freq.*	*%*
Yes	36	72	35	70	32	64
No	14	28	15	30	18	36

TABLE 5.19 Clients' Perceptions of Methods That Mitigate Defaults and/or Enforce Loan Contracts

Method	*Quotes*
Threats of legal action and/or legal action	"*The mere mention of the court is enough for most people to find the money to pay. Nobody like court, court matters*" *FC_RCB_Sandema*
Threats to air and/or airing of loan defaulters' names on the local radio	"*People don't want their names mentioned at the radio station, so they honour their part of the contract quickly when they are told that*" *FC_F_RCB_Garu*
Outsourcing loan recovery to third parties	"*The use of third parties for debt collection makes people avoid defaults*" *SFC_M_S & L_Bolga*
Guarantors co-signing contracts	"*The use of guarantors (third parties that co-sign as surety to repay in case of default) help avoid or reduce default rates and disputes between the clients and the bank*" *FC_RCB_Navrongo*
Use of traditional social structures and systems	"*We usually inform the chief about the very 'stubborn' clients and he will then invite the defaulter for dialogue and later with some bank staff at his palace. You know people do have respect for the chief, especially when he tries to let them know that the bank is our own*" Operations Manager Bessfa Rural Bank, Garu.
Lending to close social networks	"*As for my clients, I know all of them, their strengths and weaknesses. There are some clients I will never lend high amounts to and there are some that I will give any amount they ask for it. It's all about your experiences with them and the trust level*" Manager Tarasum Moneylending and Leverage

contracts does influence borrower behaviour. For the formal and informal MFIs, enforcements start with the issuance of demand notices up to three times to the defaulting customer. Upon failure to comply, the Loans Recovery Committee kick-start a series of actions aimed at ensuring compliance. However, the mere threat or actual announcement of the names of defaulting clients on the local radio usually triggers repayments.

Moreover, co-opting the presence of a police officer, threats of legal action, outsourcing loan recovery to third parties and the use of third-party guarantors were some of the mechanisms of reducing moral hazards and improving repayment rates. An unusual mechanism for enforcing contracts was the reliance of MFIs on customary practices embedded in traditional structures and systems. These included summoning defaulting clients at the local chief palace and swearing oaths to deities not to default. These probably need further exploration and incorporation in contexts deemed practical. For informal clients, personalized relationships between providers and clients were found to limit information asymmetries. The study also found that the limited product and service scope in informal credit markets was a strength, as tailor-made contracts enhanced clients' experiences and ensured high repayments. Across all three groups of MFIs, the amicable resolution of default problems had the unintended consequence of reducing moral hazards and increasing product uptake and repayment rates. Clients claimed it was in the interest of both management and clients to resolve default issues amicably. In short, designing microfinance products and services that ensure efficient screening, default risk differentiation, reduced information asymmetry, as well as adequate incentives to induce repayments is critical for sustainable microfinance intermediation in the Northern Savannah of Ghana. Designing products and services that ensure efficient screening, default risk differentiation, reduced information asymmetry, as well as adequate incentives to induce repayments is important. These measures will reduce, if not eliminate, the need to compel borrower repayments. Traditional alternative dispute resolutions rooted in the culture and traditions of clients are becoming important in financial contract enforcements in the Northern Savannah of Ghana and need further exploration and incorporation (see Appendix VI under '*Contract Enforcement*' and II, III and IV).

The next and last section assesses the role of *microfinance plus* in microfinance intermediation in the Northern Savannah of Ghana.

5.2.9 Client's Perceptions of the Role of Add-ons in Microfinance Intermediation and Livelihoods in the Northern Savannah of Ghana

Add-on services (microfinance plus) as a function of product design have a significant variation in focus and objective. In both theory and practice of microfinance, the integration of non-financial services (usually education) with financial services is not uncommon. While some add-ons provide useful secondary skills in sectors such as health, education, energy or environment, where the explicit objective is to lessen the impacts of disruptive events on clients' income, others aim to equip them with business or financial management skills. These add-ons are usually provided by the MFIs, linked to the core financial products or as stand-alone products and/or services. In other cases, they are provided in partnership with specialized organizations, designed to widen impacts through increased uptake, worth of access and customer satisfaction. Smith (2002) finds that clients working with integrated MFIs and programmes experienced improved family health than those working with minimalist MFIs and programmes. Business development training has also been found to significantly improve microenterprise performance and micro-entrepreneur empowerment (Cook et al., 2001; Dumas, 2001; Edgecomb, 2010; Karlan and Valdivia, 2011). Also, micro-entrepreneurs given minimal rules-of-thumb training have been found to apply sound accounting principles and report other positive outcomes than those who were taught traditional accounting principles (Drexler et al., 2014). Add-ons are assessed via key informant interviews with officials of the MFIs and with clients.

In the Northern Savannah of Ghana, most of the formal MFIs provided integrated services to group clients. An example was the Out-grower value chain fund (OVCF) implemented by the BESSFA Rural Bank that led to the facilitation of dialogue among cereal and legume farmers, marketers (wholesalers and retailers), input suppliers, tractor service providers and the bank. This was noted to have diversified livelihoods and increased incomes. The semi-formal and informal MFIs were oriented towards the minimalist approach to providing basic financial services to their clients.

Table 5.20 presents the pair-wise ranking of clients' perceptions of what constituted add-ons (microfinance plus) in the segmented industry of the Northern Savannah of Ghana. For the formal MFI clients, the experiences of friendly management and staff were ranked first. This suggested the importance of treating clients like partners. The respect and dignity of clients when compromised can have negative repercussions on participation and product uptake. The need to maintain friendly customer relations was followed by easy access to credit, easy access to savings and the citing of MFIs that made it easily reachable.

The fact that easy access to credit and loans came in second and third suggests the primacy of these two in the microfinance poverty reduction toolkit, even for the formal MFI clients. Friendly customer relations were also ranked first among the semi-formal clients, further suggesting the value clients placed on being valued as partners in development. This was followed by the easy access to loans, the compulsory savings contracts and the on average lower interest rates on loans. On compulsory savings contracts, clients said it helped them develop savings culture and curbed frugality in their spending habits. The informal clients, however, said easy access to savings facilities was fundamental to the positive outcomes of their livelihood strategies. This was followed by affordable interest rates on loans, support from group members in the case of the VSLAs and the dividends obtained at the end of the group cycle. Also, for the informal Susu and VSLA groups, the opportunity to securely safe was paramount. Though providing credit and opportunities for clients to save securely by microfinance institutions in the Northern Savannah of Ghana is key, the importance of prioritizing the respect and dignity of clients as partners in development cannot be overestimated. The promotion of financial inclusion must lead to the achievement of the dual goals of financial self-sufficiency and increased outreach that impact clients through livelihood diversification.

In conclusion, add-ons (microfinance plus) is a critical design factor for the attainment of increased outreach and financial self-sufficiency of MFIs. Many microfinance clients of the Northern Savannah of Ghana generally perceived well-designed products that match their livelihood needs as add-ons (microfinance plus). Factors perceived as microfinance plus by clients included friendly customer relations, easy access to loans and savings, reliability of intermediation, the use of mobile staff, input credit for farmers, support from group members and even flexible contracts. Pieces of training in group dynamics and sometimes enterprise developments are important in building the capabilities of clients to make the most use of microfinance. Research and development in microfinance remains critical, especially in product design, so that clients' livelihoods are better leveraged in the Northern Savannah of Ghana.

TABLE 5.20 Pair-wise Ranking of Client's Perceptions of Microfinance Plus

Ranked first three things clients like about their MFIs: Formal (N = 50)

Concern area	*First*	*Second*	*Third*	*Total*	*Rank*
Mobile agents coming to us	6	0	0	6	5
Friendly customer relation	12	4	8	24	1
Easy access to loan	6	6	3	15	2
Quick payments of salaries	1	0	1	2	7
Input credit for farmers	4	0	0	4	6
Moderate interest rates on loans	4	3	0	7	5
MFI proximity (mobile staff)	6	6	0	12	3
Easy Access to savings	5	8	2	15	2
Flexible contracts (savings can service loans)	1	0	0	1	8
SMS Alerts	1	0	0	1	8
Can be relied upon (non-financial services included)	0	6	5	11	4

Ranked first three things clients like about their MFIs: semi-formal (N = 50)

What liked	*First*	*Second*	*Third*	*Total*	*Rank*
Mobile agents coming to us	4	1	0	5	6
Friendly customer relation	13	13	11	37	1
Easy access to loan	15	9	4	28	2
Quick payments of salaries	0	0	1	1	10
Moderate interest rates on loans	3	5	1	9	4
MFI proximity	2	0	0	2	9
Easy access to savings	4	3	0	7	5
Compulsory savings contracts (savings can service loans)	2	5	5	12	3
High Interest on savings	2	2	0	4	7
Can be relied upon (non-financial services included)	0	2	1	3	8

Ranked first three things clients like about their MFIs: informal (N = 50)

Concern area	*First*	*Second*	*Third*	*Total*	*Rank*
Mobile agents coming to us	2	1	0	3	8
Friendly customer relation	0	1	0	1	10
Easy access to loan	6	0	0	6	6
Support from group members	7	6	5	18	2
VSL very good for poorer people	3	2	0	5	7
Moderate interest rates on loans	10	2	2	14	3
MFI proximity	3	2	1	6	6
Easy Access to savings	12	8	3	23	1
Flexible contracts (savings can service loans)	1	4	3	8	5
High Interest on savings	5	6	0	11	4
Can be relied upon (non-financial services included)	0	2	1	3	8
Developed discipline in saving	0	1	1	2	9

5.3 Summary and Conclusion

The chapter sets out to assess perceived gaps between the design of microfinance products and services (microcredit, micro-savings, micro-insurance and payment services) and the livelihood needs and wants of those with access. Microfinance product and service design is underpinned by the normative approach adopted by the MFI. While the financial systems approach advocates full cost recovery and margins for MFIs based on market principles, MFIs adopting the poverty-lending approach have poverty alleviation efforts at the core of their mandate, even if subsidies are required. In both cases, the double bottom goals of financial sustainability and outreach remain imperative. However, prioritizing one goal over the other is the inflection point where these two approaches diverge. Schreiner (2002) argued that the adoption of either of these two approaches must address six fundamental issues in the design of products and services to achieve the dual goals of financial sustainability and increased outreach. These six indices are scope, length, worth, cost, breadth and depth. Add-ons (microfinance plus) and contract enforcement mechanisms were incorporated and assessed in this study because these two factors also influence the incentive structure of both the MFI and the client.

While Schreiner (2002) used data reported to MIX Market by a group of MFIs mostly in Latin America for the estimation of the extent of incorporation of his proposed six indices and their implications on clients' livelihoods, this chapter focused on the assessment of all eight design indices in a segmented industry of the Northern Savannah of Ghana using data obtained from clients via household interviews, focus group discussions and case studies. A change in the social benefits of access to microfinance is underpinned by the interaction of all eight factors and the extent of their incorporation in the design of products and services. The extent to which each variable underpinned product and service design and their implications for product uptake, outreach and the sustainability of MFIs were assessed.

For those with access, designing microfinance products and services that simultaneously reduce the cost of access and match the livelihood needs of resource-poor populations gives weight to the poverty-reducing effects of microfinance. While the cost of access varies across the three different tiers of microfinance institutions in the Northern Savannah of Ghana, the least costs incurred by clients, in terms of interest and fees, were empirically found among the formal MFIs. However, two-thirds of clients here perceived it as unaffordable – limiting the non-cash opportunity costs and indirect cash expenses, via the use of mobile staff increased outreach, product uptake and sustainability of MFIs in the Northern Savannah of Ghana. MFIs must estimate these transactional costs generally and transmit the same efficiently into charged interest and fees, without upsetting the demand and supply dynamics of rural financial markets.

The scope of product offerings was much broader for clients of the formal microfinance institutions. These formal MFI clients had greater exposure to varieties of financial products and services and the delivery was much integrated. Deploying mobile staff by the formal and semi-formal MFIs had the positive effect of increasing outreach, product uptake and sustainability of MFIs as non-cash opportunity costs and indirect cash expenses incurred by clients for access were drastically reduced.

Over 80% of clients of microfinance institutions in the Northern Savannah of Ghana believed current business models and the design of products and services made MFIs profitable and, therefore, sustainable. However, over 70% of the clients also claimed existing MFIs in the Northern Savannah of Ghana do not have special preferences for women, the formally educated, those living in rural localities and ethnic minorities. This implies compromising the depth of outreach. Populations at the bottom of the microfinance pyramid, especially those in hard-to-reach, marginalized communities and groups, were severely excluded.

According to 87% of microfinance clients of the Northern Savannah of Ghana, it is people capable of using the financial products and services that are targeted, not just the poor per se. Donor partnerships involving USAID and World Vision International were observed with the formal and informal MFIs, respectively, in the Northern Savannah of Ghana. However, the goals and objectives of these partnerships were found not to be adequately and transparently communicated to clients. There was a need for the goals and objectives of such partnerships to be clearly communicated to enhance buy-ins and cooperation, as well as alignment with broader development policies and goals without compromising key industry standards.

Designing microfinance products and services that ensure efficient screening, default risk differentiation, reduced information asymmetry, and provide adequate incentives to induce repayments is essential. These measures will reduce, if not eliminate, the need to compel borrower repayments. Traditional alternative dispute resolutions rooted in the culture and traditions of target populations were becoming important in financial contract enforcements in the Northern Savannah of Ghana. Further assessment and incorporation as well as adaption in different geospatial areas need exploration.

The management and boards of the MFIs in the Northern Savannah of Ghana need to prioritize the creation of organizational cultures encompassing governance structures and systems and conducive working environments, where staff and clients see one another as equal partners in development. This was noted as key to sustainable microfinance intermediation in the Northern Savannah of Ghana, as it profoundly influenced participation, product uptake and repayment behaviours of clients.

Many microfinance clients of the Northern Savannah of Ghana generally perceived well-designed products that met their livelihood needs as add-ons (microfinance plus). These microfinance-plus activities, apart from training of clients in group dynamics and financial literacy, were limited to product and service design and were perceived at that level. It remains critical for the continual evolution of industry practices and product innovations that meet the needs of the dynamic livelihoods of the Northern Savannah of Ghana, especially in the wake of climate change and weather variability that are intensifying vulnerabilities (see Appendix VI under '*Add-ons*' and also II, III and IV).

The next chapter assesses the determinants of microfinance uptake in the Northern Savannah of Ghana.

6

DETERMINANTS OF MICROFINANCE UPTAKE IN GHANA

6.1 Introduction

There is a constant need for microfinance institutions (MFIs) to reach out to many clients (breadth of outreach) and ensure coverage for the poorest of the poor (depth of outreach) for purposes of consumption smoothening and enterprise development. The adoption of better lending methodologies, deposit mobilization, and the application of information and communication technologies (ATMs, internet and mobile banking) have made MFIs more efficient and sustainable (Hermes et al., 2011) and consequently led to a reduction in transaction costs for clients. The value of loan portfolios, the number of savers and the number of borrowers have recorded dramatic increases in absolute terms over the years in Ghana (Demirguc-Kunt et al., 2018). However, absolute outreach in relation to demand in the Northern Savannah of Ghana remains low (Service, 2007, 2014). Criticisms related to limited evidence of impacts on clients' livelihoods are commonplace (Rogaly, 1996; Chowdhury, 2009; Roodman and Morduch, 2009; Banerjee et al., 2010; Karlan and Zinman, 2011; Banerjee et al., 2015). The few studies that have analysed factors influencing microfinance outreach are from the macro-level perspective (Vanroose, 2008; Ahlin et al., 2011; Hudak, 2012). For example, Osotimehin et al. (2011) examine the determinants of MFIs in South Western Nigeria using firm-level variables.

While studies on the effects of macro-economic variables on the performance of microfinance activities are common in mainstream literature, three broad categories can be identified. The first group focuses on the determinants of microfinance institutional performance involving contract designs, lending methodologies and corporate governance (Hartarska, 2005; Hartarska and Nadolnyak, 2007; Caudill et al., 2009; Hermes et al., 2009; Hermes et al., 2011). The second concentrates efforts on the impact of macro-economic aggregates

DOI: 10.4324/9781003318873-6

such as GDP, inflation, poverty and economic growth on the spatial distribution patterns of the industry (Honohan, 2004; Aliaga et al., 2005; Honohan, 2008; Vanroose, 2008; Vanroose and D'Espallier, 2009). Third, but not least, others align the impact of macro-institutional factors on the performances of service providers. Most disentangle the impact of industry sustainability elements from the external environment (Ahlin and Jiang, 2008; Ahlin et al., 2011) in which providers operate. This chapter assesses broadly macro-economic and macro-institutional variables, the MFIs' (firm) level factors, and the individual clients and their household characteristics that drive microfinance product and service uptake in the Northern Savannah of Ghana.

In-depth household interviews that involved the use of semi-structured questionnaires were the primary instrument for data collection. Questions on sources of motivation for participation (both push and pull factors) involving uptake of products and services from MFIs were solicited. There is a constant need for microfinance institutions (MFIs) to reach out to a large number of clients (breadth) and the poorest of the poor (depth) for purposes of consumption smoothening and enterprise development. The adoption of better lending methodologies, deposit mobilization, and the application of information and communication technologies (ATMs, internet and mobile banking) have made MFIs more efficient and sustainable (Hermes et al., 2009; Hermes et al., 2011). The value of loan portfolios, the number of savers and the number of borrowers have recorded dramatic increases. Yet overall, those with access remain fewer than expected. Few studies have analysed the factors influencing microfinance outreach from a macro-level perspective (Vanroose, 2008; Ahlin et al., 2011; Hudak, 2012). However, that of Osotimehin et al. (2011) examines the determinants of uptake in South Western Nigeria using firm (MFI) level variables. In the achievement of this objective, data gathered from clients, their households, perceptions of MFI level factors, and macro-economic as well as macro-institutional variables driving microfinance product and service uptake were solicited. The insights are expected to inspire improvements of service provision at the MFI level and macro-level policies for increasing access to financial services and inclusion for poverty reduction in the Northern Savannah of Ghana. While a logistic regression model provided the quantitative estimations of the relevant factors determining microfinance product uptake, the qualitative key informant interviews (KIIs) and focus group discussions (FGDs) provided depth behind the numbers. While the focus group discussions (FGDs) provided the means to learn about the subject of interest from the target audience (Debus, 1988), the rapid assessment, semi-structured data gathering procedure employed allowed gathered participants to discuss issues and concerns based on a list of key themes drawn up by the researcher (Kumar, 1987). More detailed accounts of factors influencing participation in programmes were recorded with permission and later transcribed. Field diaries and observations were also kept in order to support the presentation of results.

Using a logistic regression model on responses of 150 clients (Table 5.1), where loans were proxied for all other microfinance product and service uptake, provided the basis for the quantitative analysis. The independent variables were initially 31, but correlation analysis led to the inclusion of only 13 variables deemed relevant (see Appendix VI). This was expected to positively influence firm (MFI) programmes for increased outreach and macro-policies for increased access and inclusion for the optimization of client livelihood experiences in the Upper East Region and the Northern Savannah as a whole. The chapter addresses the research question: what are the determinants of microfinance product and service uptake in the Northern Savannah of Ghana? The chapter ends with the presentation of disaggregated and compressed data on the perception of the three-tiered industry's household livelihood transitional status in the Northern Savannah of Ghana.

6.2 Determinants of Clients' Product and Service Uptake in Ghana

Loan product uptake is a binary decision that requires the application of binary choice models in its analysis, although binary dependent variables can be analysed using several methods, e.g., the linear probability model (LPM), the Linear Discriminant Function, and the Probit and Logit Models (Maddala and Jeong, 1992). The closely related linear probability model and linear discriminant functions (Maddala and Jeong, 1992) are unable to generate predicted values outside the relevant probability range (i.e., 0 and 1) when estimated by the maximum likelihood method and were thus not considered for the estimation of clients' product(s) and service(s) uptake. Moreover, the assumptions of discriminant analysis are rarely met, making its use less relevant in this analysis.

Probit and logistic regression do not feature as many assumptions and restrictions as discriminant analysis. Logit and probit models are argued to produce similar estimates (see Maddala and Jeong, 1992; Greene, 2003; Gujarati and Porter, 2004; Hill et al., 2018) as they both assume the existence of an underlying latent variable for which a dichotomous realization is observed (Gujarati and Porter, 2004). However, the logit model is generally preferred to the probit model due to its simpler mathematical structure and the cumulative distribution function that yields results that are not sensitive to the distribution of sample attributes when estimated by the maximum likelihood method. Thus, to examine which variable significantly explains a dependent dummy variable, the logit model helps to solve the problem associated with disproportionate sampling, as it only affects the constant term and not the estimated slope coefficients (Maddala and Jeong, 1992). The next section describes the variables used in the econometric analysis.

6.3 Description of the Variables Used in the Econometric Analyses

Based on studies of utility theories (McFadden, 1968; Carman, 1970; Pekelman and Sen, 1974; Shocker and Srinivasan, 1974; McFadden, 1975; Watson and

Westin, 1975; McGuire and Weiss, 1976; Manski and Lerman, 1977; Maddala and Jeong, 1992; Greene, 2003; Gujarati and Porter, 2004; Hill et al., 2018), it was assumed that in the case of binary choice models, the response variable (y_i = loan product(s) uptake) takes the value $y = 1$ for individual clients taking loans and $y = 0$ for those not taking loans. There is however an underlying unobserved latent variable y_i^* which defines the probability of loan product uptake. The latent variable is defined as $y_i^* = \beta x_i + \varepsilon_i$

where x_i = vector of explanatory variables determining y_i^* (the underlying unobserved latent variable), β = vector of unknown parameters and ε_i = random error term. The unobserved latent variable is related to the observed response variable as follows: $y_i = \begin{cases} 1 \text{ if } y_i^* > 0 \\ 0 \text{ if } y_i^* \leq 1 \end{cases}$

$$y_i^* = \beta_0 + \beta_1 X_1 + \beta_2 X_2 + \beta_3 X_3 + \beta_4 X_4 + \beta_5 X_5 + \beta_6 X_6 + \beta_7 X_7 + \beta_8 X_8 + \beta_9\ X_9 + \beta_{10} X_{10} + \beta_{11} X_{11} + \beta_{12} X_{12} + \varepsilon_i \tag{6.1}$$

where y_i^*= latent continuous variable for loan product(s) uptake, such that $y = 1$ if $y_i^* > 0$, and $y = 0$ if $y_i^* \leq 0$; β = vector of unknown parameters to be estimated and ϵ_i = random error term.

Data for 33 explanatory variables were initially collected from clients but upon a correlation regression, 11 of these were dropped, as they had no correlation with the dependent variable (loan uptake). Thus, the 13 variables included in the logit model were X_1 = Perceptions of Client Targeting (1, Targeted, 0, Not Targeted); X_2 = Perceptions of a Growing Economy (1, Affect, 0, Does Not Affect); X_3 = Perceptions of Product Scope (0 Individual, 1, Groups, 2, both Individual and Groups); X_4 = Sex of Client (1, Male, 0, Female); X_5 = Perceptions of Other Poverty Reduction Intervention (1, Benefiting, 0, Not Benefiting); X_6 = Education Level of Client (Continuous Variable); X_7 = Household Size of Clients (Continuous Variable); X_8 = Number of Livelihood Strategies (1, Many 0, Single); X_9 = Perception of Inflation (1, affect, 0, Does Not Affect); X_{10} = Perception of the Rule of Law (1, Affect, 0, Does Not); X_{11} = Perception of Start-up Requirements (1, Affect, 0, Does Not Affect); X_{12} = MFI Governance (1, Affects, 0, Does Not Affect).

However, the independent variable of Product Scope was coded into three categories: 0, for MFIs offering only individual products; 1, for MFIs offering only group product(s); and 2, for MFIs offering both groups and individual product(s). Model 1 was then transformed into Model 2:

$$y_i^* = \beta_0 + \beta_1 X_1 + \beta_2 X_2 + \beta_3 X_3 + \beta_4 X_4 + \beta_5 X_5 + \beta_6 X_6 + \beta_7 X_7 + \beta_8 X_8 + \beta_9\ X_9 + \beta_{10} X_{10} + \beta_{11} X_{11} + \beta_{12} X_{12} + \beta_{13} X_{13} + \varepsilon_i \tag{6.2}$$

where y_i^* = latent continuous variable for loan product(s) uptake, such that $y = 1$ if $y_i^* > 0$, and $y = 0$ if $y_i^* \leq 0$; β = vector of unknown parameters to be estimated and ε_i = random error term.

The explanatory variables in the logit model 6.2 for the estimation of product(s) uptake are presented in Table 6.1.

As shown in Table 6.1 the averages observed for the variables were Client Targeting (28%), Perceptions of a Growing Economy (over 81% of respondents said it influences loan product uptake), Perceptions of Product Scope (groups only) (over 39% said it influences product uptake), Perceptions of Product Scope (groups and individuals) (over 35% said it influences product uptake), Sex of Client (over 41% of respondents were male), Benefiting in other poverty intervention (only 7% were benefiting directly from other poverty intervention, either government or NGOs), Formal Education level of Client (the majority had up to ten years of formal schooling), Household Size of Client (most respondent households had on average four people), Number of Livelihood Strategies of Client (about 68% were engaged in multiple livelihood strategies), Perceptions of the Rule of Law (66% said it affects loan product uptake), Inflation (83% said it doesn't affects), Enterprise Start-up Requirements (12% said it doesn't affect) and MFI Governance (over 94% of respondents said it affected product uptake) (see Appendix VI for results of correlation of all independent variables).

6.4 Logistic Regression Results and Discussion of the Determinants of Product Uptake in Ghana

Table 6.2 presents the results of the logistic regression of the determinants of microfinance product uptake. Targeting specific sub-groups of clients in the Northern Savannah of Ghana had a positive (1.023) relationship with the product(s) and service(s) uptake but statistically significant at 10%. Thus, access to microfinance services in the Northern Savannah of Ghana is still largely supply-led rather than demand-driven. A change in targeting certain client niches has the probability of increasing product uptake by about 11%. Though not statistically significant, the potential to increase the depth of outreach could be immense. Targeting of the marginalized who are essentially out of government plans and budgets, economists' models, bankers' portfolios and national policies (Acemoglu et al., 2001) is key to financial inclusion. Targeting is particularly important in the light of earlier assertions that MFIs are failing to meet the needs of the very poor and destitute with a special need for microfinance services, especially savings (Rogaly, 1996; Dichter, 1999; Markowski, 2002; Littlefield et al., 2003a). Halder and Mosley (2004) found that BRAC in Bangladesh targeted poorer segments of society sustainably. Rigorous and professional management of MFIs is key to balancing the social and financial self-sufficiency goals of the industry. Targeting that ensures loan sizes match client needs at price points they can afford, uses compulsory savings as entry points for loan disbursement, ensures durations for repayments are based on client needs and that scaling up best practices can contribute significantly to sustainability goals of MFIs (Havers, 1996).

TABLE 6.1 Data Description and Summary Statistics of Variables Used in Econometric Analyses

Variable	*Description*	*Definition*	*Mean*	*SD*	*Min*	*Max*	*Average*
X_1	Client targeting	Dummy (1, if client was targeted; 0 for otherwise)	0.280	0.451	0	1	28%
X_2	Growing economy	Dummy (1, affects; 0, does not affect)	0.813	0.391	0	1	81%
X_3	Product scope (groups only)	Dummy (1, if group; 0, if only individuals)	0.387	0.489	0	1	39%
X_4	Product scope (both group and individual)	Dummy (1, if both; 0, if individual)	0.347	0.478	0	1	35%
X_5	Sex of client	Dummy (1, if male; 0 for otherwise)	0.407	0.492	0	1	41%
X_6	Other poverty intervention	Dummy (1, if benefiting; 0 for otherwise)	0.067	0.250	0	1	7%
X_7	Formal education level of client	Total number of years in formal education (continuous)	9.973	6.759	0	16	10 years
X_8	Household size of client	Total number of household members (continuous)	4.140	2.114	1	9	4 people
X_9	Number of livelihood strategies of client	Dummy (1, if more than one; 0 if otherwise)	0.680	0.468	0	1	68%
X_{10}	Perceptions of inflation	Dummy (1, if affects; 0 for otherwise)	0.827	0.380	0	1	83%
X_{11}	Perceptions of the rule of law	Dummy (1, if affects; 0 for otherwise)	0.660	0.475	0	1	66%
X_{12}	Enterprise start-up requirements	Dummy (1, if affects; 0 for otherwise)	0.127	0.334	0	1	13%
X_{13}	MFI governance	Dummy (1, if affects; 0 for otherwise)	0.940	0.238	0	1	94%

TABLE 6.2 Logistic Results of Determinants of Client Product(s) and Service(s) Uptake

Variable	*Coefficient*	*Standard Error*	P-*Value*	*Marginal Effect*	*Standard Error*	P-*Value*
Constant	0.685	1.372	0.618	–	–	
Client targeting	1.023	0.713	0.152	0.110*	0.065	0.090
Growing economy	1.560**	0.661	0.018	0.266**	0.135	0.049
Perception of P. Scope (groups only)	1.207***	0.612	0.049	0.140***	0.069	0.042
Perceptions of P. Scope (India and groups)	2.409***	0.666	0.000	0.250***	0.064	0.000
Sex of client	−0.959*	0.561	0.088	−0.129*	0.078	0.097
Perception of other Poverty intervention	−1.287	0.926	0.165	−0.228	0.206	0.263
Formal education Level of client	0.046	0.042	0.272	0.006	0.005	0.263
Household size of Client	0.094	0.136	0.265	0.012	0.017	0.488
Number of livelihood strategies	1.562***	0.554	0.005	0.238***	0.093	0.010
Perceptions of inflation trends	−0.576	0.734	0.432	−0.063	0.069	0.358
Perceptions of the rule of law	−0.340	0.541	0.530	−0.041	0.062	0.510
Perceptions of enterprise start-up Req'ts	−1.224*	0.706	0.083	−0.205	0.143	0.150
Perceptions of MFI Governance/Mgt	−2.512**	1.281	0.050	−0.151***	0.040	0.000
Log-Likelihood	−58.031					
LR chi^2 (13)	46.92***					
Prob >chi^2	0.0000					
No. of observations	150					

***, **, *, indicate values statistically significance at 1%, 5% and 10%, respectively.

Moreover, targeting women's income generation activities has the potential to increase both the welfare of households and repayments in the Northern Savannah of Ghana. This confirms similar findings in Bangladesh (Pitt and Khandker, 1998; Pitt, 2014), though Kevane and Wydick (2001) found that men generate slightly more employment outcomes than females in the United States of America.

The relationship between a growing rural economy and product uptake was positive (1.560) and statistically significant at a 5% level. This meant that a unit change in the growth of the rural economy had the probability of increasing product uptake by as much as 27%. A growing economy raises households' current or expected future incomes and, therefore, their willingness to take on debt and risk in investments. Moreover, increasing the availability of physical infrastructure, human capital, strengthened institutions and technological advancement at the macro-level all have a positive impact on the demand and supply dynamics of the microfinance industry. Franks (2000) concluded that macro-economic stability could ultimately be very beneficial to the microfinance sector.

Perceptions of clients on only group products and services offered by MFIs in the Northern Savannah of Ghana also had a positive (1.207) relationship with uptake and was statistically significant at the 1% level. A change in the offering of group products and services had the probability of increasing uptake by about 14%. Those offering both individual and group products and services had a greater positive relationship (2.409) with uptake, which was also statistically significant at the 1% level. An MFI change in both group and individual products and services on offer had the probability of increasing uptake by as much as 25%. Group lending improves uptake, but MFIs need to offer both group and individual products to meet the needs of different clients' transitioning out of poverty. This was succinctly stated by a female group client of an RCB in the Garu study site:

> The groups are very good for those of us in villages that do not have what the bank needs to give you personalized loans. We don't have a government salary or all of those things the bank will be asked as a guarantee. So, we the poor ones are making good use of the groups in our own small way to have access to the loans to do our business even though some group members can sometimes disappoint.
>
> *FC_F_RCB_Garu*

Increasing Product Scope that fulfils different needs of clients was crucial for uptake. The study noted that MFI group products were more associated with clients at the bottom of the pyramid, with no suitable collaterals and were enlisting the joint liability concept to curtail adverse selection and moral hazards. When loans were staggered in size for group members, it was also reported that it improved the incentive to monitor other group members' projects that reduced default rates (KII_RCB Credit Officer_Navrongo). Marr (2012), however, found that it is important not to assume group lending dynamics as existing in a vacuum but to perceive the process as embedded in social, economic and cultural spheres as group behaviour is conditioned by power structures, evolving risks, constraints and opportunities. According to the manager of one of the sampled RCBs, "the joint liability in group products had the added advantage of reducing credit risk exposure in our portfolios".

Sex of respondents had a negative (−0.959) relationship with MFI product and service uptake and this was statistically significant at the 10% level. From the model, being female increases the probability of access and uptake by about 13%. This suggests that barriers to female product uptake, mostly rooted in the cultural norms and socio-economic spheres of everyday life when eliminated, have the potential to increase product uptake by women, and that MFIs targeting women increase uptake. Targeting women was also noted to be good for business and the welfare of households, especially the nutrition of children (KII_Credit Officer_RCB). This confirms similar findings by Pitt and Khandker (1998), where access correlated with improved nutrition of children in Bangladesh. However, women were noted to be predominantly involved in low-value informal activities such as agro-processing and the sale of cooked food and local beverages.

Client engagement in more than one livelihood strategy had a positive (1.561) relationship with MFI product and service uptake and was statistically significant at the 1% level. Diversification of client livelihood strategies was associated with increased product uptake. A client engaged in more than one livelihood activity in the Northern Savannah of Ghana has the probability of increasing product uptake by as much as 24%. Multiple livelihood strategies come with varying needs for the client in terms of amounts needed, timing and investment requirements. Based on the fungibility of cash, liquidity management instruments from MFIs must be available to provide needed products and services that increase the success of broader investment and outcomes in the Northern Savannah of Ghana. The shifting of livelihood activities from on-farm to off-farm strategies (owing to shorter wet seasons and increasingly longer dry seasons) could also explain the importance of financial services to diversification, adaptation and household resilience. The following quote from a client mirrored the realities of engaging in multiple livelihood strategies:

> I own a small piggery and I manufacture sachet water. I started by saving for about 8 months and then I used those savings to start the piggery. When I started selling some pigs for pork the following year, some of the profits were saved with the bank. Then I rented a shop, took a loan, and added it to the savings and bought the equipment for manufacturing the sachet water.
>
> I also do some crop farming in the Rainy Season for subsistence. The harvest from the farm also makes me buy fewer foodstuffs for the family, making me save money. In this area, you cannot depend on one activity to survive. You will be in financial stress all the time and even debt if you are not careful.
>
> *FC_M_S&L_Bolgattanga*

However, the relationship between business start-up requirements and product and service uptake was negative (−1.224) and significant at the 10% level. This implies that MFI products are used for sustaining rather than starting new enterprises, especially the use of debt (loans). The probability of starting new enterprises using debt was as low as 21%. However, the negative relationship could further be explained by the limited availability of credit facilities for on-farm livelihood activities. On-farm activities were exposed to risk, especially in the wake of climate change and weather variability. Poor agricultural infrastructure such as irrigation and processing facilities in the Northern Savannah of Ghana was also a hindrance to on-farm and off-farm activities.

The prevailing MFI governance and management systems (i.e., MFI-customer relationship) had a negative (−2.512) relationship with client product and service uptake in the Northern Savannah of Ghana and was significant at the 5% level. Poor customer relationships, which result from poor governance and management systems, had the potential to decrease product and service uptake by as much as 15% in the Northern Savannah of Ghana. The need for boards of directors of MFIs to continually invest in improving good governance and management systems that produce positive outcomes via the organizational culture to optimize customer satisfaction and experiences is important to ensuring sustainable service provision. The need to handle clients as partners in development and respect their dignity can be crucial to product uptake and repayment behaviours of clients in the Northern Savannah. Thus, good governance and management systems that produce cordial MFI-customer relationships do yield dividends for all stakeholders of the microfinance industry. The below view of an RCB customer showed the importance of good MFI-customer relationships:

> If the bank managers make sure that the staff are friendly and patient with customers, they will feel free coming to take loans and save their monies. Some may even bring their friends to the bank without being afraid of anything because they will be attended to with patience and understanding and not shouted at and disrespected.
>
> *FC_F-RCB_Navrongo*

Education levels and household sizes had positive relationships with microfinance product and service uptake but were not significant. The perceptions of clients about the state of the rule of law, inflation and participation in other poverty interventions all had negative relationships with microfinance product and service uptake. The implication here was that an increased perception of an ineffective rule of law, of an upward inflationary trend, and the non-availability of other poverty reduction interventions could potentially trigger a downward trend in microfinance product and service uptake in the Northern Savannah of Ghana. However, such increases would usually not be statistically significant.

The compressed and disaggregated data of the transitional household status of the informal, semi-formal and formal MFI clients are presented in Table 6.3. Though variations existed across the three groups of microfinance client types in terms of the transitional status overall, only 16% of clients of the total sampled viewed their transitional household status to be that of *falling down and out*. These were those who had accessed credit and were finding it difficult to repay due to several reasons. Thirty-one percent felt they were *hanging in* with their

TABLE 6.3 Household Livelisystem Transitioning in the Northern Savannah of Ghana

Household Transitioning Status	***Informal Clients (46)***		***Semi-formal Clients (50)***		***Formal Clients (50)***		***Total Sampled (146)***	
	Number	*%*	*Number*	*%*	*Number*	*%*	*Number*	*%*
Falling down and out	7	15.2	9	18	4	8	24	16.43
Hanging in	20	43.5	12	24	9	18	45	30.8
Stepping up	14	30.4	19	38	26	52	59	40.41
Stepping out	5	10.8	10	20	11	22	26	17.81
Total	46	100	50	100	50	100	146	100

household livelihood activities status. Here, credit was mostly used for consumption smoothening. However, approximately 40% of sampled clients felt they were *stepping up* and had mostly production activities that are both market-led and household consumption. About 18% felt they were *stepping out* with their household livelihood activities and production was mostly market targeted. These results corroborated earlier findings that 93% of clients claimed the overall benefits of participation in microfinance exceeded all cost considerations (see Chapter 5, Section 5.2.2; Table 5.3). This suggests that microfinance may be doing more to keep households from *falling down and out* than the empirical evidence might suggest.

6.5 Summary and Conclusion

In summary, the findings in this chapter show that access to microfinance services remained supply-driven in the Northern Savannah of Ghana rather than demand-led. They also showed that targeting client niches does influence product uptake. The perception of a booming rural economy significantly increases MFI product and service uptake. While group lending significantly increases uptake, the combination of group and individual product offerings by an MFI was noted to improve uptake further significantly. This was because an expanded scope of products and services meets more client needs than a limited scope of products that are offered. Being female was associated with increased product uptake in the Northern Savannah of Ghana, and this was as a result of targeting female clients with the presumption that it had the added advantages of improving the depth of outreach and improving family welfare and sustainability goals of MFIs through increased repayment rates.

The diversification of livelihoods was associated with improved product uptake. However, many microfinance products were used for the sustenance of existing enterprises and not for starting new ones, which reinforced inequalities in communities. Moreover, many of the products were more suited for off-farm and/or non-farm livelihood strategies rather than farmed activities. Good customer relationships, guaranteed by good governance and management systems, yield dividends for both MFIs and clients. There is, therefore, the need to invest in building governance and management systems that aim to understand what matters to clients and facilitate the incorporation of the same in the organizational culture, policies and procedures for the optimization of customer satisfaction and experiences in microfinance provision and financial inclusion in the Northern Savannah of Ghana.

Education levels and household size of clients had positive relationships with microfinance product and service uptake, but such influences were not significant. The perceptions of clients of the state of the rule of law, of inflation, and the availability of other poverty interventions all had a negative relationship with microfinance product uptake. The implication here was that the perception of the prevailing ineffective rule of law, of an upward inflationary trend, and the availability of other poverty reduction interventions had the potential to trigger downward trends in microfinance product and service uptake in the Northern Savannah of Ghana. However, such decreases were usually not statistically significant.

Even though about 16.4% of all the sampled microfinance clients perceived their household livelihood transitional status as *falling down and out*, participation in microfinance is certainly impacting household livelihoods transitioning in the Northern Savannah of Ghana where around 87% of clients claimed they were either hanging in (31%), stepping up (40%) or stepping out (18%).

The next chapter assesses the impact of access to microfinance on client household livelihood diversification, asset accumulation and welfare outcomes in the segmented industry of the Northern Savannah of Ghana.

7

IMPACTS OF HOUSEHOLD ACCESS TO MICROFINANCE IN GHANA

7.1 Introduction

Globally, the impact of microfinance as an anti-poverty tool is at best mixed. Debates are rife among academics, practitioners and policymakers about the real impact of the industry. The need for a deeper understanding of how microfinance works to reduce poverty through the livelihoods of populations in sub-Saharan Africa has gained currency, not least because it is one of the poorest regions of the world, but also where a large share of both development aid inflows (Grabel, 2008) and majority non-profit service providers (Yanguas and Hulme, 2015) work. Moreover, there are substantial investment inflows through an array of microfinance initiatives in the region (Capital, 2011; El-Zoghbi et al., 2011), a region with a long history of microfinance activities, including credit unions of the 1950s and 1960s (Raftopoulos and Lacoste, 2001), and group-based savings and lending (Assets, 2011, p. 3). Overall, the modern microfinance industry in the region is still in its infancy, with a high concentration in a relatively few countries (Capital, 2011; El-Zoghbi et al., 2011). There is, therefore, the need for research to shape policy, especially considering new initiatives targeting capacity development (Yanguas and Hulme, 2015) to drive effectiveness (Eyben, 2010). In Sub-Saharan Africa (SSA), Ghana was ranked the highest recipient (about US$186 million) of development partner donor funding for the microfinance industry (Arun and Hulme, 2008).

The 2012/2013 Ghana Living Standards Survey also shows that while under a tenth of the Ghanaian population lives in extreme poverty, about a quarter overall is poor. However, even though the number of those in extreme poverty is relatively low, it remains a rural phenomenon and is concentrated in the Rural Savannah (the three northern regions), where a quarter of the Ghanaian population lives (Service, 2014). Microfinance promises to reduce poverty

DOI: 10.4324/9781003318873-7

within a wider scope of building peoples' financial, physical, human and social capital. However, these promises have received mixed reactions from the public mostly due to the inconclusive evidence from impact studies across time and space (Khandker, 2005; Roodman and Morduch, 2009; Imai et al., 2010; Imai and Azam, 2012; Banerjee et al., 2015).

Various studies have examined the impact of microfinance institutions on the populations served. Some have found positive effects on consumption and income (Khandker, 2005; Kondo et al., 2008; Berhane, 2009; Collins et al., 2009; Berhane and Gardebroek, 2012; Imai and Azam, 2012), housing (Berhane, 2009; Berhane and Gardebroek, 2011), wages and agricultural investments (Kaboski and Townsend, 2012), savings (Kondo et al., 2008; Dupas and Robinson, 2013), and health and food security (Stewart et al., 2010). Others such as Chowdhury (2009) have been sceptical about the effectiveness of microfinance as a poverty reduction tool. Chowdhury argues that business skills and marketing information are important to enable the leverage of loans enterprise development and job creation; otherwise, microfinance remains only a consumption smoothing tool. Copestake and Williams (2011) further argued that selection bias faults the magnitude of reported positive impacts of programmes on households' welfare. Buera and Kaboski (2012) built an economy-wide model of entrepreneurship of the industry outside the formal financial sector and further explored the extent to which MFIs influence output, capital, total factor productivity, wages and interest rates and concluded that, in some cases, microfinance institutions not only raise output but decrease disparities between the rich and the poor. Ahlin and Jiang (2008) and Yusupov (2012) also find that MFIs promote development on a wider scale via tangible and intangible spill-over effects.

As debates are beginning to shift marginally to the demand end of the microfinance industry, researchers have begun questioning how product and service design innovations are effectively mitigating the livelihood constraints of households and its impact on institutional sustainability (Banerjee et al., 2010; Feigenberg et al., 2013; Iyer et al., 2015). According to Ledgerwood et al. (2013), the attention of the microfinance community is now focused on how to address the diverse needs of clients of the industry within the broader financial system and the transformational role of technology in delivering better products and services.

Assessing the impact of microfinance on poverty reduction continues to remain difficult. Although most studies suggest a positive impact (Pitt and Khandker, 1998; Imai et al., 2010), others have indicated either negative or 'zero' impact (Rogaly, 1996; Chowdhury, 2009; Roodman and Morduch, 2009). The multiple dimensional nature of poverty and measurement criteria, the country-specific contexts and the mixed outcomes are contributing to the continuing debate (Datt and Ravallion, 1992; Pitt, 2014; Roodman and Morduch, 2014). For instance, the 2009 release of the first randomized studies in Hyderabad, India, and Manila, the Philippines, was met with mixed reactions (Banerjee et al., 2010; Karlan and Zinman, 2011). This chapter, therefore, assesses the impact of access on households' livelihoods of clients in the segmented microfinance industry of the Northern Savannah of Ghana.

The survey methodology involving the use of a semi-structured questionnaire elicited information from the study participants. Focus group discussions, an indispensable tool for social science research (Krueger, 2014), provided the platform for purposeful interaction with groups of research participants in the collection of needed data (Kitzinger, 1996) and information. Insights of target audience perceptions, needs, beliefs and reasons for certain decisions allowed the accommodation of heterogeneity in target populations and the obtaining of representative patterns of social interactions (Otoide et al., 2001). The FGDs particularly enabled the capturing of externalities associated with development interventions including credit delivery (Hulme, 2000). The case study methodology, according to Yin (1994), is an empirical inquiry into contemporary phenomena within their real-life context, and was employed for the understanding of access and clients' livelihood diversification, asset accumulation patterns and household welfare outcomes. While the intrinsic case study examined individual clients, the instrumental case study focused on the categories of formal, semi-formal and informal MFI clients' patterns of behaviour that related to diversification, asset accumulation and household welfare. The collective case study methods used allowed the combination of data from all three client categories in addressing the research question (Stake, 1995). The positivist, critical and interpretive case study methods (Klein and Myers, 1999) allowed the examination of pieces of evidence for the drawing of inferences from the sampled clients of MFIs in the study region and subsequent generalization – thus, allowing the study to uncover different socio-economic and politico-cultural phenomena shaping each group of clients and the interpretation of interest of the research related to the study objectives, respectively. Tables are mostly used to present both the descriptive and inferential statistical results and analysis.

While Section 7.2 assesses access and livelihood diversification, Section 7.3 focuses on household asset accumulation patterns among clients of the three-tier microfinance industry. Section 7.4 assesses the impact of access on household welfare outcomes.

7.2 Access and Household Livelihood Diversification in Ghana

7.2.1 Introduction

From the conceptual framework of the microfinance livelisystem (Figure 2.1) developed by the author, rural households are exposed to a broad resource base, called 'assets, properties and attributes' (including microfinance services). A household's access to the material, relational and informational properties and attributes of these assets directly or indirectly determines, to a large extent, its transitional status. These transitional statuses include the following: *falling down and out* (i.e., household failed to maintain the status quo and falling to a worsened situation); *hanging in* (i.e., household maintained the status quo); *stepping up* (i.e., household focused on investments in assets to expand productivity and income) or *stepping out* (i.e., where existing activities are meant to accumulate productive assets to ensure higher and/or more stable income in the future). Under constraints conditioned by vulnerabilities emanating from shocks (e.g., droughts, floods, crop/livestock pests and diseases and even death in the family), trends (e.g., migration, climate change, declining natural resource-based, inflation, currency devaluations, structural unemployment, technology change, market change, trade and globalization) and seasonality (e.g., changing rainfall patterns, price variations and production cycles), the household undertakes diversification, specialization, substitution, adaptation and accumulation of assets, properties and attributes.

However, the quality of the household's human and physical resources is critical for the effective and efficient use of accessed microfinance for production, consumption and investment. The household relations with the extended family, affiliations with social networks, public authorities, markets and member institutions can and do play significant roles in determining the success of the household production, consumption and investment outcomes. This was unpacked in the household livelisystem model (Figure 2.2) developed by the author. It is worth noting that the iteration of households' livelihood activities with these five welfare organizations is further contiguous with the evolving broader economic and financial transformational structures and processes concurrently taking place from the local sub-national, national, regional, global and external spheres (e.g., the relationship between the domestic and international financial eco-system – the use of microfinance investment vehicles (MIVs) in the microfinance industry).

7.2.2 Access and Household Livelihood Diversification in a Three-Tiered Microfinance Industry of the Northern Savannah

In Table 7.1, almost two-thirds (59.3%) of the microfinance client respondents of North-eastern Ghana said access to financial services was instrumental to their livelihood's diversification.

However, analysing the poverty reduction function of microfinance in the study area revealed that most were used in the expansion of existing off-farm and/or non-farm livelihood activities, as presented in Table 7.2. The use of microfinance for liquidity management of off-farm and/or non-farm activities was dominant across all three client groups of the segmented microfinance industry of North-eastern Ghana.

Thus, most microfinance product designs were suited to financing clients' off-farm and/or non-farm livelihood activities. While investment in non-farm and/or off-farm activities was the dominant push factor for product uptake among all client categories, it was consumption smoothening that ranked second for both the formal and semi-formal clients. However, it was investments in

TABLE 7.1 Access and Client Livelihood Diversification

	Frequency	*Percent*
Yes	89	59.3
No	61	40.7
Total	150	100

TABLE 7.2 Ranked Use of Financial Products for Livelihood Diversification in Ghana

Category of Activity	*Number*	*Ranked Results*
Formal MFI Clients Application of Products and Services (N = 50)		
Expanded on-farm activities	7	3
Expanded off-farm/non-farm activities	25	1
Education expenses for children	5	4
Consumption smoothening	11	2
Semi-formal MFI Clients Application of Product(s) and Service(s) (N = 39)		
Expanded on-farm activities	6	4
Expanded off-farm/non-farm activities	14	1
Education expenses for children	9	3
Consumption smoothening	10	2
Informal MFI Clients Application of Product(s) and Services (N = 33)		
Expanded on-farm activities (IGAs)	11	2
Expanded off-farm activities (IGAs)	15	1
Education	7	3
Health expenses	6	4

on-farm activities that were ranked second by the clients of the informal MFIs. The education of family members was also ranked as the third most important use of accessed microfinance products and services by the semi-formal and informal clients. For the formal clients, it was investments in on-farm activities that ranked third. The fourth highest ranked use of accessed products and services included education of household members and on-farm activities for the formal and semi-formal clients, respectively. The informal clients ranked health expenditure as the fourth most important use of accessed products and services from their MFIs.

All these results suggest the importance of short-term liquidity instruments for managing the iterations between household resources and activities involving production, consumption and investments. The financial needs of clients vary, and the demand for different product features and payment and delivery systems and structures is imperative for enabling the poor to cope with risks of irregular cash flows, smoothening of consumption, seizure of opportunities, payment for children's education, expansion of enterprises, and the utilization of crop and health insurance, where available, to stave off risks. However, inflexible withdrawals associated with deposit facilities of the informal MFIs were said to be inimical to household welfare, especially during emergencies. However, it was acknowledged that in the household livelisystem, individual members may have separate (if not competing) preferences, constraints and access to resources that dictate whether separate or joint decisions and activities are undertaken or not. This usually involves negotiation, bargaining and sometimes conflict. As a result, extensive conflicts and pervasive cooperation may be the norm rather than the exception in the household livelisystem (Sen, 1987). The nature and extent of inter-relationships that exist between the household and the five core welfare institutions – the larger family, membership institutions, public authorities, markets and social networks – can be critical for the success of households' production, consumption and investments.

7.2.3 Access and Household Livelihood Diversification: A Comparative Analysis of the Formal, Semi-formal and Informal Microfinance Participants of the Northern Savannah of Ghana

In Table 7.3, averagely half of all microfinance clients of North-eastern Ghana, irrespective of category, had engaged in crop cultivation during the past 12 months as a livelihood diversification strategy. However, it was the semi-formal clients who had the highest percentage (68%) of on-farm livelihood diversification. The crops were mostly cereals and legumes grown under rainfed conditions. However, the Vea and Tono irrigation schemes near Bolgatanga and Navrongo, respectively, are two important irrigation facilities in the study region for the cultivation of tomatoes and rice. Vegetable production along riverine bodies across the study region is also common during the dry season. Vegetables produced are mostly for commercial market purposes, though their perishable nature remains a challenge. Crop cultivation as a livelihood diversification strategy, coupled with irrigation farming, has been critical in limiting the tide of emigration out to the southern regions of the country. It is not uncommon to find migrants return to undertake crop farming or send down remittances for crop farming during the rainy seasons of the study region. This phenomenon underscores the importance of on-farm crop activities in a country where an estimated 60% of the population is engaged in agriculture.

In Table 7.3, the results showed that five out of every ten formal and informal MFI clients, respectively, raised animals as a livelihood diversification strategy. This was four out of ten for the semi-formal MFI clients. The smaller percentages of the semi-formal clients engaged in animal rearing buttresses the fact that most were either traders or professional waged workers who have little disposable time for the time-consuming animal raising business. The importance of animals, especially small ruminants such as sheep and goats, including pigs in the study region, cannot be overemphasized. As capital stocks, small ruminants

TABLE 7.3 Descriptive Statistics of Livelihood Activities of Microfinance Clients in Ghana

Type of Activity	*Formal MFI Clients (N = 50)*		*Semi-formal MFI Clients (N = 50)*		*Informal MFI Clients (N = 50)*	
	Freq.	*%*	*Freq.*	*%*	*Freq.*	*%*
On-farm (crops – cereals and vegetables) in the last 12 months						
Yes	26	52	34	68	29	58
No	24	48	16	32	21	42
On-farm (animal raising) in the last 12 months						
Yes	25	50	22	44	26	52
No	25	50	28	56	24	48
Off-farm/non-farm activities in the last 12 months						
Yes	27	54	26	52	24	48
No	23	46	24	48	26	52
Wage employment in the last 12 months						
Yes	20	40	24	48	5	10
No	30	60	26	52	45	90
Increased number of livelihood strategies in the last 12 months						
Yes	22	44	30	60	29	58
No	28	56	20	40	21	42
Increased allocation to profitable livelihood strategies in the last 12 months						
Yes	41	82	36	72	34	68
No	9	18	14	28	16	32
Increased access to land (crop/animal production) in the last 12 months						
Yes	32	64	22	44	43	86
No	18	36	28	56	7	14
Previous experience working with debt on livelihood activities						
Yes	20	40	22	44	17	34
No	30	60	28	56	33	66

are easy to convert into cash in local meat markets. They are insurance against income risks among resource-poor households. This is particularly critical in the light of aggravated climate change and weather variability in the region, increasingly making crop farming precarious. Shortened and unpredictable rainfall patterns have become very common in recent decades. Poultry, such as guinea fowl rearing, though largely small scale, has become an important alternative source of income for resource-poor households in the Northern Savannah as a whole, for the mitigation of income risks and uncertainties.

Approximately five out of every ten clients of microfinance institutions in North-eastern Ghana were engaged in off-farm and/or non-farm activities. This further confirms the earlier qualitative findings of this study that showed that, irrespective of the MFI category, most accessed products were used for non-farm and/or off-farm activities. While access within a 12-month period saw an average of 60% each of the semi-formal and informal clients increasing the number of livelihood strategies of their households, for the formal clients, it was only four out of ten clients who reported additional livelihood activities. This implies that access was associated with marginally higher livelihood diversification outcomes for the semi-formal and informal clients and probably more concentration for formal clients. However, about 80% of the formal clients and 70% each of the semi-formal and informal clients asserted that accessed funds were allocated profitably. The higher percentage of the formal clients meant they were associated with high-value investments that are characterized by quick turn-over.

On average, 90% of informal clients reported access to microfinance led to increased acreage of land for on-farm livelihood activities. This was approximately 60% and 40% for the formal and semi-formal clients, respectively. Thus, access to microfinance for the informal clients had more to do with increases in on-farm land use than for the formal and semi-formal clients. Client experiences with previous debt use saw 40% of the semi-formal clients constituting the highest client group with this experience among the three groups of clients. This further buttressed the finding that most semi-formal clients were either salaried professionals or traders in the informal economy.

7.2.4 Access and Household Livelihood Diversification: A Comparative Analysis of the Formal and Informal Microfinance Clients of the Northern Savannah of Ghana

The *t*-test statistic tested whether statistically significant differences exist between the formal and informal and then the semi-formal and informal clients with regard to the predominant livelihoods' strategies of the study region. Table 7.4 presents the results of the *t*-tests and descriptive statistics conducted for formal and informal clients. The positive sign of wage employment (0.3) implied that more formal clients were wage earners than the informal clients, and the differences were statistically significant. Thus, a client who earns wages was more likely to access financial services from the formal rural and community banks and savings and loans companies.

The sign for acreage of land for on-farm activities was negative (−0.22) and significant. This implied that clients who were predominantly engaged in on-farm livelihood activities were more likely to access financial services from informal sources such as moneylenders and VSLAs, including friends, family and relations. Informal credit was more flexible in the duration of repayments and interest rate charges, and the high risk associated with on-farm activities of poorer households with irregular income sources explains the outcome. Climate change and weather variability exacerbate the risk of on-farm activities in the region.

TABLE 7.4 Results of *t*-test and Descriptive Statistics of Livelihood Diversification: Formal versus Informal MFI Clients

Livelihood Strategy	*Formal MFI Clients (N = 50)*	*Informal MFI Clients (N = 50)*	*95% CI for Mean Difference*	*p-value (H0≠0)*
Crop cultivation	0.52	0.58	−0.06	0.552
	(0.505)[a]	(0.499)[a]	(0.100)[b]	(−0.598)[c]
Animal rearing	0.50	0.52	−0.02	0.843
	(0.505)	(0.505)	(0.101)	(−0.198)
Off-/non-farm activities	0.54	0.48	0.6	0.553
	(0.503)	(0.505)	(0.101)	(0.595)
Wage employment	0.40	0.10	0.3	0.0004
	(0.495)	(0.303)	(0.082)***	(3.655)
Previous experience with debt	0.40	0.34	0.06	0.539
	(0.495)	(0.479)	(0.0974)	(0.616)
Increased no. of livelihood strategies	0.44	0.58	−0.14	0.165
	(0.501)	(0.499)	(0.100)	(−1.400)
Increased allocation to profitable strategy	0.82	0.78	0.4	0.621
	(0.388)	(0.418)	(0.081)	(0.495)
Increased access to land	0.64	0.86	−0.22	0.012
	(0.485)	(0.351)	(0.085)***	(−2.598)
Land size used	4.46	3.4	1.06	0.062
	(2.712)	(2.893)	(0.501)	(1.89)

***, **, * mean significant at 1%, 5% and 10%, respectively.

a Standard deviation.

b Standard errors.

c t-values.

Moreover, most formal and semi-formal credit was designed for financing off-farm and/or non-farm activities. Informal credit markets were also found with inbuilt co-insurances (where interest payments were dependent on whether the lender or borrower suffered shocks to income). The following quote from an informal client of a moneylender explains the phenomenon of co-insurance in informal credit markets.

> When I took a loan from Tarasum Moneylending and Leverage and lost my mother and could not attend to my sheep and goats trading business for a long time, Mr. John reduced the interest amount for me to pay. That is why I prefer to work with him. There is an understanding when there is a genuine problem that affects your business and profits here. The banks will never understand you.
>
> *IC_M_ML_Bolgatanga*

The results of the mean differences for crop (−0.06) cultivation and animal (−0.02) rearing as on-farm livelihood diversification strategies showed that informal clients cultivated more crops and raised more animals than the formal clients, but in both cases the differences were not significant. This reaffirms the continuation of the earlier finding that informal credit markets were more associated with on-farm livelihood activities (both crop and animals) in Northeastern Ghana. It could also be confirming the fact that the design of formal microfinance products does not adequately address on-farm livelihood diversification strategies and most were rationed out. Though not significant, the formal clients were more likely to engage in off-farm and/or non-farm activities, had previous experiences with debt and invested in more profitable ventures. Those formal clients that have diversified into on-farm activities had larger absolute land sizes than the informal clients.

While access was associated with an increased number of livelihood strategies and land use for the informal clients, though not statistically significant, the results for the association of access to microfinance and access to land were negative and significant.

This implied that access to informal microfinance institutions and other sources significantly increases the client's ability to access land for on-farm activities. With a majority of informal clients engaged in on-farm livelihood activities, accessed products and services naturally went into expanding and diversifying such activities.

7.2.5 Access and Household Livelihood Diversification: A Comparative Analysis of the Semi-formal and Informal Microfinance Clients of the Northern Savannah of Ghana

For those same variables, the *t*-test results of the semi-formal and informal clients showed similar trends presented in Table 7.5. However, significantly, many of the semi-formal clients were also wage earners. Access to financial services was also significantly associated with increased access to land use by informal clients. Professional government workers and religious groups were at the forefront of initiating and establishing many of the semi-formal MFIs, including the credit unions and financial NGOs. Thus, these MFIs were poverty-lending orientated and featured an approach that served both these workers and the wider community. Although the informal clients claimed that investment of accessed financial resources was profitable, the difference between them and the semi-formal clients was not statistically significant. These investments were also centred on on-farm crop and animal production. Keeping small ruminants was particularly prominent among informal clients. Sheep and goats, including pigs, were more or less considered capital stocks and insured the poorer informal clients' households against income fluctuations.

Results for crop cultivation, off-farm/non-farm activities, previous experiences with debt, addition to livelihood strategies and absolute land size for on-farm activities showed greater association with the semi-formal clients, but were not statistically significant with the informal clients.

TABLE 7.5 Results of *t*-test and Descriptive Statistics of Livelihood Diversification: Semi-formal versus Informal MFI Clients

Livelihood Strategy	*Semi-formal MFI Clients (N = 50)*	*Informal MFI Clients (N = 50)*	*95% CI for Mean Difference*	*p-value (H0≠0)*
Crop	0.68	0.58	0.1	0.305
	(0.471)[a]	(0.499)[a]	(0.097)[b]	(1.031)[c]
Animal	0.44	0.52	−0.08	0.428
	(0.501)	(0.505)	(0.101)	(−0.795)
Off-/non-farm	0.52	0.48	0.04	0.693
	(0.505)	(0.505)	(0.101)	(0.396)
Previous experience	0.44	0.34	0.1	0.310
with debt	0.501	0.479	(0.098)	(1.020)
Wage employment	0.48	0.10	0.38	0.000
	(0.505)	(0.303)	(0.083)***	(4.562)
Increased no. of	0.60	0.50	0.1	0.317
livelihood strategies	(0.495)	(0.499)	(0.099)	(1.01)
Increased allocation to	0.72	0.78	−0.06	0.494
profitable strategy	(0.455)	(0.418)	(0.087)	(0.687)
Increased access to	0.56	0.86	−0.3	0.001
land	(0.501)	(0.351)	(0.087)***	(−3.468)
Land size used	4.18	3.4	0.78	0.231
	(3.549)	(2.893)	(0.648)	(1.205)

***, **, * mean significant at 1%, 5% and 10%, respectively.

a Standard deviation.

b Standard errors.

c t-values.

The fact that animal rearing is more time-consuming throughout the year meant crop farming (usually seasonal) better matched the semi-formal clients that had waged employment and trade as their primary livelihoods' activities. The incentive for animal rearing was limited among semi-formal clients.

In summary, whereas the formal and semi-formal clients significantly diversified into wage jobs, the informal clients significantly diversified into on-farm livelihood activities. While access by the informal clients was associated with greater crop cultivation than the formal clients, access by the formal and semi-formal clients was associated with greater absolute acreage of land use for on-farm activities but these were both not significant. Moreover, animal rearing as a livelihood diversification strategy was more associated with informal clients than with both the formal and semi-formal clients. Small ruminants are regarded as capital stocks for poorer households and insured families against livelihood risks and uncertainties in the fragile socio-economic and environmental context of North-eastern Ghana. Small ruminants could easily be converted into cash when sold in the local meat market, and demand remains relatively high throughout the year. This meant that the majority of the informal clients invested in on-farm crop and animal production. However, when semi-formal clients invested in on-farm crop and animal production, the land acreage used was larger in absolute terms, and production was usually for the market rather than subsistence. Household production for the market usually involved larger capital requirements, specialized skills and some level of risk tolerance. The relatively better off semi-formal clients and their households had the advantage of steady income sources mostly from waged employment or savings from enterprise operations.

The formal and semi-formal MFI clients mostly invested their accessed financial resources in off-farm and/or non-farm production and in the acquisition of modern consumer goods. They also tended to have gathered more previous experiences working with debt. This lends credence to the assertion that most informal clients are usually the most financially excluded. While access was associated with an increased number of livelihood strategies engaged in by the semi-formal and informal clients, increased allocations to existing profitable ventures were associated with the formal and informal clients, but in both cases these were not significant. Access to land as a result of access to financial services was significantly associated with informal clients than with both the formal and semi-formal clients. However, the formal and semi-formal clients that went into on-farm livelihood activities had significantly larger land in absolute terms than the informal clients. The formal and semi-formal clients probably took on-farm activities as a business (where they are either stepping up or stepping out) rather than a way of life (hanging in). The large capital outlay required for commercial production, the specialized skills needed and the level of risk tolerance coupled with existing relationships with the other welfare institutions (the larger family, social networks, membership institutions, decentralized government structures and other markets) probably favoured the formal and semi-formal clients more than the informal clients.

7.3 Access and Household Asset Accumulation Patterns in Ghana

7.3.1 Introduction

This section sought to document selected household assets common in the study region: first for those with access and those without access, and second, among those with access in the segmented microfinance industry of the Northern Savannah of Ghana. This enabled the establishment of common patterns. The *t*-test statistic further enabled statistical inferences to be drawn between households with access and those without access and among those with access in the tiered industry. Plausible implications of the findings are expected to support policy and practice for the financial inclusion of the productive poor and enhance the use of microfinance as a poverty reduction tool in the Northern Savannah in general.

Common assets included in the assessment were large ruminants (cattle, horses and donkeys), small ruminants (sheep, goats and pigs), cars, motorcycles, bicycles, tricycles, donkey carts, lorries/buses/trucks, television sets, DVD players, radio/tape recorders, refrigerators, washing machines, sewing machines, fans, living room furniture, irons, beds/mattresses, deposit accounts, insurance policies held, remittances (money transfers received) and loans (debt).

The percentages of the ownership of large ruminants (e.g., cattle and donkeys), vehicles (e.g., cars) and bicycles across both participants and non-participants of microfinance were approximately the same in the Northern Savannah of Ghana. However, ownership of small ruminants and donkey carts was 15 and 9 percentage points, respectively, higher for the non-participants. While, on average, nine and seven out of ten microfinance participants owned television sets and DVDs, respectively, only six and four out of ten non-participants owned the same, respectively. None of the non-participants owned a sewing machine, a bus or a washing machine. Ownership of refrigerators for the participants was averagely five out of ten. For the non-participants, it was only three out of ten who owned refrigerators. Living room furniture and beds/mattresses ownership saw six and eight out of ten participants, but only three and four out of ten for the non-participants, respectively. The comparative analysis of the rest of the identified assets between participants and non-participants in percentage terms is presented in Appendix VIII (columns 4 and 14) for microfinance participants and non-participants, respectively.

The next section assesses whether or not significant differences exist in household asset ownership between participants of microfinance and non-participants using the *t*-test statistic.

7.3.2 Household Asset Accumulation: A Comparative Analysis of Microfinance Participants and Non-participants of the Northern Savannah of Ghana

In determining the differences in asset ownership among those with access and those without access to microfinance services in the Northern Savannah of Ghana, the *t*-test statistic tested mean differences of each asset class and the results are presented in Table 7.6. The results showed that the mean differences were all positive and statistically significant at 1% for the ownership of cars, motorbikes, DVDs, refrigerators, electric fans, living room furniture, irons and beds/mattresses. The implication is that significantly more microfinance participants owned these assets than the non-participants. For the ownership of small ruminants such as sheep and goats, including pigs, and television sets, the signs were positive and significant at 10%. The positive coefficients further meant that a significantly higher proportion of microfinance participants owned small ruminants and television sets than non-participants. Though the ownership of large ruminants (cattle, horses and donkeys), tricycles and sewing machines was also positive, the mean differences were all significant. This points to a likelihood that access to microfinance maybe has little association with the acquisition of large ruminants, tricycles and sewing machines in North-eastern Ghana. Apart

TABLE 7.6 Results of *t*-test and Descriptive Statistics for Household Asset Holding: MFI Clients Versus Non-participants

Variable	*(A) Total Sampled MFI Clients (n = 150)*	*(B) Non-clients (n = 50)*	*(A − B) 95% CI for Mean Difference*	*p-value (H0≠0)*
Cattle	0.26	0.26	0	1.000
	(0.44)[a]	(0.443)[a]	(0.072)[b]	(0.000)[c]
Sheep/goats/pigs	0.607	0.74	−0.133	0.091
	(0.490)	(0.443)	(0.0782)*	(−1.701)
Horses/donkeys	0.147	0.14	0.007	0.904
	(0.355)	(0.351)	(0.058)	(0.121)
Cars	0.6	0.1	0.5	0.000
	(0.238)	(0.303)	(0.042)***	(11.978)
Motorcycles	0.64	0.36	0.28	0.001
	(0.482)	(0.485)	(0.079)***	(3.552)
Bicycles	0.78	0.80	−0.02	0.767
	(0.416)	(0.404)	(0.067)	(−0.297)
Tricycles	0.087	0.08	0.007	0.879
	(0.282)	(0.274)	(0.046)	(0.153)
Donkey carts	0.067	0.16	−0.093	0.047
	(0.25)	(0.37)	(0.046)***	(−2.002)
TVs	0.74	0.54	0.2	0.095
	(0.455)	(0.503)	(0.076)*	(2.621)
DVDs	0.693	0.42	0.273	0.001
	0.463	0.499	(0.077)***	(3.541)
Radios/tapes	0.533	0.72	−0.187	0.0204
	(0.501)	(0.454)	(0.080)***	(−0.187)
Refrigerators	0.533	0.26	0.273	0.0007
	(0.501)	(0.44)	(0.080)***	(3.431)
Sewing machines	0.26	0.14	0.12	0.0815
	(0.44)	(0.351)	(0.069)	(1.751)
Fans	0.613	0.36	0.253	0.0017
	(0.489)	(0.485)	(0.080)***	(3.175)
Living room furniture	0.587	0.3	0.287	0.0004
	(0.494)	(0.463)	(0.079)***	(3.613)
Irons	0.613	0.44	0.173	0.0325
	(0.489)	(0.501)	(0.080)***	(2.153)
Beds/mattresses	0.807	0.58	0.227	0.0012
	(0.396)	(0.499)	(0.069)***	(3.280)
Land size ownership	4.013	4.34	−0.327	0.508
	(3.085)	(2.797)	(0.493)	(−0.664)

***, **, * mean significant at 1%, 5% and 10%, respectively.

a Standard deviation.

b Standard errors.

c t-values.

from the economic function, both large and small ruminants have cultural and ceremonial functions in the socio-cultural practices of the populations of the study region. Cattle, sheep and goats are used for dowry payments for wives and were all integral to ceremonies related to the rites of passage of the population irrespective of tribe. For most tribes of the Northern Savannah, chiefs and the royal classes mostly rode horses during festivals and other cultural performances.

However, in terms of the absolute size of land and bicycle ownership, the mean differences between participants and non-participants were both negative but not significant. This implied more non-participants owned more land in absolute sizes and the majority relied on bicycles for their transportation. Marginalized and in hard-to-reach communities, the only abundant resource for most of the non-participants was land for on-farm activities. However, weather variability and climate change continue to exact a toll furthering vulnerabilities and inequality.

In summary, while non-participants in microfinance services significantly kept more small ruminants such as sheep and goats, including pigs, participants in microfinance services kept more of the large ruminants, but not significantly more than the non-participants. Overall, microfinance participants significantly owned more cars for both private and commercial purposes, but their absolute numbers were very few. Significantly more participants also owned motorcycles for private transport, television sets for information and entertainment, DVD players that gave a choice for entertainment, refrigerators that were mostly used for commercial purposes; had more fans installed in their properties; and owned more beds/mattresses, living room furniture and irons. In short, microfinance participants had better consumer asset profiles than the non-participants. Two interpretations could be deduced from this finding. First, it could mean participation in microfinance was helping reduce poverty prevalence through clients' ownership of these high-end consumer goods through investments in capital-intensive, high-valued and less risky non-farm and/or off-farm activities. It could also mean that participation in microfinance, especially those from the formal and semi-formal MFIs, was restricted to clients already better off economically and socially. Thus, the excluded non-participants had little or no access. This means that the depth of outreach was not deep enough and microfinance institutions have to do more to increase access and inclusion and thereby address widening inequalities.

The results also pointed out that the non-participants significantly made more use of bicycles for transportation, donkey carts for the conveyance of farm produce, fuelwood and construction materials, and owned more radio sets from which information and entertainment were obtained. Moreover, the non-participants of microfinance programmes also owned more land from which on-farm crop cultivation and animal raising constituted their primary livelihood activities. With participants having better asset profiles than non-participants of microfinance, especially in modern consumer goods, this points to participants being economically better off than non-participants in the Northern Savannah of Ghana.

The next sections focus on analysing trends and patterns of asset accumulation and whether there exist significant differences between the formal and informal and the semi-formal and informal participants. Deposit accounts, insurance policies held, remittances (money transfers received) and loans (debt) are included to the ownership of the physical assets stated in the previous section. The percentages are also presented in Appendix VII. While Section 7.3.3 discusses the results of the comparative analysis of household asset ownership for the formal and informal MFI clients, Section 7.3.4 discusses those of the semi-formal and informal MFI clients.

7.3.3 Access and Household Asset Accumulation: A Comparative Analysis of Formal and Informal Microfinance Participants of the Northern Savannah of Ghana

Comparative analysis of household physical asset ownership among the disaggregated client groups in percentage terms is presented in Appendix IX (from columns 7 to 12). The results showed that cattle ownership was highest among formal clients. Almost three out of every ten formal clients kept the large ruminants. Culturally, keeping cattle was symbolic of being wealthy. For sheep and goats, including pigs, the highest of eight out of ten came from the informal clients. This was understandably capital stocks, easy to convert to cash via local meat markets. Keeping small ruminants had risk-mitigating functions especially in matters of food security for households of the relatively poorer informal clients. While horses served important cultural functions, more so for the traditional ruling classes in the study region, donkeys were predominantly used as a beast of burden in the transportation of farm and other commodities. However, the ownership of donkeys among microfinance participants is relatively negligible. Concerns were raised regarding the increasing rate of decline in the donkey population in the study region, attributed to a commercial Chinese factory located in Walewale in the newly created neighbouring North-east region, that buys, slaughters and processes the skins and meat for the Chinese market. Local traders also kill and process the meat under the guise of big game for the consuming public in the southern parts of Ghana.

The ownership of cars and other vehicles such as trucks and buses was also negligible among microfinance participants in North-eastern Ghana. The initial capital outlay for their acquisition was way beyond the means of most of the inhabitants participating in microfinance. It could also be that the MFIs do not offer such facilities for the acquisition of such asset. Approximately eight out of ten semi-formal and informal clients, respectively, owned motorcycles and bicycles. These two groups made up the largest with these assets. The ownership of tricycles and donkey carts was also negligible among the three microfinance client's groups of North-eastern Ghana. However, while the former was mostly owned by the formal clients' use for commercial human transport, the latter, mostly owned by the informal clients, were mostly used for carting farm produce, fuelwood and construction materials in conjunction with donkeys, especially in rural settings. On the ownership of television sets, it was the formal and semi-formal clients that owned the majority, while the informal clients owned the majority of radio sets. However, the semi-formal clients emerged as the largest holders of refrigerators, and most were used for commercial purposes. Moreover, washing machines, fan installation on property and living room furniture also saw the semi-formal clients having the majority of ownership. In terms of financial assets for those with access, while the semi-formal clients dominated in savings accounts, loans (debt) and insurance policy ownership, the informal clients made the most use of money transfer services (remittances).

In determining whether or not clients used accessed microfinance products to acquire the physical household assets by the participants directly, columns 5 and 6 of Appendix VII revealed that the majority were not acquired directly using the accessed finances from the microfinance institutions. Expensive household cartels requiring high initial capital outlay meant loans were directly used for the purchase of such chattels. For example, 44% and 33% of car and bus owners, respectively, directly used loans in their purchases. Overall, under 20% of clients acquired the other assets directly using loans obtained from their MFIs. With regard to financial asset holdings for those with access, 73% had some deposits and 80% had received credit. Only 17% and 10% held insurance and payment services, respectively

Results of the patterns of household asset accumulation between the formal and informal clients of microfinance institutions in North-eastern Ghana using the *t*-test statistic are revealed that the mean differences in the ownership of household chattels such as motorcycles, tricycles, television sets, DVD players, refrigerators, sewing machines, irons and beds/mattresses were all positive and significant at the 1% level (Table 7.7). This implied that significantly more of the formal clients reported owning these physical asset classes than the informal clients. In North-eastern Ghana, owning these high-end consumer goods had status implications. This suggested that there may exist a cause-and-effect relationship between the category of financial institutions through which a household accesses financial resources and the types of physical assets it is capable of accumulating. Moreover, microfinance may be influencing redistribution among certain segments of the population but is doing little in terms of redistribution from the privileged to the less privileged and excluded segments of the population in North-eastern Ghana.

However, the mean differences in the ownership of small ruminants such as sheep and goats, including pigs, the frequency of loan uptake and having installed electric fans were all negative and significant at the 1% level. This meant that informal clients reported significant ownership of these asset classes than formal clients.

Small ruminants were largely kept by the relatively resource-poor and marginalized as capital stock for income security. Their easy conversion into cash via local meat product markets means they insure households against livelihood risk and uncertainties. It is not surprising therefore that many of the informal clients placed at the bottom of the microfinance pyramid kept more small ruminants in the economically and fragile environment of the study region. The frequency of borrowing was also higher among this group of clients as they borrow from friends and family members to meet daily basic expenses, i.e., smoothening consumption.

TABLE 7.7 Results of *t*-test and Descriptive Statistics of Household Asset Holding: Formal versus Informal MFI Clients

Variable	*(A) Formal MFI Clients (n = 50)*	*(B) Informal Clients (n = 50)*	*(A − B) 95% CI for Mean Difference*	*t-value*
Cattle	0.28	0.26	0.02	0.824
	(0.454)[a]	(0.44)[a]	(0.089)[b]	(0.224)[c]
Sheep/goats/pigs	0.56	0.76	−0.20	0.037
	(0.501)	(0.443)	(0.0946)***	(−2.115)
Horses/donkeys	0.16	0.14	0.02	0.782
	(0.37)	(0.351)	(0.072)	(0.277)
Cars	0.08	0.02	0.60	0.172
	(0.274)	(0.141)	(0.044)	(1.377)
Motorcycles	0.7	0.46	0.24	0.015
	(0.463)	(0.503)	(0.097)***	(2.482)
Bicycles	0.76	0.86	−0.10	0.206
	(0.431)	(0.351)	(0.079)	(−1.272)
Tricycles	0.16	0.04	0.12	0.046
	(0.37)	(0.198)	(0.059)***	(2.022)
Donkey carts	0.10	0.08	0.02	0.730
	(0.303)	(0.274)	(0.346)	(0.346)
TVs	0.92	0.44	0.48	0.000
	(0.34)	(0.501)	(0.086)***	(5.606)
DVDs	0.84	0.48	0.36	0.000
	(0.37)	(0.505)	(0.089)***	(4.066)
Radios/tapes	0.5	0.66	−0.16	0.107
	(0.505)	0.479)	(0.098)	(−1.625)
Refrigerators	0.58	0.26	0.32	0.001
	(0.499)	(0.443)	(0.094)***	(3.391)
Sewing machines	0.16	0.34	0.24	0.038
	(0.37)	(0.479)	(0.097)***	(−2.103)
Fans	0.68	0.44	−0.18	0.015
	(0.471)	(0.501)	(0.086)***	(2.468)
Living room furniture	0.52	0.48	0.04	0.693
	(0.505)	(0.505)	(0.101)	(0.396)
Irons	0.62	0.38	0.24	0.016
	(0.49)	(0.49)	(0.098)***	(2.449)
Beds/mattresses	0.88	0.72	0.16	0.046
	(0.328)	(0.454)	(0.079)***	(2.02)
Land size ownership	4.095	3.4	0.695	0.242
	(3.012)	(2.893)	(0.591)	(1.177)
Savings	0.16	0.10	0.06	0.377
	(0.39)	(0.303)	(0.068)	(0.887)
Insurance	0.12	0.02	0.1	0.102
	(0.404)	(0.141)	(0.0605)	(1.653)
Loans	0.40	0.62	−0.22	0.028
	(0.495)	(0.490)	(0.099)***	(−2.234)
Remittances	0.3	0.08	0.08	0.222
	(0.463)	(0.274)	(0.065)	(1.229)

a Standard deviation.

b Standard errors.

c t-values.

Those living in urban centres tended to either own shops or work as apprentices in informal trade sectors that are often equipped with electric fans necessary in environments where temperature can reach as high as 40 degrees centigrade.

However, the results of the mean differences in the ownership of big ruminants (e.g., cattle, horses and donkeys), cars, donkey carts, living room furniture, land in terms of absolute size, and the uptake rates of savings, insurance and remittances (money transfer) between the formal and informal clients gave positive signs but were not significant. The implication was that though the ownership of these asset classes by the formal clients was more than the informal clients, the differences were not statistically significant.

The signs of the results of assets such as bicycles and radios were also negative, but not significant. Though the ownership of these assets was found more with informal clients than with formal clients, the differences were not statistically significant. The initial capital outlay in acquiring these assets was said to be low and therefore affordable for many of the poorer and marginalized informal clients.

In summary, though the formal clients owned more large ruminants (cattle, horses and donkeys), cars, donkey carts, living room furniture, had larger land sizes, more savings, held more formal insurance policies and carried out more money transfers than the informal clients, the differences were not significant. However, significantly more of the formal clients owned high-valued modern consumer goods such as motorcycles, tricycles, TV sets, DVDs, refrigerators, sewing machines, irons and beds/mattresses than the informal clients. The formal clients were therefore considered better off and could be placed on higher layers of the microfinance pyramid (see Appendix IX).

The informal clients, however, significantly owned more small ruminants, had electric fan installations and had frequent loan uptake than the formal clients. While the possession of more small ruminants served as capital stock and insured the relatively poorer households of the informal clients, most of them also frequently take out loans from family and friends for purposes of consumption smoothening rather than investment capital. The ownership of electric fans correlated with shop ownerships in the informal trade economy for groceries or apprenticeships. While the informal clients had more bicycles and radio sets than the formal clients, the differences were not significant as most families, irrespective of wealth status, kept bicycles for use by children and tended to consume news and information from the local radio stations.

7.3.4 Household Asset Accumulation: A Comparative Analysis of the Semi-formal and Informal Microfinance Participants of the Northern Savannah of Ghana

This section also sought to determine the patterns of household asset accumulation between the semi-formal and informal clients of microfinance institutions in North-eastern Ghana. The data description and summary statistics of variables are provided in Appendix IX. The *t*-test results in Table 7.8 revealed that the

TABLE 7.8 Results of t-test and Descriptive Statistics for Household Asset Holding (Semi-formal Versus Informal MFI Clients)

Variable	*(A) Semi-formal MFI Clients (n = 50)*	*(B) Informal Clients (n = 50)*	*(A − B) 95% CI for Mean Difference*	*p-value (H0≠0)*
Cattle	0.24	0.26	−0.02	0.400
	(0.431)[a]	(0.44)[a]	(0.087)[b]	(−0.230)[c]
Sheep/goats/pigs	0.5	0.26	−0.26	0.007
	(0.505)	(0.443)	(0.095)***	(−2.737)
Horses/donkeys	0.14	0.14	0.0	1.000
	(0.351)	(0.351)	(0.070)	(0.000)
Cars	0.08	0.02	0.06	0.172
	(0.274)	(0.141)	(0.044)	(1.377)
Motorcycles	0.76	0.46	0.3	0.002
	(0.431)	(0.503)	(0.094)***	(3.202)
Bicycles	0.72	0.86	−0.14	0.088
	(0.454)	(0.351)	(0.081)	(−1.725)
Tricycles	0.06	0.04	0.02	0.650
	(0.240)	(0.198)	(0.044)***	(0.455)
Donkey carts	0.02	0.08	0.06	0.172
	(0.1414)	(0.274)	(0.044)	(−1.376)
TVs	0.86	0.44	0.42	0.000
	(0.351)	(0.501)	(0.087)***	(4.855)
DVDs	0.76	0.48	0.28	0.004
	(0.431)	(0.505)	(0.094)***	(2.981)
Radios/tapes	0.44	0.66	−0.22	0.027
	(0.501)	(0.479)	(0.098)	(−2.243)
Refrigerators	0.76	0.26	0.5	0.000
	(0.431)	(0.443)	(0.087)***	(5.720)
Sewing machines	0.28	0.34	−0.06	0.523
	(0.454)	(0.479)	(0.093)***	(−0.643)
Fans	0.72	0.44	0.28	0.0042
	(0.454)	(0.501)	(0.096)***	(2.928)
Living room furniture	0.76	0.48	0.28	0.004
	(0.431)	(0.505)	(0.094)	(2.981)
Iron	0.84	0.38	0.46	0.000
	(0.370)	(0.49)	(0.087)***	(5.296)
Beds/mattresses	0.82	0.72	0.1	0.084
	(0.388)	(0.454)	(0.084)	(1.184)
Land size	4.18	3.4	0.78	0.231
	(3.55)	(2.893)	(0.648)	(1.204)
Savings	0.8	0.1	0.06	0.000
	(0.404)	(0.303)	(0.068)	(9.802)
Insurance	0.3	0.02	0.28	0.000
	(0.463)	(0.141)	(0.068)	(4.091)
Loans	0.22	0.62	−0.4	0.000
	(0.418)	(0.490)	(0.0911)***	−(4.392)
Remittances	0.6	0.08	0.52	0.000
	(0.2398)	(0.274)	(0.05)	(10.098)

***, **, * mean significant at 1%, 5% and 10%, respectively.

a Standard deviation.

b Standard errors.

c t-values.

mean differences between the semi-formal and informal clients in the ownership of motorcycles, tricycles, television sets, refrigerators, electric fans, electric irons and DVD players were all positive and significant. This implies that a significantly higher proportion of the semi-formal clients owned these assets than the informal clients. Most of these assets were considered high-valued modern luxury consumer goods in the Northern Savannah of Ghana. Thus, the semi-formal clients, most of whom were professional wage earners and informal traders, concentrated in the urban centres, could afford them. It also suggests that products and services offered by the semi-formal microfinance institutions such as the credit unions were tailored to make it easy for clients to acquire these assets.

However, the mean differences in the ownership of small ruminants such as sheep and goats, including pigs, sewing machines and the frequency of loan uptake were all negative and significant at the 1% level. The implication being that significantly more of the informal clients owned these assets than their semi-formal counterparts. Owning small ruminants was considered savings, as these could easily be sold in the local meat market. It was, therefore, rationale that more informal clients considered poorer and marginalized kept these animals for income security and livelihood risk mitigation (e.g., in the event of crop failure). Being poor can be said to be associated with irregular and infrequent income flows. Sewing machines for dressmaking (considered an alternative livelihood strategy) are usually acquired for young females who either lacked formal education or dropped out altogether and therefore choose dressmaking as a career path.

Results of the *t*-test of the ownership of horses/donkeys, cars, donkey carts, living room furniture, beds/mattresses, absolute land size, savings, insurance and money transfers between the semi-formal and informal clients were all also positive, but not significant. This implied that although the semi-formal clients owned more of these asset classes than the informal clients, the differences were all not significant in each case. Moreover, ownerships of cattle, bicycles, and radio sets were all also negative, but not significant.

Thus, these assets could be found more in the households of the informal clients, but not significant from the households of the semi-formal clients. Keeping cattle required considerable time and effort that professional government workers and informal traders cannot easily afford. However, it was easy for informal clients to meet the demands of keeping cattle. Besides, many lived in peri-urban and rural settings where vast amounts of communal and un-used lands provided grazing grounds. However, the initial capital outlay and maintenance costs of bicycles were considered generally low and therefore affordable by the informal clients. Their livelihoods were characterized by irregular and unpredictable income flows. And radio sets presented a convenient source of information for the informal clients, most of whom lived in off-grid areas.

In summary, while the semi-formal clients owned more large ruminants (horses and/or donkeys excluding cattle), cars, donkey carts, living room furniture, beds/mattresses, absolute land size, savings uptake, formal insurance policies held and remittance transactions (money transfers) than the informal clients, the differences were not significant. However, significantly more of the semi-formal clients owned high-valued modern luxury consumer goods such as cars, tricycles, TV sets, DVDs, refrigerators and irons than the informal clients.

However, significantly more of the informal clients owned small ruminants and sewing machines, and took out more loans than semi-formal clients. While the small ruminants served as capital stocks and insured informal clients' households against livelihood risks, they also frequently took out loans from friends and family members for consumption smoothening purposes rather than their semi-formal counterparts. Owning more sewing machines by informal clients suggested that such households have low education outcomes for girls who never had the opportunity of formal education or dropped out altogether and turned to dressmaking as a career path.

Moreover, while the informal clients had more cattle, bicycles and radio sets than the semi-formal clients, the differences were not significant. This also suggested that keeping cattle was more of a socio-cultural phenomenon rather than an economic venture and the majority were mostly passed down from generation to generation. Semi-formal clients also kept bicycles probably for children to transport themselves to and from schools and most preferred consuming news and information from local radio stations (see Appendix IX).

7.4 Access and Household Welfare in Ghana

7.4.1 Introduction

This section focuses on access to financial products and services and household welfare outcomes in the segmented microfinance industry of the Northern Savannah of Ghana. Using the *t*-test statistic, the section also compares selected household welfare outcomes of those accessing financial services from the formal MFIs and those from the informal sources. Those accessing financial services from the semi-formal MFIs and the informal sources were also compared. The data description and summary statistics of variables are provided in Appendix VIII. Results of the tested means are presented in Tables 7.9 and 7.10 and provided the bases for the analysis of trends and patterns.

7.4.2 Access and Household Welfare: A Comparative Analysis of the Formal and Informal Microfinance Participants of the Northern Savannah of Ghana

Table 7.8 presents the results of *t*-tests conducted for selected household welfare indicators between those with access to formal microfinance services and those with access to informal sources. The results showed that mean differences of clients' reporting ability to afford education and training of household members (row 2), afford orthodox healthcare needs of household members (row 4), of taking within 30 minutes (row 6) and greater than an hour to the nearest healthcare facility (row 9), of improved housing (row 10), open defecation (row 14), improved gender relations (row 18), having homes connected to the national grid (row 21), and land ownership through outright purchase (row 25) all yielded positive signs and were all significant. The implication of these results is that the outcomes were significantly associated with the formal clients.

The significantly improved gender relations within households of the formal clients were probably a result of higher social and economic status, better education outcomes of household members and their higher average wage employment numbers. Salaried employment meant stable household finances and limited impact of shocks emanating from life-cycle and crisis events. Access to formal credit has not supported the need to avoid open defecation. This suggests that the formal rural and community banks and the savings and loans companies operating in the study region probably have limited social intermediation portfolios, especially in water and sanitation, despite the known health risks (Gertler and Karadi 2015). The drier and hotter weather conditions of the region have not helped much in the fight against open defecation. Faecal matter easily dries up and/or is picked up by free-range domestic animals, especially pigs. Access by the formal clients was also significantly associated with their ability to maintain the home connection to the national grid. That is the uninterrupted supply of electricity. Land ownership via outright purchase was significantly associated with the formal clients, which suggests this group of clients was better off as a result of owning high-valued assets generally and/or enterprises. It could also mean that accessed products and services were adequate and suitable for the acquisition of land that required extensive capital outlays. Land purchases, mostly in urban and peri-urban settings, have huge investment capital implications that the economically better-off can afford and the results provide further evidence of a generally higher social and economic status of the formal clients over their informal counterparts.

Though the signs of the mean differences in welfare outcomes of patronage of the Kumasi Improved Ventilated Pit (a public toilet facility for the prevention of open defecation) (row 13), general improvements in household food security (row 15), the extensive use of fuelwood (row 20) and land ownership via gifts (row 26) were all also positive, but insignificant statistically. This implied that although the formal clients reported better outcomes associated with these outcome variables than the informal clients, the differences were not significant.

Those welfare outcome variables that the informal clients showed superiority over the formal clients as a result of access to financial services included the ability to reach the nearest health facility within 15 minutes (row 5), the use of water closets (WCs) in the management of household sanitation and sewage (row 12), the use of liquified petroleum gas (LPG) (row 19), generator sets (gen sets) for electricity supply (row 22) and the ownership of land via inheritance (row 26). The signs of the results of all these outcomes were negative and significant at the 1% level. Many of the informal service providers (*Susu* individuals or companies and moneylenders) mostly operate in urban settings, where high business turn-overs can be guaranteed. Thus, apart from the VSLA groups, many informal microfinance providers and clients were concentrated in the urban areas.

Also, the high concentration of health facilities, both public and private, in these urban environments made it possible for household members to reach out to the nearest health facility in less than 30 minutes. For these same reasons, the use of water closets (WCs) for household sewage management, liquified petroleum gas (LPG) for cooking and generators (gensets) for powering homes and enterprises were all significantly associated with households of informal MFI clients.

The smaller loans that characterized informal credit irrespective of rural or urban settings probably made it difficult to acquire land in urban and peri-urban settings where huge capital outlays are required to purchase land. Thus, with many of these clients at the fringes in urban settings and mostly rural migrants etching out a living in the urban centres, it was not surprising that land acquisition via inheritance was significantly associated with clients of this category. It further reinforces the relative placements of this group against the formal clients on the microfinance pyramid and inequality in the study region.

The signs of results of household outcome variables such as access and general improvements in education and training of household members (row 1), the use of concrete blocks as primary materials in home construction (row 11), being food secured in the last 12 months (row 16) and fortnight ago (row 17), and the use of lanterns and/or torchlights for lighting at night (row 23) were all negative. These results suggest that these were more associated with the informal clients and their households and were all not significantly different from the situation of the formal clients and their households.

In summary, access to financial services by the formal clients was significantly associated with households' ability to afford children's school fees, orthodox healthcare services as well as reaching out to the nearest health facility in less than 30 minutes and shortly after an hour. Access was further significantly associated with improved housing, gender relations, affordability of electricity in homes via the national grid and purchased land ownership. However, access did little to discourage the practice of open defecation among formal clients and their households. This implied that formal MFIs had little or no water and sanitation interventions in their non-financial and/or social intermediation portfolios. However, their breadth of outreach was extensive in the rural areas of the study region, where open defecation was very common.

For informal clients, access to financial services was associated with the ability to reach out to the nearest health facility in less than 15 minutes. This suggests that most informal clients and their service providers were concentrated in urban settings where health facilities were also concentrated. Moreover, the informal clients were also associated with the use of liquified petroleum gas, mostly used in the cooked food businesses common in urban settings, the use of generators (gensets) for supplying electricity (to both businesses and homes) and land ownership through inheritance. Furthermore, access to microfinance was not only significantly associated with reduced open defecation practice among the informal clients and their households (e.g., the VSLA groups in rural areas) but was also significantly associated with higher use of water closets (WCs) in the densely populated urban settings.

7.4.3 Access and Household Welfare: A Comparative Analysis of the Semi-formal and Informal Microfinance Participants of the Northern Savannah of Ghana

Results of the *t*-test statistic of household welfare outcomes for the semi-formal and informal clients are presented in Table 7.9. Signs for client's reported ability to reach out to the nearest health facility within 30 minutes (row 6), improved housing (row 10), use of Kumasi Ventilated Improved Pit (KVIP toilets) (row 13), the practice of open defecation (row 14), gendered household relations (row 18) and home connection to the national grid (row 21) were all positive signs and significant at the 1% level. These results implied that the semi-formal clients were significantly more associated with these outcome variables than their informal counterparts.

Taking less than 30 minutes to the nearest healthcare facility by the formal clients suggests either the possession of superior means of transport or the ability to afford superior means of transport than their informal counterparts. This could also reflect the preference of the semi-formal clients for orthodox healthcare, in turn, shaped by income, economic status and formal education. In the study region, improved homes were basically and generally interpreted to mean homes constructed with concrete blocks and roofed with corrugated aluminium or iron sheets. Owning houses built with such materials was a status symbol, but because most of the semi-formal clients were professional government employees and urban traders most lived in homes constructed with such materials, either rented or owned. Most teachers, like other public servants, lived and worked in rural communities and the absence of KVIPs in such communities was probably a reason for the practice of open defecation. The families of these professionals mostly resided in the urban centres where social amenities are concentrated, and visits were conducted during weekends. Besides, social intermediation in general and water and sanitation were either little or non-existent in the portfolios of most of the semi-formal microfinance institutions, especially the credit union associations. Most were minimalist, offering only basic financial services such as credit and savings facilities.

However, the semi-formal clients reported significant association in improved gender relationships within their households, explained by high literacy rates and joint livelihood ventures, in which conservative norms, ethos and practices have little tolerance. Being more involved in waged employment also meant that there was a lower probability of experiencing financial stress at home with potential positive spill-over effects for gender relations. Having a home connected to the national grid was a status symbol, and therefore, the significant association with the semi-formal clients suggests most enjoyed better social and economic status and lived in urban centres than their informal counterparts.

TABLE 7.9 Results of t-test and Descriptive Statistics of Household Welfare Outcomes: Formal versus Informal MFI Clients

Row No.	*Variable*	*(A) Formal MFI Clients (n = 50)*	*(B) Informal MFI Clients (n = 50)*	*(A − B) 95% CI for Mean Difference*	*p-value (H0≠0)*
1	Education and training (access improved generally)	0.58 (0.499)[a]	0.64 (0.485)[a]	−0.06 (0.098)[b]	0.544 (−0.610)[c]
2	Education and training (afford children school fees)	0.900 (0.303)	0.680 (0.471)	0.22 (0.079)***	0.007 (2.778)
3	Health of household (access improved generally)	0.640 (0.485)	0.600 (0.495)	0.04 (0.098)	0.684 (0.408)
4	Afford household orthodox healthcare needs	0.740 (0.443)	0.480 (0.505)	0.61 (0.095)***	0.007 (2.737)
5	Time to nearest health facility – 15 minutes	0.200 (0.404)	0.740 (0.44)	−0.54 (0.084)***	0.000 (−6.392)
6	Time to nearest health facility – 30 minutes	0.300 (0.463)	0.100 (0.303)	0.2 (0.078)***	0.012 (2.556)
7	Time to nearest health facility – 45 minutes	0.120 (0.328)	0.040 (0.198)	0.08 (0.054)	0.143 (1.477)
8	Time to nearest health facility – 60 minutes	0.060 (0.240)	0.060 (0.240)	0 (0.048)	1.000 (0.000)
9	Time to nearest health facility –greater than 60 minutes	0.320 (0.471)	0.060 (0.240)	0.26 (0.075)***	0.0008 (3.478)
10	Housing and improved housing (improved structures)	0.420 (0.499)	0.160 (0.370)	0.26 (0.088)***	0.0039 (2.960)
11	Primary home construction materials (cement)	0.720 (0.454)	0.820 (0.388)	−1 (0.084)	0.239 (−1.18)
12	Sanitation (use of W/C)	0.640 (0.485)	0.820 (0.388)	−0.18 (0.0878)***	0.04 (−2.049)
13	Sanitation (use of KVIP)	0.260 (0.443)	0.180 (0.388)	0.08 (0.083)	0.339 (0.961)
14	Sanitation (open defecation)	0.100 (0.303)	0.000 (0.000)	0.1 (0.043) ***	0.022 (2.334)
15	Food security (improved generally)	0.680 (0.471)	0.560 (0.501)	0.12 (0.097)	0.220 (1.234)
16	Food security (enough food at home in last 12 months)	0.040 (0.198)	0.120 (0.328)	−0.08 (0.054)	0.143 (−1.476)

(Continued)

TABLE 7.9 Continued

Row No.	*Variable*	*(A) Formal MFI Clients (n = 50)*	*(B) Informal MFI Clients (n = 50)*	*(A − B) 95% CI for Mean Difference*	*p-value (H0≠0)*
17	Food security (ate less in last 2 weeks due to inadequate food at home)	0.080 (0.274)	0.100 (0.303)	−0.02 (0.058)	0.7299 (−0.346)
18	Gender relation (improved generally)	0.56 (0.501)	0.280 (0.454)	0.28 (0.096)***	0.0042 (2.928)
19	Energy for cooking (LPG use)	0.200 (0.404)	0.540 (0.503)	−0.34 (0.091)***	0.0003 (−3.727)
20	Energy for cooking (fuelwood use – firewood/charcoal)	0.580 (0.454)	0.460 (0.503)	0.12 (0.096)	0.213 (1.252)
21	Energy for household lighting – electricity (mains)	0.880 (0.328)	0.280 (0.471)	0.6 (0.081)***	0.000 (7.392)
22	Energy for household lighting – electricity (gen set)	0.080 (0.274)	0.280 (0.454)	−0.2 (0.075)***	0.009 (−2.667)
23	Energy for household lighting – (lanterns/ torchlight)	0.00 (0.00)	0.040 0.198	−0.04 0.028	0.156 (−1.429)
24	Land ownership (inherited)	0.62 0.490	0.920 0.274	−0.3 (0.079)***	0.0003 (−3.779)
25	Land ownership (purchased)	0.34 0.479	0.040 0.198	0.3 (0.0733)***	0.000 (4.093)
26	Land ownership (gifted)	0.04 0.198	0.020 0.141	0.02 0.044	0.562 (0.582)

***, **, * mean significant at 1%, 5% and 10%, respectively.

a Standard deviation.

b Standard errors.

c *t*-values.

Although the mean differences of such welfare variables including the ability to afford children's school fees (row 2), orthodox healthcare services for household members (row 4), taking under an hour to get to the nearest health facility (row 8), being food secure in the last 12 months (row 16) and the last two weeks (row 17), the use of fuelwood (row 20), lanterns and/or torch lights at night (row 23), land ownership through outright purchase (row 25) and as gifts (row 26) all produced positive signs, they were all not significant. This implied that even though the semi-formal clients were associated with higher outcomes related to these variables, the differences with the informal clients could be said to be marginal and negligible.

TABLE 7.10 Results of *t*-test and Descriptive Statistics for Household Welfare Outcomes: Semi-formal versus Informal MFI Clients

Rows No.	*Variable*	*(A) Semi-formal MFI Clients (n = 50)*	*(B) Informal MFI Clients (n = 50)*	*(A − B) 95% CI for Mean Difference*	*p-value (H0≠0)*
1	Education and training of household	0.340 (0.479)[a]	0.640 (0.485)[a]	−0.300 (0.096)[b] ***	0.0024 (−3.112)[c]
2	Afford children school fees	0.720 (0.454)	0.680 (0.471)	0.040 (0.093)	0.666 (0.432)
3	Health of household improved	0.440 (0.501)	0.600 (0.495)	−0.160 (0.099)	0.1114 (−1.606)
4	Afford household orthodox healthcare bills	0.640 (0.485)	0.480 (0.505)	0.160 (0.099)	0.109 (1.616)
5	Time to nearest health facility –15 minutes	0.440 (0.501)	0.740 (0.443)	−0.300 (0.095)***	0.002 (−3.172)
6	Time to nearest health facility –30 minutes	0.320 (0.471)	0.100 (0.303)	0.220 (0.079)***	0.007 (2.778)
7	Time to nearest health facility –45 minutes	0.000 (0.000)	0.040 (0.198)	−0.04 (0.028)	0.156 (−1.429)
8	Time to nearest health facility –60 minutes	0.100 (0.303)	0.06 (0.239)	0.04 (0.055)	0.465 (0.733)
9	Time to nearest health facility –greater than 60 minutes	0.140 (0.351)	0.060 (0.239)	0.080 (0.060)	0.186 (1.332)
10	Housing and housing improved	0.5600 (0.501)	0.1600 (0.370)	0.400 (0.050)***	0.000 (4.541)
11	Primary home construction materials (cement)	0.760 (0.431)	0.820 (0.388)	−0.06 (0.082)	0.466 (−0.732)
12	Sanitation (use of WC)	0.260 (0.443)	0.82 (0.388)	−0.560 (0.083)***	0.000 (−6.724)
13	Sanitation (use of KVIP)	0.4 (0.070)	0.18 (0.054)	0.22 (0.889)***	0.015 (2.473)
14	Sanitation (open defecation)	0.34 (0.068)	0 (0)	0.34 (0.068)***	0.000 (5.019)
15	Food security improved generally	0.520 (0.505)	0.560 (0.501)	−0.040 (0.101)	0.692 (−0.398)
16	Enough food at home in last 12 months	0.140 (0.351)	0.120 (0.328)	0.020 (0.068)	0.769 (0.294)
17	Ate less in last 2 weeks due to inadequate food at home	0.120 (0.328)	0.100 (0.303)	0.020 (0.063)	0.752 (0.317)
18	Gendered relation (improved generally)	0.560 (0.501)	0.280 (0.454)	0.280 (0.096)***	0.004 (2.928)
19	Energy for cooking (LPG use)	0.360 0.485	0.540 0.503	−0.180* 0.099	0.072 (−1.822)

(Continued)

TABLE 7.10 Continued

Rows No.	*Variable*	*(A) Semi-formal MFI Clients (n = 50)*	*(B) Informal MFI Clients (n = 50)*	*(A − B) 95% CI for Mean Difference*	*p-value (H0≠0)*
20	Energy for cooking (fuelwood use – firewood/charcoal)	0.580 0.499	0.460 0.503	0.120 0.100	0.234 (1.198)
21	Energy for household lighting – electricity (mains)	0.860 (0.351)	0.680 (0.471)	0.180 (0.083)***	0.033 (2.167)
22	Energy for household lighting – electricity (genset)	0.060 (0.240)	0.280 (0.454)	−0.220 (0.073) ***	0.003 (−3.029)
23	Energy for household lighting –(lanterns/ torchlight)	0.080 (0.274)	0.040 (0.197)	0.040 (0.048)	0.404 (0.838)
24	Land ownership (inherited)	0.820 (0.388)	0.920 (0.274)	−0.100 (0.067)	0.1398 (−1.489)
25	Land ownership (purchased)	0.100 0.303	0.040 0.198	0.060 0.051	0.244 (1.172)
26	Land ownership (gifted)	0.08 (0.274)	0.02 (0.141)	0.06 (0.044)	0.172 (1.377)

***, **, * mean significant at 1%, 5% and 10%, respectively.

a Standard deviation.

b Standard errors.

c t-values.

However, results of the outcome variables such as the general improvements in the education and training of household members (row 1), taking less than 15 minutes (row 5) and 45 minutes (7) to the nearest health facility, the use of generator sets (gen sets) for the supply of electricity (row 22) and the use of water closets, i.e., WCs (row 12), for the management of household sewage all had negative signs and significant at the 1% level. This implies that the informal clients and their households showed a significant association with these outcome variables compared to the semi-formal clients.

Access to financial services was significantly associated with improvements in educational outcomes for the informal client's household members compared to the semi-formal clients. This suggests that access by the most excluded groups not only smoothened consumption generally but impacted children's education with long-term implications on vertical social mobility and inter-generational poverty reduction as educated children unlock opportunities in the future. It also suggests the need to design microfinance products and services that improve both depth and breadth of outreach on the backdrop of access and long-term poverty reduction among poorer segments of the population.

Although the sign of the use of liquid petroleum gas was also negative, it was significant at the 10% level. This reflects the use of liquid petroleum gas in the burgeoning cooked food businesses by informal clients. The results of others – including access and general improvements in household health, household food security, taking less than 45 minutes to the nearest health facility and land ownership through inheritance – were also negative, but not significant and could be described as marginal between the two groups of clients.

In summary, access to microfinance services by the semi-formal clients was significantly associated with quality housing, the ability to reach out to the nearest health facility in less than 30 minutes, increased usage of KVIPs, improved household gender relations and the affordability of electricity from the mains at homes. However, access did little to discourage open defecation among the semi-formal clients from the limited or no social intermediation portfolios of semi-formal MFIs, especially in water and sanitation.

In contrast, access for the informal clients was significantly associated with improved access to education and training of household members, the ability to reach out to the nearest health facility in less than 15 minutes, the use of generators (gensets) for the supply of electricity and the use of liquid petroleum gas particularly in the cooked food businesses. Moreover, access was associated not only with limited open defecation among informal clients in rural settings but with improved use of water closets (WCs) in the urban settings for the management of household sewage and sanitation.

7.5 Summary and Conclusion

In summary, this chapter sets out to assess the patterns of asset accumulation between participants and non-participants in microfinance in North-eastern Ghana. Moreover, the chapter assesses the livelihood diversification, asset accumulation and welfare outcomes among those with access to the segmented microfinance industry of North-eastern Ghana.

While significantly more non-participants of microfinance services kept small ruminants such as sheep and goats, including pigs, the participants kept more large ruminants but not significantly different from the non-participants. Although the absolute numbers were generally few, significantly more households of microfinance participants owned cars, motorcycles, television sets, DVDs, refrigerators, installed electric fans, beds/mattresses, living room furniture and electric irons. In short, microfinance participants had better consumer asset profiles than the non-participants. This meant access either was helping to reduce poverty or was restricted to the economically better off, excluding poorer and marginalized groups, with the implication that the depth of outreach by microfinance institutions in the region has not been deep enough and is, therefore, doing little to reduce existing inequalities. Also, significantly more of the non-participants reported making use of bicycles, donkey carts and radio sets. They also made use of more land for on-farm activities. Thus, generally, microfinance participants had better asset profiles than the non-participants in North-eastern Ghana.

Two-thirds of all microfinance clients in North-eastern Ghana claimed households' livelihood diversification influenced access. All client groups ranked the expansion of off-farm/non-farm livelihood activities as the first use of access to microfinance products and services. While consumption smoothening ranked second for the use of access products and services for the formal and semi-formal clients, it was on-farm investments that ranked second for the informal clients.

Whereas the formal and semi-formal MFI clients were associated with significant diversification into wage jobs, the informal clients significantly diversified into on-farm livelihood activities. Also, while access for the informal clients was associated with on-farm crop and animal production but was not significant, the formal and semi-formal clients were associated with the significant absolute land size used for on-farm crop and animal production. This meant that, those of the formal and semi-formal clients, when investing in on-farm crop and animal production, the land acreage involved was larger in absolute terms than the informal clients land sizes. However, access to microfinance services by the informal clients was significantly associated with increased access to land for the on-farm livelihood activities. The formal and semi-formal clients probably took on-farm activities as a business (where they were either stepping up or stepping out) rather than a way of life (hanging in). The large capital outlay required for commercial production, the specialized skills needed and the level of risk tolerance coupled with households' existing relationships with other welfare institutions (the larger family, social networks, membership institutions, decentralized government structures and other markets) probably favoured the formal and semi-formal clients over the informal clients. The formal and semi-formal MFI clients mostly invested in off-farm and/or non-farm activities and the acquisition of modern consumer goods. They also tended to have gathered more previous experiences working with debt. This lends credence to the assertion that most informal clients are usually the most financially excluded. While access was associated with an increased number of livelihood strategies engaged in by the semi-formal and informal clients, increased allocations to existing profitable ventures were associated with the formal and informal clients, but in each case, were not significant.

Overall, significantly more microfinance participants owned consumer assets such as cars, motorcycles and television sets among others that reflect their higher social status than non-participants. And among those with access to microfinance services, the semi-formal and formal clients dominated in the ownership of these consumer goods. Investments for informal clients were more in livestock for economic and socio-cultural purposes. Easy to convert into cash at the local meat markets, small ruminants dominated the livestock asset class for the informal clients.

The formal clients significantly reported more ownership of high-valued modern consumer goods such as motorcycles, tricycles, TV sets, DVDs, refrigerators, sewing machines, irons and beds/mattresses than informal clients. Significantly more of the semi-formal clients also owned cars, tricycles, TV sets, DVDs, refrigerators and irons than the informal clients. These results suggest better economic and social status for the formal and semi-formal clients relative to the informal clients. However, while significantly more of the informal clients owned small ruminants, electric fan installations, and frequently take out loans than the formal clients, they also significantly reported owning small ruminants, sewing machines, as well as take up more credit than the semi-formal clients.

The possession of small ruminants served as capital stock and insured the relatively poorer households of the informal clients against livelihood risks and uncertainties. The frequency of loan uptake by informal clients is for consumption smoothening. Owning electric fans correlated with the informal client's ownership of shops in the space of the informal urban trade in groceries and repair works. Significantly higher ownership of sewing machines by the informal clients suggested that such households probably have low education outcomes, especially for girls who never had the opportunity of formal education or dropped out altogether and considered dressmaking as a career path.

Though the informal clients also reported owning more bicycles and radio sets than the formal clients, and more cattle, bicycles and radio sets than the semi-formal clients, these differences were altogether not significant. Most families kept cattle mostly inherited and predominantly used for socio-cultural purposes such as dowry payments and funeral performances. Furthermore, irrespective of wealth status, most families kept bicycles for use by children and consumed news and information from the local radio stations via the radio set.

On welfare outcomes among clients of the segmented microfinance industry of North-eastern Ghana, access was significantly associated with improvements in households' gender relations, quality housing, maintenance of homes' power supply from the national grid and the ability to reach out to the nearest health facility in less than 30 minutes for the formal and semi-formal client and their households. However, access by the formal and semi-formal clients significantly did little to discourage the widely practiced open defecation in the study region. While access was significantly associated with households' ability to afford children's school fees, access to orthodox healthcare services and purchased land ownership for the formal clients, it was only significantly associated with increased usage of KVIP toilets by the semi-formal clients. For the informal clients, access was significantly associated with improved access to education and training of household members compared to the semi-formal clients, but not with the formal clients. Access by the informal clients was also significantly associated with access to improved use of liquified petroleum gas (LPG), enterprise and home power supply from generators (gensets) and an increased ability to reach out to the nearest health facility in less than 15 minutes than the formal and semi-formal clients. Moreover, access was not only significantly associated with decreased open defecation but also significantly associated with the use of water closets (WCs) for the management of household sewage and sanitation by the informal clients, particularly in the rural and peri-urban localities, compared to the formal and semi-formal clients (see Appendix VIII).

The next chapter provides a summary of the findings of the research, conclusions drawn and implications of the study.

8

CONCLUSIONS

8.1 Introduction

The study aims to assess the role of microfinance as an anti-poverty tool in the Northern Savannah of Ghana. While Chapter 4 assessed the microfinance landscape and current levels of financial services provisioning in the context of the broader historical and financial eco-system developments, Chapter 5 addressed the first objective, which sought to assess the factors underpinning the design of microfinance products and services for greater outreach and enhanced sustainability. Chapter 6 addressed the third objective which sought to establish the determinants of microfinance uptake in the Northern Savannah of Ghana, especially for those with access. Finally, Chapter 7 addressed the last objective i.e., the assessment of the impact of access on the client's livelihood diversification, asset accumulation patterns and welfare outcomes in the prevailing three-tiered microfinance industry of the Northern Savannah of Ghana. In achieving these set objectives, a combination of pluralist theoretical and methodological approaches was employed to gather and analyse qualitative and quantitative data from sampled clients using multi-layered sampling techniques across the geographical boundaries of the case study region. The main quantitative method was the econometric estimation of the determinants of microfinance product and service uptake for those with access, using data collected from MFI clients and their household livelihood activities. The t-statistic was employed in the testing of means in the determination of differences in livelihood diversification, asset accumulation patterns and welfare outcomes. The qualitative methods employed were key informant interviews, focus group discussions and household case studies that provided depth behind the numbers. Key findings on the research objectives and conclusions drawn are presented in Chapter 8.

DOI: 10.4324/9781003318873-8

It does so by giving an outline of the findings in Section 8.2 (the evolution of the microfinance landscape in the Northern Savannah of Ghana in the context of the broader historical, economic and financial sector developments), Section 8.3 (types of financial institutions supplying microfinance services and current levels of services provisioning), Section 8.4 (factors underpinning microfinance product and service design), Section 8.5 (determinants of microfinance product and service uptake) and Section 8.6 (the impact of access on household livelihood diversification, asset accumulation and welfare outcomes). The chapter concludes with a brief discussion of the contribution of the study to knowledge on microfinance, livelihoods and development, and the implications of the findings for policy and practice and further research in Section 8.7.

8.2 How Has the Microfinance Industry Evolved in the Northern Savannah?

The evolution of efforts to increase access to financial services and financial inclusion started during the colonial era with the establishment of the Post Office Savings Bank in 1905 to provide deposit services and the Cooperative Bank in 1935 for thrift and lending activities among cocoa farmers and cooperative societies. After independence in 1957, many state-sponsored banks were established to develop the financial sector to drive industrialization, economic growth and development. Over the years, these various policies have substantially improved access to financial services through commercial, development and cooperative banking, and through the introduction of the rural banking concept in 1976. The establishment of rural and community banks (RCBs) throughout the country made banking possible in most rural and hard-to-reach areas. The establishment of these RCBs substantially improved access to financial services and financial inclusion in the Northern Rural Savannah. Over the years, several programmes implemented of the Government of Ghana together with bilateral and multilateral development partners have facilitated access to financial services in the Northern Rural Savannah (see Chapter 4, Section 4.3 and Appendix I). During the 1980s, the Economic Recovery Programme saw the liberalization of the Ghanaian economy and financial system. Though the financial sector adjustment programme (FINSAP I and II) and the Non-Bank Financial Institutions Project improved the financial sector regulatory framework, the efficient allocation of credit, the development of the country's capital markets and eliminated other market distortionary policies, they created other imbalances within the financial eco-system. The financial sector strategic plan (FINSSP) launched in 2003 promoted the integration of the bank and non-bank financial sub-sectors that further deepened financial intermediation, inclusion and the integration of the domestic economy with the global financial infrastructure that has continued to spur economic growth and development.

Ghana's financial eco-system currently comprises state-owned, private, domestic and foreign commercial banks; rural and community banks; and other quasi-banking institutions such as savings and loans companies, mortgage houses, leasing finance companies and discount houses. The rest is the non-bank financial institutions including life and non-life insurance and reinsurance companies, public pension funds such as the social security and national insurance trust (SNITT), other public and private pension funds and the securities industry including broker-dealers, investment advisors, custodians and trustees. The Bank of Ghana and the Securities and Exchange Commission are the primary regulatory bodies of the financial system of Ghana (see Chapter 3, Section 3.4).

Despite these earlier reforms, the financial stability risks remained heightened as of 2011. According to the international monetary fund (IMF) Financial Stability Report for Ghana released in June 2011, although the banking system remained liquid, profitable and highly capitalized at the aggregate level, the high non-performing loans (NPLs) had exposed a significant segment of the banking industry to vulnerabilities. The government initiated several measures to address the challenges in the banking sector (see Chapter 4, Section 4.3).

At a full-blown crisis level in Ghana's banking sector in 2019, nine universal banks had their licences revoked by the Bank of Ghana. There were forced mergers into a newly established bank, i.e., Consolidated Bank Ghana Limited (CBG). These developments negatively impacted the (non-bank) specialized deposit-taking institutions (SDIs) that accounted for about 14% of financial institutions in the country (see Chapter 4, Section 4.3).

In response to the challenges of the non-bank specialized deposit-taking institutions and microfinance sub-sector, the BoG further revoked the licences of 347 microfinance companies (of which 155 had already ceased operations), 39 microcredit companies/moneylenders (ten of which had already ceased operations), 15 savings and loans companies, eight finance houses, and two non-bank financial institutions that had already ceased operations. Fifty-five fund management companies also had their licences revoked by the Ghana Securities and Exchanges Commission for various infractions during the last quarter of 2019. To ensure that the surviving institutions remain resilient, the Bank of Ghana committed to proactive vigilance, the intensification of on-site examinations and the enforcement of compliance with statutory prudential and other requirements. The regulator further intimated that it would ensure the prompt resolution of early warning signs of distress of the microfinance sub-sector and work in collaboration with the association of rural banks (ARB) Apex Bank to reposition the rural and community banking sector to better support rural economic development.

The Bank of Ghana (BoG) is further strengthening its regulatory and supervisory framework for specialized deposit-taking institutions (SDIs), including reviewing the licencing and supervisory policies, capital requirements, enhancing governance directives and increasing resources available for supervision purposes (BoG, 2019b).

However, additional efforts were required from 2019 to reduce the financial sector vulnerability in short to medium term. In total, an additional GH¢5.5

billion (equivalent to 1.6% of GDP) was needed in 2019 to resolve all the challenges related to the MFIs, savings and loans, and another resolution bond for the CBG in support of the closure of the last two of the nine banks that took place in January 2019 (IMF 2019). The establishment of a Financial Stability Council by the government that integrates financial regulators and the Ghana Deposit Protection Corporation to, among other things, assess the vulnerability of the financial system on an ongoing basis is commendable. Strengthening the resilience and stability of the banking system will require the authorities to strengthen the regulatory and supervisory framework and the introduction and roll-out of deposit insurance schemes. Though the world bank (WB) supported the reform agenda for the specialized deposit-taking institutions (SDIs) by the Bank of Ghana (BoG), the fundamental factors restraining broader financial inclusion remain prevalent with substantial inefficiencies in savings mobilization and allocation of resources and commercial banks continue to lack proven methodologies for the financing of small-scale enterprises (SMEs) for resilient livelihoods, especially in the Northern Savannah (see Chapter 3, Section 3.4).

Though the financial sector clean-up will address structural and systemic weaknesses, the challenges in short to medium term are best described as enormous. The exercise will have negative impacts on access to financial services by SMEs and limit economic activities in general. The announcement by the BoG that it had reduced primary reserves ratios of banks from 10% to 8% in November 2019 is commendable. This, the regulator said, will enable regulated financial institutions to expand credit to SMEs. The impact of this policy cannot be predicted with certainty, especially in the wake of the declaration of the coronavirus pandemic in early 2020. The solvent MFIs will need to redesign their business models to make them sustainable and responsive to the needs of their constituents. There is a need for a paradigm shift towards the capacity building of key personnel and staff of these MFIs to enable them to manoeuvre the operational dynamics and challenges of the industry.

While there is also the need to comply with financial sector frameworks, policies, regulations and directives, the future sustainability of MFIs also depends on reliable and cheaper funding sources. The Ghana alternative market (GAX) operated by the Ghana Stock Exchange financing options need to be explored by MFIs as a source of loanable funds, apart from deposits, owners' equity. Exploring GAX will enable MFIs to broaden their investor base and provide liquidity for their business activities. This will further build public trust and confidence in the microfinance sub-sector following the financial sector clean-up.

Also, the ability of the government and the closed financial institutions to reimburse depositors and investors has been called into question. It is estimated that a combined investment of $1.6 billion could be affected by the closures. The launch of the Ghana Deposit Protection Scheme in September 2019 will serve as a conduit to further strengthen the protection of depositors not only in the microfinance sub-sector but in the broader financial system in Ghana.

8.3 What Types of Financial Institutions Supply Microfinance Products and Services in the Northern Savannah and What Is the Current Level of Provisioning in the Region?

The microfinance industry in Ghana comprises seven groupings of organizations broadly classified into the formal (rural and community banks and the savings and loans companies), the semi-formal (credit unions, financial NGOs and microfinance companies) and the informal (Susu companies/individuals and moneylenders). The drive to increase deposit mobilization has led many commercial banks operating in the area to engage in microfinance activities, especially among informal economic actors in the urban centres (see Chapter 4, Section 4.4.1).

Households' uptake of financial institution accounts in the Northern Rural Savannah showed that household institutional account ownership irrespective of locality and gender remains low. According to the Ghana Statistical Service (2013) and the GLSS VI report, household uptake of formal accounts in financial institutions in the Northern Savannah remains low. Only 5% of households in the Northern Savannah have accounts with commercial banks, 2% with investment/mortgage houses, 9% with rural and community banks and 3.5% with savings and loans schemes. Cooperative/credit unions, '*Susu*' schemes and other informal sources such as family, friends and the VSLAs were approximately 11%, 10% and 6%, respectively. The gender dynamics of household account ownership further revealed that men owned 62.1% of all institutional account types against 37.9% for women (see Chapter 4, Section 4.4.2). It can be concluded that microfinance service provision in the Northern Savannah comprises a diverse mix of providers, including microfinance institutions and some commercial banks, but uptake remains puzzlingly low.

On access to credit, approximately 1% of households have access to institutional credit in the Northern Rural Savannah and several factors accounted for the low levels of uptake. The lack of collateral, accumulated household indebtedness, financial institutions not granting the loan amounts needed (credit rationing), the lack of need for institutional credit (low market economic activities) and high interest rates constituted key barriers to access to credit. Most of the credit products were mostly secured through third parties, employers, friends and relations. Properties such as buildings, cattle, land and payment of salary via financial institutions are used by households to securitize loans in the Northern Rural Savannah. On the use of accessed credit, while the purchase of agricultural equipment and inputs was the major use of credit in the Northern Rural Savannah, the acquisition of modern consumer goods and socio-cultural functions such as weddings and travel made up other important uses. Education and training of household members, vehicle/motor purchase, business capital and other undefined uses were also common. The low levels of credit uptake from financial institutions by households in the Northern Rural Savannah is indicative of low levels of formal credit availability and accessibility, the prevailing large informal economy, a vibrant informal credit market and low levels of financial inclusion of the productive poor in the region and the country at large. Also, the high percentage of uncollateralized loans further suggests the dominance of an informal economy, the limited accessibility of institutional credit and the inherent ability of informal credit markets better to serve the livelihood needs of the productive poor (see Chapter 4, Section 4.4.3).

On savings, approximately 18% of households in the Northern Rural Savannah have deposits with financial institutions or contributes to saving schemes. While not having adequate money or income, irregular income flow and no need to save were key barriers to household savings in the Northern Rural Savannah, the complex processes of saving with financial institutions and the long distances that needed to be covered by customers were contributory factors to the poor savings culture in the study region. These results were proof that poverty remains endemic in the Northern Savannah, exacerbated by unfavourable climatic conditions, particularly rainfall patterns and institutional and infrastructural under-development (see Chapter 4, Section 4.4.4).

Surprisingly, at 22%, insurance product uptake was marginally higher among households of the Northern Rural Savannah than those of credit and savings uptake. Approximately two out of every ten households held one form of insurance or the other. The lack of knowledge of the workings of insurance, the unaffordability of insurance products and the perception that there is no need to hold insurance, as well as the lack of trust between insurance companies and their customer or potential customer bases, constituted major barriers to insurance access – both long term (e.g., endowments/savings plans, life and education) and short term (e.g., medical, funeral, property, commercial/business, travel and vehicle/motor). Uptake of insurance products also remains averagely low in the Northern Rural Savannah compared to other parts of the country (see Chapter 4, Section 4.4.5).

However, making and receiving digital payments continues to increase, and domestic remittances via mobile phones and mobile payment platforms are at the forefront of this revolution. For instance, the mobile money penetration rate increased from 13% in 2012 to 38.9% in 2017. Boosted by the adoption of an interoperability platform that enables transfers from mobile money accounts across different mobile networks and from mobile networks to banks in Ghana, the mobile money revolution is emerging as an important channel for financial inclusion. Mobile money services via domestic remittances are also creating jobs for the Ghanaian population. About 17.2% and 13% of the adult population users are sending and receiving remittances, respectively, via mobile money operators in Ghana (see Chapter 4, Section 4.4.6).

8.4 What Factors Underpin the Design of Microfinance Products and Services in the Northern Savannah of Ghana?

The section presents key findings of Chapter 5 that addressed the second objective of the study, i.e., the assessment of the factors underpinning microfinance product and service design from the demand-side perspective. The results showed that all eight identified features of product design featured prominently with those of the formal MFIs (rural and community banks and the savings and loans companies) than was the case with the semi-formal (credit union associations, financial NGOs and microfinance companies) and informal (moneylenders, microcredit companies and VSLA groups) MFIs. Though the design of products and services by the formal MFIs generally followed the financial systems approach, there were significant others that were poverty lending in outlook. Most of the formal MFIs offered group products designed to meet the needs of poorer clients in hard-to-reach and marginalized communities. The formal MFIs also had more ongoing partnerships, with government, bilateral and multilateral agencies as well as NGOs and the private sector geared towards sustainable microfinance intermediation in the Northern Rural Savannah (see Chapter 5, Section 5.2.1).

The cost of access in the form of interest rates across the formal, semi-formal and informal providers was found to be marginally lower in the Northern Rural Savannah than the national averages. While those of the Northern Savannah extraction averaged 32%, 35%, and 40% per annum for the formal, semi-formal and informal MFIs, respectively, the national averages recorded 36%, 45% and 65% per annum for same categories, respectively. In the Upper East Region, for instance, the variation in interest spread was prominent among the informal MFIs. '*Susu*' collectors could offer negative rates as low as −39.6% per annum, but members of the VSLA groups could earn dividends on purchased equities (shares) to as much as 60% or more per annum. Group products were particularly critical for financial intermediation with poorer clients (women and rural localities) by MFIs. Designing products and services that simultaneously reduce the cost of access, including interest and fees paid to MFIs, the non-cash opportunity cost and indirect cash expenses incurred by clients, while at the same time matching the livelihood needs and wants, added weight to microfinance as an anti-poverty tool in the Northern Rural Savannah. Though the cost of access varies across the three-tiered microfinance industry in the region, these were perceived differently. Interest and fees paid by clients of the formal MFIs were empirically the lowest in the market but were perceived by two-thirds of patrons as unaffordable. The larger loan amounts involved, and the inflexibility of formal MFI loan contracts largely explained the differences in these perceptions. Clients of the semi-formal MFIs had the highest acceptability rate on the perception of the cost of access being low. This was explained mostly by the predominant flexibility of loan contracts within this group and this was even more pronounced among clients of the informal MFIs, though empirically established as having the highest variation in interest rates among the three MFI client groups. Among clients of the informal MFIs such as the village savings and loans (VSL), groups bought equity (shares) which is put into a common pool, and groups set their interest and fees for members and self-manage credit disbursement and repayments. Lower interest and fees have implications for outreach especially on depth (numbers of poorer clients reached with microfinance services).

Limiting the non-cash opportunity costs and indirect cash expenses incurred by clients was the critical determinant of increased outreach, product uptake and MFI sustainability in the Northern Rural Savannah. The use of mobile staff tooled with motorbikes and vehicles across the study region by MFIs suggests the importance of cutting down these transactional costs on both the supply and demand side of the microfinance livelisystem framework of the microfinance industry. However, MFIs need to estimate these additional cost elements effectively and efficiently transmit the same through contract designs without up-setting existing dynamics within the rural financial markets they operate. While the deployment of mobile staff constrained non-cash opportunity costs and indirect cash expenses for clients of the formal and semi-formal MFIs, it was the proximity to providers that limited such transactional costs for the informal clients. The cost of access also has profound implications for length (sustainable microfinance intermediation) as well as depth and breadth of outreach. Bridging the interest spread has the potential of increasing savings mobilization for the formal and semi-formal MFIs and can have knock-down effects on interest and fees charged to deposit takers.

MFIs' profitability and/or donor partnerships have implications for sustainable microfinance intermediation (length). Most MFIs continue to partner with bilateral and multilateral development agencies to extend credit for poverty reduction in the Northern Rural Savannah. For instance, while the United States agency for international development (USAID) had ongoing collaborations with some rural and community banks (RCBs), world vision international (WVI) (an INGO) was continuing to partner with communities in the formation and training of village savings and loans associations (VSLAs). Some of these groups were then linked to the RCBs to enable access to broader product scope and improve financial inclusion. In terms of perception of profitability, clients of the formal MFIs perceived their MFIs to be more profitable than clients of the semi-formal and informal MFIs. Open communication between MFIs and their client bases (e.g., during annual general meetings) aimed at improving customer loyalty in terms of uptake and repayments and minimizing moral hazards is important for length (i.e., sustainable microfinance intermediation with clients by MFIs) (see Chapter 5, Section 5.2.2).

Results on product scope also showed that clients of the formal MFIs had access to the most varied financial products and services and were more integrated into services delivery approaches. Products and services accessed by clients of the informal MFIs were the least varied and integrated (i.e., more minimalist in approach to service delivery). Across all three microfinance institutional types, credit and savings dominated the product scope in the Northern Rural Savannah. This was indicative of the primacy of these two in the arsenal of microfinance as an anti-poverty tool, even though households' access to institutional credit remains abysmally low, at only 1% with savings at 18%. However, compulsory savings were widely reported among clients of the semi-formal MFIs than the formal and informal MFI clients. Debt (loans) mostly constituted the entry point for clients of the formal MFIs.

Moreover, micro-insurance penetration remained very low at only 22% of households, suggesting a large niche exists for the broadening and deepening of micro-insurance products and services in the Northern Savannah. However, this will require extensive partnerships and collaboration with insurance companies as well as with government and international development partners in the design, development, testing and roll-out of such products. Collaborations only existed between the formal MFIs and the insurance companies in offering various insurance products, including weather-indexed crop insurance, credit risk insurance (that protected the provider more than clients) and life assurances. The semi-formal MFIs offered only credit risk insurance on loans, but the informal MFIs had no such formal arrangements. However, some form of co-insurance existed where the interest was paid, depending on whether the lender or borrower suffered a loss. Traditional payment services such as Western Union and MoneyGram provided to clients by the formal MFIs were fast being disrupted by mobile money transfers considered cheaper and more convenient. The recent introduction of the interoperability services that enable mobile money transfers across different mobile network operators (MNOs) and from the platforms of the MNOs to banks is boosting mobile money services. As the MNOs are not allowed to keep cash, the phenomenon is offering a unique opportunity for deposit mobilization by existing and functional microfinance institutions across Ghana (see Chapter 5, Section 5.2.3).

On what increases the willingness of clients to pay for the uptake of microfinance products and services (i.e., worth), maintenance of good customer relationships and flexible contracts was much highly rated among clients of the semi-formal MFIs than the formal MFIs. The high sense of ownership and perception of management accountability, including giving extensive voice to clients of the semi-formal MFIs, positively influenced worth (Woller et al., 1999). Innovations in product design, such as duration of repayments (term to maturity), consistency with the livelihood needs of clients, contributed to the positive perception of worth. Other factors that drove worth for the formal and semi-formal MFI client's perception of worth were identified as obtaining loan amounts when needed (i.e., the absence of credit rationing), flexibility of deposit withdrawals, the ability to diversify livelihood activities, achievement of personal goals and employment creation in the wider community. Moreover, while friendly customer relationships and stress-free access to loans and savings facilities drove worth for the formal and semi-formal clients, it was bad staff attitude, disproportionate client to staff ratio, the lack of automated teller machines (ATMs) for weekend banking, much lower interest on deposits and unreliable internet connectivity in the banking halls that depressed worth for these two groups of MFI clients in the Northern Savannah of Ghana. For the informal clients, embedded devices and mechanisms made product and contract design inherently flexible, while the social support obtained from other group members, among the VSLA groups, promoted worth. However, the fear of theft of cash boxes or armed robbery, restriction in the withdrawals of deposits and limited product scope depressed worth. Overall, these findings suggest that the incorporation of relevant socio-cultural values and norms in the management of MFIs in product and service design and delivery does have implications for the outreach and sustainability goals of the industry in the Northern Savannah of Ghana. Thus, the approval of loan amounts as requested by clients, tailored durations for repayments (term to maturity), products that match the dominant livelihood needs, especially the regular repayment amounts (size of instalment), narrowed interest spreads (differences between interest on loans and savings), products that promote clients' livelihood diversification, employment generation for others in the wider community and facilitating the achievement of client personal and household goals all contribute to the willingness of clients to pay for financial inclusion (i.e., worth) (Woller et al., 1999) (see Chapter 5, Section 5.2.5).

On the depth of outreach of the microfinance industry in the Northern Rural Savannah, loan sizes showed trends of a continuum from generally larger loans of formal MFI clients to smaller loans of the informal clients. However, the sampling methodologies employed by the researcher across all three institutional types meant that the differences in loan sizes were not very pronounced. Nevertheless, the loan sizes mirrored the socio-economic status of the clients from a generally wealthier formal MFIs client base to a poorer informal MFIs client base. The institutional types from which clients sourced microfinance services have little or no correlation with the dominant construction materials of client homes in the Northern Savannah, as over 73% of all three MFI client groups had their homes constructed with cement blocks and roofed with either corrugated iron or aluminium sheets. Constructing homes with cement blocks and aluminium roofing sheets was considered prestigious, and household members usually pooled resources for such endeavours, irrespective of their participation in the microfinance industry. The results further revealed that all three MFI groups had no special preferences for women, the formally educated people living in rural localities and ethnic minorities in the study region. These findings suggest that the depth of outreach was probably being compromised as MFIs target individuals and groups capable of repaying. Therefore, microfinance activities could be worsening inequalities rather than redistribution across the population of the Northern Rural Savannah (see Chapter 5, Section 5.2.6).

On contract enforcement, the study established that mere threats of publishing names of defaulting clients over the local radio usually trigger repayments. This suggests that privacy is valued when it comes to debt issues in the Northern Rural Savannah. Local norms and ethics surrounding debt were used randomly by MFIs to increase repayment rates. The results further revealed that co-opting the presence of a police officer to visit defaulting clients alone was enough to trigger repayment. The threats of legal action, outsourcing loan recovery to third parties and the demand for third-party guarantors to under-write loan contracts were some of the mechanisms used by MFIs in the study region to reduce both *ex ante* and *ex post* moral hazards and to improve repayment rates. The study found that customary practices embedded in the traditional structures and systems of communities in the Northern Rural Savannah were used to improve repayment rates. For example, summoning a defaulting client at the local chief palace and making the clients swear oaths to local deities promising to repay improved repayment rates. These methods though unconventional need further exploration and incorporation in contexts and communities where informal institutions remain strong. The phenomenon of co-insurance, where interest rates paid depended on whether the client or borrower suffered losses, was common among the informal MFIs and their clients. MFI clients believed that amicably resolving default problems had the unintended consequences of reducing moral hazards and increasing product uptake and repayment rates in the Northern Savannah of Ghana (see Chapter 5, Section 5.2.8).

On add-ons, the study found that clients of MFIs in the Northern Rural Savannah generally perceived well-designed products and services that matched their livelihood needs as add-ons (microfinance plus). These included friendly customer relations, easy access to loans and savings, predictable and sustainable financial intermediation, the use of mobile staff who reach out to clients and reduce transaction costs, input credit for farmers, group member support among VSLAs as well as flexible contract designs. Both staff and clients had no clear understanding of what constituted add-ons or microfinance plus. The study further established that training in group dynamics and enterprise development were important in building the capabilities of clients to better work with accessed microfinance products and services and to build resilient livelihoods in the Northern Rural Savannah (see Chapter 5, Section 5.2.9).

Research and development in microfinance remain critical, especially regarding client-centric product and service design. Innovations that encompass effective screening, default risk differentiation, reduction in the information asymmetry between lenders and borrowers, and the incentivization of both the demand and supply sides of the microfinance industry remain important for sustainable microfinance intermediation in the Northern Rural Savannah of Ghana. Forging linkages and collaborations between these three institutional types, as well as between them and relevant government, bilateral and multilateral development agencies and NGOs in the design of products and services, remain crucial for the financial self-sufficiency of MFI increased outreach, improved financial inclusion and poverty reduction.

With over 90% of clients claiming that benefits of participation exceeded all cost considerations, microfinance is certainly working in the Northern Rural Savannah of Ghana by supporting livelihoods transitioning to better standards (Dorward, 2014) (see Chapter 2). For the minority, it has been transformational where households *stepped up* or *stepped out and* produced for the market. Few households *fell down and out* and missed out on the promise of poverty reduction through microfinance intermediation. Yet the majority of households are transitioning from *hanging in* to *stepping up* where they produce for both the market and household consumption. The need for broad-based rural development policies and programmes is critical for the development of rural financial markets and the results suggest that despite the challenges limiting the transformational role of microfinance as an anti-poverty tool, the goals of the industry are being achieved.

8.5 What Are the Determinants of Microfinance Product and Service Uptake in the Northern Savannah of Ghana?

Section 6.4 presented the results of the third objective, i.e., an assessment of the determinants of microfinance uptake, especially by those with access in the Northern Savannah of Ghana. The study established that access to microfinance services remained highly supply-driven rather than demand-led in the Northern Savannah of Ghana. The results showed that targeting particular niches of population groups or sectors, broader policies and programmes that expanded the rural economy, good MFI corporate governance and management systems aimed at improving customer relationships and experiences, being female, diversified client-based livelihood activities, and the adaptation and combination of both group and individual lending methodologies were perceived by clients to have significant associations with the uptake of microfinance products and services in the Northern Rural Savannah of Ghana.

Broad-based rural development policies with expansionary effects on the rural economy were perceived to be positive and significantly associated with microfinance uptake in the Northern Savannah of Ghana. A growing rural economy raises prospects of higher incomes and increases the risk tolerance of individuals and households to invest using debt from MFIs. While the relationship between group lending was positive and significantly associated with increased uptake, the combination of group and individual methodologies was also positive and much more strongly associated with increased uptake. Group lending methodologies are encouraged to ensure poor but productive groups in hard-to-reach and marginalized communities have access to financial services.

Clients' engagement in more than one livelihood activity had a positive and significant association with microfinance uptake. Livelihood diversification increases microfinance product and service uptake, but these went into expanding existing enterprises that were also off-farm and/or non-farm in the Northern Savannah. This development was part of a broader trend of diversification out of on-farm activities in the region. This result also broadly explains the importance of microfinance on livelihood diversification, adaptation and resilience-building in fragile environments.

The study also found that the relationship between enterprise start-up and microfinance uptake was negative and significant. This suggests that microfinance clients do not usually start new enterprises with accessed products and services. The increased risks associated with on-farm activities, especially in the wake of heightened climate change and weather variability, continue to constitute a barrier, not only to access but also to product innovation for on-farm livelihood activities. Being female had a negative and significant association with microfinance uptake. MFIs target female clients in the Northern Savannah of Ghana because of the social goal of including poorer segments of the population, their higher repayment rates and the improved household welfare outcomes associated with women, especially related to the nutrition of children.

The results further showed that the association of MFI governance and management systems, including customer relationship with uptake, was perceived as negative and significant. Therefore, MFI boards and management need to continually invest in improving the governance and management systems and in building organizational cultures that optimize customer satisfaction and experiences. Moreover, MFIs targeting specific sub-groups of clients (i.e., certain client niches in specific rural sectors) were perceived to have a positive and significant association with uptake. Targeting such niche clients such as food crop processors, shea-butter extractors, smock weavers and straw basket manufacturers in the study region has the potential to increase uptake by poorer clients, i.e., the depth of outreach. Results of education and household size of clients showed a positive association with product and service uptake in the Northern Rural Savannah but were not statistically significant. This suggests that education may not be a necessary condition for entrepreneurial activities that characterize increased uptake in the Northern Savannah. Besides, the educated may have had disproportionate access to waged employment which might improve their access, not due to entrepreneurial activities in the overall livelihoods' portfolios in the study region.

8.6 Access and Impact on Clients' Livelihoods: Diversification, Asset Accumulation and Household Welfare

Chapter 7 presents the results of the fourth objective, which sought to assess the impact of access on clients' household livelihoods in the Northern Rural Savannah of Ghana, with the Upper East Region as a case study. While Section 7.2 presented results on access and household livelihood diversification in a segmented industry, Section 7.3 presented results on access and household asset accumulation patterns. Section 7.4 presented that of access and household welfare outcomes. In all three cases, means were tested in the determination of significant differences between client groups using the t-statistic.

8.6.1 Does Access in a Segmented Industry Have Differential Impacts on Clients' Household Livelihood Diversification in the Northern Savannah?

Results of the study found that three-fifths of all microfinance clients in the Northern Rural Savannah invested accessed products and services in off-farm and/or non-farm livelihood activities. While off-farm and/or non-farm activities were the dominant push factors for the uptake of microfinance, the unintended consequences were the stifling of innovation in product and service design meant for on-farm livelihood activities (Section 7.2.2). The longer gestation periods and high risk of on-farm activities resulting from climate change and rainfall variability coupled with the increasingly commercialized microfinance industry made up the key causal factors. However, while the use of accessed products for consumption smoothening came in second for clients of both the formal and semi-formal MFIs, modern consumer goods (household chattels) dominated the consumption basket in both cases. On-farm investments came second for the informal clients, suggesting the better socio-economic status of the formal and semi-formal MFI clients, as these two groups diversify out of on-farm activities at a much higher rate. Also, while the education of household members ranked third for the semi-formal and informal MFI clients, it was on-farm investments that came in third for clients of the formal MFIs. Apart from the dominance of off-farm and/or non-farm livelihood activities, the results showed the importance of how access to financial services by households from the three groups of providers in the Northern Rural Savannah of Ghana related to different pathways of households' livelihood diversification and preferences in production, consumption and investment choices.

Though averagely half of all client groups had engaged in crop production and animal raising, the highest crop producers were clients of the semi-formal MFIs. However, most were into commercial production of rice and vegetables, unlike their informal counterparts. As many of the semi-formal MFI clients were also waged employees. The results further underscored the importance of crop production in the livelihood portfolios of households in the study region. In the case of animal raising, the semi-formal MFI clients were the least, confirming the dominance of waged employment and non-farm activities in the livelihood's portfolios of the majority of the semi-formal MFI clients. For clients of the informal MFIs, 90% reported that access to microfinance services enabled increases in the acreage of land use for on-farm activities, suggesting more informal clients were diversifying into on-farm activities as a result of the access (see Chapter 7, Section 7.2.3).

In addition, tested means using the *t*-test statistic revealed that whereas the formal and semi-formal clients significantly diversified into wage-earning jobs, the informal clients significantly diversified into on-farm activities (crop and animals). This trend was again repeated when the semi-formal and informal clients were compared. However, clients were more associated with larger land size use, suggesting that the formal and semi-formal were probably seen as a business (stepping out) by the few formal and semi-formal MFI clients that were diversifying into on-farm activities rather than the way of life (hanging-in) experiences of the informal clients. Market-focused production usually involves larger capital outlays, specialized skills and some level of risk tolerance that favoured the economically and socially better-off formal and semi-formal MFI clients. Access to larger loans, to product markets, and the means of production favoured the few formal and semi-formal MFI clients that ventured into on-farm livelihood activities.

Animal raising as a livelihood diversification strategy, however, was more associated with the informal clients compared to both the formal and semi-formal ones. However, the animals kept were mostly small ruminants that served as capital stocks and insured the highly unpredictable and irregular income flows of households of the informal clients against livelihood risks. Keeping animals was considered a risk management strategy that supported such households' weather their vulnerability contexts of pervasive shocks, trends and sensonalities.

Furthermore, the results showed that exposure to previous debt was more common among the formal and semi-formal MFI clients. The divergence was, however, not significantly different from those of the informal MFI clients. Thus, irrespective of wealth and income status, households borrow, save, invest and insured to starve-off risks and uncertainties associated with their livelihoods' activities of production, consumption and investments. The results also pointed out that access to microfinance was more associated with increased numbers of livelihood strategies engaged in by the semi-formal and informal MFI clients compared, respectively, to the formal clients. However, reports of profitability of investments made with accessed financial resources from the MFIs were more associated with the formal and informal MFI clients compared to the informal and semi-formal MFI clients, respectively (see Chapter 7, Sections 7.2.4 and 7.2.5).

8.6.2 Does Access in a Segmented Industry Have Differential Impacts on Clients' Household Asset Accumulation?

The results first compare the asset accumulation patterns of microfinance participants and non-participants; second, the formal and informal MFI clients; and third, the semi-formal and informal clients of the prevailing segmented microfinance industry of the Northern Rural Savannah.

The comparative analysis of microfinance participants and non-participants of the study region showed that ownership of small ruminants such as sheep and goats, including pigs, was significantly associated with the non-participants compared to the microfinance participants. This confirmed the earlier finding that poorer households keep small ruminants in the Northern Rural Savannah as capital stocks that insured against livelihoods and income risks and uncertainties. The unpredictability and irregular cash flows that characterize poorer households meant income risks are usually prevalent. However, the ownership of large ruminants was more associated with the microfinance participants compared to the non-participants, but this was not statistically significant. Overall, the range of household chattels was significantly associated with the microfinance participants compared to the non-participants, implying microfinance participants had better profiles of these asset classes of household chattels. Two interpretations could be deduced from this finding. First, that microfinance was helping reduce poverty, evidenced by the significant ownership of these asset classes by the microfinance participants. Second, it could be that the participants were already economically and socially better-off and therefore had disproportionate access to microfinance services. If the latter view holds true, it means that poorer segments of the population (depth of outreach) have been seriously compromised, and that microfinance may be entrenching existing inequalities rather than ensuring redistribution.

Moreover, the results also revealed that the ownership of low-value asset classes that were inherently productive but inferior, such as donkey carts, was also significantly associated with the non-participants of microfinance programmes in the Northern Rural Savannah, further confirming their poorer economic and social status (see Chapter 7, Section 7.3.2).

Within the microfinance participants (clients), the disaggregated results showed that the ownership of high-value household chattels (modern consumer goods) was significantly associated with the formal clients compared to the informal clients. This suggests that the microfinance participants who source products and services from the formal MFIs (i.e., rural and community banks and savings and loans companies) were generally more economically and socially better-off than those sourcing products and services from the informal MFIs (i.e., moneylenders, *Susu* and the VSLA groups).

Others such as small ruminant rearing, installed electric fans and frequency of loan uptake were significantly associated with the informal MFI clients compared to clients of the formal MFIs. While the possession of significant numbers of small ruminants served as capital stock for the informal households easily converted into cash via local meat markets, the frequency of loan uptake, mostly from relatives and friends, was commonly used for consumption smoothening rather than as investment capital. With the majority of informal clients engaged in the informal economy, most of the installed fans were found in stalls and groceries owned by these informal clients in the urban and peri-urban localities of the Northern Rural Savannah (see Chapter 7, Section 7.3.3).

The comparison of the household asset accumulation patterns of the semi-formal and informal clients also revealed similar trends. Those that access microfinance from the semi-formal MFIs (credit unions and FNGOs) significantly owned the high-value modern consumer goods (household chattels) compared to clients of the informal MFIs (moneylenders, *Susu* and the VSLA groups). This also implied that the former was generally more economically and socially better-off than the latter.

As was also expected, the ownership of small ruminants, sewing machines and frequency of loan uptake were also significantly associated with the informal clients compared to the semi-formal clients. The small ruminants remained capital stocks for the less economically and socially connected households of clients of the informal MFIs in the Northern Rural Savannah. The significant frequency of loan uptake also suggests either the unreliable household cash flows or the high demand for short-run liquidity management instruments in the informal economy, where most etch out their living. Sewing machines were mostly acquired for young girls who either dropped out of school or had no formal education and its significance among households of the informal clients suggests low educational outcomes and human capital formation compared to those of the semi-formal clients. Until recently, keeping cattle was more of a cultural phenomenon rather than an economic venture in the Northern Rural Savannah and the majority of cattle were mostly inherited and not acquired via outright purchase (see Chapter 7, Section 7.3.4 and Appendix VIII).

8.6.3 Does Access in a Segmented Industry Have Differential Impacts on Clients' Household Welfare Outcomes (e.g., education and training, health, housing and housing improvement, food security, sanitation) in the Northern Savannah?

The results showed that though variations in household welfare outcomes as a result of access to microfinance services existed between client groups, broader outcomes were largely a continuum from high among clients of the formal MFIs through to those of the semi-formal and informal MFIs in the Northern Rural Savannah. A comparative analysis of the formal and informal clients showed that access did little or nothing to discourage the practice of open defecation by clients of the formal MFIs. This result suggests the limitation of the social intermediation portfolios of the formal MFIs (rural and community banks and savings and loans companies), especially on water and sanitation in the Northern Rural Savannah. The informal MFIs' clients also significantly reached out to the nearest health facility in less than 15 minutes compared to those of the formal MFIs, suggesting a more urban and peri-urban client base for the moneylenders (individuals and companies). Moreover, access among the informal MFI clients was found to be significantly associated with reduced open defecation practices and high usage of water closets (WCs) in the management of household sewage and sanitation in the urban and peri-urban settings (see Chapter 7, Section 7.4.3).

Also, though variations in household welfare outcomes were prevalent between the semi-formal and informal MFI clients in comparative terms, open defecation among the former remained significantly high. This suggests that the semi-formal MFIs (credit union associations and FNGOs) also had limited social intermediations in their portfolios, especially that related to water and sanitation.

The significant use of generators (gensets) for the supply of electricity and liquified petroleum gas (LPG) in homes and businesses among the informal clients compared to the semi-formal clients suggests higher levels of involvement of the former in informal economic activities such as cooked food businesses and apprenticeship shops in the Northern Savannah. Moreover, access was also significantly associated with limited open defecation practices and higher use of water closets (WCs) in the management of household sewage and sanitation by the informal clients in urban settings compared to the semi-formal clients. Accessing microfinance by households from the three institutional types produced varying welfare outcomes based on the prevailing household livelihood activities leveraged by the accessed resources (see Chapter 7, Section 7.4.3 and Appendix IX).

8.7 Contribution to Knowledge on Microfinance, Livelihoods and Development

The study made contributions in pushing the frontiers of knowledge on microfinance, livelihoods and poverty reduction and to the existing literature. First, the study adopted the meta-theoretical livelisystem framework that integrates social, eco-systems, development and evolutionary theories onto the workings of the microfinance industry and situates same within national and the global financial and economic systems. Defined as

> a combination of the functions provided by assets (or resources) and activities undertaken in and by open, structured and actively self-regulating systems in maintaining negentropy (negative entropy) and/or increasing it with informational, material and relational mechanisms for maintenance, growth or multiplication"
>
> *(Dorward, 2014, p. 7)*

the livelisystem framework draws on conceptualizations of livelihoods (Chambers and Conway, 1992), living systems (Miller, 1978) and generative replication in complex population systems (Hodgson and Knudsen, 2010). Thus, the livelisystem framework, according to Dorward (2014), describes how material, informational and relational assets, asset services and asset pathways interact in systems with embedded and emergent properties that are constantly undergoing structural transformations (spatial, temporal or sectoral changes, physical, ecological, institutional, political, economic or trophic changes) and transformational processes (changes in social organization, belief systems, values, knowledge and the decisions involving consumption, production, investment and inheritance, shaped by the changing values and knowledge systems) from the local sub-national, to the national, regional, global and external levels (see Chapter 2, Section 2.6).

Therefore, the author conceptualized the microfinance livelisystem framework to describes how the microfinance industry and its financial and non-financial assets, with the material, informational and relational properties and attributes when accessed, contribute to poverty reduction through the client's household's livelihood activities (see Chapter 2, Section 2.3). The framework presents the scenarios of how access to microfinance products and services can lead to unsustainable household debt burdens (*falling down and out*), consumption smoothening (*hanging in*), production activities for mostly the market (*stepping up*) and those exclusively for the market (*stepping out*) (see Chapter 2, Section 2.6).

For instance, the microfinance industry and its financial services and products (financial assets) have material (e.g., loans, savings, insurance, payment services), informational (e.g., product and service scope, training in health, water and sanitation, energy and linkages to agricultural value chains) and relational (e.g., inter- and intra-households relationships versus inter- and intra-institutional partnerships and cooperation) all aimed at supporting those with access to microfinance working themselves out of poverty. The evaluation of the impact of access on the client's livelihood activities then spurs further innovations in product design to better match those livelihood activities with the ultimate twin goals of poverty reduction and financial sustainability of the MFIs. Microfinance exists in continuity with the broader economic and financial system transformational structures such as national and international capital markets and microfinance investment vehicles (MVIs) and transformational processes including national and cross-border policies, regulatory and legal frameworks that are occurring simultaneously in the local sub-national, national, regional, global and external spheres (e.g., climate change-induced livelihood mitigation strategies with financial services).

The second was the author's development of the household livelisystem model (HLM) that extended the understanding of other existing pooled income intra-household decision-making models. It borrowed from the household economic portfolio (HEP) model (Chen and Dunn, 1996) and livelihood portfolio (LP) (Chambers and Conway, 1992) model, among others, to unpack how accessed financial products and services from microfinance institutions interact with other household's resources (human, physical and financial) and allocation decisions in livelihood activities of production, consumption and investments. While the HEP extensively discussed the interactions of household resources with exogenous credit, the LP model discusses the relationship between the households and the larger family, markets, public authorities, social networks and membership institutions in the construction of livelihoods. However, the HLM is defined by the author as the process by which households re-arrange over time its mix of resources (human, physical, financial) and activities (production, consumption, investments), separately or jointly, in relationship with the larger family, social networks, membership institutions, markets and public authorities in coping with its changing economic and social objectives. Moreover, household livelisystem transitioning capability depends on the composition and structure of the household; its collective and individual constraints and preferences in the theatre of the household; and the individual or collective relationships with the five-welfare enhancing localized institutions – the family, social networks, membership institutions, markets and public authorities. The household also exists and operationalizes livelihood activities through diversification, specialization, substitution, adaptation and accumulation in the wider context of vulnerabilities that encompasses shocks, trends and seasonalities.

The third involved the use of data from microfinance clients and their households' livelihood activities (the demand side) in expanding Schreiner's (2002) framework for the design of microfinance products and services (supply side) under the constraints of increased outreach and sustainable financial intermediation. According to Schreiner (2002), the normative approach (poverty-lending or financial systems) adopted by a microfinance institution matters when designing microfinance products and services. However, in order to achieve the twin goals of increased outreach and financial self-sufficiency of MFIs, Schreiner

(2002) proposed a framework for the design of microfinance products and services by MFIs. He used empirical data from a group of Latin American MFIs and identified six indices that should underpin the design of microfinance products and services. This study diverged from Schreiner's by the use of empirical quantitative and qualitative data directly solicited from microfinance clients in the Northern Savannah of Ghana in gauging the perceptions of the levels of incorporation of these six indices (and their sub-indices). Apart from looking at Schreiner's (2002) framework from the demand side, this study identified two additional indicators (contract enforcement mechanisms and add-ons) for inclusion. The study then unpacked the perception of these eight indices through the lens of microfinance clients in the context of a three-tiered industry of the Northern Savannah of Ghana and their implications for households' livelihood activities. For instance, while the cost of supply will include only interest and fees charged by MFIs, the cost of access included the cost of supply (the interests and fees) plus the transaction costs (non-cash opportunity costs and indirect cash expenses) incurred by clients in the process of accessing microfinance and financial inclusion.

The fourth involved key but interesting findings from the study. The methodological plurality involving quantitative and qualitative methods provided depth for the findings. For example, the assessment of the perception of clients on the level of incorporation of all eight factors of microfinance product and service design identified (cost, scope, worth, depth, breadth, length, enforcement and add-ons) for the Upper East Region, in particular, and the Northern Savannah, in general, revealed that these were highly perceived among clients of the formal MFIs (rural and community banks and the savings and loans companies), moderate among clients of the semi-formal MFIs (credit union associations and financial NGOs) and low among clients of the informal MFIs (moneylenders 'Susu' and VSLAs). The formal MFIs offered varied scope of product and service, reached out to poorer (depth), larger numbers (breadth) through group products/services and had ongoing partnerships with some government ministries departments and agencies, bilateral and multilateral development agencies, and the private sector than was the case with the semi-formal and informal MFIs. However, factors that increase the willingness to pay (Woller et al., 1999) such as the maintenance of cordial relationships between clients and MFIs' staff and flexible duration of repayments were more commonly observed among clients of the semi-formal MFIs compared to the formal MFI clients. This shows that having a clear sense of ownership, a voice and a perception of MFI accountability influences the client's product uptake, helping to curtail moral hazards and increase repayment rates. However, worth in terms of loan amounts accessed, the flexibility of deposit withdrawals, and the ability to diversify income sources (livelihoods), employ others and achieve personal goals were more widespread among the formal clients compared to the semi-formal and informal clients. The formal MFIs also had varied contract enforcement mechanisms and add-ons (microfinance plus), especially group products. The study further established that forging linkages and collaborations between these three institutional types is key to achieving financial sustainability, increasing outreach and financial inclusion and likely to have more impact on poverty reduction.

Also, a growing rural economy had a positive relationship with product uptake and was significant. This reinforces the need to complement microfinance with other poverty reduction interventions for sustainability and rural financial market development. However, the relationship between gender and product uptake was negative and also statistically significant. This result suggests that when barriers to access by females are eliminated, product uptake increases significantly. Key informant interviews further revealed that MFIs favourably targeted women's economic activities in the Northern Savannah because it was good for both business and the improvement of household living standards, especially the nutrition of children (see Chapter 7, Section 7.3). The study further tested the association between access to microfinance and households' livelihood diversification, asset accumulation and welfare outcomes between the formal, semi-formal and informal MFI clients of the Northern Savannah. The use of the quantitative *t*-test statistic in estimating the mean differences in household livelihood diversifications, asset accumulation and welfare outcomes across the three-tiered industry provided objectivity and validity to the findings. The qualitative methods provided a wealth of reasons behind the statistic results. For example, accessing microfinance from informal sources was significantly associated with general improvements in access to education and training of household members, the ability to take to the nearest health facility in less than 15 minutes, and the use of generators (gensets) and liquified petroleum gas (LPG) in enterprises and homes. Focus group discussion revealed most informal service providers and clients were found in urban centres, where they have mostly engaged in informal trade and income generation activities. Steady electricity supply and LPG use were crucial in some of these livelihoods' activities. The informal MFI clients were less likely to practice open defecation even in rural localities and were significantly associated with the use of water closets (WCs) in the management of household sewage and sanitation in the urban settings (see Chapter 7, Sections 7.5.2 and 7.5.3).

8.8 Implication for Policy and Practice

The Ghana Statistical Service in 2014 reported that access to financial services by households in the Northern Savannah (Northern, Upper East and Upper West) was not only below the national average but that the area was severely underserved. There was, therefore, the need to find out the factors underpinning the unfortunate development. In exploring Objective 1, i.e., the evolution of the microfinance sub-sector in the Northern Savannah vis-à-vis the broader financial sector eco-system, it was obvious that historical legacies (colonial neglect), policy neglect by successive governments, macro-economic (e.g., economic growth and inflationary pressures), macro-institutional factors (e.g., the rule of law), MFI (firm-level) factors (e.g., the scope of lending methodologies and targeting orientation) and client characteristics (e.g., being male or female and educational levels), as well as household circumstances (e.g., household size, number of livelihood activities engaged and enterprise start-up requirements), all need careful consideration in designing policies and programmes aimed at promoting access to financial services and financial inclusion. Thus, the study revealed that targeting niches of populations in particular sectors of the rural economy, complemented by broad-based rural development programmes, the provision of group or both group and individual financial products and services by MFIs, deliberate targeting of women livelihood activities, the promotion of livelihood diversification in general and designing products that match the enterprise start-up requirements of clients as well as MFIs adherence to good corporate governance and management that is sensitive to local socio-cultural norms and values does have a significant association with microfinance participation and uptake in the Northern Savannah. These factors need consideration in policy and programme design by service providers, including government agencies, and in bilateral and multilateral development partnership programmes aimed at improving access to microfinance and financial inclusion in the Northern Savannah (see Chapter 6, Section 6.3).

Furthermore, in designing financial products and services for sustainable microfinance intermediation by the plurality of institutional types operating in the Northern Savannah see Chapter 5, Table 5.1, eight key indices need to be taken into consideration. The mainstreaming of these eight indices is critical for sustainable financial intermediation and increased outreach regardless of the approaches these microfinance institutions adapt, i.e., whether they adopt the poverty-lending approach (Welfarist) or the financial systems approach (Institutionists). The cost of access that involved fees and interest payments, the opportunity cost of time lost from other livelihood activities and the indirect cash expenses clients incur on transport and documentation, among others, are critical factors that must be given the necessary attention in the design of microfinance products and services for sustainable intermediation (see Chapter 5, Section 5.2.2). The scope of lending methodologies and product offerings must be broad enough to meet the diverse needs of clients. The scope also influences participation and product uptake (see Chapter 5, Section 5.2.3). Integrated services delivery produces better livelihood outcomes for microfinance clients and the sustainability of MFIs. Social or non-financial intermediation such as enterprise development training impacts positively on the capabilities of clients, the success of project choices and rates of repayment, with direct implications on the financial self-sufficiency of MFIs. Flexibility in contract terms and conditions that allow easy adjustments to loan amounts when needed, the duration of repayments (term to maturities), regular repayment amounts (size of instalments), variation in interest spreads that favour both depositors and loan takers, limited restrictions on withdrawal allowances for client savings, tailored products and services targeting localized livelihood diversification activities, and the promotion of forwarding and backward linkages such as employment creation, all increase worth for clients (i.e., the willingness of clients and potential clients to pay for access to financial services) (Woller et al., 1999) (see Chapter 5, Section 5.2.5).

In designing products and services for long-term sustainable intermediation (length), there is a need to build customer loyalty. This is because the longer the number of years of access, the better the success rate of clients' project choices and therefore repayment rates. Donor partnership engagements must be encouraged to support the development of the non-financial services portfolios of microfinance institutions and product innovation, especially in micro-insurance. Social intermediation does have a direct impact on financial intermediation and vice versa. These two are complementary and must be weighed and optimally balanced to reflect the different contexts under which microfinance services are provided. This is one area where microfinance institutions can partner with decentralized government ministries, departments and agencies promoting microfinance and financial inclusion and also with health, education, water and sanitation, and enterprise development, among others. Increasing sustainable microfinance intermediation (length) implies effectively balancing the pricing of products and services without compromising margins for MFIs or upsetting the demand and supply dynamics of credit markets in the Northern Rural Savannah of Ghana (see Chapter 5, Section 5.2.4).

In consideration of the most marginalized and excluded groups (depth of outreach), MFIs must consciously include tailor-made products and services targeting the dominant livelihood activities of women, rural and peri-urban populations, ethnic minorities and the productive poor economic actors concentrated at the fringes of urban informal sectors. These actors usually require much smaller loan sizes, but the impact on household welfare can almost always be certainly significant (see Chapter 5, Section 5.2.6).

Increasing the absolute number of clients accessing microfinance from MFIs (breadth of outreach) requires that the average interest rates and fees charged must make for reasonable margins while minimizing adverse selection and ensuring the incentive structures of contracts do not facilitate moral hazards among clients. The transactional costs of non-cash opportunity costs and the indirect cash expenses incurred by clients need careful consideration and amelioration when designing microfinance products and services. The widespread use of mobile staff equipped with vehicles (motorcycles in most cases) in the study region mitigated these transactional costs considerably. While mitigating the effects of these transactional costs on outreach also improved repayment rates, forging donor partnerships has the potential of reducing the interest rates charged to microfinance borrowers. Yet, there are other benefits to MFIs via integrated services delivery with social intermediation. Group-based products and services promoted both breadth and depth of outreach (see Chapter 5, Section 5.2.7). Limiting the information asymmetries between lenders and borrowers that frequently resulted in increased default rates requires linkages between the three institutional types (formal, semi-formal and informal) in the provision of appropriate and desired financial products and services. Synergy can then be established, when the inherent advantages of each can be made available to all. The three different mechanisms for establishing synergy include linkages between the informal VSLA groups and moneylenders and the formal rural and community banks as well the semi-formal credit unions; the formal rural and community banks and semi-formal credit unions mimicking the activities of the informal Susu and VSL group operations; and in both cases, the use of small group peer monitoring mechanisms.

The study also found some interesting contract enforcement mechanisms commonly used by MFIs in the study region. Apart from the threats of legal actions and airing of names of defaulters on the local radio, outsourcing of loan recovery to third parties and the use of third-party guarantors in co-signing contracts, there were incidences where loan defaulters were summoned to the local chief palace or made to swear oaths to local deities believed to have the power to invoke curses if loans were not repaid. The use of these traditional social structures and systems was, however, a measure of last resort. The study further found that lending to close networks common with informal service providers limited the information asymmetry and increased repayments (see Chapter 5, Section 5.2.8).

Moreover, the study found that there was no clear understanding of the differences between what constituted add-ons (microfinance plus) by the staff of microfinance institutions and clients alike in the Northern Savannah. However, both staff and clients could distinguish between financial and non-financial intermediation. For example, good customer service was understood as an add-on by clients in the study region. The need to make this clear is important for the promotion of best practices in know-your-customer (KYC) standards and in product design considerations that optimize outreach and sustainability goals (see Chapter 5, Section 5.2.9).

Diversification out of on-farm activities was found as a trend in the Northern Savannah. Although on-farm activities remain the primary source of livelihoods for the majority of microfinance clients and, by extension, the population at large, most were diversifying out of on-farm activities. With over 60% of MFI clients engaged in one form of off-farm activity or the other, MFIs are encouraged to explore appropriate product design and services that better meet the needs of current and emerging livelihood activities as pathways to expand outreach and diversify livelihoods in the region that is vulnerable to risks associated with climate change and weather variability. However, the identification of on-farm activities with the potential to both improve living standards and achieve financial self-sufficiency goals must receive adequate attention and support from stakeholders. Pro-poor microfinance programmes must target the livelihoods of those with the least access, i.e., the informal client groups that are mostly engaged in on-farm crop and animal production. Small ruminant raising is a significant livelihood risk mitigation strategy for the population groups with irregular income sources such as clients of the informal MFIs. This is because small ruminants are easily converted into cash via local meat product markets of the study region. Skills training such as apprenticeship, tailoring, dressmaking and weaving made up critical household livelihood diversification portfolios for the poor and vulnerable households, including clients of the informal MFI clients. MFI products and services must be tailored to meet such livelihood activities to build human capital with long-term impact on poverty reduction. They can be considered in the social intermediation efforts of MFIs and policies and programmes of government targeting resource-poor, but productive populations. Education on the effects of open defecation (OD) must be made an essential component of the social intermediation portfolios of all MFIs' operations in the study region. The implementation of these open defecation free programmes in partnership with government ministries, departments and agencies and NGOs must be strongly encouraged.

8.9 Further Research

Further research will be needed involving time-series or panel data sets in the determination of factors influencing financial product and service uptake in the long term. Building up panel and time-series data on how all 31 dependent variables affect microfinance product uptake in the long term and how that influences Ghanaian household livelihood diversification, asset accumulation and welfare outcomes in a tiered microfinance industry is recommended.

Future research on product and service design should focus on the financial and management data from the MFIs (supply side) and then be supported by qualitative data from the clients. A robust econometric estimation was possible with data from the microfinance institutions operating in the Northern Savannah in line with Schreiner's (2002) study. However, this study diverges by focusing on the demand side of the microfinance industry and the microfinance livelisystem framework by only assessing the perceptions of clients on the levels of incorporation of the eight identified factors that should underpin the design of products and services and the implications of each on clients' livelihood activities of production, consumption and investments interacting with the five localized institutions – markets, membership institutions, social networks, family and local authorities.

A number of factors placed limitations on this study. Inadequate resources limited the study to the Upper East Region of the Northern Savannah. This limitation was overcome by the use of the GLSS VI data, reports of the Ghana Statistical Services, among others, for the extraction of vital information and data on financial services in the Northern Savannah.

It is also acknowledged that the sample size of the household survey was also small, constraining the robustness and validity of the logistic regression estimation of determinants of uptake and its generalization for the Northern Savannah. Thus, the use of non-experimental data sets and cross-sectional research meant the study is subject to the limitations of cross-sectional studies. Product uptake decisions are dynamic in nature, implying they are better modelled using time-series or panel data (see, for example, Besley and Case, 1993). Given that cross-sectional data comprises data on a number of households for just a given time, the study was unable to capture the dynamic elements. It was therefore not possible to holistically and accurately examine the long-term effects of all 31 independent variables on microfinance product and service uptake in the study area and the Northern Savannah as a whole.

REFERENCES

Acemoglu, D., Johnson, S. & Robinson, J. A. 2001. *Reversal of fortune: Geography and institutions in the making of the modern world income distribution*. National Bureau of Economic Research (Cambridge, MA) Working Paper No. 8460, April 2001.

Acemoglu, D., Johnson, S. & Robinson, J. A. 2002. Reversal of fortune: Geography and institutions in the making of the modern world income distribution. *The Quarterly Journal of Economics*, 117; 1231–1294.

Ackah, C. & Asiamah, J. P. 2016. Financial regulation in Ghana: Balancing inclusive growth with financial stability. In *Achieving Financial Stability and Growth in Africa* (pp. 123–137). Routledge.

Adaawen, S. A. & Owusu, B. 2013. North-South migration and remittances in Ghana. *African Review of Economics and Finance*, 5(1); 29–45.

Adams, D. W., Graham, D. H. & Von Pischke, J. D. 1984. Undermining rural development with cheap credit, Westview. *Special Studies in Social, Political, and Economic Development*. Boulder, CA: Westview Press.

Adams, D. W. & von Pischke, J. 1992. Microenterprise credit programs: Deja vu. *World Development*, 20; 1463–1470.

Adams, R. H. & Page, J. 2005. Do international migration and remittances reduce poverty in developing countries? *World Development*, 33; 1645–1669.

Adjei, J. K., Arun, T. & Hossain, F. 2009. *The role of microfinance in asset-building and poverty reduction: The case of Sinapi Aba Trust of Ghana*. University of Manchester.

Afrane, S. 2002. Impact assessment of microfinance interventions in Ghana and South Africa: A synthesis of major impacts and lessons. *Journal of Microfinance/ESR Review*, 4; 4.

Afrane, S. K. and Adusei, M. 2014. The Female Superiority in Loan Repayment Hypothesis: Is it Valid in Ghana? *Advances in Management and Applied Economics*, 4(2); 81.

Aghion, D., Armendariz, B. & Gollier, C. 2000. Peer group formation in an adverse selection model. *The Economic Journal*, 110; 632–643.

Aghion, B.A.D. and Morduch, J., 2004. Microfinance: Where do we stand?. In *Financial Development and Economic Growth* (pp. 135–148). London: Palgrave Macmillan.

Ahlin, C. & Jiang, N. 2008. Can micro-credit bring development? *Journal of Development Economics*, 86; 1–21.

Ahlin, C., Lin, J. & Maio, M. 2011. Where does microfinance flourish? Microfinance institution performance in macroeconomic context. *Journal of Development Economics*, 95; 105–120.

Ahlin, C. & Townsend, R. M. 2007. Using repayment data to test across models of joint liability lending. *The Economic Journal*, 117; F11–F51.

Akerlof, G. A. (1970). The market for "Lemons": Quality, uncertainty and the market mechanism. *Quarterly Journal of Economics*, 84(3); 488–500.

Akudugu, M. 2012. Estimation of the determinants of credit demand by farmers and supply by rural banks in Ghana's upper East Region. *Asian Journal of Agriculture and Rural Development*, 2; 189–200.

Akudugu, M.A., Egyir, I.S. and Mensah-Bonsu, A., 2009. Access to rural bank credit in Ghana: the case of women farmers in the Upper East Region. *Ghana Journal of Development Studies*, 6(2), pp.142–167.

Akudugu Mamudu, A. 2009. Women farmers' access to credit from rural banks in Ghana. *Agricultural Finance Review*, 69; 284–299.

Akula, V. 2008. Business basics at the base of the pyramid. *Harvard Business Review*, 86; 53.

Aleem, I. 1990. Imperfect information, screening, and the costs of informal lending: A study of a rural credit market in Pakistan. *The World Bank Economic Review*, 4; 329–349.

Aliaga, I., Marconi, R. & Mosley, P. 2005. Microfinance networks and the evaluation of social performance: The case of FINRURAL, Bolivia. *Money with a Mission Volume 2-Managing the Social Performance of Microfinance*. Practical Action Publishing in association with GSE Research.

Amin, R. & Becker, S. 1998. NGO-promoted microcredit programs and women's empowerment in rural Bangladesh: Quantitative and qualitative evidence. *The Journal of Developing Areas*, 32; 221–236.

Anane, G. K., Cobbinah, P. B. & Manu, J. K. 2013. Sustainability of small and medium scale enterprises in rural Ghana: The role of microfinance institutions. *Asian Economic and Financial Review*, 3; 1003.

Anderson, C. L., Locker, L. & Nugent, R. 2002. Microcredit, social capital, and common pool resources. *World Development*, 30; 95–105.

Antwi-Asare, T. O. & Addison, E. K. Y. 2000. *Financial sector reforms and bank performance in Ghana*. London: Overseas Development Institute.

Appiah-Konadu, P., Churchill, R.Q., Agbodohu, W. and Frimpong, H.K., 2016. Evaluating the credit risk management practices of microfinance institutions in Ghana: Evidence from Capital Line Investment Ltd. and Dream Finance Ltd. Archives of Business Research (ABR) Vol, 4(5), Accra. Ghana.

Armendáriz, B. & Morduch, J. 2010. *The economics of microfinance*. Cambridge, MA: MIT Press.

Armendariz de Aghion, B. & Morduch, J. 2005. *The economics of microfinance*. Cambridge, MA: MIT Press.

Arun, T. G. & Hulme, D. 2008. *Microfinance-A way forward*. Available at SSRN 1297187.

Aryeetey, E., 1994. *Supply and demand for finance of small enterprises in Ghana* (No. 251). World Bank Publications.

Aryeetey, E. & Nissanke, M. 1998. *Financial integration and development: Financial gaps under liberalization in four African countries*. London: Routledge.

Assets, M.T. 2011. Foreign capital investment in microfinance: Reassessing financial and social returns. Washington, DC: C-GAP.

Azariadis, C. & Stachurski, J. 2005. Poverty traps. *Handbook of Economic Growth*, 1; 295–384.

Balassa, B. A. 1971. *The structure of protection in developing countries*. Baltimore, MD: Johns Hopkins University Press.

Bandyopadhyay, S. & Skoufias, E. 2012. Rainfall variability, occupational choice, and welfare in rural Bangladesh. *World Bank Policy Research Working Paper* 6134.

Banerjee, A., Duflo, E., Glennerster, R. & Kinnan, C. 2010. The miracle of microfinance? Evidence from a randomized evaluation. http.economics.mit.edu/files/5993.

Banerjee, A., Duflo, E., Glennerster, R. & Kinnan, C. 2015. The miracle of microfinance? Evidence from a randomized evaluation. *American Economic Journal: Applied Economics*, 7; 22–53.

Banerjee, A. V., Besley, T. & Guinnane, T. W. 1994. Thy neighbor's keeper: The design of a credit cooperative with theory and a test. *The Quarterly Journal of Economics*, 109; 491–515.

Bank, W. 2018. *The Global Findex Database 2017: Measuring financial inclusion and the Fintech revolution*. Washington, DC: Author.

Bank of Ghana 2019a. https://www.bog.gov.gh/news/bank-of-ghana-2019-annual-report/ [Accessed 11 March, 2020].

Bank of Ghana 2019b. https://www.bog.gov.gh/news/bank-of-ghana-2019-annual-report/ [Accessed 19 June, 2020]

Barker, K. K., Bosco, C. & Oandasan, I. F. 2005. Factors in implementing interprofessional education and collaborative practice initiatives: findings from key informant interviews. *Journal of Interprofessional Care*, 19; 166–176.

Barnes, C., Keogh, E. & Nemarundwe, N. 2001. *Microfinance program clients and impact: An assessment of Zambuko Trust, Zimbabwe*. Washington, DC: AIMS.

Barnes, C., Morris, G., Gaile, G., Kibombo, R., Kayabwe, S., Namara, A., Waalwo-Kajula, P. & graham, K. 1999. An assessment of clients of microfinance programs in Uganda. *International Journal of Economic Development*, 1; 80–122.

Barnum, H. N. & Squire, L. 1979. An econometric application of the theory of the farm-household. *Journal of Development Economics*, 6(1); 79–102.

Barrett, C. B., Reardon, T. & Webb, P. 2001. Nonfarm income diversification and household livelihood strategies in rural Africa: concepts, dynamics, and policy implications. *Food Policy*, 26; 315–331.

Barry, T. A. & Tacneng, R. 2014. The impact of governance and institutional quality on MFI outreach and financial performance in Sub-Saharan Africa. *World Development*, 58; 1–20.

Basu, S. 1997. The conservatism principle and the asymmetric timeliness of earnings 1. *Journal of Accounting and Economics*, 24; 3–37.

Bateman, M. & Chang, H. J. 2009. *The microfinance illusion*. Available at SSRN 2385174.

Baydas, M. M., Meyer, R. L. & Aguilera-Alfred, N. 1994. Discrimination against women in formal credit markets: Reality or rhetoric? *World Development*, 22; 1073–1082.

Bebbington, A., Guggenheim, S., Olson, E. & Woolcock, M. 2004. Exploring social capital debates at the World Bank. *Journal of Development Studies*, 40; 33–64.

Beck, T., Demirgüç-Kunt, A. & Levine, R. 2004. Finance, inequality, and poverty: Cross-country evidence. *NBER Working Paper* w10979.

Beck, T., Demirgüç-Kunt, A. & Levine, R. 2007. Finance, inequality and the poor. *Journal of Economic Growth*, 12; 27–49.

Beck, T., Demirgüç-Kunt, A. & Maksimovic, V. 2008. Financing patterns around the world: Are small firms different? *Journal of Financial Economics*, 89; 467–487.

Bell, C. 1988. Credit markets and interlinked transactions. *Handbook of Development Economics*, 1; 763–830.

Belnye, F. 2011. Financial inclusion and regulatory policy: The case of Ghana's informal and semiformal financial institutions. *Innovations*, 6(4); 99.

Bening, R. B. 1971. The development of education in Northern Ghana 1908–1957. *Ghana Social Science Journal*, 1; 21–42.

Bening, R. B. 1990. *A history of education in Northern Ghana, 1907–1976*. Accra: Ghana Universities Press.

Bennaceur, S. & Ghazouani, S. 2005. Does inflation impact on financial sector performance in the MENA region? *Review of Middle East Economics and Finance*, 3; 219–229.

Bennett, L. & Goldberg, M. 1993. *Providing enterprise development and financial services to women, a decade of bank experience in Asia*. World Bank-Technical Papers.

Berhane, G. 2009. *Econometric analysis of microfinance group formation, contractual risks and welfare impacts in Northern Ethiopia*. Netherlands: Wageningen University.

Berhane, G. & Gardebroek, C. 2011. Does microfinance reduce rural poverty? Evidence based on household panel data from northern Ethiopia. *American Journal of Agricultural Economics*, 93(1); 43–55.

Berhane, G. & Gardebroek, C. 2012. *Assessing the long-term impact of microcredit on rural poverty: Does the timing and length of participation matter?* (No. 43). International Food Policy Research Institute (IFPRI).

Besley, T. & Case, A. 1993. Modeling technology adoption in developing countries. *The American Economic Review*, 83(2); 396–402.

Besley, T. & Coate, S. 1995. Group lending, repayment incentives and social collateral. *Journal of Development Economics*, 46; 1–18.

Beverly, S. G. & Sherraden, M. 1999. Institutional determinants of saving: Implications for low-income households and public policy. *The Journal of Socio-Economics*, 28; 457–473.

Bhaduri, A. 1973. A study in agricultural backwardness under semi-feudalism. *The Economic Journal*, 83; 120–137.

Bhaduri, A. 1977. On the formation of usurious interest rates in backward agriculture. *Cambridge Journal of Economics*, 1; 341–352.

Bhagwati, J. N. 1988. Poverty and public policy. *World Development*, 16; 539–555.

Bhatt, N. & Tang, S.-Y. 2001. Designing group-based microfinance programs: Some theoretical and policy considerations. *International Journal of Public Administration*, 24; 1103–1125.

Bhatt, N. & Tang, S.-Y. 2002. Determinants of repayment in microcredit: Evidence from programs in the United States. *International Journal of Urban and Regional Research*, 26; 360–376.

Binks, M. 1979. Finance for expansion in the small firm. *Lloyds Bank Annual Review*; 134; 33–45.

Binswanger, H. P. & Rosenzweig, M. R. 1986. Behavioural and material determinants of production relations in agriculture. *The Journal of Development Studies*, 22; 503–539.

Bittencourt, M. 2012. Financial development and economic growth in Latin America: Is Schumpeter right? *Journal of Policy Modeling*, 34; 341–355.

BoG. 2017. https://www.bog.gov.gh/annual_report/annual-report-2017/ [Accessed July 2019].

BoG. 2018. https://www.bog.gov.gh/annual_report/annual-report-2018/ [Accessed 19 April, 2019]

Boehe, D. M. & Cruz, L. B. 2013. Gender and microfinance performance: Why does the institutional context matter? *World Development*, 47; 121–135.

Bolnick, B. R. & Nelson, E. R. 1990. Evaluating the economic impact of a special credit programme: KIK/KMKP in Indonesia. *The Journal of Development Studies*, 26; 299–312.

Bottomley, A. 1964. Monopoly profit as a determinant of interest rates in underdeveloped rural areas. *Oxford Economic Papers*, 16; 431–437.

Boyd, J. & Smith, B. 1996. The coevolution of the real and financial sectors in the growth process. *The World Bank Economic Review*, 10; 371–396.

Boyd, J. H. & de Nicolo, G. 2005. The theory of bank risk taking and competition revisited. *The Journal of Finance*, 60; 1329–1343.

Boyd, J. H. & Smith, B. D. 1998. The evolution of debt and equity markets in economic development. *Economic Theory*, 12; 519–560.

Braverman, A. & Stiglitz, J. E. 1982. Sharecropping and the interlinking of agrarian markets. *The American Economic Review*, 72; 695–715.

Braverman, A. & Stiglitz, J. E. 1986. Cost-sharing arrangements under sharecropping: Moral hazard, incentive flexibility, and risk. *American Journal of Agricultural Economics*, 68; 642–652.

Brownbridge, M. & Gockel, A. F. 1996. The impact of financial sector policies on banking in Ghana. *Institute of Development Studies Working Paper* 38.

Brune, L., Giné, X., Goldberg, J. & Yang, D. 2011. Commitments to save: A field experiment in rural Malawi. *World Bank Policy Research Working Paper*, 5748.

Bryceson, D. F. 1996. Deagrarianization and rural employment in sub-Saharan Africa: A sectoral perspective. *World Development*, 24; 97–111.

Bryceson, D. F. 1999. African rural labour, income diversification & livelihood approaches: A long-term development perspective. *Review of African Political Economy*, 26; 171–189.

Buckley, G. 1997. Microfinance in Africa: Is it either the problem or the solution? *World Development*, 25; 1081–1093.

Buera, F. J. & Kaboski, J. 2012. The rise of the service economy. *The American Economic Review*, 102; 2540–2569.

Burns, F., Imrie, J. Y., Nazroo, J., Johnson, A. M. & Fenton, K. A. 2007. Why the (y) wait? Key informant understandings of factors contributing to late presentation and poor utilization of HIV health and social care services by African migrants in Britain. *AIDS Care*, 19; 102–108.

Campaign, M. S., Rao, D. S. K. & Daley-Harris, S. 2015. State of the microcredit summit campaign report. *Microcredit Summit Campaign*.

Carman, J. M. 1970. Correlates of brand loyalty: Some positive results. *Journal of Marketing Research*, 7; 67–76.

Carney, D. Sustainable rural livelihoods: What contribution can we make? Papers presented at the Department for International Development's Natural Resources Advisers' Conference, July 1998. Department for International Development (DFID).

Carney, D. 2003. *Sustainable livelihoods approaches: Progress and possibilities for change*. London: Department for International Development.

Carroll, T. 2012. Working on, through and around the state: The deep marketisation of development in the Asia-Pacific. *Journal of Contemporary Asia*, 42(3): 378–404.

Caudill, S. B., Gropper, D. M. & Hartarska, V. 2009. Which microfinance institutions are becoming more cost effective with time? Evidence from a mixture model. *Journal of Money, Credit and Banking*, 41; 651–672.

Cavatassi, R., Lipper, L. & Winters, P. 2012. Sowing the seeds of social relations: Social capital and agricultural diversity in Hararghe Ethiopia. *Environment and Development Economics*, 17; 547–578.

Chambers, R. 1994. The origins and practice of participatory rural appraisal. *World Development*, 22; 953–969.

Chambers, R. 1997. *Whose reality counts* (Vol. 25). London: Intermediate technology publications.

Chambers, R. and Conway, G.R., 1992. Sustainable rural livelihoods: practical concepts for the 21st century. *Discussion paper-institute of development studies, University of Sussex*, Sussex United Kingdom.

Chaskin, R. J. 2001. Building community capacity: A definitional framework and case studies from a comprehensive community initiative. *Urban Affairs Review*, 36; 291–323.

Chen, M. A. & Dunn, E. 1996. Household economic portfolios, assessing the impact of microenterprise services (AIMS). *Office of Microenterprise, USAID.*

Chowdhury, A. 2009. Microfinance as a poverty reduction tool—A critical assessment. *United Nations, Department of Economic and Social Affairs (DESA) working paper*, 89.

Chowdhury, A., Mahmud, M. & Abed, F. 1991. Impact of rural credit for the poor: The case of BRAC in Bangladesh. *Small Enterprise Development*, 2; 4–13.

Chowdhury, A. M. R. & Bhuiya, A. 2004. The wider impacts of BRAC poverty alleviation programme in Bangladesh. *Journal of International Development*, 16; 369–386.

Christen, R. P. 2001. Commercialization and mission drift. *Occasional paper.* Washington, DC: CGAP.

Claessens, S. 2006. Access to financial services: A review of the issues and public policy objectives. *The World Bank Research Observer*, 21; 207–240.

Cleveland, D. A. 1991. Migration in West Africa: A savanna village prespective. *Africa*, 61; 222–246.

Coase, R. H. 1992. Contracts and the activities of firms. *Journal of Law and Economics*, 34; 451–452.

Cole, R. A., Goldberg, L. G. &White, L. J. 2004. Cookie cutter vs. character: The micro structure of small business lending by large and small banks. *Journal of Financial and Quantitative Analysis*, 39(2); 227–251.

Coleman, B. E. 1999. The impact of group lending in Northeast Thailand. *Journal of Development Economics*, 60; 105–141.

Coleman, B. E. 2006. Microfinance in Northeast Thailand: Who benefits and how much? *World Development*, 34; 1612–1638.

Collins, D., Morduch, J., Rutherford, S. & Ruthven, O. 2009. *Portfolios of the poor: How the world's poor live on $2 a day.* Princeton: Princeton University Press.

Conning, J. 1999. Outreach, sustainability and leverage in monitored and peer-monitored lending. *Journal of Development Economics*, 60; 51–77.

Conning, J. & Udry, C. 2005. *Rural financial markets in developing countries* (Discussion Paper No. 914). Yale University, Economic Growth Center.

Cook, P. 2001. Finance and small and medium-sized enterprise in developing countries. *Journal of Developmental Entrepreneurship*, 6(1); 17.

Copestake, J. 2002. Inequality and the polarizing impact of microcredit: Evidence from Zambia's copperbelt. *Journal of International Development*, 14; 743–755.

Copestake, J., 2007. Mainstreaming microfinance: Social performance management or mission drift?. World development, 35(10), pp.1721–1738.

Copestake, J., Bhalotra, S. & Johnson, S. 2001. Assessing the impact of microcredit: A Zambian case study. *Journal of Development Studies*, 37; 81–100.

Copestake, J. & Williams, R. 2011. What is the impact of microfinance and what does this imply for microfinance policy and for future impact studies? *Dutch National Platform on Microfinance*, 29.

Cornwall, A. 2000. Beneficiary, consumer, citizen: Perspectives on participation for poverty reduction. Sida Studies No. 2. Stockholm: International Development Cooperation Agency.

Coulter, J. & Onumah, G. 2002. The role of warehouse receipt systems in enhanced commodity marketing and rural livelihoods in Africa. *Food Policy*, 27; 319–337.

Cowles, D. L., Kiecker, P. & Little, M. W. 2002. Using key informant insights as a foundation for e-retailing theory development. *Journal of Business Research*, 55; 629–636.

Crépon, B., Devoto, F., Duflo, E. & Pariente, W. 2011. *Impact of microcredit in rural areas of Morocco: Evidence from a Randomized Evaluation* (No. 6659). MIT Working paper.

Csáki, C. & Lerman, Z. 2000. *Structural change in the farming sectors in Central and Eastern Europe: Lessons for the EU accession: Second World Bank/FAO Workshop* 27–29 June 1999, World Bank Technical Paper No. 465, Europe and Central Asia environmentally and Socially Sustainable Development Series, Washington, DC.

Cull, R., Demirgüç-Kunt, A. & Morduch, J. 2009. Microfinance meets the market. *The Journal of Economic Perspectives*, 23; 167–192.

Cull, R. & Morduch, J. 2007. Financial performance and outreach: A global analysis of leading microbanks. *The Economic Journal*, 117; F107–F133.

Datt, G. & Ravallion, M. 1992. Growth and redistribution components of changes in poverty measures: A decomposition with applications to Brazil and India in the 1980s. *Journal of Development Economics*, 38; 275–295.

Davis, B., Winters, P., Carletto, G., Covarrubias, K., Quiñones, E. J., Zezza, A., Stamoulis, K., Azzarri, C. & Digiuseppe, S. 2010. A cross-country comparison of rural income generating activities. *World Development*, 38; 48–63.Debus, M. 1988. *A Handbook for Excellence in Focus Group Research*, HEALTHCOM Project special Report Series. Washington, DC: Porter/Novelli.

Delgado, C. L. & Siamwalla, A. 2018. Rural economy and farm income diversification in developing countries. In *Food Security, Diversification and Resource Management: Refocusing the Role of Agriculture?* (pp. 126–143). Routledge.

Demirguc-Kunt, A., Klapper, L., Singer, D. & Ansar, S., 2018. *The Global Findex Database 2017: Measuring financial inclusion and the fintech revolution.* World Bank Publications.

Diaz-Serrano, L. & Sackey, F. G. 2016. *Empowering the Vulnerable to Be Entrepreneurs: An Empirical Test on the Effectiveness of the Ghana Microfinance Policy 2006* (No. 10323). IZA Discussion Papers.

Díaz Serrano, L. & Sackey, F. G. 2015. *Microfinance and credit rationing in Ghana: Does the microfinance type matter?*. Universitat Rovira i Virgili, Department of Economics.

Diccicco-Bloom, B. & Crabtree, B. 2006. The qualitative research interviews. *Medical Education*, 40; 314–321.

Dichter, T. W. 1999. NGOs in microfinance: Past, present and future. *Microfinance in Africa*, 2; 12–37.

Dickson, K. 1968. Background to the problem of economic development in Northern Ghana. *Annals of the Association of American Geographers*, 58; 686–696.

Diop, C., Dorsner, C. & Gross, D. M. 2003. *Understanding savings mobilisation by mutual savings and loan institutions in WAEMU Countries*. ILO.

Diop, A., Hillenkamp, I. and Servet, J.M., 2007. Poverty versus inequality. In *Microfinance and Public Policy* (pp. 27–46). Palgrave Macmillan, London.

Drexler, A., Fischer, G. & Schoar, A. 2014. Keeping it simple: Financial literacy and rules of thumb. *American Economic Journal: Applied Economics*, 6(2); 1–31.

Duflo, E. & Banerjee, A. 2011. *Poor economics* (Vol. 619). Public Affairs.

Dumas, C. 2001. Evaluating the outcomes of microenterprise training for low income women: A case study. *Journal of Developmental Entrepreneurship*, 6(2); 97.

Hall, P.D., 1987. A historical overview of the private nonprofit sector. *The Nonprofit Sector: A Research Handbook*, 12; 341–361.

Dorward, A.R. 2014. Livelisystems: a conceptual framework integrating social, ecosystem, development, and evolutionary theory. *Ecology and Society*, 19(2)

Dunford, C. 2000. In search of "sound practices" for microfinance. *Journal of Microfinance/ESR Review*, 2; 2.

Dunn, E. 2002. It pays to know the customer: addressing the information needs of client-centered MFIs. *Journal of International Development*, 14(3); 325.

Dunn, E. & Arbuckle JR, J. G. 2001. *The impacts of microcredit: A case study from Peru. USAID Office of Microenterprise Development*. Washington, DC: USAID AIMS Project.

Dupas, P. & Robinson, J. 2013. Savings constraints and microenterprise development: Evidence from a field experiment in Kenya. *American Economic Journal: Applied Economics*, 5; 163–192.

Edgecomb, E. 2010. *Looking good and taking care: Consumer culture, identity and poor, minority, urban tweens*. Doctoral dissertation, University of South Florida.

Edison, H. J., *Levine*, R., Ricci, L. & Sløk, T. 2002. International financial integration and economic growth. *Journal of International Money and Finance*, 21; 749–776.

El-Zoghbi, M., Gähwiler, B. & Lauer, K. 2011. Cross-border funding of microfinance. *CGAP Focus Notes*, 70; 1–12. Elahi, K. Q. & Danopoulos, C. P. 2004. Microcredit and the Third World: Perspectives from moral and political philosophy. *International Journal of Social Economics*, 31; 643–654.

Ellis, F. 1998. Household strategies and rural livelihood diversification. *The Journal of Development Studies*, 35; 1–38.

Ellis, F. 1999. *Rural livelihood diversity in developing countries: Evidence and policy implications*. London: Overseas Development Institute.

Ellis, F. 2000. *Rural livelihoods and diversity in developing countries*. Oxford University Press.

Ellis, F. & Allison, E. 2004. Livelihood diversification and natural resource access, Livelihood Support Programme. LSP Working Paper 9, FAO, Rome.

English, W. B. 1999. Inflation and financial sector size. *Journal of Monetary Economics*, 44; 379–400.

Evans, T. G., Adams, A. M., Mohammed, R. & Norris, A. H. 1999. Demystifying nonparticipation in microcredit: A population-based analysis. *World Development*, 27; 419–430.

Eyben, R. 2010. Hiding relations: the irony of 'effective aid'. *The European Journal of Development Research*, 22; 382–397.

Eyiah, A. K. 2001. An integrated approach to financing small contractors in developing countries: A conceptual model. *Construction Management and Economics*, 19; 511–518.

Fafchamps, M. 1997. Trade credit in Zimbabwean manufacturing. *World Development*, 25; 795–815.

Fafchamps, M., Mckenzie, D., Quinn, S. & Woodruff, C. 2014. Microenterprise growth and the flypaper effect: Evidence from a randomized experiment in Ghana. *Journal of Development Economics*, 106; 211–226.

Fafchamps, M. & Pender, J. 1997. Precautionary saving, credit constraints, and irreversible investment: Theory and evidence from serniarid India. *Journal of Business & Economic Statistics*, 15; 180–194.

Feigenberg, B., Field, E. & Pande, R. 2013. The economic returns to social interaction: Experimental evidence from microfinance. *Review of Economic Studies*, 80(4); 1459–1483.

Ferber, M. A. & Birnbaum, B. G. 1977. The "new home economics:" Retrospects and prospects. *Journal of Consumer Research*, 4(1); 19–28.

Field, E., Pande, R., Papp, J. & Rigol, N. 2011. *Term structure of debt and entrepreneurship: Experimental evidence from microfinance.* Manuscript, Harvard University, Princeton University and MIT. Princeton, United States of America.

Fischer, G. and Ghatak, M., 2011. Spanning the Chasm: Uniting Theory and Empirics in Microfinance Research. World Scientific Book Chapters, pp. 59–75.

Fleisig, H. & de la Peña, N. 1996. Creating a legal and regulatory framework to promote access to rural credit. *trabajo sin publicar*, Washington, DC: Center for the Economic Analysis of Law.

Franks, J. R. 2000. Macroeconomic stabilization and the microentrepreneur. *Journal of Microfinance/ESR Review*, 2; 5.

Fugelsang, A. & Chandler, D. 1993. Participation as process—process as growth: What we can learn from Grameen Bank Bangladesh. Dhaka: *Grameen Trust.*

Gangopadhyay, S., Ghatak, M. & Lensink, R. 2005. Joint liability lending and the peer selection effect. *The Economic Journal*, 115; 1005–1015.

Gart, A. 2012. *MIX and CGAP analysis of key trends - 2011 Sub-Saharan Africa regional snapshot*, Opportunity International. United States of America. Retrieved from https://policycommons.net/artifacts/1736419/mix-and-cgap-analysis-of-key-trends/2468093/ on 06 Oct 2022. CID: 20.500.12592/rc6h2j.

Gertler, M. & Karadi, P. 2015. Monetary policy surprises, credit costs, and economic activity. *American Economic Journal: Macroeconomics*, 7(1); 44–76.

Ghana Statistical Service. 2007. *Pattern and trends of poverty in Ghana, 1991–2006.* Accra: Ghana Statistical Service.

Ghana Statistical Service, 2013. *2010 Population & Housing Census Report: Children, adolescents & young people in Ghana.* Accra: Ghana Statistical Service.

Ghana Statistical Service. 2014. *2010 population and housing census report: Urbanisation in Ghana.* Accra: Ghana Statistical Service.

Ghana Statistical Service, 2015. *Ghana poverty mapping report.* Accra: Ghana.

Ghatak, M. 1999. Group lending, local information and peer selection. *Journal of Development Economics*, 60; 27–50.

Ghatak, M. 2000. Screening by the company you keep: Joint liability lending and the peer selection effect. *The Economic Journal*, 110; 601–631.

Ghatak, M. & Guinnane, T. W. 1999. The economics of lending with joint liability: Theory and practice. *Journal of Development Economics*, 60; 195–228.

Gibson, J., Mckenzie, D. & Rohorua, H. 2014. Development impacts of seasonal and temporary migration: A review of evidence from the Pacific and Southeast Asia. *Asia & the Pacific Policy Studies*, 1; 18–32.

Giné, X., Goldberg, J. & Yang, D. 2012. Credit market consequences of improved personal identification: Field experimental evidence from Malawi. *American Economic Review*, 102(6); 2923–2954.

Godquin, M. 2004. Microfinance repayment performance in Bangladesh: How to improve the allocation of loans by MFIs. *World Development*, 32; 1909–1926.

Goldmark, A., 2003. Fewer Loans for the Lonely: Can Social Capital Improve Access to Credit for the Poor? *GEO. PUB. POL'Y REV.*, 9; 49–53.

Gomez, R. & Santor, E. 2001. Membership has its privileges: the effect of social capital and neighbourhood characteristics on the earnings of microfinance borrowers. *Canadian Journal of Economics*, 34(4); 943–966.

Gonzalez-Vega, C. 1977. Interest rate restrictions and income distribution. *American Journal of Agricultural Economics*, 59; 973–976.

Goodland A., Onumah G. & Amadi O. (1999) "Rural finance", DFID/NRI Policy Series No. 1.

Grabel, I. 2008. The political economy of remittances: What do we know? What do we need to know? *PERI Working Papers*; 172.

Grasmuck, S. & Espinal, R. 2000. Market success or female autonomy? Income, ideology, and empowerment among microentrepreneurs in the Dominican Republic. *Gender & Society*, 14; 231–255.

Greene, W. H. 2003. *Econometric analysis*. India: Pearson Education.

Grosh, B. & Somolekae, G. 1996. Mighty oaks from little acorns: Can microenterprise serve as the seedbed of industrialization? *World Development*, 24; 1879–1890.

Grosh, M. & Glewwe, P. 2000. *Designing household survey questionnaires for developing countries: Lessons from 15 years of the living standards measurement study*, Volume 3. Washington, DC: World Bank Publications.

Gubert, F. & Roubaud, F. 2005. *Analyser l'impact d'un projet de Micro-finance: l'exemple d'ADéFI à Madagascar* (No. DT/2005/14). DIAL (Développement, Institutions et Mondialisation).

Guiso, L., Sapienza, P. & Zingales, L. 2004. Does local financial development matter? *The Quarterly Journal of Economics*, 119; 929–969.

Gupta, S., Pattillo, C. A. & Wagh, S. 2009. Effect of remittances on poverty and financial development in Sub-Saharan Africa. *World Development*, 37; 104–115.

Gustafsson, B. & Makonnen, N. 1993. Poverty remittances in Lesotho. *Journal of African Economies*, 2; 49–73.

Hadi, N. A. & Kamaluddin, A. 2015. Social collateral, repayment rates, and the creation of capital among the clients of microfinance. *Procedia Economics and Finance*, 31; 823–828.

Haggblade, S., Longabaugh, S. and Tschirley, D. L. 2009. *Spatial patterns of food staple production and marketing in South East Africa: Implications for trade policy and emergency response* (No. 54553). Michigan State University, Department of Agricultural, Food, and Resource Economics.

Halder, S. R. & Mosley, P. 2004. Working with the ultra-poor: Learning from BRAC experiences. *Journal of International Development*, 16; 387–406.

Hart, K. 1971. Migration and tribal identity among. *Asian and African Studies*, 6; 21.

Hartarska, V. 2005. Governance and performance of microfinance institutions in Central and Eastern Europe and the newly independent states. *World Development*, 33; 1627–1643.

Hartarska, V. & Nadolnyak, D. 2007. Do regulated microfinance institutions achieve better sustainability and outreach? Cross-country evidence. *Applied Economics*, 39; 1207–1222.

Havers, M. 1996. Financial sustainability in savings and credit programmes. *Development in Practice*, 6; 144–164.

Hermes, N., Lensink, R. & Meesters, A. 2009. *Financial development and the efficiency of microfinance institutions*. Available at SSRN 1396202.

Hermes, N., Lensink, R. & Meesters, A. 2011. Outreach and efficiency of microfinance institutions. *World Development*, 39; 938–948.

Hill, R. C., Griffiths, W. E. & Lim, G. C. 2018. *Principles of econometrics*. Hoboken, NJ: Wiley & Sons.

Hill, R. C. & Sarangi, S. 2012. Repayment performance in group lending: Evidence from Jordan. *Journal of Development Economics*, 97; 404–414.

Hodgson, G. M. & Knudsen, T. 2010. Generative replication and the evolution of complexity. *Journal of Economic Behavior & Organization*, 75; 12–24.

Hoff, K. R. & Stiglitz, J. E. 1993. *A theory of imperfect competition in rural credit markets in developing countries: Towards a theory of segmented credit markets* (No. 58). Center for Institutional Reform and the Informal Sector, University of Maryland at College Park.

Hoff, K. & Stiglitz, J. E. 1990. Introduction: Imperfect information and rural credit markets: Puzzles and policy perspectives. *The World Bank Economic Review*, 4; 235–250.

Hollis, A. & Sweetman, A. 1998. Microcredit: What can we learn from the past? *World Development*, 26; 1875–1891.

Honohan, P. 2004. Financial development, growth and poverty: how close are the links?. In *Financial development and economic growth* (pp. 1–37). London: Palgrave Macmillan.

Honohan, P. 2008. Cross-country variation in household access to financial services. *Journal of Banking & Finance*, 32; 2493–2500.

Hossain, M. 1988. *Credit for alleviation of rural poverty: The Grameen Bank in Bangladesh* (Vol. 65). Intl Food Policy Research Institute.

Hossain, S. 2013. Does external stakeholder orientation in corporate governance influence in sustainability and outreach of microfinance institutions. *Research Journal of Finance and Accounting*, 4; 25–33.

Huang, J.-K. & Wang, Y.-J. 2014. Financing sustainable agriculture under climate change. *Journal of Integrative Agriculture*, 13; 698–712.

Huang, Y. & Temple, J., 2005. *Does external trade promote financial development?* (No. 05/575). School of Economics, University of Bristol, UK.

Hudak, K. 2012. What next for microfinance? How the broader financial context matters for effective microfinance outreach. *Journal of Developmental Entrepreneurship*, 17; 1250023.

Hudon, M. and Seibel, H.D., 2007. Microfinance in post-disaster and post-conflict situations: turning victims into shareholders (No. 2007, 8). University of Cologne, Development Research Center.

Hulme, D. 2000. Impact assessment methodologies for microfinance: Theory, experience and better practice. *World Development*, 28; 79–98.

Hulme, D. & Moore, K. 2006. *Why has microfinance been a policy success in Bangladesh (and beyond)?* (No. GPRG-WPS-041). University of Oxford, Department of Economics.

Hulme, D. & Mosley, P. 1996. *Finance against poverty* (Vol.2). London: Psychology Press.

Huybens, E. & Smith, B. D. 1998. Financial market frictions, monetary policy, and capital accumulation in a small open economy. *Journal of Economic Theory*, 81; 353–400.

Huybens, E. & Smith, B. D. 1999. Inflation, financial markets and long-run real activity. *Journal of Monetary Economics*, 43; 283–315.

IFAD (2011). *New realities, New Opportunities for Tomorrow's generation. Rural Poverty Report 2011.* Rome: IFAD.

Im, J. & Sun, S. L. 2015. Profits and outreach to the poor: The institutional logics of microfinance institutions. *Asia Pacific Journal of Management*, 32; 95–117.

Imai, K. S., Arun, T. & Annim, S. K. 2010. Microfinance and household poverty reduction: New evidence from India. *World Development*, 38; 1760–1774.

Imai, K. S. & Azam, M. S. 2012. Does microfinance reduce poverty in Bangladesh? New evidence from household panel data. *Journal of Development studies*, 48; 633–653.

Islam, M. M.-U. 1996. Peer monitoring in the credit market. *Journal of Contemporary Asia*, 26; 452–465.

Ivatury, G. & Mas, I. 2008. The early experience with branchless banking. *CGAP Focus Note*, 46.

Iyer, R., Khwaja, A. I., Luttmer, E. F. & Shue, K. 2015. Screening peers softly: Inferring the quality of small borrowers. *Management Science*, 62; 1554–1577.

Jalilian, H. & Kirkpatrick, C. 2002. Financial development and poverty reduction in developing countries. *International Journal of Finance & Economics*, 7; 97–108.

Jalilian, H. & Kirkpatrick, C. 2005. Does financial development contribute to poverty reduction? *Journal of Development Studies*, 41; 636–656.

Jeanneney, S. G. & Kpodar, K. 2011. Financial development and poverty reduction: Can there be a benefit without a cost? *The Journal of Development Studies*, 47; 143–163.

Johnson, S. 2004. The impact of microfinance institutions in local financial markets: A case study from Kenya. *Journal of International Development*, 16; 501–517.

Johnson, S. & Rogaly, B. 1997. *Microfinance and poverty reduction*. Oxford: Oxfam.

Jones, J. H. M. & Sakyi-Dawson, O. 2002. Linking formal and informal financial intermediaries in Ghana: A way to increase women's access to financial services?. *Women and Credit, Researching the Past and Refiguring the Future* (pp. 271–294). Oxford University Press.

Kaboski, J. P. & Townsend, R. M. 2012. The impact of credit on village economies. *American Economic Journal: Applied Economics*, 4; 98–133.

Kane, E. J. 1977. Good intentions and unintended evil: The case against selective credit allocation. *Journal of Money, Credit and Banking*, 9(1); 55–69.

Karlan, D. & Valdivia, M. 2011. Teaching entrepreneurship: Impact of business training on microfinance clients and institutions. *Review of Economics and statistics*, 93(2); 510–527.

Karlan, D. & Zinman, J. 2010. Expanding credit access: Using randomized supply decisions to estimate the impacts. *The Review of Financial Studies*, 23(1); 433–464.

Karlan, D., Mcconnell, M., Mullainathan, S. & Zinman, J. 2016. Getting to the top of mind: How reminders increase saving. *Management Science*, 62; 3393–3411.

Karlan, D., Osei, R., Osei-Akoto, I. & Udry, C. 2014. Agricultural decisions after relaxing credit and risk constraints. *The Quarterly Journal of Economics*, 129; 597–652.

Karlan, D. & Zinman, J. 2004. The price elasticity of demand for credit: Evidence and implications from a randomized field experiment. Working paper Princeton University and Federal Reserve Bank of New York.

Karlan, D. & Zinman, J. 2009. Observing unobservables: Identifying information asymmetries with a consumer credit field experiment. *Econometrica*, 77; 1993–2008.

Karlan, D. S. & Zinman, J. 2009. *Expanding microenterprise credit access: Using randomized supply decisions to estimate the impacts in manila* (No. 1858-2016-152715).

Karlan, D. & Zinman, J. 2011. Microcredit in theory and practice: Using randomized credit scoring for impact evaluation. *Science*, 332; 1278–1284.

Kaufmann, D., Kraay, A. & Mastruzzi, M. 2009. Governance matters VIII. *Policy Research Working Paper*, 4978; 2–6.

Keho, Y. 2009. Inflation and financial development: Cointegration and causality analysis for the UEMOA countries. *International Research Journal of Finance and Economics*, 27; 117–123.

Kevane, M. & Wydick, B. 2001. Microenterprise lending to female entrepreneurs: Sacrificing economic growth for poverty alleviation? *World development*, 29; 1225–1236.

Khalil, E. L. 2004. What is altruism? *Journal of Economic Psychology*, 25; 97–123.

Khan, M. S. & Ssnhadji, A. S. 2001. Threshold effects in the relationship between inflation and growth. *IMF Staff Papers*, 48; 1–21.

Khandker, S. R. 2005. Microfinance and poverty: Evidence using panel data from Bangladesh. *The World Bank Economic Review*, 19; 263–286.

Khavul, S., Bruton, G. D. & Wood, E. 2009. Informal family business in Africa. *Entrepreneurship Theory and Practice*, 33; 1219–1238.

Kim, J.-K. & Lee, C. H. 2010. Finance and economic development in Korea. *Seoul National University Institute for Research in Finance and Economics Working Paper Series*; 10-A05.

Kitzinger, J. 1996. Introducing focus group in qualitative research in health care. *Qualitative Research in Health Care*. London: BMJ Publishing Group.

Klein, H. K. & Myers, M. D. 1999. A set of principles for conducting and evaluating interpretive field studies in information systems. *MIS Quarterly*, 23; 67–94.

Kondo, T., Orbeta, A., Dingcong, C. & Infantado, C. 2008. Impact of microfinance on rural households in the Philippines. *IDS Bulletin*, 39; 51–70.

Kostova, T. & Zaheer, S. 1999. Organizational legitimacy under conditions of complexity: The case of the multinational enterprise. *Academy of Management Review*, 24; 64–81.

Krueger, R. A. 2014. *Focus groups: A practical guide for applied research*. California: Sage Publications.

Krugman, P., 1994. Competitiveness: a dangerous obsession. Foreign Aff., 73, p. 28.

Kumar, K. 1987. *Conducting focus group interviews in developing countries. AID Program design and evaluation methodology*. Report No. 8. Washington, DC: US Agency for International Development. Retrieved September, 17; 2012.

Kusterer, K. 1989. Small Farmer Attitudes and Aspirations.@ USAID Program Evaluation Discussion Paper No. 26. Washington, DC: US Agency for International Development.

Kwankye, S. O. 2012. Independent North–South child migration as a parental investment in Northern Ghana. *Population, Space and Place*, 18(5); 535–550.

Ledgerwood, J., Earne, J. & Nelson, C. 2013. *The new microfinance handbook: A financial market system perspective*. Washington, DC: World Bank Publications.

Lee, J. & Wong, K.-Y. 2005. Vertical integration and strategic trade policies. *The North American Journal of Economics and Finance*, 16; 93–117.

Lentz, C., 2022. Ethnicity and the Making of History in Northern Ghana. In Ethnicity and the Making of History in Northern Ghana. Edinburgh University Press. United Kingdom.

Lipper, L., Anderson, C.L. & Dalton, T. J., 2010. Seed trade in rural markets. *Implications for Crop Diversity and Agricultural Development*. London: Earthscan.

Litchfield, J., Lipton, M., Blackman, R., de Zoysa, D., Qureshy, L. & Waddington, H. 2002. The impact of irrigation on poverty. *Poverty research unit*. Brighton: University of Sussex. United Kingdom.

Littlefield, E., Morduch, J. & Hashemi, S. 2003a. Is microfinance an effective strategy to reach the Millennium Development Goals? *Focus Note*, 24; 1–11.

Littlefield, E., Morduch, J. & Hashemi, S. 2003. Is microfinance an effective strategy to reach the Millennium Development Goals. *Focus note*, 24(2003); 1–11.

Madajewicz, M. 1999. Capital for the poor: The effect of wealth on the optimal credit contract. New York: Mimeo, Columbia University.

Maddala, G. S. & Jeong, J. 1992. On the exact small sample distribution of the instrumental variable estimator. *Econometrica*, 60; 181–183. Magill, J. H. & Meyer, R. L. 2005. *Micrenterprise and microfinance in Ecuador*. Washington, DC: USAID, March.

Makina, D. & Malobola, L. M. 2004. Impact assessment of microfinance programmes, including lessons from Khula Enterprise Finance. *Development Southern Africa*, 21; 799–814.

Manski, C.F. and Lerman, S.R., 1977. The Estimation of Choice Probabilities from Choice Based Samples. *Econometrica*, 45(8).

Markowski, P. 2002. Microfinance innovations in the Gulf of Guinea region. In *Food Security in a Changing Africa. Centre for Applied studies in International Negotiations*, Geneva.

Marr, A. 2002. Studying group dynamics: An alternative analytical framework for the study of microfinance impacts on poverty reduction. *Journal of International Development*, 14; 511–534.

Marr, A. 2012. Effectiveness of rural microfinance: What we know and what we need to know. *Journal of Agrarian Change*, 12; 555–563.

Mas, I. and Radcliffe, D., 2011. Mobile payments go viral: M-PESA in Kenya. *Capco Institute's Journal of Financial Transformation*, 32, 169.

Mcfadden, D. 1968. *The revealed preferences of a government bureaucracy*. Economic Growth Project. Technical Report.

Mcfadden, D. 1975. The revealed preferences of a government bureaucracy: Theory. *Bell Journal of Economics*, 6; 401–416.

Mcguire, T. W. & Weiss, D. L. 1976. Logically consistent market share models II. *Journal of Marketing Research*, 13; 296–302.

Mcintosh, C. & Wydick, B. 2005. Competition and microfinance. *Journal of Development Economics*, 78; 271–298.

McKenzie, D. J. & Gibson, J. 2010. The development impact of a best practice seasonal worker policy. *World Bank Policy Research Working Paper*, 5488.

Mckernan, S.-M. 2002. The impact of microcredit programs on self-employment profits: Do noncredit program aspects matter? *Review of Economics and Statistics*, 84; 93–115.

Mersland, R. & Strøm, R. Ø. 2009. Performance and governance in microfinance institutions. *Journal of Banking & Finance*, 33; 662–669.

Mersland, R. & Strøm, R. Ø. 2010. Microfinance mission drift? *World Development*, 38; 28–36.

Meyer, R. L. 2002. *Track Record of Financial Institutions in Assisting the Poor in Asia* (No. 49). ADBI Research Paper Series. Miller, J. G. 1978. Living systems.

MkNelly, B., Watetip, C., Lassen, C.A. and Dunford, C., 1996. Preliminary evidence that integrated financial and educational services can be effective against hunger and malnutrition. Freedom From Hunger. Davies, California. United States of America

McNelly, B. and Dunford, C., 1998. Impact of Credit with Education on mothers' and their young children's nutrition: lower Pra rural bank Credit with Education program in Ghana (Research paper No. 4). Davis, Calif, USA: Freedom from Hunger.

Morduch, J. 1998. *Does microfinance really help the poor?: New evidence from flagship programs in Bangladesh*. Princeton, NJ: Research Program in Development Studies, Woodrow School of Public and International Affairs.

Morduch, J. 2000. The microfinance schism. *World Development*, 28; 617–629.

Mosley, P. 2001. Microfinance and poverty in Bolivia. *Journal of Development Studies*, 37; 101–132.

Mosley, P. & Hulme, D. 1998. Microenterprise finance: is there a conflict between growth and poverty alleviation? *World Development*, 26; 783–790.

Mosley, P. & Rock, J. 2004. Microfinance, labour markets and poverty in Africa: A study of six institutions. *Journal of International Development*, 16; 467.

Moyo, J., Nandwa, B., Council, D.E., Oduor, J. & Simpasa, A., 2014. Financial sector reforms, competition and banking system stability in Sub-Saharan Africa. *New perspectives*, 14(1); 1–47.

Murdoch, J., *1999*. The microfinance promise. *Journal of Economic Literature*, 36; 1569–1614. Mustafa, S., Ara, I., Banu, D., Hossain, A., Kabir, A., Mohsin, M., Yusuf, A. & Jahan, S. 1996. *Beacon of hope*. Dhaka: BRAC.

Nagarajan, G. 2003. —Microfinance in Conflict-Affected Environments,‖ in: Date-Bah, E. (ed.) Jobs After War: A critical challenge in the peace and reconstruction puzzle. ILO.

Nampewo, D., Munyambonera, E. & Lwanga, M. M. 2013. Sectoral effects of monetary policy in Uganda. *Journal of Empirical Economics*, 1; 43–58.

Narayan-Parker, D. and Patel, R. 2000. *Voices of the poor: Can anyone hear us?* (Vol. 1). World Bank Publications. Navajas, S., Schreiner, M., Meyer, R. L., Gonzalez-Vega, C. & Rodriguez-Meza, J. 2000. Microcredit and the poorest of the poor: Theory and evidence from Bolivia. *World Development*, 28; 333–346.

Neumark, D. & Wascher, W. 2002. Do minimum wages fight poverty? *Economic Inquiry*, 40; 315–333.

Newsham, A. & Thomas, D. 2009. Agricultural adaptation, local knowledge and livelihoods diversification in North-Central Namibia. *Tyndall Centre for Climate Change Research Working Paper*, 140.

North DC. Institutions, institutional change and economic performance. Cambridge university press; 1990 Oct 26. United Kingdom.

Nourse, T. H. 2001. The missing parts of microfinance: Services for consumption and insurance. *SAIS Review*, 21; 61–69.

Nunan, F. & Satterthwaite, D. 2001. The influence of governance on the provision of urban environmental infrastructure and services for low-income groups. *International Planning Studies*, 6(4): 409–426.

Nwanna, G. I. 1989. Stimulating savings in the informal financial sector of less developed countries. *The Journal of Social, Political, and Economic Studies*, 14; 351.

Nwanna, G. I. 1996. *Rural financial markets in West Africa: Roles, experiences, constraints and prospects for promoting rural Development*. Accra: Center for Economic Research on Africa.

Nyamukapa, C. & Gregson, S. 2005. Extended family's and women's roles in safeguarding orphans' education in AIDS-afflicted rural Zimbabwe. *Social Science & Medicine*, 60; 2155–2167.

Obeng, S. K. & Sakyi, D. 2017. Macroeconomic determinants of interest rate spreads in Ghana. *African Journal of Economic and Management Studies*, 8; 76–88.

Olivares-Polanco, F. 2005. Commercializing microfinance and deepening outreach? Empirical evidence from Latin America. *Journal of Microfinance/ESR Review*, 7; 5.

Onumah, G. 2003. *Improving access to rural finance through regulated warehouse receipt systems in Africa*. United States Agency for International Development–World council of credit unions conference on paving the way forward for rural finance: An international conference on best practices. Washington, DC, June, 2003; 2–4.

Onumah, G. 2010. Implementing warehouse receipt systems in Africa potential and challenges. fourth African agricultural markets program policy symposium, organized by the Alliance for Commodity Trade in Eastern and Southern Africa (ACTESA) of the Common Market for Eastern and Southern Africa (COMESA), 2010.

Onumah, G., Davis, J., Kleih, U. & Proctor, F. 2007. *Empowering smallholder farmers in markets: Changing agricultural marketing systems and innovative responses by producer organizations MPRA*. Munich.

Opare, N. 2001. Commercial banks must help micro-financing. *Accra, Ghana: Daily Graphic, October*, 29; 33.

Osei-Assibey, E. 2010. Microfinance in Ghana: A comparative study of performance of the formal versus informal rural financial institutions. *Forum of International Development Studies*, Forthcoming.

Osei-Assibey, E. 2011. Microfinance in Ghana: A comparative study of performance of the formal versus informal rural financial institutions, Nagoya University Press, Japan.

Osei-Assibey, E. 2013. Source of finance and small enterprise's productivity growth in Ghana. *African Journal of Economic and Management Studies*, 4(3); 372–386.

Osmani, L. N. K. 1998. Impact of credit on the relative well-being of women: Evidence from the Grameen Bank. *IDS Bulletin*, 29; 31–38.

Osotimehin, K., Jegede, C. A. & Akinlabi, B. 2011. Determinants of microfinance outreach in South-Western Nigeria: An empirical analysis. *International Journal of Management and Business Studies*, 1; 001–007.

Otero, M. 1999. Bringing development back, into microfinance. *Journal of Microfinance/ESR Review*, 1; 8–19.

Otoide, V. O., Oronsaye, F. & Okonofua, F. E. 2001. Why Nigerian adolescents seek abortion rather than contraception: Evidence from focus-group discussions. *International Family Planning Perspectives*, 27(2); 77–81.

Park, A. & Ren, C. 2001. Microfinance with Chinese characteristics. *World Development*, 29; 39–62.

Paulson A. 2002. Human Capital and the Development of Financial Institutions: Evidence from Thailand, *Working Paper*, Federal Reserve Bank of Chicago. Pekelman, D. & Sen, S. K. 1974. Mathematical programming models for the determination of attribute weights. *Management Science*, 20; 1217–1229.

Peng, M. W., Wang, D. Y. & Jiang, Y. 2008. An institution-based view of international business strategy: A focus on emerging economies. *Journal of International Business Studies*, 39; 920–936.

Perez-Moreno, S. 2011. Financial development and poverty in developing countries: A causal analysis. *Empirical Economics*, 41; 57–80.

Perry, D. 2002. Microcredit and women moneylenders: The shifting terrain of credit in rural Senegal. *Human Organization*, 61; 30.

Pickbourn, L. J. 2011. *Migration, remittances and intra-household allocation in northern Ghana: Does gender matter?* (Doctoral dissertation, University of Massachusetts Amherst).

Pingali, P. L. & Rosegrant, M. W. 1995. Agricultural commercialization and diversification: processes and policies. *Food Policy*, 20; 171–185.

Pitt, M. M. 2014. Response to 'The impact of microcredit on the poor in Bangladesh: Revisiting the evidence'. *Journal of Development Studies*, 50; 605–610.

Pitt, M. M. & Khandker, S. R. 1998. The impact of group-based credit programs on poor households in Bangladesh: Does the gender of participants matter? *Journal of Political Economy*, 106; 958–996.

Plange, N. K. 1979. Underdevelopment in northern Ghana: Natural causes or colonial capitalism? *Review of African Political Economy*, 6; 4–14.

Raftopoulos, B. & Lacoste, J.-P. 2001. Savings mobilisation to micro-finance: a historical perspective on the Zimbabwe savings development movement. International Conference on "Livelihood, Savings and Debts in a Changing World: Developing Sociological and Anthropological Perspectives". Wageningen, Netherlands.

Reardon, T. 1997. Using evidence of household income diversification to inform study of the rural nonfarm labor market in Africa. *World Development*, 25; 735–747.

Reardon, T., Berdegué, J., Barrett, C.B. and Stamoulis, K., 2007. Household income diversification into rural nonfarm activities. *Transforming the rural nonfarm economy: opportunities and threats in the developing world*, pp. 115–140.

Reardon, T., Pingali, P. and Stamoulis, K.G., 2006. *Impacts of Agrifood Market Transformation during Globalization on the Poor's Rural Nonfarm Employment: Lessons for Rural Business Development Programs* (No. 11572). Michigan State University, Department of Agricultural, Food, and Resource Economics.

Reed, L. R., Marsden, J., Ortega, A., Rivera, C. and Rogers, S. 2011. State of the microcredit summit campaign report 2011. *Microcredit Summit Campaign. Washington DC.*

Reille, X., Forster, S. & Rozas, D. 2011. *Foreign capital investment in microfinance: Reassessing financial and social returns* (No. 63334), pp. 1–16. The World Bank.

Remenyi, Joe and Quinones, Benjamin. 2000. Microfinance and Poverty Alleviation: Case studies from Asia and the Pacific. New York. 79. p. 131-134, 253–263.

Rhyne, E. 2001. *Mainstreaming microfinance: How lending to the poor began, grew, and came of age in Bolivia*. Bloomfield, CT: Kumarian Press.

Rhyne, E. & Christen, R. P. 1999. *Microfinance enters the marketplace*. Washington, DC: USAID. Richter, P. *The integration of the microfinance sector in the financial sector in developing countries*. The Role that Apex Mechanisms Play in Uganda. WIDER Conference, Finland, 2004.

Robinson, M. S. 1996. Addressing some key questions on finance and poverty. *Journal of International Development*, 8; 153–161.

Robinson, M. S. 2001. *The microfinance revolution: Lessons from Indonesia* (Vol. 2). Washington, DC: World Bank Publications.

Rodrik, D. 1997. *Globalization, social conflict and economic growth*. Conferencia de Raúl Prebisch. Ginebra. Versión revisada (en inglés) disponible en http://www.ksg.harvard.edu/rodrik/global.pdf.

Rogaly, B. 1996. Micro-finance evangelism, 'destitute women', and the hard selling of a new anti-poverty formula. *Development in Practice*, 6; 100–112.

Roodman, D. & Morduch, J. 2009. The impact of microcredit on the poor in Bangladesh: Revisiting the evidence. *Center for Global Development Working Paper*.

Roodman, D. & Morduch, J. 2014. The impact of microcredit on the poor in Bangladesh: Revisiting the evidence. *Journal of Development Studies*, 50; 583–604.

Rose, G. 1997. Situating knowledges: positionality, reflexivities and other tactics. *Progress in Human Geography*, 21; 305–320.

Rousseau, P. L. & Wachtel, P. 2002. Inflation thresholds and the finance–growth nexus. *Journal of International Money and Finance*, 21; 777–793.

Rutherford, S. 1998. The savings of the poor: Improving financial services in Bangladesh. *Journal of International Development*, 10; 1–15.

Rutherford, S., 2011. Boosting the Poor's Capacity to Save: A Note on Instalment Plans and their Variants (pp. 517–535). World Scientific Publishing Co. Pte. Ltd.

Sachs, J. 2005. *The end of poverty: How can we make it happen in our life time*. London: Penguin Books.

Sakyi-Dawson, O., Odonkor, C. & Al-Hassan, R. M. 2014. Downgrading financial service delivery and institutional sustainability: A case study of Akwapim rural bank, Ghana. *Ghana Journal of Development Studies*, 11; 19–37.

Samuelson, P. A. & Modigliani, F. 1966. The Pasinetti paradox in neoclassical and more general models. *The Review of Economic Studies*, 33; 269–301.

Schreiner, M. 2002. Aspects of outreach: A framework for discussion of the social benefits of microfinance. *Journal of International Development*, 14; 591–603.

Schreiner, M. & Colombet, H. H. 2001. From urban to rural: Lessons for microfinance from Argentina. *Development Policy Review*, 19; 339–354.

Schreiner, M. & Woller, G. 2003. Microenterprise development programs in the United States and in the developing world. *World Development*, 31; 1567–1580.

Scoones, I. 2008. A new start: Challenging the Myths about Zimbabwean Agriculture and Land Reform. Institute of Development Studies, University of Sussex, Sussex, September, 2008 UK.

Scott, W.R., 1995. Institutions and organizations (Vol. 2). Thousand Oaks, CA: Sage.

Sehrawat, M. & Giri, A. 2015. Financial development and economic growth: empirical evidence from India. *Studies in Economics and Finance*, 32; 340–356.

Seibel, H. D. 2001. Rural finance: Mainstreaming informal financial institutions. *Journal of Developmental Entrepreneurship*, 6; 83.

Sen, A. 1993. Capability and well-being73. *The quality of life*, 30; 1–445.

Sen, A. K. 1985. Commodities and capabilities. Oxford: Oxford University Press.

Sen, A. K. 1987. *The standard of living (edited by Geoffrey Hawthorn)*. Cambridge University Press, Cambridge UK.

Sen, A. K. 1997. From income inequality to economic inequality. *Southern Economic Journal*, 64; 384–401.

Sen, A. K. 1999. *Development as Freedom (DAF)*. Oxford, UK: Oxford University Press.

Senbet, L. W. & Otchere, I. 2006. *Financial sector reforms in Africa: perspectives on issues and policies*. Annual World Bank conference on development economics 2006: Growth and integration; 81–120.

Shocker, A. D. & Srinivasan, V. 1974. A consumer-based methodology for the identification of new product ideas. *Management Science*, 20; 921–937.

Simanowitz, A. 2001. From event to process: Current trends in microfinance impact assessment. *Small Enterprise Development*, 12; 11–21.

Simtowe, F. and Zeller, M., 2008. *The Impact of Access to Credit on the Adoption of hybrid maize in Malawi: An Empirical test of an Agricultural Household Model under credit market failure* (No. 307-2016-4874), pp. 21–35.

Singh, K., 1983. Structure of Interest Rates on Consumption Loans in an Indian Vil lage. Rural Financial Markets in Developing Countries. Baltimore and London: Johns Hopkins. United States of America.

Skoufias, E., Bandyopadhyay, S. & Olivieri, S. 2017. Occupational diversification as an adaptation to rainfall variability in rural India. *Agricultural Economics*, 48; 77–89.

Smith, A. 1776. *The wealth of nations*. New York: The Modern Library.

Smith, S. C. 2002. Village banking and maternal and child health: Evidence from Ecuador and Honduras. *World Development*, 30; 707–723.

Snow, D. R. & Buss, T. F. 2001. Development and the role of microcredit. *Policy Studies Journal*, 29; 296–307.

Songsore, J. & Denkabe, A. 1995. *Challenging rural poverty in Northern Ghana: The case of the upper-west region*. Norway: University of Trondheim, Trondheim, Norway.

Sriram, M. and Radha, K., 2005. *Conditions in Which Microfinance has Emerged in Certain Regions and Consequent Policy Implications* (No. WP2005-05-03). Indian Institute of Management Ahmedabad, Research and Publication Department.

Stake, R. E. 1995. *The art of case study research*. California: Sage, Thousand Oaks, United States of America.

Steele, F., Amin, S. & Naved, R. 2001. Savings/credit group formation and change in empowerment in Bangladesh. *World Development*, 24; 635–653.

Stewart, R., van Rooyen, C., Dickson, K., Majoro, M., & de Wet, T. (2010b). What is the impact of microfinance on poor people? A systematic review of evidence from sub-Saharan Africa (Technical report). London: EPPI-Centre, Social Science Research Unit, University of London.

Stigler, G. J. 1967. Imperfections in the capital market. *Journal of Political Economy*, 75; 287–292.

Stiglitz, J. E. 1987. Competition and the number of firms in a market: Are duopolies more competitive than atomistic markets? *Journal of political Economy*, 95(5); 1041–1061.

Stiglitz, J. E. 1989. Markets, market failures, and development. *The American Economic Review*, 79; 197–203.

Stiglitz, J. E. 1990. Peer monitoring and credit markets. *The World Bank Economic Review*, 4; 351–366.

Stiglitz, J. E. 1993. The role of the state in financial markets. *The World Bank Economic Review*, 7; 19–52.

Stiglitz, J. E. & Weiss, A. 1981. Credit rationing in markets with imperfect information. *The American Economic Review*, 71; 393–410.

Stiglitz, J. E. & Weiss, A. 1983. Incentive effects of terminations: Applications to the credit and labor markets. *The American Economic Review*, 73; 912–927.

Strøm, R. Ø., D'espallier, B. & Mersland, R. 2014. Female leadership, performance, and governance in microfinance institutions. *Journal of Banking & Finance*, 42; 60–75.

Stugler, G. 1987. *The theory of price*. New York: Macmillan Publishing Company.

Swift, J. 1989. Why are rural people vulnerable to famine? *IDS Bulletin*, 20; 8–15.

Tejerina, L., Bouillon, C. P. & Demaestri, E. C. 2006. *Financial services and poverty reduction in Latin America and the Caribbean*. Washington, DC: Inter-American Development Bank.

Thomas, R. G. 1973. Forced labour in British West Africa: The case of the Northern Territories of the Gold Coast 1906–1927. *The Journal of African History*, 14; 79–103.

Thompson, B. 2015. Cost of capital and economic development: The case of Ghana's liberalized capital market. *Journal of Finance and Bank Management*, 3; 1–10.

Toulmin, C. & Quan, J. 2000. *Evolving land rights, policy and tenure in Africa*. Sussex: DFID/IIED/NRI.

Townsend, P. 1979. *Poverty in the United Kingdom: A survey of household resources and standards of living*, University of California Press.

Tribe, K. 1999. Adam Smith: Critical theorist? *Journal of Economic Literature*, 37; 609–632.

Udry, C. 1994. Risk and insurance in a rural credit market: An empirical investigation in northern Nigeria. *The Review of Economic Studies*, 61; 495–526.

Udry, C. 1995. Risk and saving in Northern Nigeria. *The American Economic Review*, 85; 1287–1300.

United Nations. 2005. *Microfinance and the millennium development goals international year of microcredit 2005*. Washington, DC.

Van Tassel, E. 1999. Group lending under asymmetric information. *Journal of Development Economics*, 60; 3–25.

Vanroose, A. 2008. Which macro factors make microfinance institutions reach out? *Savings and Development*, 17(3); 153–174. Vanroose, A. & D'Espallier, B. 2009. Microfinance and financial sector development. *Centre Emile Bernheim. Research Institute in Management Sciences: CEB Working Paper*, 9; 040.

Varian, H. 1990. Monitoring agents with other agents. *Journal of Institutional and Theoretical Economics*, 146; 153–174.

Von Pischke, J. D. 1991. *Finance at the frontier: debt capacity and the role of credit in the private economy* (No. 332.74/V94f). Walker, C. 2004. A charitable view of altruism: Commentary on 'What is altruism?' by Elias Khalil. *Journal of Economic Psychology*, 25; 129–134.

Walpole, M. & Wilder, L. 2008. Disentangling the links between conservation and poverty reduction in practice. *Oryx*, 42; 539–547.

Wärneryd, K. E. 1988. The psychology of innovative entrepreneurship. In *Handbook of economic psychology* (pp. 404-447). Dordrecht: Springer.

Watson, P. L. & Westin, R. B. 1975. Transferability of disaggregate mode choice models. *Regional Science and Urban Economics*, 5; 227–249.

WCED, S. W. S. 1987. World commission on environment and development. *Our Common Future*, 17(1); 1–91.Weber, H. 2010. Politics of global social relations: Organising 'everyday lived experiences' of development and destitution. *Australian Journal of International Affairs*, 64(1); 105–122

Weiss, J. and Montgomery, H., 2005. Great expectations: microfinance and poverty reduction in Asia and Latin America. Oxford Development Studies, 33(3-4), pp. 391–416.

Wenner, M. D. 1995. Group credit: A means to improve information transfer and loan repayment performance. *The Journal of Development Studies*, 32; 263–281.

Westley, G. D. 2005. *Microfinance in the Caribbean: How to go further.* Washington, DC: Inter-American Development Bank.

Williamson, O. E. 2006. *The economic institutions of capitalism.* New York: Free Press.

Witztum, A. 1998. A study into Smith's conception of the human character: Das Adam Smith problem revisited. *History of Political Economy*, 30; 489.

Wodon, Q. T. 1997. Targeting the poor using ROC curves. *World Development*, 25; 2083–2092.

Woller, G. 2002. Introduction to the second microfinance revolution: Creating customer centred microfinance institutions. *Journal of International Development*, 16; 1–5.

Woller, G. & Parsons, R. 2002. Assessing the community economic impact of microfinance institutions. *Journal of Developmental Entrepreneurship*, 7; 133.

Woller, G. M., Dunford, C. & Woodworth, W. 1999. Where to microfinance. *International Journal of Economic Development*, 1; 29–64.

Woller, G. M. & Woodworth, W. 2001. Microcredit and third world development policy. *Policy Studies Journal*, 29; 265-265.

Wood, G. D. & Sharif, I. A., 1997. *Who needs credit? Poverty and finance in Bangladesh.* Zed Books.

Woolcock, M. 2001. The place of social capital in understanding social and economic outcomes. *Canadian Journal of Policy Research*, 2; 11–17.

Woolcock, M. J. 1999. Learning from failures in microfinance: What unsuccessful cases tell us about how group-based programs work. *American Journal of Economics and Sociology*, 58; 17–42.

World Bank, 1997. *World development report 1997: The state in a changing world.* Washington, DC: The World Bank.

World Bank. 2015. *Global monitoring report 2015/2016: Development goals in an era of demographic change.* Washington, DC.

World Bank, 2016. *World development report 2016: Digital dividends.* Washington, DC: World Bank Publications.

World Bank, 2019 \ [accessed July, 2020].

Wright, G.A. 2005. Understanding and Assessing the Demand for Microfinance. *Expanding Access to Microfinance: Challenges and Actors, Paris, MicroSave Africa.*

Wydick, B. 1999. Can social cohesion be harnessed to repair market failures? Evidence from group lending in Guatemala. *The Economic Journal*, 109; 463–475.

Wydick, B. 2001. Group lending under dynamic incentives as a borrower discipline device. *Review of Development Economics*, 5; 406–420.

Wydick, B. 2002. Microfinance among the Maya: Tracking the progress of borrowers. *Development and Change*, 33; 489–509.

Yang, D. 2008. International migration, remittances and household investment: Evidence from Philippine migrants' exchange rate shocks. *The Economic Journal*, 118; 591–630.

Yanguas, P. & Hulme, D. 2015. Barriers to political analysis in aid bureaucracies: From principle to practice in DFID and the World Bank. *World Development*, 74; 209–219.

Yaron, J. 2004. Rural Microfinance: The Challenge and Best Practices. *Best Practise*; 2 Tanzania.

Yaron, J., Benjamin, M. P. & Piprek, G. L. 1997. *Rural finance: Issues, design, and best practices.* Washington, DC: World Bank.

Yin, R. K. 1994. *Case study research: Design and methods*, 2d ed. Thousand Oaks, CA: Sage.

Yunus, M. 1998. Poverty alleviation: Is economics any help? Lessons from the Grameen Bank experience. *Journal of International Affairs*; 47–65.

Yunus, M. 1999. The Grameen Bank. *Scientific American*, 281; 114–119.

Yunus, M. 2009. Creating a world without poverty: social business and the future of capitalism. *The Electronic Journal of Sustainable Development*, 1(3); 125.

Yusupov, N. 2012. Microcredit and development in an occupational choice model. *Economics Letters*, 117; 820–823.

Zeller, M. & Meyer, R. L. 2002. Improving the performance of microfinance: Financial sustainability, outreach and impact. *The Triangle of Microfinance, Baltimore, Maryland*, 2002; 1–18.

Zeller, M. and Sharma, M., 1998. Rural finance and poverty alleviation (No. 8). International Food Policy Research Institute (IFPRI).

Zeller, M., Sharman, M. & Mcclafferty, B. 1997. Commentary: Making rural microcredit work for the poor. *IFPRI Report*, 19.

Zohir, S. & Matin, I. 2004. Wider impacts of microfinance institutions: Issues and concepts. *Journal of International Development*, 16; 301–330.

APPENDIX I

GOVERNMENT AND MULTILATERAL DEVELOPMENT PARTNER INITIATIVES FOR FINANCIAL INCLUSION AND POVERTY REDUCTION IN GHANA: 1980S–TO DATE

Name of Initiative and Duration	*Funding Source(s) and Sector*	*Core Objectives*	*Scale and Funding Amount*
The Economic Recovery Programme (Phase 1: 1983–1986; Phase 2: 1987–1989; Phase 3: 1990–1993)	GoG/WB/IMF (1983–1993)	Reduction in public expenditures; incentives for private production, especially in the export sectors; government divested itself of many public assets through privatization; instituted radical foreign exchange reforms to devalue the cedi further; intensified monetary reforms and reduced private corporate taxes to boost private-sector growth	Country-wide
Programme of Action to Mitigate the Social Costs of Adjustment (PAMSCAD)	Government/WB/ IMF	Aimed at the poorest individuals, small-scale miners and artisans, communities were to be helped to implement labour-intensive self-help projects	Country-wide. Total project costs US$85 million
Ghana Vision 2020: The First Step (1996–2020)	GoG	Overall objective: by the year 2020 Ghana will have achieved a balanced economy and a middle-income country status and standard of living	Country-wide

Achievements/Gaps	Challenges
Initial expenditure cuts and improved tax collection brought the budget deficit down from 6.3% of GDP in 1982 to 0.1% by 1986; reduced government pressure on the banking system freeing capital for the private sector; series devaluations boosted export activity; improved the country's international financial reputation because of its ability to make loan repayments in 1991; first entry onto the international capital market in almost two decades	Privatization was sluggish, the hard-currency black market was nearly eliminated with the introduction of foreign exchange bureaus in 1988; failed to bring about a fundamental transformation of the economy, which still relied on income earned from cocoa and other agricultural commodities; no significant improvements in living standards of the majority Ghanaians; a shift in resources was towards cocoa rehabilitation and other export sectors, not towards food production; government employees, especially those in state enterprises, were actively targeted, and many lost their jobs
Improving water supply, sanitation, primary education, and health care; redeployment and end-of-service benefits for those who had lost their jobs in civil service and parastatal reorganizations	
From 1996 to 2000, medium-term coordinated programme of economic and social development policies (CPESDP) based on five themes: human development; economic growth; rural development; urban development; an enabling environment were developed. The 5-year sectoral and district development plans were developed and coordinated, rationalized and harmonized by the national development planning commission (NDPC) in order to reduce poverty, increase employment opportunities and average incomes, and reduce inequities in order to improve the general welfare and the material well-being of all Ghanaians	Changes in government led to changes in policy which made the Vision 2020 document not followed through by preceding governments

(Continued)

Name of Initiative and Duration	*Funding Source(s) and Sector*	*Core Objectives*	*Scale and Funding Amount*
Ghana Poverty Reduction Strategy (GPRS I) (2003–2005)	GoG; IMF; WB	Prepared as a precondition for Ghana under the highly indebted poor country (HIPC) initiative and focus on human development – targets improvement in access to basic needs and essential services	Country-wide
The Growth and Poverty Reduction Strategy (GPRS II) (2006–2009)		Shifted focus and context to accelerate growth of the economy towards sustained poverty reduction and the attainment of middle-income status	Country-wide
The Ghana Shared Growth and Development Agenda (2010–2013)	Government/ Multilateral (WB & IMF)	Was aimed at addressing seven thematic development issues: sustainable macro-economic stability; competitive private sector; modernization of agriculture in a well-managed natural resource setting; the development of the oil and gas sector; infrastructure and human settlement development; human development, employment and productivity; and transparent and accountable governance systems	Country-wide

Achievements/Gaps	*Challenges*
A positive and significantly stabilized macro-economic environment, with a potential for attaining higher rates of growth; economic stability and international creditworthiness. Economic reconstruction: under the HIPC compact the MDGs were transformed into the mandatory framework of domestic economic policy in return for the grant of debt relief; proportionate allocation of budgetary resources to basic pro-poor services, such as primary education, water supply and public health; measures to plans (SMTDP), the corresponding medium-term expenditure framework (MTEF) and annual budgets. It ensured macro-economic stability and a framework for sustainable economic growth to support poverty reduction in line with sectoral medium-term development	
Achieved the Millennium Development Goal in times; improved shared benefits of growth within a measurable time. Achieved lower middle-income status in the medium term	
Achieve and sustain macro-economic stability while placing the economy on a higher path of shared growth and poverty reduction	

(*Continued*)

Name of Initiative and Duration	*Funding Source(s) and Sector*	*Core Objectives*	*Scale and Funding Amount*
The National Board for Small Scale Industries (NBSSI) (1985–to date)	Government initiative NBSSI established in 1985 by an Act of Parliament (Act 434 of 1981)	Under the direction of the Ministry of Trade and Industry, the NBSSI is the apex government body promoting the development of micro and small enterprises (MSE) to maximize the sector's potential for growth, poverty reduction and development	Country-wide
Export Trade, Agriculture and Industrial Development Fund (EDAIF) (2000–to date)	EDAIF is a public investment fund operating as an agency of the Ministry of Trade and Industry and governed by an Act of Parliament (Act 872 of 2014)	To provide financial resources for the development and promotion of: export trade; Agro-processing and industrial development for both public and private sectors, especially SMEs in agro-processing	Country-wide
National Entrepreneurship and Innovation Plan (NEIP)		Set within the context Ghana's long-term strategic vision of consolidating its middle-income status, NEIP is to provide integrated national support for start-ups and small businesses in the form of business development services; start-up incubators and funding building an industry-driven economy capable of providing decent jobs	

Achievements/Gaps	Challenges
Established in 1985 by an Act of Parliament (Act 434 of 1981) and currently, under the direction of the Ministry of Trade and Industry, the NBSSI is the apex government body promoting the development of micro and small enterprises (MSE) to maximize its potential for poverty reduction throughout the country. Entrepreneurial skills development for employment generation is the key component of the NBSSI programmes. It has secretariats in all ten regional capitals and the business advisory centres (BACs) are located in almost all the district capitals to ensure access to business support services (BDS) is made available	
Development and promotion of agricultural products for exports; development of agriculture relating to agro-processing and agro-processing industry; capacity building, market research relating to exports and development of infrastructure; export trade and agriculture-oriented activities of institutions and bodies both in the public and private sector.	0.75% of value of non-petroleum commercial imports. 10% of net divestiture proceeds Parliamentary approvals; recovered loans and interest payments
Fostering the development of SMEs equity funding	
The NEIP Greenhouse Estate Project is the largest greenhouse estate in Africa, which has installed 75 greenhouse domes at the Dawhenya irrigation site in the Greater Accra Region to produce fruits and vegetables in a controlled environment; the national entrepreneurship and innovations fund (NEIF) is special purpose vehicle (SPV) targeting start-ups. An established marketplace where freelance talent can be tapped into projects, e.g., web designers, graphic designers, Digital Marketers, Writers and Proof Readers, Video Editors; local services provide a platform to make it easier to find trusted local services providers such as plumbers, electricians, air-condition technicians and architects; the formation of the email is an online marketplace to find truly rare but quality handmade products in Ghana	

(Continued)

Name of Initiative and Duration	*Funding Source(s) and Sector*	*Core Objectives*	*Scale and Funding Amount*
The Microfinance and Small Loan Centre (MASLOC) (2006–to date)	Government of Ghana/World Bank	The objective of sustainable poverty reduction by making credit available for the productive poor, especially women, the physically challenged and the youth	Country-wide
Livelihood Empowerment Against Poverty (2008–to date)	Government of Ghana/ UK DFID/UN International Children's Emergency Fund/World Bank National Social Protection Strategy (NSPS)	Social safety net where cash is transferred to targeted extremely poor households and vulnerable groups living below the bottom third of the poverty-line on a medium- to long-term basis	Country-wide
Savannah Accelerated Development Authority (SADA)	Established by an Act of Parliament; SADA Act 805 on 17 September 2010	The agency responsible for coordinating a comprehensive development agenda for the savannah ecological zones ((Northern, Upper East and Upper West and stretches of Brong Ahafo and Volta regions that are contiguous to the Northern region of Ghana)	Limited to the Savannah ecological zones of Ghana

Achievements/Gaps	*Challenges*
Policy reforms that strengthen the microfinance sub-sector for poverty reduction; serving as the administrative wing of government on fiduciary basis; collaborate with bilateral and multilateral development partners on micro and small-scale enterprises' development programmes; complement the work of non-bank microfinance institutions; institutional capacity building of sub-sector actors and carrying out research to inform policy and practice	Subsidized programmes and their poor repayment performance distorted the rural finance market with implications for widening and deepening the rural financial sector; political interference in the form of elite capture, limited capacity in management and programme implementation are key issues the institution has been grappling with over the decades
Beneficiaries are linked to complementary services to make them productive. Also, registered onto the National Health Insurance Scheme so healthcare shocks do not erode benefits	
SADA mandate is to assist in the development of agriculture and industry in the Savannah ecological zone so as to bridge the development gap between the area and the rest of the country. The focus is to coordinate projects, programmes and policies aimed at stimulating growth and addressing the human and social development needs of the area	

(*Continued*)

Name of Initiative and Duration	*Funding Source(s) and Sector*	*Core Objectives*	*Scale and Funding Amount*
Northern Rural Growth Programme (2007–2015)	Government of Ghana/ AfDB funded. Project was consistent with the millennium development goals (MDGs) and the NEPAD's comprehensive African agricultural development Programme (CAADP)	The overall goal is to contribute to an equitable and sustainable poverty reduction and food security among rural households (especially women and other vulnerable groups) living on marginal lands, via agricultural and rural livelihoods in northern Ghana	Limited to the three northern savannah regions. Total project costs US$103.55 million
The Food and Agricultural Sector Development Policy (FASDEP)/ the Medium-Term Agricultural Sector Investment Plan (METASIP) (2009–2015)	Government of Ghana	Overall objective is the achievement of a target agricultural GDP growth of at least 6% annually, halving poverty by 2015 in line with then MDG 1 and based on government expenditure allocation in the national budget of at least 10% within the Plan's period (2011–2015)	Country-wide
A Tiered Regulatory Environment (2011–to date)	Government/Bank of Ghana	Overall goal is to take care of the different needs and segments of the population served	Country-wide
Rural Finance Support Project (RFSP) (2002–2008)	Co-financed by IFAD, the World Bank and the African Development Bank (AfDB)	Complement government efforts in reducing poverty by broadening access to rural finance	Country-wide but sub-sector specific at the macro, meso and micro level

Achievements/Gaps	*Challenges*
NGRP has strengthened linkages among the various actors in agricultural value chains – including producers and their organizations, suppliers, service providers, financial institutions, aggregators, 'off-takers' (such as processors, traders and exporters), researchers and administrators. Several private-public partnership arrangements are supported to ensure smallholders' access to finance and markets. Technical assistance and institutional support, as well as investments in productive infrastructure and technology, have been provided	
METASIP fell in line with the ECOWAS agriculture policy and NEPAD's comprehensive Africa agriculture development programme (ECOWAP/CAADP), which provided an integrated framework to support agricultural growth, rural development and food security in the African region. As an outcome of the consultative, technical and budgetary process, METASIP identified results and resource requirements and roles that the stakeholders in the sector should play. It considered ongoing projects and adopted the sector-wide approach (SWAp) in its implementation, bringing on board sector stakeholders' ineffective coordination and participation.	
The tiered regulatory environment facilitated the development of the microfinance sub-sector, targeting different populations and sectors of the economy. The tiered approach to external regulation also takes into account the different categories and types of MFIs	
Was consistent with national policies, IFAD's country strategy and rural finance policy, and national micro and rural finance development needs. It covered micro, meso and macro aspects of the financial sectors and emphasized the development of sustainable financial institutions	Linkages between informal and formal financial institutions did not consider the Ghanaian context and the project design did not articulate coordination with other IFAD interventions in Ghana that could have benefited from enhanced access to rural financial services

(*Continued*)

Name of Initiative and Duration	*Funding Source(s) and Sector*	*Core Objectives*	*Scale and Funding Amount*
The Rural Financial Services Project (RAFiP) (2010–2016)	Government of Ghana, the Italian Government and IFAD	Provide poor rural people and smallholder farmers with improved access to financial services, technical assistance and risk management instruments in collaboration with rural finance institutions for sustainable livelihoods particularly women and young people	Country-wide. Total project costs: US$41.86 million
The Social Investment Fund (SIF) Project (1998–to date)	Established by the Government of Ghana in 1998 under the Companies Code 1963 (ACT 179) supported by the AfDB/UNDP / OPEC Fund for International Development	Provide a rapid, reliable and flexible mechanism for channelling resources for delivering targeted assistance to impoverished urban and rural communities. Economic and social infrastructure investments that improve access by the poor	Country-wide

Achievements/Gaps	*Challenges*
As RAFiP partners, Ghana's rural microfinance institutions (MFIs) have so far demonstrated an enhanced capacity to support an inclusive rural finance environment. RAFiP promotes product development and innovation in the microfinance sector, and tailor-made financial approaches, products and services that address specific needs of the rural poor have been rolled out. The wider rural financial system institutional performance, public outreach and client orientation are been enhanced considerably via capacity building in institutional processes and human resources; financial and agricultural linkages and support systems; policy, regulation, supervision and monitoring; and knowledge development and dissemination among and between stakeholders in the sub-sector	
SIF employs effective institutional collaborations and cooperation with both private and government institutions to objectively target beneficiaries and gender mainstreaming in order to create opportunities for the poor and vulnerable, e.g., SIF has already completed a consultancy assignment for the Ministry of Water Resource, Works and Housing on the Establishment of Baseline Data for the Measurement of Capacity Development.	
Facilitated credit investment and agriculturally oriented financing in partnership with strategic investors and Partner Financial Institution for small- medium- and large-scale enterprises (SMiLEs) in northern Ghana. Through the FinGAP 5-year Programme funded by USAID funded initiative.	
It improves the capacity of microfinance institutions and local governance structures, as well as community-based organizations (CBOs) and non-governmental organizations (NGOs), to improve the livelihoods of vulnerable groups in hard-to-reach areas	

(*Continued*)

Name of Initiative and Duration	*Funding Source(s) and Sector*	*Core Objectives*	*Scale and Funding Amount*
IFAD Land Conservation and Smallholder Farmer Project (LACOSREP) (1990–1996)	IFAD; GoG; WFP	The overall objective of LASCOSREP was to increase farm household income of the rural poor while protecting the environment and improving access to water. Potential health hazards of irrigation, such as malaria, bilharzia and other water-borne diseases, were also addressed by the project	Limited to the North-Eastern Ghana (the Upper East Region) US$15.04 million
IFAD Upper West Agricultural Development Project (UWADEP) (1995–2005)	IFAD; GoG	The overall goal was to improve food security and increase the income of smallholders	Limited to North-western Ghana (the Upper West Region). Total project costs US$11.3 million. Supervised: the united nations office for project services (UNOPS)

Achievements/Gaps	*Challenges*
The project addressed the broad challenges of high and expanding rural populations; the increasingly unreliable rainfall patterns, aggravated by climate change and variability; the worsening low adaptive capacity of farm households by providing and improving irrigation facilities, other infrastructure, services, marketing outlets, cottage industries, agro-processing and traditional crafts	LACOSREP introduced and promoted the cultivation of improved maize, millet and soybean varieties, currently prevalent in the region; helped farmers control pest outbreaks threatening sorghum, millet, maize, rice and onion, and provided assistance in production techniques and marketing; increased the income of women groups and smallholder farmers by disseminating improved breeds of sheep and goats
The UWADEP project helped build the capacity and strengthened project delivery and management skills of key implementing agencies; expanded water resources development (rehabilitation of dams, formation and support to Water Users' Associations, catchment area protection and promotion of manually operated tube wells); accelerated agricultural development through farmer training and demonstrations, technology generation and research, marketing and processing, and livestock development; and thus increased incomes by increasing access to rural financial services. Rural infrastructure such as roads networks and water and sanitation were also improved	There were omissions in major areas of agricultural production, e.g., tuber cultivation and diversification into higher humidity crops, tree crops and riverside gardens, owing to a transposition of the LACOSREP project design. Training, particularly in animal traction, was emphasized at the expense of implement supply, which farmers wanted. Issues of marketing were not adequately addressed. Agricultural and credit extension were limited as expenditure weighted heavily towards infrastructure

(*Continued*)

Name of Initiative and Duration	*Funding Source(s) and Sector*	*Core Objectives*	*Scale and Funding Amount*
Upper Region Agricultural Development Project (URADEP) (1976/77–1980/81)	IFAD; GoG	Two principal objectives: (1) to increase agricultural production and farm incomes; (2) to establish permanent farmer support services	Limited to Northeast and Northwest (present Upper East and West Regions) US$21 million
Northern Region Poverty Reduction Programme (2001–2009)		The overall objective was to strengthen government institutions and promote a more participatory approach to local development in Ghana's northern region	Northern Region Total project cost: US$59.58 million
IFAD Ghana Agriculture Sector Investment Programme (GASIP) (2014–2020)	IFAD; GoG Credit and Financial Services	Provide an institutional framework that facilitates long-term private sector investments in pro-poor agricultural value chains in Ghana	Country-wide US$112.99 million

Achievements/Gaps	*Challenges*
Expanded farm development through the establishment of service centres, farm input and improved on-farm grain storage provisions, better animal health services and improved animal husbandry, applied research and demonstration units, pilot functional literacy scheme, expanded Ghana Broadcasting Corporation's facilities, and improved the nutrition and health of the population; expanded the physical infrastructure by constructing and rehabilitating existing dams and village wells and two cotton ginneries; institutional support such as the establishment of the Farmers Services Company (UR) Ltd, the regional branch of the agricultural development bank (ADB), and the upper regional development corporation (URDECO), particularly its transport and wholesale divisions	Subsidies in both inputs and production placed a greater fiscal burden on government; the policies generally favoured large-scale farmers; subsidy structure distorted market prices and sustained economically and financially nonviable farms
Improved community awareness; empowered and built the capacity of institutions; improved sustainable agricultural development; increased rural microenterprise and financial support services and upgraded village-level community infrastructure	
Build on four strategic prongs, GASIP works to build a win-win nationwide smallholder farmer and agribusinesses networks; scale up successful investments approaches in agricultural value chains, mainstream climate change resilience, which is funded the adaptation for smallholder agriculture programme (ASAP); and target specific policies and knowledge management strategies among vulnerable food crop farmers and value chains such as cassava, yam, maize, sorghum, fruits and vegetables value chains based on market, demand, technical and commercial viability, and the potential for private-sector investment for income growth of target groups – smallholder farmers and resource-poor rural households, in particular women, young people (15–24 years of age) and young adults (25–34 years of age)	

(*Continued*)

Name of Initiative and Duration	*Funding Source(s) and Sector*	*Core Objectives*	*Scale and Funding Amount*
Rural Enterprises Programme (Crépon et al.) 2011–2019	IFAD, GoG and AfDB Credit and Financial Services	The overall programme objective is to boost and improve the livelihoods of micro and small entrepreneurs by increasing the number of rural enterprises that generate profit, growth and employment opportunities	Country-wide. Total costs: US$225.13 million
The Ghana Luxembourg Social Trust project (GLST) was a 5-year technical Cooperation Project	International labour organization (ILO) and the Government of Ghana	Aims to provide health insurance and pension coverage, such that evidence of the impact of cash transfers on maternal and child health status of vulnerable populations can be gathered	Funding from the OGB-LONG Solidarité Syndicale to pregnant women and mothers with young children from vulnerable households in Ghana. Limited to the Dangme West District
(ASAP) (Start Date:2012–End Date: Multi-year and Multi-donor)		With the ministry of food and agriculture (MOFA) as the implementing agency, the project aimed at increasing resilience and profitability of participating smallholder farmers in the wake of climate change and variability	Government of the Republic of Ghana (GoG) and the international fund for agricultural development (IFAD)

Achievements/Gaps	*Challenges*
Programme is mainstreamed within the public and private institutional system across Ghana and designed to improve the target population's access to business development services, appropriate technology and skills, and financial services. REP has created an institutional, regulatory and policy environment for the growth of rural micro and small enterprises	
Transfers' beneficiaries also access reproductive and child health-related services from designated health facilities. Expanded access to services such as pre-natal and post-natal services; safe delivery; birth registration of new-borns; immunizations; periodic health checks; and compulsory registration on the National health insurance scheme (NHIS). Over a 3-year period, between 3,000 and 4,000 poor people in the Dangme West district will benefit from a 75% subsidy on their health insurance premiums. It is a long-term partnership expected to be extended to the rest of the country as part of the National Social Protection Strategy as more donors from Luxembourg are mobilized	
In the three northern regions, adaptive trials of modern conservation agricultural techniques under rain-fed conditions were carried out with farmers for subsequent commercialization. Systematic integration of IFAD climate resilience programmes into its overall portfolio. ASAP funding was in line with the agricultural sector improvement programme (ASIP) focused in areas with low adaptive capacity, but considerable exposure to climate risks. ASIP basically focus on addressing the effects of dry spells, drought and land degradation issues working with nucleus farmers, farmer-based organizations and with specialist farm service providers to adopt and adapt conservation farming technologies to local conditions. Maximizing farm output for improve food and income security underpinned the ASIP programme.	

(*Continued*)

Name of Initiative and Duration	*Funding Source(s) and Sector*	*Core Objectives*	*Scale and Funding Amount*
IFAD Agribusiness Systems International (ASI), Agricultural Value Chain Mobile Finance (AgFin) Project and the Smallholder Financial Inclusion (SFIN)	IFAD; agribusiness systems international (ASI), relevant government agencies and in partnership with Open Revolution – a cross-border entity with specialty in launching and scaling-up mobile money platforms	To expand mobile money transfers in rural communities with improved financial literacy by smallholders via sourcing and payment systems and leverage new mobile technologies and private partnerships to improve savings and investments abilities of smallholder farmers in the three northern regions of Ghana	Funded by IFAD and implemented by the Agribusiness Systems International with Mobile Network Operator Tigo Cash and Open Revolution
Government of Ghana and Bilateral Development Partner Initiatives for Financial Inclusion and Poverty Reduction			
The Deutsche Gesellschaft für Internationale Zusammenarbeit (GIZ) GmbH or GIZ (English: German Corporation for International Cooperation GmbH (GIZ))	GoG/GTZ	Improving small and medium-sized enterprises' access to financial services and boosting job creation by targeting high-performance structures such as mobile banking or deposit insurance systems	

Achievements/Gaps	*Challenges*
Payments deposited directly into farmers' mobile wallets mitigating the risks of robbery associated with cash payments. The privacy, efficiency and accountability of mobile money transfers (MMT) were valued especially by women farmers. From the previous Rice Mobile Finance (RiMFin), other services added to farmers' mobile wallets included payments of utility bills, insurance premiums and loan repayment. The AgFin project has so far scaled out RiMFin's MMT successes to different groups and value chains, including the smallholder financial inclusion (SFIN) project. SFIN with funding from the alliance for a green revolution in Africa (AGRA) financial inclusion for smallholder farmers in africa project (FISFAP) leverages new mobile technologies and private partnerships to improve savings and investment abilities of smallholder farmers in the three northern regions of Ghana	Limited in scale
MFIs facilitated to access debt and equity funding for product diversification increased outreach and improved capacity to comply with guidelines of Responsible Finance. Ghana's cashless payment system supported with the 'E-zwich' to facilitate access to the formal financial system has reduced costs of entrepreneurial activity. The introduction of deposit insurance system boosted confidence in banks and shifted informal savings to regulated savings; it expanded employability skills of most business and professional lines along value chains, e.g., maize, citrus fruits, mangoes and pineapples through its market-oriented agriculture programme (MOAP). Established farmer business schools for the cashew, cotton and cocoa value chains are also supported in collaboration with the European Union and the Bill and Melinda Gates Foundation through trainings in farmer business schools	The Deutsche gesellschaft für internationale zusammenarbeit (GIZ) GmbH or GIZ (English: German corporation for international cooperation GmbH (GIZ))

(*Continued*)

Name of Initiative and Duration	*Funding Source(s) and Sector*	*Core Objectives*	*Scale and Funding Amount*
DFID Market Development in Northern Ghana (MADE) (2013–2020)	GOG/UK GOV	Objective leveraging markets for the development of selected agricultural value chains for the improvement of livelihoods by producers and marketers	Three northern regions
DFID Ghana Business Enabling Environment Programme (BEEP) (2015–2018)	GOG/UK GOV	Provide research outcomes to support public-private dialogue (PPD) to implement reforms for the improvement of private sector investment to create economic opportunities for the poor population	Country-wide
The Support Programme for Enterprise Empowerment and Development (SPEED I and SPEED II) October 2006–June 2010	GoG/GTZ/ DANIDA	Micro-enterprises and SME (MSME) have improved access to adequate and demand-oriented financial and non-financial services. An increased effort to coordinate, harmonize and streamline existing Danish and German support to private sector development (PSD) in Ghana	Country-wide
Ghana Private Sector Development Fund (GPSDF): Phase I (2004–2007) and Phase II (2007–2040)	GoG and the Italian government	Promotion of private sector development	Country-wide EUR 33 million
The Japanese Non-Project Type Grant	Government of Japan; MoFEP; Crown Agents	Promote the expansion of Small and Medium Enterprises (SMEs) in Ghana by importing Japanese capital goods	

Achievements/Gaps	*Challenges*
Exclusively in the Northern Savannah Economic Zone supporting the generation of sustainable incomes of smallholder farmers made resilient with sharpened entrepreneurial skills taking advantage of markets to improve incomes and food security	
Strengthen capacities of institutions of government to enact and implement reforms that reduce the time and cost of doing business in Ghana	
Focused on private sector development. The coordination, harmonization and streamlining of existing Danish and German government projects for private sector development (PSD) and balancing the social and geographical development of micro, small and medium enterprises (MSMEs) through market-oriented financial and non-financial business support instruments. Increased MSMEs' sector assets by boosting the rate of turnover and market interlinkages. Implemented in three phases, the project had three components, namely: technical assistance to microfinance institutions; a wholesale funding facility and a business development services	
It supported the economic and structural adjustment efforts of the Government of Ghana through the importation of Japanese capital goods for the expansion of Small and Medium Enterprises (SMEs) in manufacturing, services and production sectors in Ghana.	

(Continued)

Name of Initiative and Duration	*Funding Source(s) and Sector*	*Core Objectives*	*Scale and Funding Amount*
Private Enterprises and Export Development (PEEP) Project	The GoG; the International Development Association (Hollis and Sweetman)	Promote non-traditional exports by making export credits available through the banking systems to non-traditional exporters	IDA and GoG
Financing Ghanaian Agriculture Project (USAID- FinGAP)	A 5-year USAID-funded initiative implemented by CARANA Corporation of USA. FinGAP addresses key constraints restricting development of commercial agriculture and thus food security in Ghana	Supported by Feed the Future, USAID-FinGAP provides a comprehensive and integrated approach to financing actors and increasing competitiveness in the maize, rice and soy value chains in northern Ghana	

Achievements/Gaps	*Challenges*
The two categories: short-term credits in foreign exchange or cedis accessed via participating banks are repayable within a year; and the term loan facility is medium term and repayable over 5 years with up to a year's moratorium, thereby expanding the production and increasing export volumes of non-traditional exports such as bananas	
Through incentives, training and technical assistance, FinGAP builds the capacity of financial institutions (FIs) and Business Advisory Services (Basu) providers to facilitate private finance and investment to thousands of micro, small, medium, including large enterprises (SMiLEs) in the target value chains.	
FIs and BAS providers are reducing loan processing time, increasing the likelihood that funds are approved, and building trust and cooperation between actors, enabling the financial sector to engage more deeply in agriculture.	
Under the Partnership for Growth mandate, the capacity of Ghana's Securities and Exchange Commission and the Ghana Alternative Stock Exchange are strengthened to improve regulation, supervision and enforcement to minimize risks and to facilitate small, medium and large-scale enterprises (SMiLE listings) so as to expand alternative sources of financing to actors in the target value chains.	
Specifically, 25 strategic partnerships within target value chains; 250 transactions developed by project advisors and business advisory Support providers; $75 million in finance at an average transaction size of $200,000; and 80 SMEs and farmer organizations linked to 120,000 smallholder farmers in target value chains gaining access to finance	
Hords Ltd listed on the Ghana Stock Exchange with support of FinGAP; introduction of smart subsidies expanded rural agribusiness finance; successfully organized the Ghana Agribusiness Investment Summit in 2014	

(*Continued*)

Name of Initiative and Duration	*Funding Source(s) and Sector*	*Core Objectives*	*Scale and Funding Amount*
Non-Governmental Organization Initiatives for Financial Inclusion and Poverty Reduction			
Financial Non-Governmental Organizations (FNGOs) (1980s–to date)	Financial NGOs took roots in the 1980s during the implementation of the Economic Recovery Programme when it was thought of as an alternative to provide financial and non-financial services for poverty reduction	Dissemination of financial and non-financial services in collaboration with relevant government agencies to improve livelihoods and reduce poverty	Various donors and government agencies. FNGOs are excluded from mobilizing savings from the public and therefore rely on external funding sources for their operations
Responsible finance through local leadership in sub-Saharan Africa	SEEP Network Four-year partnership to improve management capacity of microfinance associations, advance financial transparency and promote consumer protection through strong local leadership	Support greater consumer protection and financial transparency as the industry increasingly adopts the financial systems approach in scale and commercialization	Country-wide funding from the SEEP Network and The MasterCard Foundation
The Credit Union Association of Ghana (CUAG)	Umbrella organization of all credit unions in Ghana. Founded in 1968, the CUAG is affiliated with the African confederation of co-operative savings and credit association (ACCOSCA) and the world council of credit unions (WOCCU); BoG	The credit union association of Ghana (CUAG) regulate and supervise all the credit unions in the country on behalf of the Bank of Ghana and other interested groups	Country-wide funding from membership fees of more than 455 member unions as of 2014

Achievements/Gaps	*Challenges*
The association of financial non-governmental organizations (ASSFIN), the apex body of all FNGOs, is registered as a private voluntary organization in the development and regulates the activities of member entities. FNGOs are part of the semi-formal providers that are broadening access to financial products and services for the marginalized, unserved and underserved populations, mostly in hard-to-reach areas.	
Examples of FNGOs operating in the northern savannah belt include Empretec Ghana Foundation; the centre for agriculture and rural development (CARD); Grameen Ghana; Maata-n-Tudu; Simplipong; Send Fingo; Urban Agric Network; Ghana developing communities association (GDCA) and GNADO	
Market research, developed diagnostic tools for consumer protection, national code of conduct, credit information sharing forum, developed complaints system, national database, and reporting platform, NCAT for the seven-member associations and internal capacity strengthening and restructuring	
Pro-poor lending models with one of the lowest interest rates on loans in the microfinance market	

(*Continued*)

Name of Initiative and Duration	*Funding Source(s) and Sector*	*Core Objectives*	*Scale and Funding Amount*
Microcredit Association of Ghana	Apex body of microcrediting companies and individuals registered under the Companies Code 1963 (Act 179), and limited by guarantee to provide financial and non-financial services; BoG	It serves as a platform for members and other stakeholders to network and develop professional skills. It lobbies government, development partners and regulatory bodies and influences policies, capacity building, monitoring and regulation of member activities to ensure responsible financial services and impact positively the social and economic development of sustainable businesses and livelihoods	Membership fees
Ghana Cooperative Susu Collectors Association (GCSCA) (1994–to date)	Apex organization of Susu collectors in Ghana; BoG	It monitors, supervises and regulates member activities in line with set industry standards and the national prudential and regulatory frameworks with the objective of protecting service providers, users and public	Members fees from a social investment fund (SIF)
Ghana Association of Savings and Loans Companies (GHASALC) (2008–to date)	The apex body of savings and loans companies registered under the Companies Code 1963 (Act 179) and limited by guarantee (non-profits) licence by BoG	The primary objective is to serve as a platform for networking and sharing of experiences, knowledge and best practices	Fees for services, membership fees and grants

Achievements/Gaps	*Challenges*
According to an IFAD study (IFAD, 2008), formal financial service providers such as commercial banks represented about 40% of the money supply in the overall financial sector. The remaining amount (i.e., 60%) was believed to be outside the formal system and mainly in rural areas (Nair and Fissah, 2010)	
Most commercial banks and non-banking financial institutions (NBFIs) have adopted the susu model and many have linked up with informal providers with positive effects on formal bank deposits and improved outreach indices.	
The Bank of Ghana has in the past collaborated with the german development corporation (GIZ), via the rural and agriculture finance programme (RAFiP), to develop prudential reporting templates for susu operators that effectively capture monthly operational information on their businesses. The Association was also supported by the Bank of Ghana to establish a social investment fund (SIF), where licence operators contribute monthly from their interest mark-ups and the pool serves as a primary reserve and an insurance cover against industry risks and uncertainties	
As a consultative body, GHASLC has collective negotiation and bargaining rights and acts to improve information sharing and transparency through public education on the activities of the savings and loans companies	

(*Continued*)

Name of Initiative and Duration	*Funding Source(s) and Sector*	*Core Objectives*	*Scale and Funding Amount*
The Ghana Micro-Finance Institutions Network (GHAMFIN) (1998–to date)	Legally registered in August 1998 as a company limited by guarantee made up of a network of institutions of different sizes and legal structures such as commercial banks, savings and loan institutions, NGOs, cooperative, rural banks and traditional 'Susu' savings clubs	It collaborates with government and donor organizations in Ghana, particularly in the area of policy change activities and implementation of capacity building and institutional strengthening programmes, e.g., MicroStart (UNDP/AfDB), and the Social Investment Fund	GoG; donor agencies; NGOs
SEEP Network	The SEEP Network (The Small Enterprise Education and Promotion Network) founded in 1985. The SEEP Network since then has developed into a global learning community of 124 member organizations	The SEEP Network is a non-profit organization that acts as a network for practitioners working in microenterprise development and microfinance for poverty reduction via financial systems and inclusive market developments	Funding sources: Bill and Melinda Gates Foundation, Ford Foundation, Citi Foundation, USAID and Omidyar Network

Achievements/Gaps	*Challenges*
GHAMFIN's major contractors are the Government of Ghana, the World Bank, the USAID, IFAD, GTZ and Care International. It receives funding from the WWB/UNDP regional programme to build microfinance networks in Africa. Total network membership is 2,287. It presents a common platform for varied providers; advocacy issues, e.g., microfinance with MoFEP and BoG; capacity building and performance monitoring; promotion of transparency and social performance management	
SEEP documents and gathers the experience of practitioners through its Working Groups, made up of self-selected individuals, through whom SEEP members engage in participatory research, applied learning, documentation and training. Research accumulated through the Working Groups – Poverty Outreach Working Group, Social Performance Working Group, Consumer Protection Working Group and Market Facilitation Initiative – is disseminated through publications, training tools, conferences and SEEP Communities of Practice for collaboration on areas of shared interest. For instance, the SEEP Youth and Financial Services Working Group explores practical solutions to challenges in the microfinance and microenterprise sectors and share experiences to help deepen access and usage of sustainable financial and non-financial products and services for the youth; SEEP-specific initiatives in Ghana include the responsible finance through local leadership (RFLL) programme, a multi-stakeholder dialogue for information sharing on the integration of the microfinance sector into the credit information market and structures; the SEEP Network also collaborates others such MasterCard Foundation, the Rural and Agricultural Finance Project and the Ghana Microfinance Institutions	

(Continued)

Name of Initiative and Duration	*Funding Source(s) and Sector*	*Core Objectives*	*Scale and Funding Amount*
Microfinance Information Exchange (MIX)	Founded by the consultative group to assist the poor (CGAP), MIX comprised MIX Market and the Micro-Banking Bulletin	It provides data, analytics and insight to empower decision-makers to build an inclusive financial services eco-system for low-income populations globally. It promotes transparency through a detailed cataloguing of industry players' financial and social performances	Funded by the Citi Foundation, CGAP, The MasterCard Foundation, MetLife Foundation and others

Achievements/Gaps	*Challenges*
Network on projects; worked on the Shea Economic Empowerment programme that sought to restructure shea butter supply chains build capacity of producers; introduced new production technologies geared towards the development of trade hubs, storage and distribution networks, training production and business management, financial literacy and multiple stakeholder engagement for sustainable supply chains.	
The SEEP Network also develops products targeted at partners and microfinance institutions (MFIs) to streamline standards in financial reporting frameworks for a diverse and growing industry. This culminated in many training workshops organized by GHAMFIN in Ghana where microfinance information exchange (MIX) staff trained partner institutions to improve reporting capacity and standards needed and used by stakeholders	
Policymakers, regulators, microfinance institutions, donors, investors, networks and service providers associated with the industry accessed data and information through MIX Market and the MicroBanking Bulletin for informed decision-making. In 2016, MIX Market reported that 774 financial service providers (FSPs) worldwide extended microcredit to 115 million borrowers with a total gross loan portfolio of US$96.6 billion. Savings reached 98.8 million depositors with a combined US$64.0 billion in absolute terms. The figures represented an annual growth rate of 11.1% for loans and 9.8% for borrowers. In the same year, the weighted average portfolio at risk of > 30 days (i.e., PAR > 30) rose from 5.3% in 2015 to 7.2% in 2016 due to several regional challenges witnessed in the sector, particularly in Africa, Eastern Europe and Central Asia.	
In Ghana, Mix Market reported an aggregate of 289,500 active borrowers in 2016. While 144,900 were rural borrowers, 113,100 were made-up urban borrowers with a combined gross loan portfolio (GLP) of US$427.3 million. Women borrowers were approximately 75%. Also, the number of total depositors stood at 2,013,000, with combined total deposits of US$760.8 million. It's worth noting that the average deposit balance per depositor fell from US$406 in 2015 to US$378 in 2016 (MIX, 2016)	

(*Continued*)

Name of Initiative and Duration	*Funding Source(s) and Sector*	*Core Objectives*	*Scale and Funding Amount*
CGAP	Composed of 34 partner organizations working to increase financial inclusion for marginalized and low-income populations globally	The overall goal is to improve the lives of poor people by spurring innovations and advancing knowledge and solutions that promote responsible, sustainable, inclusive financial markets	GOG; private foundations; bilateral donors (USAID, DFID); multilateral donors (UN agencies, World Bank, AfDB Asia Development Bank); and development finance institutions (DFIs) such as the international finance corporation (IFC) and KfW
MasterCard Foundation Financial Inclusion Programme (2006–to date)	A global foundation established by Mastercard in 2006	The foundation works to improve educational experiences and access to financial services and programmes by the poor in the Global South. Working with financial service providers, the foundation seeks to expand financial inclusion to low-income households and populations, particularly in rural and remote areas	US$2 billion endowment fund

Achievements/Gaps	*Challenges*
In Ghana, CGAP have collaborated with the Ghana insurance commission (NIC) and the german development cooperation (GIZ) in expanding micro-insurance coverage in the predominantly informal sector. The launch of the Micro-insurance Market Conduct Rules in 2013 testified to this collaboration. Three mobile network operators MTN, Tigo and Vodafone – are currently offering insurance products. In the loyalty schemes, consumers of the network airtime obtain free insurance policies at certain thresholds. The fully paid schemes involve customers buying insurance policies via their airtime or mobile money and/or a combination of both. With limited business and operational models of micro-insurance products, these innovations are expanding outreach. A countrywide study of the mobile insurance risk market and the analysis risks to inform the review of the regulatory framework is key to eliminating barriers to entry that allow mutual funds and cooperatives to enter the micro-insurance market to expand outreach and gains	Transparency and consumer protection issues and cost are key challenges where transactions are paperless. The use of electronic texts containing terms and conditions hardly understood by consumers represents a challenge. A breakdown in collaboration between micro-insurance providers and policyholders could have far-reaching implications
By working with providers and experts to build their capacity building through staff training, state-of-the-art management and governance practices, and innovating and testing business models, service providers can improve on outreach indices. Through its flagship MasterCard Foundation Symposium on Financial Inclusion, information is disseminated to stakeholders and global leaders share scalable best practices, advocate for client-centric business practices and share key lessons across the industry worldwide. In Ghana, the foundation through its financial inclusion and skills training partnered with alliance for green revolution in Africa (AGRA) to enable young smallholder farmers to connect with new markets, increasing incomes and creating jobs and other opportunities. The foundation also works with young underprivileged girls providing them with quality education, leadership training and support services	

(*Continued*)

Name of Initiative and Duration	*Funding Source(s) and Sector*	*Core Objectives*	*Scale and Funding Amount*
International Association for Research on Income and Wealth September, 1947	September 1947, in conjunction with a meeting of the International Statistical Institute	It promotes research on financial inclusion	
FinMark Trust	Established in March 2002–to date based in South Africa and the SADC region	It makes financial markets work for the poor, by promoting financial inclusion and regional financial integration	FinMark is funded primarily by UKaid from DFID through its Southern Africa office
Centre for Financial Inclusion at Accion	Created in November 2008 by ACCION: we seek a world in which people have the financial ability to improve their lives	It engages through foras, research, publications and campaigns on financial inclusion	Accion, CGAP, MasterCard Foundation

Achievements/Gaps	*Challenges*
The IARIW has been instrumental in developing the important techniques in national income and national budgeting that had been implemented in a number of countries during the Second World War and the immediate postwar period.	
It conducts FinScope demand and supply surveys such as the creation and analysis of financial services from consumer data that supply in-depth insights on both the served and unserved populations across the developing world and the systematic programmes that promote financial inclusion and deepening so as to overcome regulatory, supplier and other market-level barriers to financial inclusion	
The center for financial inclusion at accion (CFI) is an action-oriented think tank that engages and challenges the industry to better serve, protect and empower clients. Programmes include: the Africa Board Fellowship connects board members and CEOs through peer learning and exchange to strengthen the governance of financial institutions serving low-income clients in sub-Saharan Africa; the Africa Board Fellowship; the CFI Fellows Programme was launched in July 2015 to encourage independent researchers and analysts to systematically examine some of the most important challenges in financial inclusion; financial capability promotes behaviourally informed interventions aimed at financial knowledge transfer from the classroom and is paired with well-designed products. This approach takes into account behavioural biases as well as cultural factors; investing in inclusive finance – explores the challenges and opportunities associated with the intersection of financial inclusion and commercial investment; mainstreaming financial inclusion – an initiative to facilitate learning and action on how mainstream financial institutions around the world can reach underserved populations with quality financial services; and the Smart Campaign works globally to create an environment in which financial services are delivered safely and responsibly to low-income clients	

(*Continued*)

Name of Initiative and Duration	*Funding Source(s) and Sector*	*Core Objectives*	*Scale and Funding Amount*
Gates Foundation	The Bill & Melinda Gates Foundation launched in 2000 and Seattle, Washington, United States	Generally, it works to help all people lead healthy, productive lives. It promotes low-cost digital payment systems, digital financial services, global partnerships and research and innovation	Bill and Melinda Gates Foundation
Private Sector Initiatives for Financial Inclusion and Poverty Reduction			
KfW formerly Bankengruppe	A development bank of the German government, based in Frankfurt, has collaborated with the german development cooperation (GIZ) and the Government of the Republic of Ghana in the agricultural sector development	The development of the agricultural sector for job creation and food and income security since the 1970s	German government
Microfinance Investment Vehicles	MIVs are pooled investments that target the microfinance sector. IFIs and private investors provide MIVs with the bulk of their funding. They range anywhere from direct investment in individual MFIs to investments in other MIVs	Through MIVs some MFIs have scaled-up operations and increased their financial and social impacts. MIVs act as conduits between capital markets and MFIs where debt, equity or a combination of the two is accessed by the latter in emerging and frontier markets. As intermediary investment vehicles, MIVs are growing rapidly in total assets, assets devoted strictly to microfinance and regional funding	Private investors

Achievements/Gaps	*Challenges*
The Gates Foundation is a private foundation founded by Bill and Melinda Gates. Created in 2000, it's the largest private foundation in the United States, holding $38 billion in assets. In developing countries, we focus on improving people's health and giving them the chance to lift themselves out of hunger and extreme poverty. In the United States, we seek to ensure that all people – especially those with the fewest resources – have access to the opportunities they need to succeed in school and life	
Examples of projects supported by KfW on behalf of the German government are the 'Outgrower and Value Chain Fund (OVCF)' that integrates smallholder farmers into commercial agricultural chains through access to medium- and long-term funding. Technical operators (processors, exporters) also have access to this investment funding through contract-based collaborations between the smallholder farmers, agribusinesses and local financial institutions	
The MIV market (private investment funds) was estimated at US$13.5 billion in 2016 and represents a 20% annual market growth rate since 2006. Private institutional investors constituted 52%, while retail investors made up 24% each overtaking public sector funders (20%). Though the consultative group to assist the poor (CGAP) and Symbiotics have collaborated in improving and reporting MIV activities, the practice continues to lag behind capital market standards. The assessment of risk and return profiles as well as the social orientation of individual MIVs is still contentious. In Ghana, MIV equity financing accounted for 1.9% of the global microfinance industry (Symbiotics, 2016)	

(*Continued*)

Name of Initiative and Duration	*Funding Source(s) and Sector*	*Core Objectives*	*Scale and Funding Amount*
Alliance for Financial Inclusion (Imai and Azam) (2008–to date)	Started in 2008 in Bangkok, Thailand, it was officially launched in 2009 in Kenya	It empowers policymakers intending to increase access to quality financial services for the world's poorest populations	Bill and Melinda Gates Foundation; GIZ
BIS/Basel Committee on Banking Supervision (BIS/BCBS) (1974–to date)	It was established by the central bank Governors of the Group of Ten countries at the end of 1974. The BIS has 60 member central banks as of now, representing countries from around the world that together make up about 95% of world GDP	It is primary a global standard setter for the prudential regulation of banks and provides a forum for regular cooperation on banking supervisory matters	Inter-governmental body/funding
Committee on Payment and Settlement Systems (CPSS) (1990–to date)	The committee on payments and market infrastructures (CPMI), formerly the committee on payment and settlement systems (CPSS) until 2014, is made up of the central banks of G10 countries	It provides guidance on regulation of innovations in the payment, settlement and clearing systems and contributes to its efficiency	Inter-governmental body/funding sources

Achievements/Gaps	*Challenges*
A world-leading organization on financial inclusion policy and regulation, the Maya Declaration enables Afi members to set concrete financial inclusion targets; share in-country policy changes and updates; organize the Global Policy Forum, a cardinal event for its membership, e.g., the high-quality financial inclusion data and measurement at the Bank of Ghana-AFI Joint Learning Programme; and constituted the following working groups: consumer empowerment and market conduct (CEMC) Working Group; financial inclusion strategy (FIS) Peer Learning Group; financial inclusion data (FID) Working Group; Proportionate Application of Global Standards (GSP) Working Group; digital financial services (DFS) Working Group; SME finance (SMEF) Working Group	
Principles revised to include microfinance; three main departments: Monetary and Economic Department that undertakes research and analysis to shape the understanding of policy issues concerning central banks, provides committee support, organizes key meetings for the analyses and disseminates statistical information on the international financial system; Banking Department that provides a range of financial services to support central banks in the management of their foreign exchange, gold reserves and investments in the BIS's equity; and the General Secretariat that provides comprehensive corporate services, including human resources, facilities management, security, finance, communications and IT. These departments are further supported by the legal service, as well as the risk management, internal audit and compliance units	
Hosted by the Bank for International Settlements, the CPMI is supervised by the global economy meeting (GEM). It is the global standard setter of most (if not all) financial market infrastructures, including analytical and policy work on issues of payment, clearing and settlement in world financial markets. Little wonder there was the need to revise its charter and mandate and change its name in 2014	

(*Continued*)

Name of Initiative and Duration	*Funding Source(s) and Sector*	*Core Objectives*	*Scale and Funding Amount*
Financial Action Task Force (FATF) (1989–to date)	The Financial Action Task Force (on Money Laundering) (FATF) (in French, Groupe d'action financière (GAFI)) is an inter-governmental organization founded in 1989 on the initiative of the G7	Its overall objective is to develop policies to combat money laundering. In 2001 its mandate was expanded to include terrorism financing. It sets standards and promotes effective legal, regulatory and operational issues that combat money laundering, terrorist financing and other related threats to the international financial system	Inter-governmental body/funding sources
International Association of Deposit Insurers (Azariadis and Stachurski 2005)	The International Association of Deposit Insurers (Azariadis and Stachurski 2005) was formed in May 2002 and currently represents 83 deposit insurers	It contributes to the stability of financial systems by promoting international cooperation in the field of deposit insurance and providing frameworks that guide the establishment of new and enhancing existing deposit insurance systems. It also encourages wide international networks among deposit insurers and other interested parties	IADI is a non-profit organization constituted under Swiss Law and is domiciled at the Bank for International Settlements in Basel, Switzerland

Achievements/Gaps	*Challenges*
Developed series of recommendations is recognized as the international standard for combating money laundering and terrorism financing and the proliferation of weapons of mass destruction; the recommendations then become the basis for a coordinated response to these threats to the integrity of the world financial system. Also, it helps in ensuring a level playing field for all stakeholders. The FATF monitors the implementation of necessary measures of member countries' reviews of money laundering and terrorist financing techniques and counter-measures and promotes the adoption and implementation of appropriate measures globally. In collaboration with other international stakeholders, the FATF works to identify national-level vulnerabilities to protect the international financial system from misuse. The FATF Plenary, the decision-making body, meets three times every year	
It provides training and educational programmes and produces research and guidance on matters related to deposit insurance.	
Its Executive Council has established four council committees, as well as regional committees for Africa, Asia-Pacific, the Caribbean, Eurasia, Europe, Latin America, the Middle East and North Africa, and North America to provide a voice on common interests and issues affecting members in those regions.	
The regional committees also serve as separate forums for sharing information and ideas.	

(*Continued*)

Name of Initiative and Duration	*Funding Source(s) and Sector*	*Core Objectives*	*Scale and Funding Amount*
International Association of Insurance Supervisors (IAIS) (1994–to date)	A voluntary membership organization of insurance supervisors and regulators from more than 200 jurisdictions, constituting 97% of the world's insurance premiums	It contributes to global financial stability by promoting effective and globally consistent supervision of the insurance industry in order to develop and maintain fair, safe and stable insurance markets for the benefit and protection of policyholders	
Global Partnership for Financial Inclusion (GPFI)	An inclusive platform for all G20 countries, interested non-G20 countries and relevant stakeholders to carry forward work on financial inclusion, including implementation of the G20 Financial Inclusion Action Plan, endorsed at the G20 Summit in Seoul	Platform for G20 and stakeholders on financial inclusion	

Achievements/Gaps	*Challenges*
The IADI is supported by five committees established by the by-laws – the Audit and Risk, Budget, Financial Stability, Implementation and Technical Committees – as well as by the Supervisory Forum. Committees may establish subcommittees to help carry out their duties.	
The International Association of Deposit Insurers (Azariadis and Stachurski 2005) and the basel committee on banking supervision (BCBS) issued the Core Principles for Effective Deposit Insurance Systems in June 2009.	
A Compliance Assessment Methodology for the Core Principles was completed in December 2010 and is used as a benchmark for assessing the quality of their deposit insurance systems and for identifying gaps in their deposit insurance practices and measures to address the gaps. The core principles are also used by the international monetary fund (IMF) and the World Bank, in the context of the financial sector assessment Programme (FSAP), to assess the effectiveness of jurisdictions' deposit insurance systems and practices.	
It produces monthly newsletters	
The GPFI's efforts include helping countries put into practice the G20 Principles for Innovative Financial Inclusion, strengthening data for measuring financial inclusion and developing methodologies for countries wishing to set targets.	
The GPFI is the main implementing mechanism of the action plan endorsed by G20 leaders during the Seoul Summit and functions as an inclusive platform for G20 countries, non-G20 countries and relevant stakeholders for peer learning, knowledge sharing, policy advocacy and coordination. It contributes to strengthening coordination and collaboration between various national, regional and international stakeholders. The GPFIs cooperate with the Alliance for Financial Inclusion (Imai and Azam), the consultative group to assist the poor (CGAP) and the international finance corporation (IFC). In 2012, the World Bank Group and the SME Finance Forum joined the GPFI as Implementing Partners. The organization for economic co-operation and development (OECD) also joined the GPFI as Implementing Partner in 2013. In 2014, the Better Than Cash Alliance and the international fund for agricultural development (IFAD) also joined as Implementing Partners	

APPENDIX II

MFIS' CREDIT PRODUCTS AND SERVICES IN THE NORTHERN SAVANNAH

MFI Category	*Name of MFI*	*Name of Credit Product*	*Age (years) Product*	*Product Target Group*	*Activity Expected to Finance*	*Accessed in Group or Individual*
Formal Microfinance Institutions	*Naara Rural Bank*	1. Naara Micro-Credit (NMC)	16	Low-income groups (e.g., women)	Petty trading	Groups
		2. Credit with education	10	Women groups	Trading	Groups
		3. Susu loan	7	Petty traders	Trading	Individual

Product Designed to Help Clients Achieve	*Modified in Last 3 Years?*	*How Clients Are Assessed and Arranged for Access*	*Key Contractual Terms (Repayments)*	*Contract Enforcement Procedures*
access to credit by the excluded (the productive poor)	No	Groups trained by credit officers; appraisal report is produced; manager recommends to loan committee; Loan advanced group activity serves as collateral	Repayment on a monthly basis; group leaders collect individual repayments from members; credit officers go to group leaders or group leaders visit the bank to make collective repayment	Defaulters issued first, second and third demand notices; a report is made to loans recovery committee; bank's lawyer is briefed to pursue legal case against defaulters
	No	Groups trained by credit officer on financial literacy; an appraisal report is produced; the manager recommends to loan committee; approval prioritized/quicker than all others	Repayment is made on a weekly basis. Credit officers visit groups weekly to pick up repayments until principal and interest are recovered	Defaulters issued first, second and third demand notices; a report is made to loans recovery committee; bank's lawyer is briefed to pursue a legal case against defaulters
Expand their businesses	Yes: contract terms altered to improve flexibility for client	Application stating amount and duration for repayment; application appraised by credit officer; bank manager recommends to loan committee for approval or rejection	Monthly repayment schedule; daily susu accumulate to form repayment at end of month	Defaulters issued first, second and third demand notices; a report is made to loans recovery committee; bank's lawyer is briefed to pursue a legal case against defaulters

(*Continued*)

MFI Category	*Name of MFI*	*Name of Credit Product*	*Age (years) Product*	*Product Target Group*	*Activity Expected to Finance*	*Accessed in Group or Individual*
		4. Construction business loan	15	Contractors	Construction activities	Individual
		5. Overdrafts/ business	20	Business owners	Trading and construction	Individual
		6. Salary	36	Salaried workers	Household consumption	Individual
	Builsa Community Bank	Commercial loans	20	Traders and business owners	Buying and selling commercial products	Individual
		Agricultural loans	20	Farmers	Agribusiness (stocking and selling crops and animal produce)	Individual and groups
		Microfinance group loans	20	Business partners (groups)	Groups in farming	Groups

Product Designed to Help Clients Achieve	*Modified in Last 3 Years?*	*How Clients Are Assessed and Arranged for Access*	*Key Contractual Terms (Repayments)*	*Contract Enforcement Procedures*
	Yes: contract terms altered to improve security of loan for provider	Applicant fills out a form stating amount and duration for repayment; provides collateral; collateral and construction sites visited by credit officer and appraisal reports completed; recommendation given to loan committee for approval or rejection	Deductions are made from the account when the contractor is paid to pay off the loan principal and interest	Defaulters issued first, second and third demand notices; a report is made to loans recovery committee; bank's lawyer is briefed to pursue a legal case against defaulters
	No			
Fixed income earners meet their financial obligations	Yes: contract terms to improve the security of the loan	The client fills out loan form; gets employers to endorse; returned form is appraised and reports are written by credit officer; the manager either disapproves or recommends for approval by loan committee	Repayment on a monthly basis; the monthly instalment is deducted from the applicant salary account	Defaulters issued first, second and third demand notices; a report is made to loans recovery committee; bank's lawyer is briefed to pursue legal case against defaulters
Replenishing stocks	No	Application form completed; credit officer appraise; management recommend/approve; board approval	12-month duration facility; 3months grace period; 9 months monthly instalment of interest and principal	Phone calls; physical visitation; first, second, third reminder letters; a court action to recover the loan
Support agribusinesses	No	Application form completed; credit officer appraise; Management recommend/approve; board approval; disbursement	9–12 months duration facility; 4 equal instalments of principal and interest after harvest; 12 months for agric related but not crops	Phone calls; physical visitation; first, second, third reminder letters; a court action to recover the loan
Promote partnerships	No	Application form completed by group; microfinance officer appraise; management recommend/approve; board approval; disbursement	6–9 months duration; bi-weekly repayments during group meetings; bank official pick up repayments	

(*Continued*)

MFI Category	*Name of MFI*	*Name of Credit Product*	*Age (years) Product*	*Product Target Group*	*Activity Expected to Finance*	*Accessed in Group or Individual*
		Susu loans	7	Susu clients	Petty traders	Individual
		Quick/smart loans	20	Al clients	Emergency needs	Individual
		Salary loans	20		Emergency/ household needs	Individual
		Construction loans	20	Contractors and government workers	Professional contractors and persons wishing to construct their own homes	Individual
		Individual non-salaried loan	Over 26	Traders and farmers	Trading and farming	Individual
	BESSFA Rural Bank (Garu	Individual salaried loan	Over 26	Salaried workers	Education, housing, etc.	Individual
		Farming loans	Over 26	Agriculture	Agriculture-related	Groups and individual

Product Designed to Help Clients Achieve	*Modified in Last 3 Years?*	*How Clients Are Assessed and Arranged for Access*	*Key Contractual Terms (Repayments)*	*Contract Enforcement Procedures*
Improve liquidity of petty traders	No	Application letter; amount and duration of repayment stated; credit officer appraise and submit appraisal report; bank manager and general manager review; loan committee approve or reject	6 month-duration facility; monthly instalment of principal and interest	
	No			
A variety of reasons	Yes: to allow non-salary clients access overdraft		12–36 months duration facility	
Allow contractors access funds for projects	No			
Expand businesses and increase profits	No	Must be a customer of the bank for at least 6 months; consistent deposit pattern observed; the minimum balance of 40% of the amount requested as a loan	Monthly repayment of principal and interest for the duration of the loan	Three letters of reminders, at least a month interval each, to pay-up; then the community chief invites customer for dialogue; if the customer fails then court action
Help educate themselves, and their children	No	Must have current/ salary account with the bank; deductions to service loan should not go beyond 40% of net salary	Monthly equal instalment of principal and interest; should not exceed 40% of net salary	
Food crop production for food security in the local area	Yes: insurance component introduced to mitigate risks	Group members are taken through training by credit officers; group members accept group liability conditionality	8–9 months duration; moratorium of 4 months; equal monthly instalment for 4–5 months	

(*Continued*)

MFI Category	*Name of MFI*	*Name of Credit Product*	*Age (years) Product*	*Product Target Group*	*Activity Expected to Finance*	*Accessed in Group or Individual*
		Credit with education loans	7	Women groups	IGAs	Groups
		Overdraft facilities	Over 26	Corporate bodies and individuals having current accounts	IGAs/trades that are profitable with quick turnover	Individual
		Group loans (Trust Bank & Cluster Group Loans)	22	Microbusiness owners	Low-income entrepreneurs	Groups
	SINAPI Aba	Micro-enterprise loans	18	Small and micro-enterprises	Small and micro-entrepreneurs	Individual
		Sinapi festive loan	22	All existing customers	Celebrations of festive seasons	Individual
		Sinapi agro-loans (project)	3	Farmers	Overcome challenges of the agric sector and transform agric	Group and/or individual
		Micro-school loans	15	Private schools		Institutions/ individual
		Tractor loans				Individual
		Susu loans				Individual
		Educational loans				Individual
		Asset loans				Individual
		Home improvement loans				Individual

Product Designed to Help Clients Achieve	*Modified in Last 3 Years?*	*How Clients Are Assessed and Arranged for Access*	*Key Contractual Terms (Repayments)*	*Contract Enforcement Procedures*
Assist women in IGAs to reduce poverty levels	No	Must be women groups; accept group liability conditionality; compulsory 6-week training by credit officers; abide by group by-laws	4–6 months duration; no moratorium; 16 weekly instalments for the 4 months loan and bi-weekly for 24 weeks; and 12 equal instalments if 6 months	
Expand businesses to improve living conditions	No	Must have an account with bank especially checking account; operate with the bank for at least 6 months; show quick turnover	Regular deposit is expected in customer overdraft account until the overdrawn balance is defrayed	
Working capital for low-income entrepreneurs	Yes: to meet clients' needs = what needs	6–10 months duration; pay in groups; 4–10 membership	No collateral required; doorstep delivery of service; group support in form business advisory services	
	To meet BoG policies	5–12 months duration; monthly instalment		
	To meet clients' needs	12-month duration and one-off payment after harvest		
	No	36–50 months duration; monthly instalment		
	No	36-month duration; monthly instalment		
	No			
	No			
	No			
	No			

(*Continued*)

MFI Category	*Name of MFI*	*Name of Credit Product*	*Age (years) Product*	*Product Target Group*	*Activity Expected to Finance*	*Accessed in Group or Individual*
	Navrongo Teachers Credit Union	Long-term loans	20	Farmers; traders; teachers; other salaried workers	Agricultural activities; business capital; school fees; hospitalization costs	Individual
		Loans within savings	11	Traders; teachers	Expansion of business; school fees; food security; rent	Individual
		Soft loans	5	Traders; teachers; other salaried workers		Individual
	Assemblies of CUAGod	Provident loans	9	Farmers	Inputs, e.g., fertilizers	Individual and group
		Agricultural loans	9	Teachers	Education, social events, housing	Individual and group
		Business loans	9	Traders		Individual and group
	Bolgatanga Teachers CUA	Education loan		Teachers Traders		Individual
		Business capital loan	2	Traders		Individual
		Housing loan		Workers		Individual
		Medical (healthcare loan)		Workers Traders		Individual

Product Designed to Help Clients Achieve	*Modified in Last 3 Years?*	*How Clients Are Assessed and Arranged for Access*	*Key Contractual Terms (Repayments)*	*Contract Enforcement Procedures*
Business expansion	No	Consistent savings for at least 6 months; maintain a minimum share capital of 100 cedis; loan amount is always twice as much as savings balance; monthly instalment required; maximum duration of 36 months	Monthly instalment; monthly insurance premium payments for the entire duration of loan; maximum duration of 36 months; interest rate is the proportional duration	A phone call to remind defaulter; issue reminder letter; issue demand letter; re-insurance of the loan if expired; legal action was taken against the defaulter
Educate self and children	No	Maintain a minimum share capital of 100 cedis; loan is a ratio of savings balance; reduced interest rate	The loan amount is proportional to balanced saved; maximum duration of 36 months; lower interest rate than long-term loans (2%); no insurance on loans; monthly instalment	
Emergencies such as hospitalization costs	No	Maintain a minimum share capital of 100 cedis; maximum loan amount cedis 150; one-off payment within a month	The maximum amount of 150 cedis; minimum share value of 100 cedis; one-off payment within a month	
Asset acquisition	Yes: clients now need guarantors	6-month consistent savings; minimum shares of 100 cedis	One-off repayment; monthly	First, second, third reminder letters to defaulting clients; threats of legal action
Input purchase	Yes: clients have to own shares	6-month consistent savings; minimum shares of 100 cedis	One-off repayment; monthly	Same as PL above
Business start-up capital	Yes: clients now have to own shares union	6-month consistent savings; minimum shares of 100 cedis	One-off repayment; monthly	Same as PL above
	No	Birth certificate of child required		
	No			
	No			
	No			

(*Continued*)

MFI Category	*Name of MFI*	*Name of Credit Product*	*Age (years) Product*	*Product Target Group*	*Activity Expected to Finance*	*Accessed in Group or Individual*
		Individual loans	2	All persons (adults)		Individual
		Group loans	1	Groups	Farmers	Group
		Soft loans	Less than 1	Mostly teachers	Salary earners	Individual
	GARU Teachers CUA	Business loan	1			
		Personal loan	1			
		Agri-business loan	1			
	Innovative Microfinance	Group loan	9	Petty traders; retailers; women groups	Petty traders; retailers	Groups
		Community group loan	Less than 1	Rural women	Petty traders; Basketweavers; Sheabutter processors	Groups and individual
		Individual loan	9	Business persons	Retailers; wholesalers; manufacturers; aggregators	Individuals

Product Designed to Help Clients Achieve	*Modified in Last 3 Years?*	*How Clients Are Assessed and Arranged for Access*	*Key Contractual Terms (Repayments)*	*Contract Enforcement Procedures*
	No			
	No			
	No			
		Loan committee meet to assess application using some preset criteria; if approved, loan disbursed	Weekly, fortnightly or monthly instalment; provide a guarantor	
	No	Loan committee meet to assess application using some preset criteria; if approved, loan disbursed	Weekly, fortnightly or monthly instalment; client provide guarantor	
	No	Loan committee meet to assess application using some preset criteria; if approved, loan disbursed	Weekly, fortnightly or monthly instalment; Client provide guarantor	
Easy access (group liability)	No	Type of business considered; business turnover; client commitment to the group; home visitation; members guarantee	4–5 months of duration; members guarantee for each other; collateral of defaulter seized to offset loan	
No collateral required	Yes: to cater for others who do not want group loans	Common interest groups formed; are based in communities; a chain of business assessed; loans given out in groups to individuals who take responsibility for repayment	There is group guarantee for loans disbursed	
Stabilizes cash flows	Yes: Susu to cater for individual savers	Individuals operating an existing business; cash flows are assessed; must provide guarantors (salaried) and collateral (asset or savings)	The client must provide a guarantor agrees to pay if s/he defaults; sign an undertaking agreeing for stocks to be sold to offset loan in default; must have to save with IMF	

(*Continued*)

MFI Category	*Name of MFI*	*Name of Credit Product*	*Age (years) Product*	*Product Target Group*	*Activity Expected to Finance*	*Accessed in Group or Individual*
		Susu loan	9	Adults	Petty traders; retailers; wholesalers	Individual
		Hire purchase	9		Petty traders; retailers	Individual
	BC Bencyn Susu	No Loans offered by Bencyn Susu				
	Tarasum Leverage	Tarasum microloan		Individuals and institutional	Low- to middle-income individuals; institutions	Individual and Institutions
	VSLA Groups			Individual group members	Group members	

Product Designed to Help Clients Achieve	*Modified in Last 3 Years?*	*How Clients Are Assessed and Arranged for Access*	*Key Contractual Terms (Repayments)*	*Contract Enforcement Procedures*
Lower interest rates on loans	No	Be a susu saving client; at least 3 months membership; cash flow assessed; cash collateral and a guarantor provided	Members guarantee for each other	
Provide consumer goods	No	Any individual or group with a reliable income qualifies; asset and purpose assessed; asset not client asset until payment for it completes	Asset not the property of the client until payment is complete	
School fees; funeral expenditures; capital sourcing; building materials	No	1 passport picture; valid ID; a copy of a utility bill; one most recent payslip and bank statements of the client for the past 3 months; a post-dated cheque; present a guarantor/sponsor; any amount exceeding 1,000 requires collateral; the loan cannot exceed 40–60% of salary; 40% if the net salary of the client is 1,000 and 60% if the net is more than 1,000; selected organizations with physical presence and structures such as the board of directors	Loan disbursement is made on the table; loan duration is 1–3 months; cash or cheque subject to rollover with interest charges if the client fails to repay the loan on the scheduled date	In the event of a deliberate breach, the loan beneficiary shall pay 40% interest charges on both principal and accumulated interest; the guarantor liable for repayment of the loan. To minimize default, interest rate is raised high so as to reduce volumes requested; clients apprehensive of interest rates and penalties; others sharing testimonies help
Petty trade;	No	During meetings request is made and depending on how much is in savings	Loan disbursed and recorded; loan duration between 1–3 months	No default

APPENDIX III

MFIS' SAVINGS PRODUCTS AND SERVICES IN THE NORTHERN SAVANNAH

MFI	*MFI Name*	*Insurance Products*				
	Name of	*Product*	*Age (years) of Product Roll Out*	*Insurance Product Target Group*	*Source of Funds for Insurance Product*	*Accessed in Groups or Individuals*
	Buco Bank	Susu savings-linked insurance	1	Petty traders		Individual
	BESSFA Rural Bank	Credit Life		Traders, farmers and others		Individuals and groups
		Bancassurance		Traders, farmers and others		Individuals
		Crop insurance		Traders and farmers in agric-related activities		Individuals and groups
	Naara Rural Bank	Insurance on all loans (various)		All categories		Individuals and groups
	Sinapi Abba	Insurance and welfare schemes (various)		All categories of loans		Individuals and groups

Insurance Product Designed to Help Client Achieve	*Insurance Product Modified in Last 3 Years*	*How Clients Assessed and Arranged for Insurance*	*How Clients Assessed for Claims*	*Breach of Contract Terms*
Support surviving relations by paying off loan or percentage of savings; cultivate importance of micro-insurance	No	Base on risk levels of business; income levels (inflows/outflows and nature of business	Proof of death or accident; proof of valid micro-insurance held	Termination of insurance contract with clients and denial of claims
Settle outstanding loan balance of customers	No	Must be a loan customer; total loan amount; loan duration; instalment amounts	Confirmation letter, e.g., death; medical; repayment schedule	No breach of insurance terms and conditions yet
Support funeral and hospitalization expenses	No	Must be a loan customer; total loan amount; loan duration; instalment amounts	Confirmation letter, e.g., death; valid premium payments	No breach of insurance terms and conditions yet
In the event of crop failure, insurance settles outstanding loan balance to bank	No	Must be a loan customer; total loan amount; loan duration; instalment amounts	Drought/excess rain fall; fire; pest and diseases	No breach of insurance terms and conditions yet
In case of fire or permanent disability or death	No	Must have loan with bank	Investigation of fire, permanent disability or death of the customer with loan	
Client welfare schemes	No			

APPENDIX IV

THE EIGHT FACTORS UNDERPINNING MFIS' PRODUCTS AND SERVICES DESIGN

Product Design Factors	*Sub-design Factors*
Costs of access refer to all the economic costs incurred by a client for accessing financial product(s) from an MFI	Price costs (interest and fees) are the direct cash payments in the form of interest and fees paid by the client to the MFI to access financial products and services.
	Non-cash opportunity costs refer to the time taken off by clients from other income-generating activities (IGAs) to apply and access product/service MFIs. It is a form of transaction costs borne by clients.
	Indirect cash expenses include such cost as transportation costs, costs of documentation, subsistence and taxes (where applicable) borne by clients to access financial product(s) and/or service(s).
	Cost/benefits analysis refers to the overall verdict of the benefits or otherwise of accessing financial product(s) and service(s) from an MFI
Scope is the number of different types of financial products and services (contracts) that are supplied by an MFI. Scope between products is the number of types of different products (e.g., number of loans, deposits, payments and insurance). Scope within products are the variants of the same product (e.g., different loan types) that is supplied by the MFI	Scope at MFI level
	Scope within product (microloans)
	Scope within product (micro-savings)
	Scope within product (micro-insurance)
	Scope within product (micro-payments)
	Able to employ others
	Able to achieve personal goals

Worth describes the willingness to pay in relation to the terms of the financial contract as well as the risk profile, constraints and opportunities available to the client.	Perceptions of MFI factors increasing worth of access Perceptions of MFI factors decreasing worth of access Loan amounts disbursed and worth Duration of repayment (term to maturity) and worth
Loans: worth increases for loans when terms of contracts (amount disbursed, term to maturity and instalment size) match client needs. Deposits: it is the interest paid on deposits and the flexibility of savings	Regular repayment amounts (size of instalment) and worth Interest paid on client deposits and worth Flexibility of client deposit withdrawals and worth Livelihood strategies and worth
Length is the time frame that product(s) and service(s) are targeted at populations. Length is perceived in future terms and hence difficult to gauge and measure	Years of access and livelihood outcomes Clients knowledge of donor support to MFIs Client perceptions of MFI profitability
Depth of outreach in the microfinance livelisystem refers to the value society places on the net gain of a given client. Poverty levels of targeted clients are a good proxy for depth as society would prefer that net gains from programmes should be received by the poor	Preference for women and depth Preference for rural dwellers and depth Preference for the less/no formal education and depth Ethnic minorities and depth Housing and depth Loan Sizes and depth
Breadth of outreach for an MFI is the number of clients that it serves with financial products and services. Budgetary constraints and the unlimited needs and want of the poor make breadth an imperative for analysis	Client perceptions of targeting orientation of MFI and breadth Perceptions of MFI interests' rates and breadth Perceptions of donor partnership and MFIs breadth Perceptions of MFI group products and breadth Perceptions of MFI individual products and breadth
Contract enforcement refers to the mechanisms MFIs use to ensure clients honour their side of the contract agreements in the case of default	Perceptions of MFI contract enforcement mechanisms
Add-ons are additional products or services provided by the MFI or based on the MFI's main product(s) or service(s) that enhance uptake	Perceptions of MFI relations with clients Perceptions of microloans add-ons Perceptions of micro-savings add-ons Perceptions of micro-insurance add-ons Perceptions of payment services add-ons

APPENDIX V

CLIENT RANKED PERCEPTIONS OF THE EIGHT FACTORS OF MFIS' PRODUCT AND SERVICE DESIGN

Definition of Design Facto	*Definition of Design Sub-factor*	*Formal MFI Clients' Perceptions of Design Sub-factor*	*No/ Rank*	*Semi-formal MFI Clients' Perceptions Design Sub-factor*	*N/Rank*	*Informal MFI Client's Perceptions Design Sub-factor*	*No/Rank*
		Perceptions of affordability of interest and fees (*N* = 16)		**Perceptions of affordability of interest and fees (*N* = 22)**		**Perceptions of affordability of interest and fees (*N* = 21)**	
Costs of access refer to all the economic costs incurred by a client for accessing financial product(s) from an MFI	**Price costs (interest and fees)** are the direct cash payments in the form of interest and fees paid by the client to the MFI to access financial products and services	You are made aware before taking product, so it must be moderate for you to be repeating taking loans	8 1st	Price cost (interest rate) moderate compared to others	8 1st	At that moment, there is nothing more important than getting the loan	2 4th
		That is what they (MFIs) must do to stay in business	5 2nd	Price cost lower than other MFIs	6 2nd	Interest paid on loans is agreed/accepted by all the group members	3 3rd
		To help the bank pay interest on people saving and pay interests on loanable funds borrowed	2 3rd	The institution can cover costs and administrative expenses	2 5th	Flexible services	8 1st
		Because the bank know best	2 3rd	Flexible services supersede any interest rates	3 4th	Interest are low to moderate	5 2nd
				I get interest on my savings	3 4th	The interest money comes back to us in the group	1 5th
				Good customer relations	2 5th	Interest is little compared to benefits	

(Continued)

Definition of Design Facto	*Definition of Design Sub-factor*	*Formal MFI Clients' Perceptions of Design Sub-factor*	*No/ Rank*	*Semi-formal MFI Clients' Perceptions Design Sub-factor*	*N/Rank*	*Informal MFI Client's Perceptions Design Sub-factor*	*No/Rank*
				The insurance on loans makes it possible to get help when you have a crisis	3 4th		
				One does not waste time to access the loans	5 3rd		
		Perceptions of unaffordability of interest and fees (*N* = 16)		**Perceptions of unaffordability of interest and fees Clients (*N* = 22)**		**Perceptions of unaffordability of interest and fees (*N* = 21)**	
		Interest paid is very high and you end up using all profits to support loan payment		Interest charged is very high for loans, it can be brought down a bit for us		No reason to be inappropriate	
		Since I save with the bank and that money is also used for other activities, the interest should not be that high		Loan form is costly to clients			

	They are there to serve us the poor ones and should not make extra charges					
Non-cash opportunity costs refer to the time taken off by clients from other income-generating activities (IGAs) to apply and access product/service MFIs. It's a form of transaction costs borne by clients	**Perceptions of the appropriateness of non-cash opportunity cost (N = 16)**		**Perceptions of the appropriateness of non-cash opportunity cost (N = 22)**		**Perceptions of the appropriateness of non-cash opportunity cost (N = 21)**	
	After all, I do get the loan at the end	8 1st	Achieve purpose with loan. That is no money, no business	10 2nd	Loan when needed is more important	2 4th
	Agents come around and not much time is required working with MFI	7 2nd	Benefits are more than whatever I could be doing	7 3rd	I can use loans to invest in my business	7 2nd
	At the end I can use the loan to expand my business/achieve my purpose	5 4th	I don't want armed robbers to take my money, so I go to save	4 4th	It does not require much time	11 1st
	At times like that the only thing important is getting access, all other things are put aside	6 3rd	It does not require much time as agents come around and process simple than commercial banks	18 1st	Since the fellow needs the money it's worth it	3 3rd
			It helps me save money that would have been spent	2 5th		

(*Continued*)

Definition of Design Facto	*Definition of Design Sub-factor*	*Formal MFI Clients' Perceptions of Design Sub-factor*	*No/ Rank*	*Semi-formal MFI Clients' Perceptions Design Sub-factor*	*N/Rank*	*Informal MFI Client's Perceptions Design Sub-factor*	*No/Rank*
		Perceptions of the inappropriateness of non-cash opportunity cost (*N* = 16)		**Perceptions of the inappropriateness of non-cash opportunity cost (*N* = 22)**		**Perceptions of the inappropriateness of non-cash opportunity cost (*N* = 21)**	
		I have no options	3	Affects the loan amount granted and the purpose	3	Takes longer time provide services	2
		Too much time visiting MFI for loan to be approved	4	Affects productivity	2		
		Too much time attending financial literacy trainings	3				
		Processes involved are too long and cause delays	3				
	Indirect cash expenses include such cost as transportation costs, costs of documentation, subsistence and taxes (where	**Perceptions of the appropriateness of indirect cash expenses (*N* = 16)**		**Perceptions of the appropriateness of indirect cash expenses (*N* = 22)**		**Perceptions of the appropriateness indirect cash expenses (*N* = 21)**	
		MFI's agents come around to my workplace, so there are little indirect costs	10	Agents come around so little expenses are made	3	Loan is for a purpose, e.g., expand my business and make profit	2nd 9
				Because one does not waste time at all	2	It is not much members cannot afford	4 3rd

applicable) borne by clients to access to financial product(s) and/or service(s)	Because you need the money at that time, indirect cost does not matter	7	Low costs involve in transport and documentations	6	Loan I get is well invested in my business	4 3rd
	Use loan product to achieve my goal	8	Use products to achieve purpose so indirect costs matter little	4	No walk to the meeting	11 1st
	But because I also get financial advices from the bank as a client	1				
	It's a way the bank also makes money (profit)	3				
	Once you need the product, cost matters not much	1				
	Perceptions of the inappropriateness of indirect cash expenses (*N* = 16)		**Perceptions of the inappropriateness of indirect cash expenses (*N* = 22)**		**Perceptions of the inappropriateness of indirect cash expenses (*N* = 21)**	
	I had to travel several times to the MFI to get the loan and it increased costs to clients	6	It still affects the income status of the client		No response	0
	It goes a long way to affect the amount accessed from the bank indirectly	4	It should be the cost of the bank			
	More transport cost incurred accessing loans and documentation	5				
	Sometimes those charges are high	2				

(Continued)

Definition of Design Facto	*Definition of Design Sub-factor*	*Formal MFI Clients' Perceptions of Design Sub-factor*	*No/ Rank*	*Semi-formal MFI Clients' Perceptions Design Sub-factor*	*N/Rank*	*Informal MFI Client's Perceptions Design Sub-factor*	*No/Rank*
	Cost/benefits analysis refers to the overall verdict of the benefits or otherwise of accessing financial product(s) and service(s) from an MFI	**Perceptions of C/B analysis (positives)**		**Perceptions of C/B analysis (positive)**		**Perceptions of C/B analysis (positive)**	
		Engage in multiple livelihood activities	4	Because I have improved and expanded my business	11	Use loans and savings products to pay my children's school fees	12
		Expand my business through working with the MFI products (loans)	21	Because if I hadn't joined I wouldn't have been able to save this much	15	No other place to borrow because I use not to have anywhere to turn to in times of need	7
		Pay my children's school fees	1	I have multi-livelihood activities	1	Able to buy inputs for my farm	3
		Able to save and spend use it later	10	Achieve personal development goals	1	Able to save profits for emergencies	12
		Financial and non-financial services from MFI staff	3	School fees of children	2	Loans accessed are used to invest in my business	8
		Helps me save and cut down on unplanned expenditure	2	Cut down on unplanned expenditure	1	Helps save money to prevent unplanned spending	12
				Plot of land to build house	1	My saving gets interest	7
		Perceptions of C/B analysis (negative)		**Perceptions of C/B analysis (negative)**		**Perceptions of C/B analysis (negative)**	
		Most of the loan is partly used to repay the loans due to the high regular repay	3	–	0	–	0

Scope is the number of different types of financial products and services (contracts) that are supplied by an MFI. Scope between products is the number of types of different products (e.g., number of loans, deposits, payments and insurance). Scope within products is the variants of the same product (e.g., different loan types) that is supplied by the MFI	**Scope at MFI level**	Perceptions of scope		Perceptions of scope		Perceptions of scope	
		MFIs offer variety of products and services, including group and individual ones	4	Whether individual or group products, people eventually benefit	2	Satisfied with all services savings are safe	15
		Loans and savings are the necessary products	16	Loans and deposit products are necessary	10	Limited investment opportunities around locality	3
		Clients are satisfied with product mix offered once they are saving and taking loans	16	Clients are satisfied with product mix offered	1	Other basic products such as loans and savings should be included in the product mix	15
		Clients' needs and wants are so varied that they can't all be met at the same time	6	Clients' needs and wants are so many that they can never be satisfied comprehensively	3	Inadequate capital base so many people can't take loans	5
		Interest on loans is high	6	The introduction of the Ghana agricultural insurance programme for farmers is very helpful	2		
		Duration for repayment, short	1	Insurance on loans mitigate risk	2		
		Late loan disbursal	2	MFIs have enough capital base to meet clients' needs	1		
		Loan sizes are small	2	Group loans are generally problematic	4		

(Continued)

Definition of Design Facto	*Definition of Design Sub-factor*	*Formal MFI Clients' Perceptions of Design Sub-factor*	*No/ Rank*	*Semi-formal MFI Clients' Perceptions Design Sub-factor*	*N/Rank*	*Informal MFI Client's Perceptions Design Sub-factor*	*No/Rank*
		No grace period to invest loan effectively		Loans can only be twice of savings amount	5		
				No fix deposits services			
				No grace period before commencement of repayments	1		
				Insurance should not only be on loans but should be expanded to cover crops, fire and other risks	2		
				No payment services especially for salaries	2		
				Inadequate capital base	2		
	Scope at product level (LOANS)	**Drivers of within-product scope (loans) satisfaction-formal MFIs**		**Drivers of within-product scope (loans) satisfaction-semi-formal MFIs**		**Drivers of within-product scope (loans) satisfaction-informal MFIs**	
		The financial advice	5	Non-financial advice (e.g., client project execution)	1	Low interest	17
		Loan amounts given as requested	4	Loan amounts granted as requested	4	Financial advice	1
		Convenience in transactions (e.g., mobile staff)	7	Convenient and quick transactions (e.g., mobile staff)	10	Interest from loans remains with group (end of cycle share- out)	10

	'Good' durations for repayments	6	Flexible contract terms (e.g., duration, instalment and applications)	6	Good customer relations	2
	Low interests as compared CBs	10	Low interests compared to CBs and RCBs/SLs	16	Quick access to loans	5
	Quick access to loans (no delays)	7	Quick access to loans (no delays)	5	Flexible contract terms (duration and instalment	5
	Flexible contract terms (instalment amounts)	2	Good customer relations	3	Support from group members	8
	Good customer relations	2	Loan diversity (group and individual)	1		
	Loan diversities	1	Awards to clients who repay in time	1		
	Awards to non-defaulting clients	1	Insurance on loans (credit risk management)	2		
Scope at product level (SAVINGS)	**Drivers of within-product scope (savings) by formal MFI clients**		**Drivers of within-product scope (savings) by semi-formal MFI clients**		**Drivers of within-product scope (savings) by informal MFI clients**	
	Any amount can be saved	4	Convenience (mobile staff)	13	Savings is secured	2
	Awards to high savers	2	Any amount can be saved	8	High interest on savings	12
	Proximity and convenience	6	Awards to high savers	1	Interest is shared among members	8

(*Continued*)

Definition of Design Facto	*Definition of Design Sub-factor*	*Formal MFI Clients' Perceptions of Design Sub-factor*	*No/ Rank*	*Semi-formal MFI Clients' Perceptions Design Sub-factor*	*N/Rank*	*Informal MFI Client's Perceptions Design Sub-factor*	*No/Rank*
		No restrictions on withdrawals	8	No restrictions on withdrawals	4	Local ownership and management	1
		Good customer relations	16	Deductions for savings can be automated	3	Proximity and convenience	1
		Financial advice	2	Quick services (no delays)	4	Any amount can be saved	19
		Avoidance of unplanned expenditure	1	Moderate interest on savings	6	Quick access to savings	5
		Interest paid on deposits	5	Good customer relations	6	Diverse savings products	2
		Savings to access loans	2	Savings are secured	1	Savings is secured	2
		Savings are secured	4	Savings to access loans	3	High interest on savings	12
	Scope at product level (INSURANCE)	**Drivers of within-product (insurance) scope satisfaction by formal MFI clients**		**Drivers of within-product (insurance) scope satisfaction by semi-formal MFI clients**		**Drivers of within-product (insurance) scope satisfaction by informal MFI clients**	
		Bancassurance	1	Low premiums	6		
		Low premiums	4	Loan balances covered even upon death	3		
		Livestock insurance	1	Covers all credit risks for client and MFI	1		
		Crop insurance	1	Evidence of clients benefiting when misfortunes occur	3		
		Regular deductions	1	The education policy secure children education	1		
		The evidence of payout	2	The life plan policy for funeral	1		

	Scope at product level (PAYMENTS)	**Drivers of within-product (payments) scope satisfaction by formal MFI clients**		**Drivers of within-product (payments) scope satisfaction by semi-formal MFI clients**		**Drivers of within-product (payments) scope satisfaction by informal MFI clients**	
		Charges are affordably moderate	6				
		Good customer relations	1				
		Convenience	4				
		No under-dealings/ Transparent	3				
		Quick services	12				
Worth describes the willingness to pay in relation to the terms of the financial contract as well as the risk profile, constraints and opportunities available to the client.	**Factors increasing worth of access at the MFI level**	**Formal MFI clients' perceptions of what increases worth**		**Semi-formal MFI clients' perceptions of what increases worth**		**Informal MFI clients' perceptions of what increases worth**	
		Mobile agents coming to us	6	Mobile staff coming to us	5	Mobile agents coming to us	3
		Friendly customer relation	24	Friendly customer relation	37	Friendly customer relation	1
		Easy access to loan	15	Easy access to loan	28	Easy access to loan	6
		Quick payments of salaries	2	Quick payments of salaries	1	Support from group members	18
		Input credit with farmers	4	Moderate interest rates on loans	9	VSL very good for poorer people	5
		Moderate interest rates on loans	7	MFI proximity	2	Moderate interest rates on loans	14
		MFI proximity	12	Easy access to savings	7	MFI proximity	6

(*Continued*)

Definition of Design Facto	*Definition of Design Sub-factor*	*Formal MFI Clients' Perceptions of Design Sub-factor*	*No/ Rank*	*Semi-formal MFI Clients' Perceptions Design Sub-factor*	*N/Rank*	*Informal MFI Client's Perceptions Design Sub-factor*	*No/Rank*
		Easy access to savings	15	Flexible contracts (savings can service loans)	12	Easy access to savings	23
		Flexible contracts (savings can service loans)	1	High Interest on savings	4	Flexible contracts (savings can be used to service loans)	8
		SMS alerts	1	Can be relied upon (non-financial services included)	3	High interest on savings	11
		Can be relied upon (non-financial services included)	11			Can be relied upon (non-financial services included)	3
						Developed discipline in saving	2
	Factors decreasing worth of access at the MFI level	**Formal MFI clients' perceptions of what decreases worth**		**Semi-formal MFI clients' perceptions of what decreases worth**		**Informal MFI clients' perceptions of what decreases worth**	
		Banking hall too small	5	No weekend banking	10	Scope should increase to include basic savings and loans	2
		Low interest paid on savings	5	Delayed loan disbursement	1	Charging of late fee	1
		Bad customer relations with staff	10	No grace period to repay loans especially agricultural loans	4	Mobile staff of MFI fail to turn up regularly	2
		Lower interest on loans	5	Low interest on savings	8	Delay in repaying loans	1
		Autocratic decisions during annual general meetings	4	Loan amounts tied to savings amount	4	Ceiling on number of shares allowed individuals	8

Loans: worth increases for loans when terms of contracts (amount disbursed, term to maturity and instalment size) match client needs. Deposits: it is the interest paid on deposits and the flexibility of savings	Fewer number of staff (e.g., tellers)	10	Increase scope to include payment services	7	Theft of boxes (should be deposited with bank)	9
	Instalment amounts high	3	Increase the number of workers	3	Low capital base	6
	Delays in loan disbursement	4	Increase interest on savings	4	The restrictions on withdrawal till maturity	5
	Restriction on minimum amount (>5 Ceids) that can be deposited	2	High insurance premiums on loans	2	Restrictions on membership	2
	Delays in transactions in banking hall	5	Lack of permanent office	1	Weekly savings should be made bi-weekly	8
	Short regular weekly instalment requirements	5	Demand for guarantors for loyal customers	3	Disagreements among group members making it time consuming	3
	Irregular visits by mobile staff	3	No ATMs/internet banking	6	Limited staff numbers (Bencyn Susu and Tarasum Leverage)	1
	Unreliable internet services that force the use of savings books	9	Fixed account balance requirements	1	No issues	7
	High charges on cheque clearance	1	No SMS alerts	3		
	No automated teller machines in areas with no bank branches	3	Incompetent staff (need training)	3		
	Bank liquidity issues where clients are asked to go and come the following day	2	Imposition of penalties when one skips instalment	3		

(Continued)

Definition of Design Facto	*Definition of Design Sub-factor*	*Formal MFI Clients' Perceptions of Design Sub-factor*	*No/ Rank*	*Semi-formal MFI Clients' Perceptions Design Sub-factor*	*N/Rank*	*Informal MFI Client's Perceptions Design Sub-factor*	*No/Rank*
		No separate orderly ques for depositors and deposit takers	2	Forced use of savings to defray unpaid loans	1		
		Bank not linked to controller and accountant general for quick and early payments of salaries	2	Rejection of coins	1		
		Don't know	7				
	Loan amounts disbursed	**Formal clients' perceptions of disbursed loan amounts**		**Semi-formal clients' perceptions of disbursed loan amounts**		**Informal clients' perceptions of loan amounts disbursed**	
		MFI confident I will repay loan	17	Loan amounts tied to savings (50%)	15	Always obtain the loan amount requested	13
		MFI have large capital	3	Because MFI have adequate capital base from profits made from its large client base	6	Because the group had enough (VSL) savings the day wanted loan	4
		Amount involved was small	7	Interest payments obtained by MFI, but they insure loans	2	Did not request for large amount	4
		I meet all the requirements for loan disbursement	3	Because of small size of loans involved	2	Client know the loan amount is tied to the savings amount with MFI and request accordingly	6

	They take commission and processing fees (Bebbington et al.)	4	Meet conditions for loan	1	MFI officer thinks I might not be able to repay	1
			I belong to a group		There was not enough money in the box	1
			There is a maximum limit for loans based on savings	2		
			Did not have enough savings to obtain amount requested	3		
Duration of repayment (term to maturity)	**Formal clients' perceptions of duration of repayments of accessed loans**		**Semi-formal clients' perceptions of duration of repayment of accessed loans**		**Perceptions of duration of repayment of accessed loans**	
	Duration OK/appropriate	10	Flexible repayment terms (options, negotiable, early settlement)	19	Group (VSLA) collectively agreed on the duration to repay borrowed monies	
	Client chooses duration for repayment	13	Duration OK/ appropriate	8	Duration is flexible and long enough	
	6-month duration is too short	2	Duration too short	4	Repayment done within maturity period	
	Wants an extended duration	7			Duration is too short (especially with larger amounts)	

(*Continued*)

Definition of Design Facto	*Definition of Design Sub-factor*	*Formal MFI Clients' Perceptions of Design Sub-factor*	*No/ Rank*	*Semi-formal MFI Clients' Perceptions Design Sub-factor*	*N/Rank*	*Informal MFI Client's Perceptions Design Sub-factor*	*No/Rank*
	Regular repayment amounts (size of instalment)	**Formal clients' perceptions of regular loan repayment amounts**		**Semi-formal clients' perception of regular loan repayment amounts**		**Informal clients' perceptions of regular repayment amounts**	
		Client given choices on size of instalment	18	Amounts are affordable (as size is usually determined by clients)	22	Monthly amounts payable by client is negotiated with MFI	
		Amounts involved are affordable	11	Interest plus principal instalment is high	8	It's flexible (any amount can be repaid before maturity)	
		Size of instalment too high	7	Size of instalment no matter the size is a problem for farmers	3		
	Interest paid on deposits	**Formal clients' perceptions of interest paid on deposits**		**Semi-formal clients' perceptions of interest paid on deposits**		**Informal clients' perceptions of interest paid on deposits**	
		Although less than expected I am OK savings in MFI is safer	9	Interests on savings is better than none	4	At the end of VSL cycle, dividends are paid proportional to shares held	18
		Able to withdraw any amount and time	3	Interest is moderately OK	10	Saving to enable me take loans more important	10
		The interest is quite high	7	Small interests earned is better than keeping money at home	2	It is the only 'Susu' company that pays interest on savings	3

	Just an appreciation for working with MFI	5	Interest earned is much higher than other MFIs	6	MFI incurs costs by going to meet clients at the workplaces (so why pay much interest on savings)	2
	No interest on savings	1	If a group member does not save in time it affects the interest earned in collective group savings with MFI	7	No interest is paid on savings	7
	Very low rate	7	Interest on savings much lower than loan interest	3	Do not save	2
	Interest paid quarterly	15	Interest on savings with MFI is low	5		
			No interest on savings at all with MFI			
Flexibility of deposit withdrawals	**Formal clients' perceptions on the flexibility of withdrawals of deposits**		**Semi-formal clients' perceptions on the flexibility of withdrawals of deposits**		**Informal clients' perceptions on the flexibility of withdrawals of deposits**	
	When you have emergencies or business opportunities	17	Flexibility of deposit contracts means clients can solve emergency problems	6	Client agreed with group (VSL) that only at the end of cycle one can obtain savings (share value) and dividends	18
	Even compulsory savings terms that make it easy to access loans is alright	10	Flexibility in deposit contracts makes life easy	15	No charges on withdrawals	2

(*Continued*)

Definition of Design Facto	*Definition of Design Sub-factor*	*Formal MFI Clients' Perceptions of Design Sub-factor*	*No/ Rank*	*Semi-formal MFI Clients' Perceptions Design Sub-factor*	*N/Rank*	*Informal MFI Client's Perceptions Design Sub-factor*	*No/Rank*
		Withdrawals are not flexible	6	Flexibility in savings contracts means clients can pay off loans with savings	2	A day's savings as costs of keeping your savings safe (Susu)	2
		Ask to go and come following day	4	The MFI encourages more savings	1	Inflexible withdrawal terms (BenCyn)	6
				Frequency of compulsory savings, even if for a loan, can be stressful	3	Unless in critical emergencies	2
				Not allowed withdrawals of savings until loan is fully settled	2		
				May need money in emergencies and savings is not matured yet for withdrawal	4		
	Diversified income sources	**Formal clients' perceptions on access and livelihood diversification**		**Semi-formal clients' perceptions on access and livelihood diversification**		**Informal clients' perceptions on access and livelihood diversification**	
		Diversified income sources	8	Diversified income sources	5	Not enough funds accessed	3
		Added additional business	15	Increased productive assets	4	Do not use loans/ savings on IGAs	11

	Consumption smoothing	1	Added additional business	8	Expanded existing IGAs	5
			Consumption smoothing		Added additional IGAs	
	Increased productive assets	3	Support household members education	9	Started new IGAs	6
	Have not expanded my business	9			Bought consumable assets (refrigerators, motorbikes, TV sets)	3
	Only does savings from my existing sources	3				
Employed others	**Minimum-maximum number of persons employed by formal MFI clients**		**Minimum-maximum number of persons employed by semi-formal MFI clients**		**Minimum-maximum number of persons employed by informal MFI clients**	
	Averagely employed between 1 and 6 persons		Averagely employed between 1 and 10 persons		Averagely employed between 1 and 8 persons	
Achievement of personal and household livelihood goals	**Livelihood goals achieved by formal MFI clients' access to products and services**		**Livelihood goals achieved by formal MFI clients' access to products and services**		**Livelihood goals achieved by formal MFI clients' access to products and services**	
	Expanded on-farm activities	7	Expanded on-farm activities	2	Expanded on-farm businesses (IGAs)	7
	Expanded off-farm activities	25	Expanded off-farm activities	12	Expanded off-farm businesses (IGAs)	11
	Pay school fees	5	Pay school fees	3	Tackled emergencies (health, education)	4
	Consumption smoothening	11	Consumption smoothening	8	No access to loans negatively affecting livelihoods	6
	Made losses	2			Just prevented me from unnecessary spending	2

(Continued)

Definition of Design Facto	*Definition of Design Sub-factor*	*Formal MFI Clients' Perceptions of Design Sub-factor*	*No/ Rank*	*Semi-formal MFI Clients' Perceptions Design Sub-factor*	*N/Rank*	*Informal MFI Client's Perceptions Design Sub-factor*	*No/Rank*
Length is the time frame that product(s) and service(s) are targeted at populations. Length is perceived in future terms and hence difficult to measure	**Years with MFI and livelihood outcomes**	**Minimum-maximum number of years clients worked with formal MFIs**		**Minimum-maximum number of years semi-formal clients worked with MFIs**		**Minimum-maximum number of years informal clients worked with MFIs**	
		Lowest: 1 year – Highest: 17		Lowest: 2 years – Highest: 12 years		Lowest: 1 – Highest: 17	
		Type of donor support for formal MFIs		**Type of donor support for semi-formal MFIs**		**Type of donor support for informal MFIs**	
	Donor support for sustainability	USAID partnership		Church, Ghana National Association of Teachers		World Vision International Partnership	
	Profitable sustainable	**Formal clients' perceptions of MFIs' profitability**		**Semi-formal clients' perceptions of MFIs' profitability**		**Informal clients' perceptions of MFIs' profitability**	
		Charges are made on all services	5	The MFIs have large customer base	14	If members carry out transactions, interests will accrue as profits	14
		Interest and fees made on all loan products	18	The MFI would have closed by now if no profits where been made	4	Interest made on loans (shares bought-deposits)	4
		MFIs carry out large transactions with a large customer base	12	Profits are made on loans extended to clients	27	MFIs have large customer base	5

		Investment (securities) profits from customer deposits	2	Profits from investment of customer deposits with short-term risk-free government and other securities	1	Support from group members more than profits	5
		Most customers are formal salaried workers (payment charges)	2	MFI derive revenue from renting properties (office space)	1		
				We are informed of the profit and losses made during AGMs (annual General Meetings)			
Depth of outreach in the microfinance livelisystem is the value society places on the net gain of a given client. Poverty levels of targeted clients are a good proxy for depth as society would prefer that net gains from programmes should be received by the poor	**Preference for women**	**Formal clients' perceptions on the preference for women**		**Semi-formal clients' perceptions on the preference for women**		**Informal clients' perceptions on the preference for women**	
		Women are poorer	2	Women easy to deal with	3	The group is made up of only women	15
		Women are more committed to repayment	4	Women are vulnerable	2	Most women are traders and earn daily	1
		Women are more concerned with family welfare	3	Women are more in business	2	Only group members are served;	3
						target workers with salary	5
		Women are easy to deal with	1	No discrimination	16	Non-discrimination base on gender/sex	20
		No discrimination between the sexes	19	Any member who is a client and meet the conditions	4	Come from same community as MFI	2
		Any member who is a client and meets the conditions	11				
		Based on one's ability to repay	1				

(*Continued*)

Definition of Design Facto	*Definition of Design Sub-factor*	*Formal MFI Clients' Perceptions of Design Sub-factor*	*No/ Rank*	*Semi-formal MFI Clients' Perceptions Design Sub-factor*	*N/Rank*	*Informal MFI Client's Perceptions Design Sub-factor*	*No/Rank*
	Preference for rural	**Formal clients' perceptions on the preference for rural clients**		**Semi-formal clients' perceptions on the preference for rural clients**		**Informal clients' perceptions on the preference for rural clients**	
		Clients who meet the requirement	19	Support to small businesses	2	The provider (MFI) lives in our community	6
		It's based on who can pay	9	Village people are poorer	7	Once a member, it doesn't matter where you live	13
		No discrimination between rural and urban clients	7	More given to town folks because businesses are located there with high turnovers	23	No discrimination based on locality	5
		The business people are in the towns	6	No discrimination (once a member meets conditions, and can payback)	4		
				Even though those in the villages repay faithfully, business turnover is low	3		

Preference for less/not educated	**Formal clients' perceptions on the preference for the less educated or no formal education**		**Semi-formal clients' perceptions on the preference for the less educated or no formal education**		**Informal clients' perceptions on the preference for the less educated or no formal education**	
	Most educated people have regular income which guarantee repayment	2	The educated understand issues better	2	Educated people are easy to deal with	4
	The educated just understand the processes and procedures better	1	Non-discrimination based on education level	20	They easily understand contract	2
	It's based on who can repay, not education level	10			Give more salaried workers who mostly are educated	7
	No discrimination based on education level	24			Non-discrimination base on level of education	11
Ethnic minorities	**Formal clients' perceptions on the preference for the ethnic minorities**		**Semi-formal clients' perceptions on the preference for the ethnic minorities**		**Informal clients' perceptions on the preference for the ethnic minorities**	
	They are sometimes difficult to trace and must have guarantors	1	No discrimination based on ethnic origins	19	No discrimination, provided you are a group member	18
	Non-discrimination	19			No discrimination, provided you can repay	5
	Provided you meet the requirements for access	2				

(*Continued*)

Definition of Design Facto	*Definition of Design Sub-factor*	*Formal MFI Clients' Perceptions of Design Sub-factor*	*No/ Rank*	*Semi-formal MFI Clients' Perceptions Design Sub-factor*	*N/Rank*	*Informal MFI Client's Perceptions Design Sub-factor*	*No/Rank*
	Housing	**Formal clients' main housing construction materials**		**Formal clients' main housing construction materials**		**Formal clients' main housing construction materials**	
		Cement	72%	Cement	76%	Cement	82%
		Mud (unburnt)	28%	Mud (unburnt)	24%	Mud (unburnt)	18%
	Loan sizes	**Formal clients' loan size distribution**		**Semi-formal clients' loan size distribution**		**Informal clients' loan size distribution**	
		Loan amount	**%**	**Loan amount**	**%**	**Loan amount**	**%**
		100	10	100	12	100	18
		225.5	14	225.5	4	225.5	35
		375.5	2	375.5	6	375.5	18
		525.5	15	525.5	6	525.5	12
		675.5	6	675.5	4	675.5	8
		825.5	10	825.5	2	825.5	2
		975.5	8	975.5	14	975.5	4
		>1100.5	35	>1100.5	52	>1100.5	2
Breadth of outreach for an MFI is the number of clients that it serves with financial products and services.	**Targeting orientation**	**Formal clients' perceptions on targeting of their MFIs**		**Semi-formal clients' perceptions on targeting of their MFIs**		**Informal clients' perceptions on targeting of their MFIs**	
		People who can repay	96%	People who can repay	90%	People who can repay	74%
		Very poor people MFIs' interest is to generate profits and revenues	4%	Very poor people Anyone who can save can be a member	10%	Very poor people Interested members	26%

	If one can't use the products how and why will they even join the MFI	Clients benefit according to their contributions (savings amounts)	Amounts involve means, the target is the poor
	Products are targeted at customers who make profit and can save (business women)	Government workers with salary or those with formal employment and/or running a business	Target salaried workers with payslips
	Targeted salaried workers they need more customers and not poverty alleviation	Target people who can use them products whether rich or poor	Target people with enterprises and earn income
	They want those who can use the product and benefit from it and be able to repay and make deposits	Its people are capable of doing business with the MFI	It's for group members, group target people who make efforts to help themselves
	Once customers meet the bank requirement they can access loans	Those who meet the MFI requirements to access products and services get it	
		The union (MFI) should make profits to stay in operation	
Interests rates in Ghana	**Average interest rates for formal MFIs**	**Average interest rates for semi-formal MFIs**	**Average interest rates for informal MFIs**
	Approx. 35%	Approx. 47%	Approx. 63%

(Continued)

Definition of Design Facto	*Definition of Design Sub-factor*	*Formal MFI Clients' Perceptions of Design Sub-factor*	*No/ Rank*	*Semi-formal MFI Clients' Perceptions Design Sub-factor*	*N/Rank*	*Informal MFI Client's Perceptions Design Sub-factor*	*No/Rank*
	Donor partners	USAID partnership		Church, Ghana National Association of Teachers (GNAT)		World Vision International Partnership	
	Groups	Enable poor people with no collaterals to form groups and have access		Enable poor people to also form groups and have access		Those in towns lend money from moneylenders and those of us in the villages use the VSLA	
				Generally problematic as people are not trustworthy			
	Individual	It is for those of us who can provide collateral		For those who business people and can save with the union to be able to take loans and provide collateral		During emergencies you can provide collateral	
Contract enforcement refers to the mechanisms MFIs use to ensure clients honour their side of the contract agreements in case that they default	**Enforcement methods affecting product uptake**	**Enforcement methods affecting formal MFI product uptake**		**Enforcement methods affecting semi-formal MFI product uptake**		**Enforcement methods affecting informal MFI product uptake**	
		Freq.	%	Freq.	%	Freq.	%
		36	72	35	70	32	64
		14	28	15	30	18	36
		Why enforcement methods affect formal clients		**Why enforcement methods affect semi-formal clients**		**Why enforcement methods affect informal clients**	

Enforcement methods and access	If disputes are resolved amicably, it motivates clients to take more products and vice versa	21	Amicably resolved disputes build confidence and encourage product uptake from old and new clients	22	If clients can be punished for breach of contract, they will conduct themselves well and honour their obligation and vice versa	8
	Flexibility in contract design helps avoid disputes and vice versa	3	Flexibility and transparency help to avoid disputes and vice versa	4	If disputes are fairly settled, clients will feel comfortable to take up products and vice versa	6
	People don't want their names to be mentioned at the radio station, so they honour their part of the contract	2	The use of third parties for debt collection makes people avoid defaults	3	Effective dispute resolution ensures good customer relation and satis-faction and vice versa	
	Contract terms if well explained by MFI and followed by client help avoid defaults and vice versa	4	Negotiation and persuasion with clients first before considering legal action or threats of legal action is good	2	Even with group loans, there is need to resolve defaults with the interest of the individuals taken into consideration	3
	The use of guarantors (third party that provide surety to repay in case of default) helps avoid or reduces defaults and disputes	1	Obliging all group members to pay for a defaulting member can cause people to drop out	3	It's in the interest of management to resolve disputes amicably	2
					Flexibility in contract design helps avoid disputes	

(Continued)

Definition of Design Facto	*Definition of Design Sub-factor*	*Formal MFI Clients' Perceptions of Design Sub-factor*	*No/ Rank*	*Semi-formal MFI Clients' Perceptions Design Sub-factor*	*N/Rank*	*Informal MFI Client's Perceptions Design Sub-factor*	*No/Rank*
Add-ons are additional products or services provided by the MFI or based on the MFI's main product or service that enhance uptake	**MFI level**	**Formal clients' perceptions of add-ons at the MFI level**		**Semi-formal clients' perceptions of add-ons at the MFI level**		**Informal clients' perceptions of add-ons at the MFI level**	
		Mobile agents coming to us	6	Mobile agents coming to us	5	Mobile agents coming to us	3
		Friendly customer relation	24	Friendly customer relation	37	Friendly customer relation	1
		Easy access to loan	15	Easy access to loan	28	Easy access to loan	6
		Quick payments of salaries	2	Quick payments of salaries	1	Support from group members	18
		Input credit with farmers	4	Moderate interest rates on loans	9	VSL very good for poorer people	5
		Moderate interest rates on loans	7	MFI proximity	2	Moderate interest rates on loans	14
		MFI proximity	12	Easy access to savings	7	MFI proximity	6
		Easy access to savings	15	Flexible contracts (savings can service loans)	12	Easy access to savings	23
		Flexible contracts (savings can service loans)	1	High interest on savings	4	Flexible contracts (savings can service loans)	8
		SMS alerts	1	Can be relied upon (non-financial services included)	3	High Interest on savings	11
		Can be relied upon (non-financial services included)	11			Can be relied upon (non-financial services included)	3
						Developed discipline in saving	2

	Formal clients' perceptions of add-ons on loan products		Formal clients' perceptions of add-ons on loan products		Formal clients' perceptions of add-ons on loan products	
LOANS	The financial advice	5	Non-financial advice (e.g., client project execution)	1	Low interest	17
	Loan amounts given as requested	4	Loan amounts granted as requested	4	Financial advice	1
	Convenience in transactions (e.g., mobile staff)	7	Convenient and quick transactions (e.g., mobile staff)	10	Interest from loans remain with group (end of cycle share-out)	10
	'Good' durations for repayments	6	Flexible contract terms (e.g., duration, instalment and applications)	6	Good customer relations	2
	Low interests compared to commercial banks	10	Low interests compared to CBs and CRBs/SLs	16	Quick access to loans	5
	Quick access to loans (no delays)	7	Quick access to loans (no delays)	5	Flexible contract terms (duration and instalment)	5
	Flexible contract terms (instalment amounts)	2	Good customer relations	3	Support from group members	8
	Good customer relations	2	Loan diversity (group and individual)	1		
	Loan diversities	1	Annual awards to clients who repay in time	1		
	Annual awards to non-defaulting clients	1	Insurance on loans (credit risks management)	2		
			Transparent transactions	1		

(*Continued*)

Definition of Design Facto	*Definition of Design Sub-factor*	*Formal MFI Clients' Perceptions of Design Sub-factor*	*No/ Rank*	*Semi-formal MFI Clients' Perceptions Design Sub-factor*	*N/Rank*	*Informal MFI Client's Perceptions Design Sub-factor*	*No/Rank*
	SAVINGS	**Formal clients' perceptions of add-ons on savings products**		**Semi-formal clients' perceptions of add-ons on savings products**		**Informal clients' perceptions of add-ons on savings products**	
		Any amount can be saved	4	Convenience (mobile staff)	13	Savings is secured	2
		Awards to high savers	2	Any amount can be saved	8	High interest on savings	12
		Proximity and convenience	6	Annual awards to high savers	1	Interest is shared among members	8
		No restrictions on withdrawals	8	No restrictions on withdrawals	4	Local ownership and management	1
		Good customer relations	16	Deductions from accounts for savings can be automated	3	Proximity and convenience	1
		Financial advice	2	Quick services (no delays)	4	Any amount can be saved	19
		Avoidance of unplanned expenditure	1	Moderate interest on savings	6	No restrictions on amounts that can be saved	5
		Interest paid on deposits; savings to access loan	5	Good customer relations	6	Quick access to savings	2
		Savings are secured	2	Savings are secured	1	Diverse savings products	2
				Savings to access loans	3	No restrictions on amounts that can be saved	12
				Many branches	1		

INSURANCE	**Formal clients' perceptions of add-ons on insurance products**		**Semi-formal clients' perceptions of add-ons on insurance products**	**Informal clients' perceptions of add-ons on insurance products**
	Bancassurance	1	Low premiums	
	Low premiums	4	Loan balances covered even upon death	
	Livestock insurance	1	Covers all credit risks for client and MFI	
	Crop insurance	1	Clients benefit when misfortunes occur	
	Regular deductions	1	The education policy secure children education	
	The evidence of payout	2	The life plan policy for funeral	
PAYMENT	**Formal clients' perceptions of add-ons on insurance products**		**Semi-formal clients' perceptions of add-ons on insurance products**	**Informal clients' perceptions of add-ons on insurance products**
	Charges are affordably moderate			
	Good customer relations			
	Convenience			
	No under-dealings/ transparent			
	Quick services			
	Reliable/secured			

APPENDIX VI

CORRELATION OF INDEPENDENT VARIABLES OF THE DETERMINANTS OF PRODUCTS AND SERVICES (LOAN UPTAKE)

	LoanUptal	TargetedP	Good_Bad	WageWor	MultipleLi	Inflationa	AccesstoR	OnfarmSt	NonfarmS	Regulator	RuleofLaw	GovtComm	Voice_Acc	BusinessS	AbilitytoP	Innovation
LoanUptal	1															
TargetedP	0.2036	1														
Good_Bad	0.2616	0.2225	1													
WageWor	0.1858	0.0883	0.1957	1												
MultipleLi	0.2636	0.1732	0.3683	0.3376	1											
Inflationa	0.0805	0.0894	0.3682	0.0278	0.2144	1										
AccesstoR	-0.0411	0.0464	-0.0357	-0.007	-0.0605	-0.0572	1									
OnfarmSt	0.2187	0.1193	0.1828	0.1969	0.3301	0.03	0.0457	1								
NonfarmS	-0.0469	0.041	0.0148	-0.2691	-0.0244	0.1521	0.1154	-0.1106	1							
Regulator	-0.0632	-0.041	0.0442	-0.0585	-0.1732	-0.011	0.1925	-0.0882	0.0796	1						
RuleofLaw	-0.0299	-0.0539	0.0173	-0.1097	-0.1308	-0.0312	0.0621	-0.1478	0.0549	0.336	1					
GovtComm	-0.0422	-0.0624	-0.0226	-0.0044	-0.0071	0.0406	0.1718	-0.0902	0.0959	0.2154	0.2789	1				
Voice_Acc	-0.0309	-0.0611	-0.0369	0.0814	0.0252	-0.076	0.0932	0.1614	0.069	0.1922	0.0497	0.2586	1			
BusinessS	-0.0742	0.2982	0.0281	0.0156	0.0464	0.0685	0.0086	-0.1378	0.1568	-0.1196	-0.1075	-0.1148	0.0314	1		
AbilitytoP	-0.0451	-0.005	-0.032	-0.0833	-0.0287	0.03	0.2382	-0.1087	0.1159	0.502	0.2055	0.1684	0.2024	0.0718	1	
Innovation	-0.0232	-0.0909	0.0831	-0.0692	-0.061	0.1057	0.12	-0.1318	0.0536	0.2976	0.2096	0.3167	0.276	-0.1076	0.3212	1
MFIMgT_	-0.0066	0.095	0.1671	0.0609	0.1276	0.1809	-0.0465	0.1656	-0.041	0.0925	-0.0036	0.0914	0.3138	-0.0726	0.1656	0.1159
Add_ons_	-0.0262	0.1663	-0.0621	0.1034	0.0285	0.1288	-0.0463	-0.1131	-0.0235	0.1754	-0.014	0.0622	0.0351	0.1235	0.1009	0.1016
employme	-0.1033	-0.0712	-0.1619	-0.0571	-0.2301	-0.0688	-0.0369	-0.4596	0.0321	0.0962	-0.053	-0.0026	0.0022	0.1535	0.1289	-0.0177
InterestRa	0.0873	0.1089	0.1377	0.0404	0.0742	-0.0418	0.0011	0.0718	0.007	0.0501	0.0764	0.0261	0.1539	0.1482	0.1464	0.0528
Lending_S	0.3399	0.1075	0.0053	0.0956	-0.0396	-0.0208	0.0386	0.2012	-0.1223	0.045	0.0876	0.0099	0.0151	-0.0391	0.0938	-0.0603
Commerci	0.1266	0.0217	0.084	0.1854	0.1074	-0.0181	-0.0082	0.0832	0.0496	-0.0779	-0.1062	-0.0669	0.0016	0.1589	-0.0576	-0.0376
ProductDe	0.1345	-0.0424	-0.0306	0.1217	0.1245	-0.0803	-0.0908	0.1581	-0.1024	-0.122	-0.1565	-0.1737	0.0129	0.0023	-0.0993	-0.0155
SexofResp	-0.153	-0.0931	0.0135	0.1185	0.0733	-0.1946	0.0171	-0.0695	-0.0768	0.0931	-0.0934	-0.1068	0.0452	0.0928	-0.0127	-0.093
AgeofResp	0.0834	0.1644	0.0918	-0.1082	0.1338	0.0287	0.0388	0.1812	0.1375	-0.0232	-0.046	0.0197	0.0654	-0.0285	-0.0119	0.1775
Maritalsta	0.0116	0.0197	-0.0782	-0.1757	-0.0443	-0.0052	0.1153	0.0391	0.0519	-0.1292	-0.056	0.0729	0.1012	0.0384	-0.0123	-0.0547
Household	0.0735	0.0769	0.0545	0.1743	0.1529	-0.0663	0.2023	0.3885	-0.189	-0.0097	-0.0817	-0.1725	0.0675	-0.022	0.016	-0.0374
Education	-0.0911	-0.1386	-0.1949	-0.0918	-0.2149	0.04	-0.0341	-0.2306	0.0771	-0.0025	0.0849	0.1315	0.0916	0.0551	0.0592	0.0666
OtherPove	-0.1053	-0.1071	0.0594	0.0251	0.0688	-0.0188	0.0901	-0.0261	0.0615	-0.0119	0.0226	0.044	-0.0524	-0.0214	-0.1379	0.0289
LocalitySe	0.1287	0.0667	0.2515	0.1859	0.21	0.0503	-0.1314	0.2904	-0.3095	-0.2182	-0.1321	-0.1458	0	-0.1473	-0.1936	-0.0379
ICTechnol	-0.027	0.0497	-0.1115	0.1504	-0.0502	-0.1012	0.0605	-0.1507	-0.1498	0.014	-0.0507	-0.0224	0.0168	0.1684	0.0287	-0.1711
Employed	0.0405	0.3361	0.0352	0.093	0.2561	0.0498	-0.1038	0.1782	0.0624	-0.177	-0.1714	-0.0518	0.0673	0.2973	-0.061	-0.1379

	MFIMgT_	Add_ons_	employme	InterestRa	Lending_S	Commerci	ProductDe	SexofResp	AgeofResp	Maritalsta	Household	Education	OtherPove	LocalitySe	ICTechnol	Employed
MFIMgT_	1															
Add_ons_	0.0711	1														
employme	0.0441	0.1452	1													
InterestRa	0.0578	0.0573	-0.0165	1												
Lending_S	0.134	0.0039	0.011	-0.0197	1											
Commerci	-0.1707	0.1327	0.0045	0.1255	-0.1213	1										
ProductDe	-0.047	-0.0281	-0.0306	0.0991	0.0051	0.1737	1									
SexofResp	-0.0194	0.0795	0.0732	0.0909	-0.1547	0.1275	0.1298	1								
AgeofResp	0.1028	-0.0205	-0.2151	0.0514	0.0598	-0.0847	0.1506	-0.0454	1							
Maritalsta	-0.0745	-0.2541	-0.073	0.0894	-0.0328	0.1314	0.1669	-0.056	0.1362	1						
Household	0.1604	0.035	-0.2154	0.1388	0.1504	0.036	0.1414	0.1844	0.1888	0.0018	1					
Education	-0.0093	0.1302	0.3732	-0.0747	-0.0098	-0.0706	-0.0213	0.0879	-0.095	0.0134	-0.1887	1				
OtherPove	-0.045	0.0273	-0.1594	0.0024	-0.0274	0.0157	0.057	0.0508	0.0926	0.0788	0.196	0.0487	1			
LocalitySe	0.0917	-0.0731	-0.1309	0.0073	-0.1712	0.0652	0.0737	-0.0665	0.0549	0.0903	0.0443	-0.2796	-0.1091	1		
ICTechnol	-0.1276	0.1908	0.2663	0.117	0.113	0.199	-0.019	0.2758	-0.2374	-0.0611	-0.0171	0.2233	-0.0115	-0.21	1	
Employed	0.1733	0.0811	-0.0714	0.1744	0.1497	0.1449	0.1217	0.0722	0.0278	0.0969	0.0476	-0.1246	0.1031	0.0525	0.0502	1

APPENDIX VII

DATA DESCRIPTION AND SUMMARY STATISTICS OF HOUSEHOLD ASSET OWNERSHIP OF SAMPLED CLIENTS OF MICROFINANCE INSTITUTIONS IN NORTH-EASTERN GHANA

		Overall Sample				*Disaggregated Sample*									
Asset		*Total Sample* (*N* = 150)		*Asset Bought with MFI Loan*		*Formal Clients* (*N* = 50)		*Semi-formal* (*N* = 50)		*Informal* (*N* = 50)		*Non-clients*		*Min*	*Max*
1	**2**	**3**	**4**	**5**	**6**	**7**	**8**	**9**	**10**	**11**	**12**	**13**	**14**	**15**	**16**
		Freq.	**%**	**Freq.**	**%**	**Freq.**	**%**	**Freq.**	**%**	**Freq.**	**%**	**Freq.**	**%**		
Cattle	Yes	39	26	3	8	14	28	12	24	13	26	13	26	0	67
	No	111	74	36	92	36	72	38	76	37	74	37	74		
Sheep/goats/pigs	Yes	91	61	17	19	28	56	25	50	38	76	38	76	0	82
	No	59	39	74	81	22	44	25	50	12	24	12	24		
Horses/donkeys	Yes	22	15	4	18	8	16	7	14	7	14	7	14	0	20
	No	128	85	18	82	42	84	33	86	33	86	43	86		
Cars	Yes	9	6	4	44	4	8	4	8	1	2	6	6	0	15
	No	141	94	5	56	46	92	44	92	49	98	44	94		
Motorcycles	Yes	96	64	10	10	35	70	38	76	23	46	18	36	0	3
	No	54	36	86	90	15	30	10	24	27	54	32	64		
Bicycles	Yes	117	78	12	10	38	76	36	72	40	80	41	82	0	5
	No	33	22	105	90	12	24	14	28	10	20	9	18		
Tricycles	Yes	13	9	5	38	8	16	3	6	2	4	4	8	0	2
	No	137	91	4	62	42	84	47	94	48	96	46	92		
Donkey carts	Yes	10	7	0	0	5	10	1	2	4	8	8	16	0	1
	No	140	93	7	100	45	90	49	98	46	92	42	84		
Lorries/buses/trucks	Yes	3	2	1	33	1	2	1	2	1	2	0	0	0	1
	No	147	98	2	67	49	98	49	98	49	98	50	100		
Television sets	Yes	109	93	9	8	44	88	43	86	22	44	28	56	0	2
	No	41	27	100	92	6	12	7	14	28	56	22	44		

DVDs	Yes	104	69	6	6	42	84	38	76	24	48	21	42	0	3
	No	46	31	98	94	8	16	12	24	26	52	29	58		
Radios/tape recorders	Yes	80	53	2	3	25	50	22	44	33	66	37	74	0	3
	No	70	47	78	97	25	50	28	56	17	44	13	36		
Refrigerators	Yes	80	53	8	10	29	58	38	76	13	26	13	26	0	5
	No	70	47	72	90	21	42	12	24	37	74	37	74		
Washing machines	Yes	10	7	0	0	2	4	2	4	6	12	0	0	0	3
	No	140	93	10	100	48	96	48	96	44	98	50	100		
Sewing machines	Yes	39	26	0	0	8	16	14	28	17	34	7	14	0	2
	No	111	74	39	100	42	84	46	72	33	66	43	86		
Fans	Yes	92	61	2	2	34	68	36	72	22	44	18	36	0	7
	No	58	39	90	98	16	32	24	28	28	66	32	64		
Living room furniture	Yes	88	59	3	3	26	52	38	76	24	48	15	30	0	6
	No	62	41	85	97	24	48	12	24	26	52	35	70		
Clothing iron	Yes	92	61	3	3	31	62	42	84	19	38	22	44	0	3
	No	58	39	89	97	19	38	8	16	31	52	28	56		
Beds and Mattresses	Yes	121	81	4	3	44	88	41	82	36	72	29	58	0	10
	No	29	19	117	97	6	12	9	18	14	28	21	42		
Deposit account	Yes	109	73	15	14	38	76	40	80	31	62	-	-	0	5
	No	41	27	94	86	11	22	10	20	19	38	-	-		
Insurance	Yes	26	17	8	31	10	20	15	30	1	2	-	-	0	11
	No	124	83	18	69	40	80	35	70	49	98	-	-		
Money transfer	Yes	15	10	2	13	8	16	3	6	4	8	-	-	0	22
	No	135	90	13	87	42	84	47	94	46	92	-	-		
Loans	Yes	120	80	120	100	38	76	45	90	31	62	-	-	0	3
	No	30	20	0	0	12	24	5	10	19	38	-	-		

APPENDIX VIII

DATA DESCRIPTION OF HOUSEHOLD WELFARE VARIABLES

Household Welfare Outcome		*Formal MFI Clients (N = 50)*		*Semi-formal MFI Clients (N = 50)*		*Informal MFI Clients (N = 50)*	
		Freq.	*%*	*Freq.*	*%*	*Freq.*	*%*
Education (access improved generally)	Yes	29	58	17	34	32	64
	No	21	42	33	66	18	36
Able to pay school fees of children	Yes	45	90	36	72	34	68
	No	5	10	14	28	16	32
Healthcare (access improved generally)	Yes	32	64	22	44	30	60
	No	18	36	28	56	20	40
Able to afford orthodox healthcare	Yes	37	74	32	64	24	48
	No	13	26	18	36	26	52
Time to nearest hospital in 15 minutes	5–15 min	12	24	22	44	34	74
Time to nearest health facility in 30 minutes	16–30 min	21	42	16	32	5	10
Time to nearest health facility in 45 minutes	31–45 min	10	20	16	32	2	4
Time to nearest health facility in 60 minutes	46–60 min	3	6	5	10	3	6
Time to nearest health facility > 60 minutes	>60 min	4	8	7	14	3	6

Housing and housing improvement	Yes	21	42	28	56	8	16
	No	29	58	22	44	42	84
Primary home construction materials	Cement	36	72	38	76	41	82
Sanitation (use of W/C)	WC	32	64	10	20	41	82
Sanitation (use of KVIP)	KVIP	13	26	20	40	9	18
Sanitation (open defecation)	Open defecation	5	10	17	34	0	0
Food security	Yes	34	68	26	52	28	56
	No	16	32	24	48	22	44
Not enough food at home in the past 12 months	Yes	2	4	7	14	6	12
	No	48	96	43	86	44	88
Ate less in the past 2 weeks	Yes	4	8	6	12	5	10
	No	46	92	44	88	45	90
Gendered relation with partner	Yes	28	56	28	56	16	32
	No	22	44	22	44	34	68
Energy (fuel for cooking)	LPG	10	20	19	38	27	54
	Fuelwood	29	58	29	58	23	46
Energy (household lighting)	Electricity (mains)	44	88	43	86	34	68
	Electricity (Generator)	4	8	3	6	14	28
	Lantern/ torchlight	2	4	4	8	2	4
Land acquisition	Inherited	31	62	41	82	47	92
	Purchased	17	34	5	10	2	4
	Gifted	2	4	4	8	1	2

APPENDIX IX

CLIENT ASSET CLASSES OWNED

Data description and summary statistics of household asset ownership for sampled clients Microfinance Institutions in North-eastern Ghana

		Overall Sample				*Disaggregated Sample*									
Asset		*Total Sample (N = 150)*		*Asset Bought with MFI Loan*		*Formal Clients (N = 150)*		*Semi-formal (N = 150)*		*Informal (N = 150)*		*Non-clients*		*Min*	*Max*
1	*2*	*3*	*4*	*5*	*6*	*7*	*8*	*9*	*10*	*11*	*12*	*13*	*14*	*15*	*16*
		Freq.	**%**	**Freq.**	**%**	**Freq.**	**%**	**Freq.**	**%**	**Freq.**	**%**	**Freq.**	**%**		
Cattle	Yes	39	26	3	8	14	28	12	24	13	26	13	26	0	67
	No	111	74	36	92	36	72	38	76	37	74	37	74		
Sheep/goats/ pigs	Yes	91	61	17	19	28	56	25	50	38	76	38	76	0	82
	No	59	39	74	81	22	44	25	50	12	24	12	24		
Horses/ donkeys	Yes	22	15	4	18	8	16	7	14	7	14	7	14	0	20
	No	128	85	18	82	42	84	33	86	33	86	43	86		
Cars	Yes	9	6	4	44	4	8	4	8	1	2	6	6	0	15
	No	141	94	5	56	46	92	44	92	49	98	44	94		
Motorcycles	Yes	96	64	10	10	35	70	38	76	23	46	18	36	0	3
	No	54	36	86	90	15	30	10	24	27	54	32	64		
Bicycles	Yes	117	78	12	10	38	76	36	72	40	80	41	82	0	5
	No	33	22	105	90	12	24	14	28	10	20	9	18		
Tricycles	Yes	13	9	5	38	8	16	3	6	2	4	4	8	0	2
	No	137	91	4	62	42	84	47	94	48	96	46	92		
Donkey carts	Yes	10	7	0	0	5	10	1	2	4	8	8	16	0	1
	No	140	93	7	100	45	90	49	98	46	92	42	84		

Lorries/ buses/ trucks	Yes	3	2	1	33	1	2	1	2	1	2	0	0	0	1
	No	147	98	2	67	49	98	49	98	49	98	50	100		
Television sets	Yes	109	93	9	8	44	88	43	86	22	44	28	56	0	2
	No	41	27	100	92	6	12	7	14	28	56	22	44		
DVDs	Yes	104	69	6	6	42	84	38	76	24	48	21	42	0	3
	No	46	31	98	94	8	16	12	24	26	52	29	58		
Radio/tape recorders	Yes	80	53	2	3	25	50	22	44	33	66	37	74	0	3
	No	70	47	78	97	25	50	28	56	17	44	13	36		
Refrigerators	Yes	80	53	8	10	29	58	38	76	13	26	13	26	0	5
	No	70	47	72	90	21	42	12	24	37	74	37	74		
Washing machines	Yes	10	7	0	0	2	4	2	4	6	12	0	0	0	3
	No	140	93	10	100	48	96	48	96	44	98	50	100		
Sewing machines	Yes	39	26	0	0	8	16	14	28	17	34	7	14	0	2
	No	111	74	39	100	42	84	46	72	33	66	43	86		
Fans	Yes	92	61	2	2	34	68	36	72	22	44	18	36	0	7
	No	58	39	90	98	16	32	24	28	28	66	32	64		
Living room furniture	Yes	88	59	3	3	26	52	38	76	24	48	15	30	0	6
	No	62	41	85	97	24	48	12	24	26	52	35	70		
Clothing irons	Yes	92	61	3	3	31	62	42	84	19	38	22	44	0	3
	No	58	39	89	97	19	38	8	16	31	52	28	56		
Beds and mattresses	Yes	121	81	4	3	44	88	41	82	36	72	29	58	0	10
	No	29	19	117	97	6	12	9	18	14	28	21	42		
Deposit account	Yes	109	73	15	14	38	76	40	80	31	62	–	–	0	5
	No	41	27	94	86	11	22	10	20	19	38	–	–		
Insurance	Yes	26	17	8	31	10	20	15	30	1	2	–	–	0	11
	No	124	83	18	69	40	80	35	70	49	98	–	–		
Money transfer	Yes	15	10	2	13	8	16	3	6	4	8	–	–	0	22
	No	135	90	13	87	42	84	47	94	46	92	–	–		
Loans	Yes	120	80	120	100	38	76	45	90	31	62	–	–	0	3
	No	30	20	0	0	12	24	5	10	19	38	–	–		

INDEX

Note: **Bold** page numbers refer to tables and *italic* page numbers refer to figures.